MYSTERY WRITER'S SOURCE BOOK
WHERE TO SELL YOUR MANUSCRIPTS
SECOND EDITION

Edited by **DAVID H. BORCHERDING**
Assisted by **DON PRUES**

WRITER'S DIGEST BOOKS
Cincinnati, Ohio

Mystery Writer's Sourcebook. Copyright © 1995 by Writer's Digest Books. Printed and bound in the United States of America. All rights reserved. No part of this book may be reproduced in any form or by any electronic or mechanical means including information storage and retrieval systems without permission in writing from the publisher, except by a reviewer, who may quote brief passages in a review. Published by Writer's Digest Books, an imprint of F&W Publications, Inc., 1507 Dana Avenue, Cincinnati, Ohio 45207. 1-800-289-0963. Second edition.

This hardcover edition of *Mystery Writer's Sourcebook* features a "self-jacket" that eliminates the need for a separate dust jacket. It provides sturdy protection for your book while it saves paper, trees and energy.

97   96   95   94   93   5   4   3   2   1

International Standard Serial Number
ISSN 1081-6747
International Standard Book Number
ISBN 0-89879-724-1

Designed by Sandy Kent
Cover illustration by Mercedes McDonald

Attention Booksellers: This directory is published every two years by F&W Publications. Return deadline for this edition is December 31, 1997.

TABLE OF CONTENTS

From the Editor   1

SECTION I

Mystery and Crime Writing Trends

A View From The Experts   4
BY JAN GRAPE

SECTION II

Craft and Technique

The Vital Importance of Setting   12
BY JACK BICKHAM

Plotting the Mystery   20
BY SHARON GWYN SHORT

Give A Clue   28
BY MICHAEL SEIDMAN

Writing a Series   34

An Interview with Margaret Maron   43

SECTION III

Novel Markets

Marketing Your Mystery Novel   49
BY ROBIN GEE

Primary Novel Markets   61

☀: *Ballantine Books (Joe Blades)*   62

☀: *Bantam Books (Kate Miciak)*   66

☀: *Berkley Publishing Group (Natalee Rosenstein)*   72

☀: *Dutton/Signet, A Division of Penguin USA (Joseph Pittman)*   76

☀: *Donald I. Fine (Jason Jacob Poston)*   79

☀: *Forge (An Imprint of Tor Books) (Camille Cline)*   84

☀: *Foul Play Press (Louis F. Kannenstine)*   88

☀: *HarperCollins Publishers (Eamon Dolan)*   91

☀: *Kensington Publishing Corp. (Sarah Gallick)*   95

☀: *Mysterious Press (Sara Ann Freed)*   98

☀: *The Naiad Press, Inc. (Barbara Grier)*   101

☀: *Random House, Inc. (Elisa Wares)*   104

☀: *St. Martin's Press (Keith Kahla)*   107

☀: *Walker & Co. (Michael Seidman)*   110

☀: *Secondary & Foreign Novel Markets*   114

SECTION IV

Magazine Markets

Marketing Your Short Story   173

BY ROBIN GEE

Primary Short Fiction Markets   178

☀: *Alfred Hitchcock Mystery Magazine (Cathleen Jordan)*   180

☀: *Ellery Queen's Mystery Magazine (Janet Hutchings)*   183

☀: *Hardboiled Magazine (Gary Lovisi)*   187

☀: *Mystery Forum Magazine (Bob Myers)*   191

☀ *New Mystery Magazine (Charles Raisch)*   195

☀ *NOIR (Christopher Mills)*   199

☀ *Over My Dead Body! The Mystery Magazine (Cherie Jung)*   202

☀ *Pirate Writings (Edward McFadden)*   206

☀ *Secondary & Foreign Short Fiction Markets*   210

☀ *Nonfiction Short Markets*   244

SECTION V

Finding An Agent

How To Find, And Keep, A Top-Notch Mystery Agent

277

BY DON MAASS

Agent Listings 291

SECTION V I

Editors At Work

Anatomy of a Sale:

☀ "Me and Mr. Harry" *to Ellery Queen's Mystery Magazine*   329

     BY JANET HUTCHINGS

☀ *The Innocents* to Walker & Company   339

     BY MICHAEL SEIDMAN

☀ *Felony Murder* to St. Martin's Press, Inc.   348

     BY RUTH CAVIN

SECTION VII

Resources

Organizations, Conventions and Awards   370
BY ROBERT J. RANDISI

Online Resources   382
BY DON PRUES

Reference Books, Periodicals and
Other References   390

Bookstore Listings   395

Must Reading   426

About the Contributors   427

Glossary of Mystery Terms   432

Editor Index   437

Category Index/Novel Markets   439

Category Index/Magazine Markets   444

Category Index/Agents   449

General Index   454

From the Editor

Today's mystery writers must be like the sleuths they create, ferreting out clues to the market, using a network of informants to find out what editors are looking for and maybe even hiring an agent for muscle.

The *Mystery Writer's Sourcebook* was created to help you solve the mystery of writing and publishing crime fiction. This second edition is a hybrid of the two types of books that we at Writer's Digest Books have been publishing for years. The **Craft & Technique** section has the kind of expert advice you find in our how-to books, while the **Markets** sections provide in-depth information similar to our annual market guides. All the clues you need to crack the mystery market are in these pages.

In the **Trends** section, for example, mystery author, columnist and bookstore owner Jan Grape puts you in the editors' shoes and lets you walk around a bit, giving you "A View from the Experts." The industry's top editors and authors tell you what current trends will last, which ones have been done to death and what will be hot tomorrow.

In the **Craft & Technique** section, you'll learn the intricacies of plotting, how to drop clues, the importance of setting and the secrets of writing a series. Established mystery writers Jeff Abbott, Jack Bickham, Joan Hess, Margaret Maron, Sharyn McCrumb and Sharon Gwyn Short, along with seasoned mystery editor Michael Seidman, are your men and women on the inside.

The editors of the top markets for mystery short stories and novels sing like canaries in the **Markets** sections. You'll discover what books and authors they grew up with, what they read now, what they're dying to see and what they never want to encounter again. In addition, you've got submission guidelines and a list of the specific categories of mystery each publisher specializes in. And you've got their mug shots, too.

Eventually, you'll want to hire some muscle. Agent Don Maass tells you how to find and keep good representation in the **Agents** section. Then we list the heavyweights, the G- men of the mystery representation field, and give you the bird's eye lowdown on their operations.

Ruth Cavin, Janet Hutchings and Michael Seidman examine two novels and an award-winning short story in the **Editors at Work** section. Their "Anatomy of a Sale" pieces tell you how three new writers made it out of the slush pile and onto the bookstore shelves.

Finally, you've got a host of informants in the **Resources** section. Robert J. Randisi gives you the scoop on mystery writers' organizations, conventions and awards. Don Prues steers you down the Infobahn in his piece on computer online services. Bookstore owners from across the U.S. and around the world give you the skinny on their stores. And there's a list of reference books and magazines to put you hot on the trail of the latest developments not only in the mystery fiction market, but in the crime and police fields as well.

The bottom line is that we've given you just what you need to crack the mystery market. And, of course, we've tried to give you the most up-to-date information possible. But no field of business is entirely static and the writing field is especially dynamic. Therefore, you should keep abreast of changes by reading mystery and writing periodicals like *The Armchair Detective*, *Mystery Scene* and, of course, *Writer's Digest Magazine*. Query publishers before sending them your work. And, if you find that something listed in this book has changed, help us keep you and your fellow mystery writers updated by letting us know.

Likewise, we want to know about your successes. When you sell that first or next short story or novel, drop us a note. Our address is:

The Marketplace Series
Writer's Digest Books
1507 Dana Avenue
Cincinnati, Ohio 45207
E-mail: wdigest@aol.com

Good luck!

MYSTERY AND CRIME WRITING TRENDS

Trends: Views From the Experts

J A N   G R A P E

Who will be the next Sue Grafton? The next Tom Clancy? The next John Grisham or Tony Hillerman? The odds of predicting what might hit the *New York Times* bestsellers list are about the same as winning the state lottery. And, while it will tell you what's already been done, reading what's on the bestseller list won't give you any indication of what is selling to editors right now.

The problem is, what's on the bookstore shelf now isn't what editors are buying. Today's bestsellers were acquired over a year ago, and editors have already bought the books they will publish in the next two years. So, while it is important to read and keep up with the market, it still is of little help in telling you what editors are buying now. For that, you need to go to the experts.

When you ask mystery editors and authors what they think the next big concept in mystery might be, most of them say the same thing: You can't go by current trends. "It's hard for me to think about trends," says Carolyn Marino, senior editor at HarperPaperbacks. "I buy what I like and what I respond to." She tries not to buy what isn't selling, but she says, "I don't worry about trends because I don't have a crystal ball to see that far into the future."

Michael Seidman, of Walker & Company, says he doesn't pay attention to trends in the marketplace, either. Personally, he doesn't care for them and never looks for trends when he buys a manuscript. He says, "If a Lynda S. Robinson book like *Murder at the Place of Anubis* or *Murder at the God's Gate* happens to be a historical/mystery at the exact time when historical/mysteries are being published and touted, then we've published the right book at just the right time. That's great for the author and great for us. But I try not to limit my choices and, when you go for what might be hot at the moment, you are definitely limited."

Although trends can't be predicted, one trend that does show amazing longevity is the series character. From Sherlock Holmes to Kinsey Milhone, hardboiled to cozy, series remain popular among readers and publishers alike.

"For a long while now," says Joe Blades, executive editor of Ballantine Books, "the only surefire way to launch a career in crime fiction has been through a series. Mystery readers love series characters for the continuity—following characters you care about through various adventures—and the chain [book]stores prefer series because they are clearcut, easy to pigeonhole. Independent mystery specialty stores don't necessarily have this prejudice."

Writing the series character presents a set of challenges all its own, and we cover those later in this book (page 34). But there are a few things to keep in mind when writing your mystery. Ruth Cavin, senior editor and associate publisher at St. Martin's Press, defines a good mystery as nothing more than a good story which just happens to have a murder or crime in it. "We have good stories with great atmosphere and which are set in numerous and various places, cities other than New York, Los Angeles and San Francisco. They're not academic mysteries nor police procedurals. They're absolutely not even classifiable. They're just good mainstream fiction." That's one trend she has seen for several years and one she expects will continue for many more years.

Cavin also says that six months after reading a good book, she probably might not remember who committed the crime, but she will remember the protagonist. "And that's why I usually buy a book—a really memorable character." What makes a character memorable often is key to what defines a trend. Characters with unusual occupations, cultural backgrounds, habits and such stand out in readers' minds and become popular. So what kinds of characters and stories do editors see developing?

Ethnic Sleuths

"Ethnic sleuths will get stronger," says Scribner's editor Suzanne Kirk. "Main characters modeled after real life—real people." Keith Kahla, editor at St. Martin's Press, says he thinks a trend is stories featuring well-thought out, well-written ethnic characters. He cites Barbara Neely's character Blanche White (*Blanche Among the Talented Tenth*) and Eleanor Taylor's Mattie MacAlister (*Slow Burn, Gone Quiet*) as examples. "I'd be excited to see a new voice, a new venue, like maybe an Asian author with an Asian character."

"No one could have ever predicted the success of Tony Hillerman," says Carolyn Marino. "His stories are set in the Southwest with a Navajo police officer as a protagonist—and Hillerman's success is phenomenal."

Regional Settings

Closely related to the ethnic sleuth trend is the popularity of books with small town or regional settings. "People like to read about different areas of the country with strong local color and characters," says Ballantine's Joe Blades. Ed Gorman, mystery author and editor of *Mystery Scene* magazine, agrees. "Different background and settings, regional novels which take you to places you've never been before, like Dana Stabenow's *A Cold Day for Murder* or *A Cold-Blooded Business*, should continue to be strong. I've never been to Alaska but I enjoy reading all about it." Other examples are D.R. Meredith's John Lloyd series (*Murder by Sacrilege*) and her sheriff series (*The Homefront Murders*), set in the Texas Panhandle. Barbara Burnett Smith set her *Writers of the Purple Sage* in a small Texas town, and Steve Womack's P.I. series (*Way Past Dead*) takes place in Nashville.

Even if the setting of your novel isn't exotic, your treatment of it can be. "Look at Earl Emerson and his Seattle heroes Thomas Black and Mac Fontana (*The Portland Laughter, Morons and Madmen*)," Gorman says. "No one else is doing what he does. Look at Bob Crais with his Elvis Cole in Los Angeles (*Lullaby Town, Free Fall*), and John Lutz with his Fred Carver in Florida (*Burn*) and how they give you new insights into their settings. Susan Rogers Cooper with her East Texas comedienne Kimmey Kruse (*Funny as a Dead Comic*) shows us a different Texas than Dallas or Houston."

New writer David Daniel set his novel, *The Heaven Stone*, in a Massachusetts fishing town with a large Cambodian population. With his fresh insights into a familiar premise of old line Yankees and new immigrants, Daniel produced an award-winner; *The Heaven Stone* won the 1993 St. Martin's Press/Private Eye Writer's of America's Best First Private Eye Novel Contest.

Characters Drawn From Real Life

"If the author has or had the same occupation as the protagonist," says Suzanne Kirk, "it helps. That gives the publisher a built-in nonfiction angle which helps with publicity. Real life experiences create a hook for

TV or radio shows to book authors to talk about their background or knowledge and plug their book at the same time."

Nevada Barr's protagonist, Anna Pigeon (*Track of the Cat, A Superior Death*), is a good example of this kind of author-character tie-in. Pigeon is a national park ranger. Guess what Barr's occupation is? Park ranger.

If you don't have the experience your hero or heroine has, try to get it. Patricia Daniels Cornwell, author of *Cruel and Unusual* and *The Body Farm*, isn't a doctor of pathology, but she went to work in a medical examiner's office and learned the terminology and the slang germane to the character of Dr. Kay Scarpetta. These little touches can make your story ring true.

The Older Sleuth

"Older sleuths are going to be the next hot trend," says Sue Grafton, author of the bestselling Kinsey Milhone series (*A is for Alibi, B is for Burglar*, etc.). She cites that the baby boomer generation is getting older, and they like to read about people nearer their own age. Joe Blades agrees. "With the graying of America and the baby boomers aging," he says, "this very well could be the next new trend. Look at Carolyn Hart's Henrie O, seen in *Dead Man's Island* and *Scandal in Fairhaven*. Henrie's past sixty and she's a very strong, very intriguing character." Bob Randisi, mystery author and co-founder of the Private Eye Writers of America, also thinks the older protagonist can be seen as a small trend. He says to look at Bill Pronzini's 'nameless' detective and Jim Burke's Dave Robicheaux, who are in their fifties. Lawrence Block's Scudder is fifty-five.

The Female P.I.

Ruth Cavin says "a trend used to be books with tough female private eyes, but those are now an institution." Keith Kahla agrees, saying that while the traditional female private eye (like Sara Paretsky's V.I. Warshawski) may be overbought, fresh and original female sleuths are still being published. He points to Wendi Lee's detective Angela Matelli (*The Good Daughter*) and S.J. Rosen's Lydia Chin (*China Trade*) as examples.

Kate Stine, editor of *The Armchair Detective*, says she'd love to see more thrillers with women protagonists, such as *The Eight* by Katherine Neville, or *One for the Money* by Janet Evonavich. "I wish there had been books like these when I was growing up," she says. "Adventure stories with self-reliant, independent women heroines. The female Indiana Jones is an exciting concept, and I'd probably buy a story like that if I could find it."

Ed Gorman mentions the works of Sandra West Prowell (*By Evil Means*, *The Killing of Monday Brown*), Karen Kijewski (*Copy Kat*, *Wild Kat*) and the work of Patricia Cornwell as examples of books with strong female heroines. "Those books have been generating good contracts and good sales," he says.

Prowell once said that when she first began *By Evil Means*, she kept hearing that absolutely no one was buying female private eye books. But she believed in her half-Catholic, half-Jewish, Montana native character Phoebe Siegal and kept on writing. Prowell's work has an original voice that gives a fresh look at the Big Sky Country. So, despite the odds, Walker & Company bought the first and second books in the series, which led to a multi-book contract for Prowell with Bantam/Doubleday for the paperback rights.

The Traditional Story

Keith Kahla sees a steady trend in the plot-driven, traditional puzzle story, like books written in the 40s and 50s, but thinks the trend is moving away from the gimmicky stuff. "A mini-resurgence could occur in the hardboiled style; the dark, Jim Thompsonesque style. For example, George Pelecanos's *Shoedog*, *Down by the River Where the Dead Men Go*." Gorman agrees, saying, "I think the most marketable type of mystery today is the traditional story. Not the cozy, not the locked room puzzler, but the old-fashioned traditional story with a strong protagonist, either male or female."

"The male amateur [sleuth] written in a slightly soft-boiled style, perhaps with a touch of humor, should come on strong," says Joe Blades. "Bill Crider's Professor Carl Burns (*One Dead Dean*, *A Dangerous Thing*) comes to mind, as does Jeff Abbott's librarian, Jordan Poteet (*Do Unto Others*, *The Only Good Yankee*)."

Along the same lines, Kahla doesn't see an end to the historicals, yet. He says the quality of historical mysteries being published is improving; therefore, sales are up. Kate Stine agrees, "I can see historicals still running strong and continuing to grow."

The Juvenile/Young Adult Mystery

One other brief note, regarding trends in the juvenile/young adult markets, comes from author Carol Gorman. She says the only trend she sees is that the crimes have become more serious. "It used to be that in juvenile mysteries, the kids would be solving the mystery of a stolen bike or jewelry or something like that. Now, as in my *Chelsey and the Green-Haired Kid*, it's more likely that the mystery will revolve around a murder connected with drug dealings or something else equally serious. Mary Downing Hahn wrote one dealing more peripherally with murder and drugs in *The Dead Man in Indian Creek*. These books are not graphic, but they are scary with realistic bad guys."

The Non-Series Novel

Joe Blades sees a tiny trend developing away from the series and towards non-series, bigger suspense novels. Laurie R. King's *A Grave Talent*, and the two Minette Walters novels, *The Sculptress* and *The Scold's Bride*, are two examples of this, with more emerging every day. The opportunity is there for current series novelists who occasionally want to break from their ongoing characters for a single-entry venture. For the reader, this provides variety—and perhaps more important for the writer, it's an opportunity to experiment and refresh his or her craft.

Ed Gorman agrees. "J.A. Jance is a good example of a writer taking a break from her series character and writing a stand alone suspense like *Hour of the Hunter*. With that book she's written a regional with a slightly different take on the Southwest than Tony Hillerman."

Joe Blades believes that in the crime fiction market the series will continue to dominate, but there will be a small shift in the status quo.

"A Fresh Voice Will Always Sell"

"The most exciting thing now is that there's a market for all types and categories of mystery," says Joseph Pittman, editor at Dutton/Signet, a division of Penguin USA. "The male P.I., the female P.I., the cozy, the regional amateurs, the suspense thrillers, the police procedurals, the older detectives, the ethnic detectives—it all works on a certain level. Our list is very diverse. I always ignore trends and buy what I like."

Keith Kahla agrees. "All of the above goes out the window in the face of the well-written, well-told story. A fresh voice will always sell."

Without exception, editors look for high-quality, well-written manuscripts. Stories fitting that criteria, says Michael Seidman, will always sell, regardless of the current trend.

"There are so many good mysteries being published today that right now is the golden age of mystery," Ed Gorman says. "Some purists will disagree, but read Sue Grafton, read Lawrence Block, read Margaret Maron . . . the work of these writers is absolutely outstanding. They write appealing stories that take a slant we have never had before; they have appealing, intriguing characters and backgrounds. But mainly they tell a good story."

Carolyn Marino advises new writers to "write what excites them, to seek their own story and their own voice and not worry about trends." Trends are pointers, usually to what not to do.

Even if what you're reading now is new and fresh to you, you can bet it is not so fresh to editors and agents. More than likely five new manuscripts similar to what you just picked off the bookstore shelf already have been bought and are in production. It's possible that the market might stand one more similar novel before it reaches saturation, and if you have a similar novel *already completed*, the odds are slightly higher that it may be bought. But you have to remember, the odds are only cut by a small margin. Agents and editors have talked to each other about nothing but that type of book for the several weeks.

So instead of your trying to guess what might sell, the experts recommend writing what *you* enjoy, what you would buy. Carolyn Marino advises new writers to "write what excites them, to seek their own story and their own voice and not to worry about trends."

In the end, it is the writers who set the trends. When a book that is fresh and original hits the market and sells like crazy, pretty soon everyone wants something similar. That's the beginning of a trend. And if you write the book that is unique to you, *yours* might be the next trend.

CRAFT AND TECHNIQUE

The Vital Importance of Setting

JACK M. BICKHAM

I t's probable that most mystery writers begin their story-planning with considerable thought about the nature of the crime, how it came about, and how the sleuth eventually will solve it. This, of course, is fundamental.

As the mystery attracted more sophisticated readers in recent years, a second serious concern developed for the mystery writer: the major characters, and how to make them vivid, complex, and completely believable. That's become a "must," too.

Now, increasingly, a third major factor has come to the fore: story setting. The mystery writer of today simply cannot afford to skimp on presentation of this major element, and it better be accurate, graphic, and properly presented!

Not that setting was less important in the past; it's just that so many writers seem to have taken it for granted. But if you look at the better mystery writers over the years, you'll see that they knew setting's importance all along—and the best ones still know it today.

It's difficult, for example, to imagine the classic mysteries of Ross Macdonald set anywhere but in the decaying urban sprawl of southern California; the look and sound and sense of the area permeate every chapter of Macdonald's best novels. The *feel* of those often-shabby motels and cafes, growing out of precise descriptions of them, makes the storyline more credible.

The Travis McGee novels of John D. MacDonald provide another excellent example of how important setting can be. Try to imagine McGee away from his Florida setting, where his houseboat, the Busted Flush, so well characterizes his whole philosophy of life. (MacDonald tried once or twice to move McGee out of Florida for a job, and the resulting novels are generally considered the weakest of the series.)

More recently, Tony Hillerman has achieved great success with his books set in the American Southwest and embedded in the Native American culture. And Eve K. Sandstrom has been well rewarded for her "Down Home" mysteries, which flourish in a unique, hot, dusty, small-town Oklahoma which she portrays well.

So today the locale of the mystery is more important than ever before. The general fiction reader wants to be drawn into an imaginary world, and entertained there. To draw the reader in, the writer has to provide good description of what the story place looks like, sounds like, possibly smells like—and feels like. The mystery reader demands no less just because she happens to be focusing also on a plot puzzle. Indeed, in many cases the mystery needs more and better handling of setting than many other kinds of stories because the writer has the additional problem of drawing the reader into a fictional situation that may border on the incredible: happenings light years from anything that reader is familiar with. A good setting can make everything else seem more acceptable.

Thus it is that a writer who wants to present an effective mystery must take story setting very seriously. But what's involved in this task?

In the first place, you must *select your setting carefully.*

Second, you must *learn to know your setting intimately.*

And third, you must *make sure it's presented vividly.*

Let's look at each of these factors.

Selection

Sometimes a setting seems to be picked almost by accident, or as an afterthought. This mistake can doom an otherwise marketable story. The setting must not only be believable; it must mesh properly with the plot and characters.

It's hard to imagine, for example, that a light-hearted cozy mystery involving the theft of a prize-winning quilt could be played out success-fully against the backdrop of a bleak and gritty city slum. The elements would not match up: the grim setting would destroy the desired light tone of the story at every step, and it would be almost impossible to get anyone to believe the quilt plot in that setting anyway.

Therefore, in evaluating a mystery setting, certain practical questions of credibility must be asked. Here are some of them:

1. Is it believable that the desired plot would take place in the setting under consideration?
2. Is it believable that this setting would have in it the kind of people

I need to make this plot work?

3. Will descriptions of this setting contribute to the kind of emotional mood I want to evoke in the reader?

Our real lives may be jarred now and then by news reports of big-city gang violence in a small rural community, or a small-town policeman solving a case by using the very latest DNA test, or a sunny ocean-front community with an atmosphere that is somehow black and miserable. Such things can happen.

In the world of fiction, however, events, people and mood should usually be tailored in a way to *fit*, not detract from one another. Thus a plot concerning gang violence would be more believable, and have more impact, if set in a gritty inner city environment; an officer with the savvy to use modern DNA testing would be much more credible if placed in a metropolitan center, and a mood of bleakness and despair would be easier to make convincing in a hostile, dirty town in the middle of a harsh winter.

Knowing the Setting Intimately

It's not enough to have chosen setting well. The next step is to get to know that setting as intimately as possible.

No one can guess all the facts about your story's physical world. But here is a list of things that almost always must be known.

- The climate at the time of year to be used.
- Details of the look of things, from terrain to buildings to quality of streets to how the residents ordinarily dress. (And if there is a particular real-life building or lake or mountain involved, exactly what the appearance or construction or height or depth of that thing really is.)
- How the place sounds—traffic noises, noon whistles, whisper of wind through trees, foghorns in the bay, coyotes yodeling in the night.
- How the place smells, if that's a factor . . . and in a town near an oil refinery or a pulp mill, it may be.
- How the place feels, in the sense of whether it seems generally happy or gloomy or isolated or open or whatever.
- Population density—whether a street or road should be crowded or empty, whether a walk down the sidewalk in the evening means

loneliness or being pushed around in a crowd, whether the office is spacious and isolated from the next, or is a cramped cubicle separated from its neighbor only by a six-foot metal partition.
- Usual quality of light—whether it's usually sunny or gloomy, or if a high hill makes sunset come prematurely, or if the office has bright windows or solid walls and blue-tinged overhead lights.

This suggestive list should provide an idea of directions that should be taken in your own research.

Learning the answers may not always be easy. But a good writer will never guess what a town looks like, how the inside of a bank appears, or what color best describes the lake. The good writer will *find out*, either by going there (the best), or looking things up in the library, or by interviewing someone who knows the answers, or a combination of all three. A single mistake in presentation of a physical setting will be caught by somebody. Count on that. And for that person who caught the error, all belief in the story is lost.

Unfortunately, editors are very smart and check everything. They are usually the ones who spot the mistake—and back goes the manuscript, rejected.

Of course some settings will be entirely fictional. But that doesn't mean anything goes. If the setting is not a real, specific place, it at least is in a region of a country, or some identifiable part of the world. Your story's Montana town in the northern Rockies may have a brief snowstorm in May or June, for example, and that's acceptable because real Montana mountain towns do have late snows sometimes. But a writer couldn't put that same June snowstorm in Florida, and then beg off by arguing that "It's not a real town! I made it up!"

The moral: when in doubt, check it out. Thoroughly.

Presenting the Setting Vividly

Once the details have been found and checked and double-checked, a big piece of setting work is done. *How* the setting will be presented is another question, however.

Ordinarily we think of description as a sentence or paragraph, or several paragraphs, which describes the physical attributes of a place in a kind of stop-action technique. And this kind of static description, whether from an omniscient viewpoint or the viewpoint of a character,

15

is good and necessary.

In all such writing, the writer should strive for strong, accurate nouns and active verbs. Color and contrast often are a key to describing something visually. Short sentences are better than long ones, and a heavy reliance on adjectives or adverbs is probably a signal that the description is going on too long, or limping. Static description often takes very careful rewriting to make it as pointed and vivid as possible.

Sometimes, however, especially in the mystery, static description is not practical. The action gets going pretty fast, and the last thing we want to do is slow down the reader's pace. In such cases it might be deadly to stop to describe something about the setting, because—after all—when we stop to describe, we *stop*. Plot development, character movement, thought, dialogue—all come to a halt while the description is rendered.

For this reason, it's wise to consider putting some of the description of the setting into *glimpses on the fly*.

In this technique, the writer does not "back off" to describe anything, but stays firmly in the viewpoint of the lead character. Then, as that character continues to talk . . . or drive the car . . . or run down the street, she has only enough story time to get a glimpse of this, hear a bit of sound there, perhaps catch a whiff of pine as she hurries past the park.

This kind of description on the fly must be planned carefully, with bits of information sprinkled through the character's movement in very small, selective bits. A general rule is that even a simple description—of a building, say, or the view from the side of the mountain—must be broken into several small compartments of information and inserted a bit at a time.

If you remember that the character in movement *does not have time* to take in more than fleeting impressions, the writing is easier and more believable. For example, a young woman fleeing a killer on foot through the city streets might glance back and spot him rushing through the dense sidewalk crowds behind her, then later look up with dismay at the clotted traffic blocking her way across the busy intersection just ahead, then—again later—hear the noon chimes of the clock tower as she runs down the side street, then (after more chase details) feel the first spatter of warm summer rain on her face as she gets to the next corner, then (later still) smell Karmelkorn at a red-and-white plywood booth across the way.

Such glimpsed details can accomplish as much as a longer view in keeping the reader aware of the looks and smells and feel of the city setting, while at the same time keeping the plot on the boil.

Now, however, before we assume our mystery setting is perfect, we have to consider just a few more complications.

In a nutshell: Setting is a lot more than physical surroundings, even though that's all we usually think about when the word "setting" is mentioned.

What else is there? For one, *factual information* is a key part in a story's setting.

Ordinarily, we tend to focus on current factual information, such data as the following:

- Geographical or topographical details. Mountain scenery or plains? Hot southern summer or the milder summer of Canada? Flat or hilly?
- The town's population, form of government, biggest building, major business.
- Kinds of plants and animals that may be seen.
- Special techniques or information that may be known or used by the main character—what he needs to know if he is a CPA, for example, as opposed to his special factual expertise if he happens to be a farmer.

Every story setting will dictate its own list of needed factual information to make the story setting seem real.

Presentation of setting facts can be handled in much the same way as descriptions of sensory details. Here, however, "dumping in" great gobs at a time is even more dangerous than it is with description. The careful writer finds ways to slip in short paragraphs of setting facts that the reader must know. But she will also develop brief scenes in which the information can be brought out by the characters themselves.

This is done by creating a felt need in the viewpoint character to learn certain facts about the environment. This character then asks one or more other story characters about the needed information. As the other story people tell the viewpoint character what he or she needs to know, the reader learns it also.

In all this, a credible story world will slowly build and transport the reader into the story's setting.

In terms of total credibility, however, still another aspect of setting must be considered: *setting intangibles.*

Here we are talking about such matters as:

Historical setting.
Cultural setting.
National or regional setting.

And here we are getting into some deep water.

The point, however, can be stated fairly simply. If plot has to fit setting, and character has to fit both, then we must remember that the history, culture and regional orientation of a setting can directly affect how people there think and live.

What do we mean by this? Consider: In Detroit not so long ago, on the night before Halloween, kids celebrated "Devil's Night," traditionally a night for pranks, by doing everything from soaping car windows to (sadly!) burning abandoned buildings. In not-so-far away Columbus, meanwhile, children went door to door in costumes, asking for candy, as part of that city's "Beggars' Night" tradition. In isolated farm homes across much of America, they didn't do anything at all that night, or possibly bobbed for apples, because the environment made anything else impossible.

In each case, if you had asked the locals why they were doing what they were doing, they would have blurted, "Because that's what we do here."

It would be a very wise answer. Tradition varies with place, or setting, just as attitudes, fears, hopes, beliefs, expectations, and all things do. If you set a story in San Francisco, that fact alone sets up a historical-cultural backdrop radically different from a setting somewhere in Utah.

And not only does place make a difference, so does time. Things change. The writer who sets a mystery in the New York of 1918 is not dealing with the same environment that would exist in a mystery set in New York today. On the very simplest level, the old-time detective would not have a fax, a cellular phone, a car radio—or a car!—a Glock sidearm, or a myriad of other things. He would not have the crime, either. And at a deeper and more meaningful level, the old-time cop's *attitudes and assumptions*—as well as his motivation—would be quite different.

So if plot, character and setting are to be in total, credible harmony, we must think of the setting's historical background, region, and culture.

At the outset we mentioned two contemporary mystery novelists, Eve K. Sandstrom and Tony Hillerman. They both work on the current scene. But their stories feel and are vastly different because of the settings they employ. It's not just that Sandstrom's southwestern Oklahoma town is out on the dusty prairie flats, while Hillerman's people live in a desert with mountains closeby. It's the part of the settings related to history and the prevailing culture that make the mysteries profoundly different. Oklahoma was settled late, mostly by Southerners, and attitudes are mostly Southern to this day. Hillerman's area around Shiprock has been Indian land for longer than anyone knows, and its history is filled with ancient native American tradition; therefore the people act differently. A characteristic Sandstrom mystery plot simply would not work in a Hillerman setting, and *vice versa*, not because the places look different, but because the "intangibles" such as history and culture have bred far different people.

How, then, is a mystery writer to proceed with that next project as far as the setting is concerned? Let's review.

First, he must realize that selection of setting is probably far more important than he may have suspected.

Second, he must pick a story setting that will help make the story believable.

Third, he must carefully mix and match setting with such other story elements as plot and characters.

Fourth, he must do whatever is necessary to get to know the selected setting intimately.

Fifth, he must present setting in the most effective ways.

Sixth, he must be alert to the often-overlooked intangible effects of setting.

It sounds like a lot of work, and sometimes it is. But thought beforehand, good research and artful presentation can make all the difference between a near miss and a sure sale.

That makes it all worth the effort, doesn't it?

It does for me.

Plotting the Mystery

SHARON GWYN SHORT

Plot is the backbone of the mystery, perhaps more important in the mystery than in any other genre. An exceptional writing style, unique characters, or a dramatic theme will not rescue a mystery novel from a weak plot. Plot is a major part of the mystery's appeal to readers because it provides a definite story, and a suspenseful one at that—a chance to indulge in a few delicious thrills and, hopefully, to feel a sense of catharsis at the end when the "bad guy" is caught, a sense of justice in a fictional world that all too often the reader doesn't get at the end of the 6 o'clock news.

The requirement of a strong plot is also what makes the mystery genre so appealing to many writers. Before even the first glimmer of an idea for a mystery, the mystery writer knows his or her plot must have a definite beginning, middle and end. Someone is a victim (most often of murder), someone is a perpetrator, and someone satisfactorily resolves the crime. This basic structure provides a framework in which to work—a comforting thought to a writer who may be wondering where to begin.

Yet, ironically, it is because the mystery not only provides but demands this framework that the mystery is also one of the most challenging genres for writers.

Early in the mystery's history, "the plot was the thing." Readers wanted a challenging, intelligent puzzle. Characters were created to move forward a cleverly conceived plot. Modern mystery readers still want the challenging, intelligent puzzle, but along with it fully-realized, richly-developed characters. The elements of plot and character—along with setting, theme, and style—must work together to create a well-integrated whole.

To provide this, mystery writers must now create what I call character-driven plots. The difficulty is that this brings up the old chicken-and-egg question—which comes first, character or plot? The answer, for me, is to develop characters and plot virtually in tandem, one playing off and enriching the other.

Another chapter in this book describes how to develop interesting characters. In this chapter, I will first describe the essential elements of the mystery plot. Then I will describe how I create character-driven plots in several stages: before actually plotting, while plotting, and while writing the story or novel. During each stage, I create tools to help me with plot development.

These stages are not rigidly divided. The creative process for developing a plot is not like following the steps for assembling a bicycle; I shift back and forth between these stages several times before I am firmly working in a new stage.

Essentials of the Mystery Plot

Besides working within the framework given above, mystery writers must follow a few "rules" to play fair with the reader. They may use red herrings to decoy readers from too easily guessing the solution, but they also must provide all the clues used to solve the mystery and introduce all the suspects early on. It's no fair to name Uncle Harry as the murderer at the end if Uncle Harry hasn't been introduced somewhere in the beginning or middle of the story. It's no fair for the fictional detective to solve the mystery by saying Uncle Harry has an in-depth knowledge of the deadly herbicide used to kill the victim if Uncle Harry hasn't been shown at least once using the herbicide to kill off pesky weeks in the garden.

Besides fair play, suspense is critical to good mystery plotting. This means revealing facts a bit at a time, giving readers just a little bit more knowledge about the crime, enough to make him or her say, "I think I'll read just one more chapter." One technique for building suspense is to end a chapter with a hint of danger or with a hint that in the next chapter a new revelation will take place. Putting the detective in danger also adds to the suspense.

Plotting Pre-Work

I stated a few paragraphs ago that the plot of the mystery requires someone to be murdered, someone to commit murder, and someone to solve the murder. These characters, as well as other supporting characters such as suspects, must be wholly realized creations, with believable motivations and personalities and lives. Plot is comprised of characters' actions, and believable, interesting actions can only arise from believable, interesting characters who live and work and love and die in believable, interesting places.

For this reason, I spend a great deal of time creating my characters and settings. The tools I use to develop these aspects of a story are *character sketches* and *setting descriptions*. As I work on these, plot images—bits of action inspired by character or settings—come to mind. I use a *plot image journal* to keep track of these images.

Character Sketches

To create Patricia Delaney, the private detective of my mystery series, I spent numerous hours writing pages about her before I even knew the kinds of adventures in which I would involve her.

I started on the surface, with the easily created characteristics—she's tall, and has green eyes and brown hair. And then I went a little deeper and gave her a family and personal background—she's the youngest of six children in an Irish Catholic family and grew up in Cleveland; now she's single and lives and works in Cincinnati.

I continued giving Patricia more depth, asking myself what is she most afraid of? What motivates her to be a detective? What kind of spiritual and emotional life does she have? What does she do when she's angry? When she's sad or happy? And now, before I begin a new Patricia Delaney adventure, I explore the question: How has her previous adventure changed her or helped her grow as a person?

I ask myself these questions about not only my detective, but also the murderers, the victims, and other characters in my novels. I use the answers to write in-depth descriptions for each character.

Setting Descriptions

Another area I develop before plotting is the settings I plan to use. My Patricia Delaney novels are set in Cincinnati, but I have also created a fictional suburb (Alliston) where Patricia lives and works, and fictional towns outside of the metropolitan area of Cincinnati.

For actual settings, I visit the areas and gather information (maps, tourism brochures and articles) about them. For fictional settings, I create a basic map and write a general description.

Plot Image Journal

For me, plot development begins as I work on character sketches and setting descriptions. For example, as I write a character sketch, images of the character in action spring to mind—perhaps I see the victim, a woman named Amy, for example, just seconds before she's murdered, lovingly watering a plant in her garden. I note this scene in what I call a plot image journal. Often, as I note one image another springs to mind. What about the murderer? Is he or she just out of Amy's view, cold-bloodedly pulling on gloves to keep from leaving fingerprints at the scene? Or recklessly driving through town to get to the victim, furious but not yet aware that fury will lead to murder? If so, will someone note the reckless driving and think to call the police? And what about the police officer who gets the call—what is he or she like?

And so on, and on. One image, spurred by simply developing a character, can bring up many plot points as well as other character possibilities. This is the creative process at work; once the conscious mind is working on an idea, the subconscious mind will offer up many possibilities for characters and plot. The plot image journal, as well as the character sketches and setting descriptions, are ways to capture these possibilities.

At some point, however, it's time to begin using the character sketches, setting descriptions, and plot image journal to construct a plot. For me, I know it's time when I feel an almost intuitive mental shift to move on to detailed plot development.

Moving on to detailed plot development does not mean that my pre-work on characters, setting, or plot images is finished. As the creator, I can (and usually do) change characters or settings as I develop my plot. But the tools I've created thus far enable me to keep a change to one aspect of a character consistent with all of his or her other aspects; a perpetually late protagonist cannot show up early in a scene for the purposes of discovering a clue just to make a plot work.

Techniques for Plot Development

Armed with my character sketches, setting descriptions, and plot image journal, I am now ready to begin constructing a plot for my story.

Actually, I plot three stories: the *"back story,"* the *"story as it happened,"* and the *"story as it is told."*

The "Back Story"

The "back story" is the motive. Let's return for a second to my earlier example of Amy, the victim. I have to know what she's done that would motivate someone to murder her. Perhaps she's blackmailing Uncle Harry because she's discovered he's cooking the books in the business he runs with her father, Joe.

Now, of course, I have quite a few details to work out—why doesn't Amy just tell her father Joe about Uncle Harry's naughty deeds? How did she discover Uncle Harry's crime? And why is Uncle Harry cooking the books? But once I've worked out the answers, I have created my back story—the story of what has happened to create a situation in which a character is motivated to murder another character.

The "Story As It Happened'"

Then comes the "story as it happened." In this story, I work out, for example, how Uncle Harry goes about murdering Amy and why he feels he must go to such extremes. Perhaps Amy has suddenly resolved a conflict with her father and Uncle Harry realizes that she will probably now feel she must turn him in. Uncle Harry knows he'll lose considerable sums of money if this happens, so he lures Amy into the garden and douses her with the deadly herbicide.

The "Story As It Is Told"

Neither the "back story" nor the "story as it happened" are revealed whole cloth to the reader. These stories are tools to help me create the story which is shared with the reader—what I call "the story as it is told." Both the "back story" and the "story as it happened" are discovered by the detective (and the reader) in "the story as it is told."

In the "story as it is told" about Amy, for example, the reader might see Amy and her father at a family reunion announcing that their rift has been mended and they are now on great terms. Let's say at the family reunion we have the suspects and the detective, who is Amy's cousin Ralph, a police officer on vacation at the family reunion. Ralph notices that everyone seems excited by Amy and her father's reconciliation—except Uncle Harry, who wanders out to the garden to pull a few weeds, and great-aunt Matilda, who storms off to the kitchen.

And on the "story as it is told" goes, with Amy eventually getting murdered, great-aunt Matilda—and a few other deadly relatives being suspected by cousin Ralph, who cleverly gathers clues and encounters danger and uncovers all sorts of skeletons in the family closet until he realizes the murderer had to be the herbicide-wielding Uncle Harry.

As I build the main plot, I also like to build a sub-plot for the detective which in some way reflects in the detective's life what is happening in the main plot of the story. Perhaps detective Ralph is himself a father, and on this family vacation is trying to deal with issues with his own child. The sub-plot gives me a chance to illuminate the detective's character, as well as the theme of the novel—perhaps, in this example, that family conflicts may be difficult, but are best dealt with lest they become deadly.

My tools for developing the "story as it is told" include a *point-of-view chart*, *scene note cards*, and *preliminary outline*.

Point-of-View Chart

Before creating the "story as it is told," the writer must decide upon point-of-view, most usually first person, third person limited, or third person multi-viewpoint. I write my Patricia Delaney novels in third person multi-viewpoint, so once I've worked out the "back story" and the "story as it happened," I make a viewpoint chart on which I very briefly synopsize the story from the main characters' points of view. I get a large piece of paper from a sketch pad, make a column for each main character, and in the column synopsize the story from that character's point of view.

This tool helps me select scenes for my novel and balance the number and mix of scenes written from various characters' viewpoints. I think it is useful for writing in first-person and limited third-person as well, as it helps keep straight what the protagonist cannot know about from first-hand experience but may need to discover from interacting with other characters.

Scene Note Cards

At this point, I get out a pack of three-by-five note cards and, referring to all the tools I've created so far—the character sketches, setting descriptions, plot image journal, "back story," "story as it happened," and viewpoint chart—I begin jotting scenes onto the cards.

To continue with my previous plot example, "Amy makes up with father" might go on one card, while "Cousin Ralph discovers Amy dead among the petunias" might go on another card, and so on. Once I'm done filling out cards, I lay them out in the order in which I think the scenes should occur—a nice expanse of floor is helpful at this point.

The advantage of this technique is that it lets me play with scenes, moving cards around to try new orders. It also lets me see where the holes in my "story as it is told" might exist. Once I have the cards in an order I like, I number them, but I always number in pencil in case I want to reorder the scenes or add scenes or take some away.

Preliminary Outline

Finally, with the scenes in some semblance of order on my note cards, I can then divide the scenes into chapters, and create a rough chapter by chapter preliminary outline. I call it a preliminary outline because I know it will change as I actually write.

We all have an image (perhaps left from school days) of the outline as a rigid device that demands we follow it. It is not. Writers create outlines; writers can change them. Many of us have had the experience of writing directions to a destination and then discovering, partway there, that a detour is necessary. This is what happens, almost inevitably, when working with an outline because an outline is simply a step in the creative process.

Plot Development While Writing

After all of the previously described spadework, I am at last ready to start writing the first draft of the "story as it is told." And yet, even with all the spadework, I find that my story inevitably changes to some degree as I am writing not only the first draft, but subsequent drafts as well.

The changes usually arise from my knowledge of my characters; by now I know Uncle Harry pretty well, and I realize that he might do or say something differently than what I've plotted.

To keep track of how the story changes, I have one final tool, the *chapter summary outline*. Once I finish the first chapter, I write a brief synopsis of it, including any pertinent clues or character developments. After finishing chapter two, I write a synopsis for it beneath the first chapter's synopsis; and so on with each chapter, thus developing an outline as I write a book.

The chapter summary outline gives me a way to check if I really did mention a pertinent clue in Chapter Three when I'm working on Chapter

Twelve and need to address that clue again.

To revamp an old cliche: the plot always thickens, but it never quite gels until I am done writing—and rewriting, and rewriting, and rewriting, and rewriting once more.

In Summary

Keep in mind that no two writers plot in quite the same way; the process I have described works for me, and it is a process which I have developed over years of trial and error. Ask me again in a few years how I plot a novel, and I'm certain something in my process will have changed. In reading about how I create my plots, I hope you will find something you can incorporate into your own creative writing process, just as I have learned from other writers.

Give a Clue

MICHAEL SEIDMAN

C lues are crucial to all fiction. When characters are trying to make decisions, to choose between the options you give them in the course of a story, their choices will be based on clues, those indicators that tell them how *other* characters will react to the decisions they make. Because reactions are what your story is about—and because every scene leads to a reaction—the clues you offer will be basic to the development of the characters and the direction of the plot.

In mystery fiction, clues are essential. They are what the sleuth uses to determine whodunit. In all forms of the traditional crime novel, the clues must be presented to the readers and the detective at the same time. If readers aren't made aware of them, they can't solve the crime (while withholding clues from readers works in some forms of crime fiction, it is *not* the way to build a loyal following). Most mystery readers view the genre as a game between the author and the audience; they want the author to win, to fool them, but they want an even chance.

A clue may be physical evidence, body language, a comment made in an unguarded moment. Whatever clues you choose—and don't forget red herrings, false clues that lead readers and characters astray—they must be obvious to the discerning and missed by the careless. You want to avoid highlighting them: A clue with a neon arrow pointing at it takes all the fun out of the game.

Let's look at some clues and the ways they might be presented. I'm not going to quote from any published works because mystery readers, rightly, resent it. If they haven't read the book and I discuss things that will reveal the solution, not only will the joy of reading be gone, but the book's would-be readers might turn violent. (That could be the setup for a clue: You learn, in the course of a story, that disappointed readers can be dangerous. Later, when a book reviewer is murdered, that recalled detail may start you thinking that an embittered reader killed the reviewer. A possible event has been foreshadowed, a possible motive given.)

Clues at the Seat of the Crime

Human nature and so-called normal behavior provide clues (and explain motives and motivations) and have the advantage of not having to be spelled out. For instance, nine times out of ten, the toilet seat in a home occupied only by a woman will be down (unless she's in the middle of housecleaning). When you think about it, most men are housebroken to the extent that they return the seat to the lowered position after use.

Knowing that, your sleuth might notice the seat is up when at the murder scene. (This might also be more noticeable to a female detective.) If you make too big a deal of it, you're going to tip your hand to the fact that a man was in the house and used the facilities sometime before or after the commission of the crime. Of course, it's possible that the victim had recently called a plumber, or that a man had been there innocently. (If she was doing housework, it's likely that some cleanser would be nearby, another clue.)

Red herring? Should your police officer ask to have the underside of the seat dusted for fingerprints? Should it be ignored? That's where the fun—and the challenge—comes in.

How do you present such information to your reader? Certainly not by writing, "I noticed that the toilet seat was up, which struck me as strange, because. . . ." Your detective might be looking through the domicile and comment, "The bathroom was generally clean, everything in order. I saw a few dark-colored spots of dried liquid on the porcelain rim of the toilet and made a note to have the technicians check it."

You've just done two things: First, you've set up those spots as potential clues. Blood? Cleaning liquid? Something else? Second, while your reader is concentrating on *that* information, he might ignore the fact that you can't see the rim of the toilet if the seat is down. You've been fair: The information is there; if the reader doesn't discern it, it's his problem.

There's an old ploy that's still viable and can be easily changed and adapted: the cigarette butt with lipstick on it. Now, if you happen to have two crushed cigarettes in the ashtray, and the lipstick stains are not quite the same, will that indicate that the visitor was there for a longish period of time, with decreasing amounts of makeup to transfer, or does it indicate that there were two women? Or did one woman change her lipstick for some reason? And was it even a woman? Is the corpse that of a cross dresser? Was the visitor a transvestite?

And you don't need to make it a cigarette butt. What about a lipstick stain on the edge of a container of milk in the fridge? (The stain on a glass has been overused.) Or on a napkin, or the victim's collar? Or neck?

Any of these "clues" can be used just as effectively for motivational and/or foreshadowing purposes in other forms of fiction. If a lover discovered a lipstick-stained cigarette in her significant other's apartment, if could be used to indicate a coming breakup, or put to whatever other plot use you'd prefer.

Such clues might become evidence. You might, for instance, use them to establish someone's presence. (Lipstick stains can be used in much the same way as fingerprints, although I don't know if that would hold up in court.) In the famous case of Dr. Sam Sheppard, a cigarette butt was accidentally flushed down the toilet by someone at the crime scene. Think of the ramifications and of how you might use that. Was the officer who flushed the toilet involved in the murder? Or just stupid?

Anything found around the house—and in cars, boats, garages, etc.— can be used in this way to boggle the mind. And that's good, because using them allows you to throw your reader off the scent. It'll be important for you to play "The Purloined Letter" with the information. As you recall, the letter in the famous Poe story was hidden in plain sight. That's what you want to do. A police detective at a crime scene lists and records everything because he can never tell what's important. Burying in that list a tube of glue used to hold a toupee in place might seem beside the point, but later, when the detective is at the autopsy and hears a comment about how someone wishes he "had a head of hair like that," you may be revealing something that astute readers will remember. (And if you mention the glue only by brand name, you're still giving the information; it's up to the reader to find out what Folliglu is.)

Taking Clues Personally

Personal behavior is another greenhouse for clue cultivation. Not only does it help develop characterization but, if you establish that someone rubs her thumb and forefinger together when she's lying, and later have your sleuth comment on a dry, rubbing sound while he's interrogating her, you can establish the lie that places the perpetrator at the scene. Again, it's not a good idea to write, "I knew she was lying because she always rubs her fingers when she lies." Approach it this way: Your detective (or narrator, or the character herself) reflects on the physical act early in the tale. At some later point, the fact that the character lied about something is brought to readers' attention by an offhand comment: "I thought you said you slept over at Giorgio's house Thursday."

"Oh, I must have been confused. I'm sorry, it was Wednesday night, now that I think of it."

If you planted that earlier clue, that's all you have to say. Later— during an exchange readers know is filled with lies—you show the nervous habit again, without authorial comment. In the final confrontation, the habit and the lie are connected; if readers have been paying attention, they'll know.

Spreading the information throughout the novel has several advantages. You'll not only avoid the pitfall of calling attention to your clue, but you'll also be forced to show, not tell. You'll prevent the slowing of the story by stopping for blocks of description that don't move the action. So, if your killer never wears a particular item of clothing—perhaps a tie—you might comment on it when you introduce your character (long before he's been identified) by writing, "Joe wasn't wearing a tie." Later, during the commission of a crime, you might mention that the perp's collar was open. Another time, you mention a gold chain. Or chest hair sticking out of the shirt. A pattern of behavior is established; again, it's up to the readers to put the pieces together. If they don't, when your detective reveals the solution at the end of the story, they can only say, "Of course! How did I miss that?" They missed it by not remembering that Joe wasn't wearing a tie during a business meeting (when one might be expected—at least outside Hollywood); they didn't remember it because you kept the mentions far enough apart, and offered lots of other information in between.

Clues in Front of Their Faces

Not every clue should be hidden; just as many jigsaw puzzle enthusiasts begin by forming the border, you have to give the reader a context in which to work. The poison you choose to use on your victims will, perhaps, leave some telltale sign. The first time it is seen, the reader probably won't know what this sign means. The second time it creates a pattern. The third time, you may spill the beans: It's evidence of oleander poisoning. Now, which of the characters might have access to oleander and know that even the water in the vase in which it is kept can be highly poisonous? And who else might know?

Much will depend on the manner in which you choose to tell the story. In a first-person tale (like most P.I. stories), the narrator sees, hears or otherwise discovers something at exactly the same time as the reader. It's in how the character puts the information to use that the fair play exists; he may be bald and thus know about Folliglu. To the reader, that brand name may appear meaningless. The detective, however, isn't allowed to uncover anything the reader doesn't also discover. He can't, when explaining the process of deductions, say, "When I spoke to Joe on Friday, he said . . ." unless the reader was privy to the conversation at the same time.

In third-person formats, information can and should be revealed through conversations and narration. Again, the fact that there *was* a conversation with Joe on Friday—as well as the substance of that conversation—must be known, but we don't have to be there; we can learn about it later that evening. (A case can be made for the first-person detective revealing the conversation in the same manner, while talking to an associate, or a police officer. The key is in the revealing.)

In a police procedural—or if your amateur detective has the background and access to a crime scene—certain things may be evident: the lipstick stains, the nature of a wound, that the residence was *tossed* (searched) or other similar pieces of evidence. The fact that the body was moved, however, may be evident only to those with some knowledge of rigor mortis or lividity; the time of death may only be guessed by knowledge of decompositon, rigor, or the breeding patterns of flies and maggots. Most mystery readers will be aware of these things. It's usually sufficient to say, for example, that the body was prone and that there was dark blotching on the backs of the legs, the shoulder blades and the buttocks; the reader who is paying attention will know that the victim has been dead for a while, originally lay on his back, and was rolled over sometime later.

(The exact timing of things like that can be learned from the books in the Writer's Digest Books Howdunit series, which offer a wealth of information about everything from poisons to weapons, forensics to crime scenes, private eyes to police officers. If you are going to be a mystery writer, the entire series—there are eight books at present—should be on your shelf. See page 391.)

A final word on foreshadowing: The old saw is that you don't show a shotgun over the fireplace in the first scene unless it's going to be fired before the last. Too much foreshadowing, however, too many hints about what may come, can be counterproductive. Too many hints about what's behind the green door will lessen the suspense rather than heighten it—except in the hands of exceptional writers. While not necessarily a minimalist, I do think that less is often more, and that you should give the reader only enough to pique interest and play fair.

You do that by mentioning everything that's necessary, and nothing more. (Red herrings, false trails and the like are necessary for the fun.) Your clues may be ambiguous, they may be disguised by misdirection—having a character dwell on one seemingly important subject and only toss off a comment about something else (which is actually more important)—or they may be spelled out so that the reader has a blueprint from which to build the case.

While reference books can give you the information you need to maintain accuracy, the best way to learn the tricks is to read the masters. That list is different for each of us, certainly, but you know the writers who amaze you as they pull killers from their deerstalkers. Look at the way they fool you—and then go them one better.

Writing a Series

Mystery readers like series. From Sherlock Holmes on Baker Street to Arly Hanks in Maggody, Arkansas, fans keep coming back to novels with familiar faces and places. And for that reason, publishers are attracted to series mysteries as well. But is a series character right for you?

The simple answer is yes, if that's what you've really wanted to write all along. You should not try to write a series just because that's what sells; you should write it because that's truly what you like to read and are interested in writing.

"My agent announced to me that it's more marketable," says Joan Hess, author of the Claire Malloy mysteries and the Arly Hanks series, "and that's what I prefer to read, also. When I'm looking for a new author to read, I look for a series, because if I like one book, I want to be able to enjoy the characters in several other books."

Jeff Abbott, whose novel *Do Unto Others* won the 1995 Agatha Award for Best First novel, didn't have a choice. "They bought two books in the series at the beginning. But, like Joan, I enjoy series characters a lot. I like to see how a character grows and changes over the course of several books, and I get involved in the lives of the secondary characters. So that's what I wanted to write."

Even if you don't *plan* on writing a series, you may find yourself coming back to a character again. "I had no intention of writing a series," says Sharyn McCrumb, author of the Elizabeth MacPherson novels and the Ballad series, "but I sold the first book, which was *Sick of Shadows*, and the publisher said, 'Where's the next one?' They do prefer to publish series books, and while I thought of it as a stand-alone, like *Pride and Prejudice*, they didn't think so."

McCrumb, whose Ballad novel, *She Walks These Hills*, won the 1995 Agatha Award for Best Novel, says publishers like to package writers, and they prefer them to keep the same style from book to book. "They want writers to be like candy bars. If you get a Snickers, there's always peanuts in it. They don't want you to have different voices." Little room is allowed for experimentation or devices that don't follow the series' pattern. "Sometimes you get ideas that do not easily fit into the mold that you have in the series. I want very much to do a book about the first woman hanged in North Carolina in 1833, but my series is set in Tennessee. How am I going to work this in so that somebody can take an interest in researching this old murder case?"

This is not the only problem you might encounter in writing a series. In fact, serial books have a whole host of unique difficulties. The recurring sleuth, his or her associates, and their surroundings all have to be carefully planned by the author from the start and closely monitored throughout. While there is no easy pattern, no magic recipe for creating the perfect series, there are some items to keep in mind at the outset.

Joan Hess

Sharyn McCrumb

Jeff Abbott

The Sleuth

One character you need to know very well is the main character—the sleuth. You and your readers will be spending a lot of time with your sleuth, so it pays to know him or her as well as, or even better than, you know yourself. Editors agree that for both writing and marketing purposes, it helps if the author has the same occupation or has shared the same background and experience as the main character. As already mentioned in the previous section (see **Trends**, page 4), shared experience gives the publishers a good way to promote the book through talk shows and interviews.

This is not to say your book is doomed to failure if the sleuth doesn't share your job or hobby or background. Jeff Abbott isn't a librarian, nor has Joan Hess lived in a small Arkansas town. Sharyn McCrumb, until recently, did not know how to build a coffin. To make their characters believable, they read, took classes and talked to people.

"I live in a university town of 45,000, in a greater metropolitan area of 100,000," Hess says. "For Maggody, I was unfamiliar with small towns. My editor suggested the series, so I hopped in my car and drove around all these little towns and talked to police departments and talked to people in antique stores and restaurants and hardware stores and gas stations. It was not a pretty experience, but that's where the characters and the town came from."

"To me, that's the fun part," McCrumb says. "I went to Berea College one December to learn how to build a coffin in their woodworking department because the people in my next book are building a coffin. I've gone on patrol with a deputy sheriff; I have been out on the Appalachian Trail with a naturalist; I wrote a guy in prison to find out how Hiram would escape. I do a lot of research."

Abbott is not a librarian, nor has he been one, but since his Jordan Poteet is, Abbott has made friends with the librarian in a small Texas town. "There's a very nice library in a small town that's not terribly dissimilar to Mirabeau in its locale and size, and the library really is the focal point of that community. It's very heavily used. And the lady who is the chief librarian there does not have an MLS; she learned the ropes by starting off as an assistant and working her way through. She's given me lots of really good information." Abbott also talks to the police department. "The librarian and the police chief are pretty good friends, so they kid about what I ask one and what I ask the other. One is quite the town gossip and the other is rather stony faced and never seems to blink, no matter how odd the question is."

Hess has no qualms about calling people to find the information she needs. "I've been known to call the police department and ask questions." She points out that, despite Arly Hanks's job, she is not a professional crime solver. "The Maggody books were once described as a police procedural series. I found that a fascinating remark. I purposefully made her an amateur sleuth with a badge. She does not have a crime lab or any of the tools of the trade."

The Secondary Characters

Part of the joy of reading a series is getting to know the many friends, lovers, children, parents, co-workers and such that the sleuth comes in regular contact with. These secondary characters often serve to lighten the tone, provide clues and further complicate the plot for the sleuth by getting captured or becoming lost or endangered. If you think of your favorite series character, you can probably name two or three recurring secondary characters as well.

While a joy for the reader, this 'supporting cast' can cause some problems for the writer. Careful records must be kept from book to book about the actions, backgrounds and names of every character. A good rule here is *write it down*. Do not rely on your memory or your editor.

"In my innocence, I thought that the copy editor would be familiar with the series," says Hess. "So not only did I not check names very carefully (which is why people's names change throughout the Maggody series just a little), but I have one character who had died, poor Mrs. Wockermann, and that's why people were living in her house. Two books later, she's doing quite well out at the nursing home. The copy editors are contracted independently, so you don't have the same copy editor over and over again," she says, which is why you can't rely on them to catch these kinds of continuity errors.

Another problem is overpopulation. "What if," Abbott says, "you start off with a character in the first book, and after three books you say, 'you know, I really don't want to keep this person around anymore. Can I get rid of him?' If I killed off one of my continuing characters, I'm not sure my editor or my agent would be too happy. One of my continuing characters is Eula May Quiff, who is a romance writer in the first book. When I turned in the first hundred pages of the second book, both my agent and my editor said 'Where's Eula May?' They liked her a lot in the first book and they wanted her to reappear. So I had to go back and put her in, and that was fine because I enjoy writing her. But there may be other characters that pop up, and you worry about whether the cast is becoming too crowded."

Hess has a similar problem with each new book in the Maggody series. "I can't kill off Jim Bob or Mrs. Jim Bob," or any other recurring character, she says. "It would be rather absurd to have them seriously suspected of anything, because we all know they are going to show up in the next book."

Which brings up another problem involved with writing a series. "With each book," Hess says, "I have to introduce the same situation and the same characters. And after nine Maggodys, it becomes very difficult to introduce the characters without making the regular readers fall over dead out of boredom." At the same time, she says, a certain amount of introduction has to be made for readers who haven't read any of the other books. Sometimes it's as simple as having your main character driving through town, noting the familiar landscapes and waving to the recurring characters. Hess admits that it's not very exciting to write, but it has to be done.

"Dell Shannon wrote something like thirty-seven of those police precinct books," McCrumb says. "And I got in on about number thirty-five of the series. Having read none of the earlier ones, the thing read like a Christmas newsletter to me. She was giving me little updates on the family life of a whole bunch of people I didn't know. These guys' kids were taking swimming lessons, and this one's dog was sick and this one's daughter was about to go off to college. And I frankly didn't care. There wasn't a lot of plot in there because we had to catch up on family."

"I've only had to mess with this twice so far," says Abbott, "in writing *The Only Good Yankee* and the third book, which is *Promises of Home*. I try to do it as quickly as possible, but there are only so many ways you can say 'Hi, I'm Jordan Poteet. I've moved back to this town to take care of my mama, who's dying of Alzheimer's.' Sometime I might have another character allude to it, but Jordan narrates the story, so generally it will be him. You want to make it as painless as possible, because you don't want to dwell on this for your previous readers, but you also don't want to confuse a new reader. You want to make it very plain and succinct and clear."

McCrumb doesn't have those problems, due to the way she structured her two series at the outset. In her Elizabeth MacPherson series, the main character is a forensic anthropologist who travels around the country to different crime scenes. The only constant is MacPherson herself, and McCrumb reintroduces her by opening each book with a letter from Elizabeth to her brother, Cameron. "I almost always begin with a letter, usually to her brother, and she's very sarcastic. And so the information is conveyed quickly, but in a very funny way. But in *If I'd Killed Him When I Met Him*, I open with a letter to Cameron, and she's talking about her therapist and how they're telling her to express her grief. The letter ends with, 'Cameron, if I knew where you were, I'd mail this.' "

"Someone suggested," says Hess, "that in the front of the book there ought to be a pocket with a list inside. You pull it out if you've never read the series before and it says 'Here's a description of the characters and the town and everything you need to know, and now we can start the story.' I don't know. I sort of like that. It would be a joy to jump right in and not have to explain the relationships between these people and what impact if any the last book has had on Maggody or Claire and Caron. But the book has to stand alone. The reader has to be able to enjoy the book without spending the entire time saying, 'Who's that?' "

No matter how you choose to re-introduce your series characters, one important consideration is to keep them from becoming sidekicks. Sidekicks, such as Sir Arthur Conan Doyle's Dr. Watson, are not really characters, but props to make the main character look smarter or cooler or better than everyone else.

"I'm in dire danger of having Junebug and Candice be Jordan's side-kicks," Abbott says, "but they are characters in their own right, and they are not there simply to serve as foils for him. Certainly they are there when he's involved in investigations, but I resist always having them pop up to make some observation or to make a wisecrack. They are part of his life and his relationship with them changes from book to book. He's drawn closer to them both as a close friend and of course with Candice being his significant other." Making them into Dr. Watson-type characters, he says, would make them less interesting people.

Hess deals with a set cast of characters in both of her series. "Some-times the focus changes and some of them become major subplots or are involved more strongly in the main plot. When I introduced Kevin and Dahlia in *Malice in Maggody*, I had no intention of making them anything but one-line characters. But I became very interested in them, so they came to be one major subplot." They cannot, however, be relied upon to take the most thoughtful approach to helping Arly. Nor can Ruby Bee, Arly's criticizing mother, and her friend Estelle. "I use Ruby Bee and Estelle to do some fairly off-the-wall things. Arly is not a particularly funny character. She will make some dry observations, but most of it's bouncing off of her while she tries to focus on the problem."

Another concern is aging. "Are they getting older?" says Hess. "If my characters age at the rate the books come out, charming Caron [Claire Malloy's daughter], who is now fifteen, would be twenty-three. She would have graduated high school, college and gone off to get a job, which makes it very hard to maintain the mother-teenage daughter relationship." Nevertheless, you don't want them to remain forever one age, either. Time lines and ages can get tricky without some forethought. Keep in mind as your series progresses how much time has passed between each novel. It doesn't have to be the same amount of time for each installment, but it should move forward consecutively, without leaping around.

Occasionally, there will be the character who's sole purpose in the story is to provide a clue or an alibi. Nevertheless, that character does not have to be one-dimensional. In Abbott's *Do Unto Others*, Jordan seeks out Chelsea Hart in order to confirm his cousin's story that he was on a date with Chelsea. As Abbott wrote the scene, he didn't have a conscious plan to make her anything more than an alibi provider. But, with just a few extra lines, she became a memorable, realized person. "She only has one scene in the whole book," Abbott says, "but she makes a statement about what it is like to be unattractive in a small town and to realize you are being courted for a reason, an ulterior motive, just to provide an alibi for a night when something bad happened. Instead of being someone who just sort of sulks about her unattractiveness, she's almost defiant about it. At one point, Jordan thinks that she will get far in life for having her sense of bravado and self-worth. Her basic role in the mechanics of the story is to further suspicion towards a certain character, but you don't have to leave it at that. You can give the reader a little something more."

The Setting

Where your novels take place is equally as important as who is in them. Earlier in this book, Jack Bickham showed you the vital importance of setting (see page 12). But, like sleuths and secondary characters, the setting in a series has some unique concerns. Some authors, like Abbott, find it easier to write about a fictional place than a real one.

"The very first book I wrote that wasn't published," he says, "was set in Houston, and I never felt that I created the setting as effectively as I did with a fictitious place. I grew up in the big cities of Texas, but I spent most of my summers in the small town that my grandparents lived in. I thought it would be more interesting to write about a small town."

Like your sleuth and your secondary characters, you must know your setting well. Many writers, including Hess, McCrumb and Abbott, suggest making a map. Hess has a map of Maggody, and Abbott has one of Mirabeau. But more important, you need to know the *culture* of your setting.

"These people should only be able to exist in this kind of setting," Abbott says. "The characters are a product of the setting. This is their native soil, so to speak, and the way they interact should convey a lot of the setting. The way small town gossip works, the way that you can't sneeze without someone on the other side of Mirabeau or Maggody knowing that you've done this. I didn't want people to read my book and say 'well, this is an American small town, or maybe even just a Southern small town.' I wanted them to feel that this is a *Texas* small town. Mirabeau itself has to contribute something to the story, the same as a major character would."

For Hess, Maggody represents small towns not just in Arkansas, but anywhere. "It's the dynamics of a community of that size and the oppressive economy more so than it is Arkansas. I've been told that this could be Connecticut. There are pockets of Connecticut that have the same characters and have the same dynamics." The same holds true for her Claire Malloy series. "Claire lives in the fairly generic small college town of Farberville. I didn't mention that it was in Arkansas in the first book. I was at the ABA show, and a bookseller came up to me and said, 'I'm so pleased to meet you. I so enjoy selling mysteries set in New England.' I said thank you. But finally, in one of the Maggody books, I admit that Arly drives into Farberville."

The Price of Fame

Writing a series has a few other problems, ones that come after the first book is published. "Once you sell one, you won't have time to write another," Abbott says. "Even being under contract. Once you write it, it doesn't just go off to the publisher and you don't have to worry about it anymore. You get involved and pulled into the other parts of the business, such as publicity and going to conferences. Those are things that I enjoy, but it wasn't really anything I ever worried about while I was writing the book. It never occurred to me that those would be concerns. Then all of a sudden, it's like a list of new responsibilities and challenges for me."

"You become a writer because you don't work and play well with others," says McCrumb, "and you like sitting off by yourself where the only people you interact with say what you tell them to say. And then suddenly you're in a business where you have to be an author and you have to dress well and be charming and go out and talk to strangers. And it's just not a job that we were necessarily suited for."

"What I should have done very early in my career is get a book like this one [*Mystery Writer's Sourcebook*]," Hess says. "Or something about the dark secrets of publishing. Something so that I would have a better understanding of the industry. I still do not have a very good understanding of the processes and the different roles. I just can't discipline myself to sit down and read something to explain it to me."

"I learned the way I learned auto repair," McCrumb adds. "What's a carburetor? $135.00. You make one mistake at a time, and you learn."

"The only reason I survived," Hess says, stressing the importance of networking, "is that I met so many other writers in the genre who were willing to give me advice or lecture me at length. At the conferences and trade shows, I met not just fellow writers, but other editors and agents who were willing to give me advice. I did have enough sense to listen, even if I didn't necessarily act upon it immediately. Eventually, I acted on all of it."

Interview: Margaret Maron

M argaret Maron's novel, *Bootleg-ger's Daughter*, is unique. No other novel has ever won the Edgar, the Agatha, the Anthony *and* the Macavity awards for best novel of the year. For a mystery novel, it's as impressive as sweeping the Oscars.

Margaret Maron

You would think that, after all the awards ceremonies were over and it came time to sit down and write the next book, there might be a certain amount of pressure involved. The world expects more brilliance, another award-winner. It might be enough to lead to, well, *writer's block*.

Not for Margaret Maron. "I think I have never been blocked," she says. "I certainly have procrastinated at times; I'm a great procrastinator. But mostly I look upon it as a job. Teachers don't get up in the morning and say, 'Gosh, I'm really blocked on gerunds, I don't think I'll go in and teach today.' Dentists don't say, 'I'm blocked on doing crown work and cavities.' You just do it. It's a job and you treat it as a job. If I waited for inspiration, I don't think I'd get anything done. I find inspiration comes best when I'm actually sitting at my desk in front of the word processor. Lovely things happen. I almost never have bolts of the blue when I'm off doing something else. It's usually when I'm sitting right here, trying to make it come. And it does come."

Maron was first prompted to write at age eleven, after reading Edna St. Vincent Millay's *Renascence*. "I was also inspired by the fact that she wrote it when she was 19. I think it was the first time it had ever dawned on me that writing was an option. And to read she had written that poem when she was a teenager really blew my mind. I thought, 'Gee, I could do this too.' Until that point I hadn't made the connection between the printed page, which I adored, and the fact that it could be written by walking-around-type people."

The other book Maron cites as a major influence is Craig Rice's *Home Sweet Homicide*. "Looking back on it now, I realize I was fascinated by the image of the mother in that upstairs bedroom banging out a novel every three months in her bathrobe. I thought that sounded like a really great working concept."

The influences of Millay and Rice led Maron to write mystery short stories, which were the entirety of her writing career for over a decade. She sold her first story to *Alfred Hitchcock Mystery Magazine* in 1968, but never attempted the monumental task of crafting a novel. "I spent the first 11 or 12 years of my writing career writing short stories. I never thought I could write a novel. I was intimidated by the whole idea of even trying to write a novel," she says. But when she wrote a long short story and couldn't find a market for it, she decided to double the length of it and make it a novelette, in hopes that she could sell it to *Hitchcock*. They mailed it right back.

"By this time, I was getting into the character of Sigrid Harald," Maron says. "She started out as Lieutenant Peter Bohr, and somewhere between the short story and the novelette she had transmuted into Sigrid Harald. So even though it was rejected as a magazine-type novelette, I had gotten interested [in the character]. I thought maybe I could double it into a book-type novelette, and at this point I found my first agent. He sent it right back, saying nobody was buying book-length novelettes, but if I could double it into book length, maybe he could place it. And so I did and he did."

That novel, *One Coffee With*, landed with Raven House and editor Margaret Woollard in 1981, after circulating for two years. Raven House was an imprint of Worldwide, which also owns Harlequin. With the mystery imprint, they were attempting to market mysteries in the same serial format they marketed romances. "They spent I don't know how much money researching the market to find out what any of us could have told them. Mystery readers don't read lines the way romance readers seem to read anything in the line. Mystery readers read specific authors. They thought they could market mysteries the way they market the Harlequin books, and of course it didn't work out. Mine was one of the books that made it into the book club part, but was never generally released to the public." When the line folded, Maron says, they were very ethical and reverted all rights to her.

Although it had a rocky start, the Sigrid Harald series thrived, and the eighth book in that series, *Fugitive Colors*, is just out. "When I finally decided to do a book-length novel, I did look at it very rationally and methodically. I knew I enjoyed reading a book about a character who grew and developed over a series, so I decided I would make her that sort of character." She began by deciding Sigrid's profession. "I liked the amateur sleuth, but I didn't think I could be that inventive to come up with reasons why an amateur gets involved with murder in every book. I decided I would make her a professional, and that way she would have a ready supply of bodies and I could just pick her an interesting case." So Sigrid became a police officer. Despite that, however, Maron did not intend to write police procedurals. "My idea was that she would function the way P.D. James's Adam Dalgliesh or Tony Hillerman's Joe Leaphorn functions, which is as an amateur sleuth that just happens to be a police officer. If you'll notice, their books are not all that concerned with the hardware and the mechanics of police procedurals, but they're used as the jumping off point. That's what I wanted to do."

After Maron established Sigrid's profession, she infused her with character flaws and personal problems which Maron could then work out over the course of the series. When she had finished the seventh novel in the series, *Past Imperfect*, she says, "I had more or less solved all the problems I had given Sigrid from the beginning, so what I'm doing in the eighth book is recapping all the things that have happened in the past. I'm going to be sending her in a new direction with this book."

Maron is moving in a new direction herself with the Deborah Knott series, of which *Bootlegger's Daughter* is the first. While the Sigrid Harald novels are set in New York, where Maron lived for ten years, the Deborah Knott books are set in North Carolina, Maron's native state and current home. And while Deborah's turf, the fictional Colleton County, is Maron's creation, the voices and the characters are drawn from the rich Carolina culture. "When I first started, I thought mysteries had to be based in either New York or California, and since I didn't know California, I used New York. Now I'm getting much more attention with the Deborah Knott books, which are set in North Carolina." Part of this, Maron says, is due to the current popularity of regional novels, a trend she enjoys. "One of the nice things about reading any novel is you want to be taken out of your own world and put into a different world. And that's what we have today. You can indulge your proclivity for just about any section of the country you want, from Alaska to Florida, and with all degrees of realism or escapism in between."

Maron researches the places her characters visit by reading a lot of magazines and by visiting with a camera and note pad. She tries to stick to the West Side/Greenwich Village area of New York, Brooklyn, Chelsea and East Flatbush for her Sigrid Harald novels, because they are the areas she knows. For the details of police work and law offices, Maron relies on knowledge she's gleaned from taking paralegal and criminalistics courses at community colleges. "Also, I have no qualms about asking the experts," Maron says, adding that most police departments and hospitals are open to answering questions. "Explain who you are and what you want to know. But you have to be specific in your questions. You can't just say, 'Tell me how you do an autopsy.' You have to know specifically the question you want to ask them." Sometimes, Maron finds a letter more appropriate. In that case, she sends a letter with the questions and enough space for the person she's querying to write the answers right on the page. She also includes a self-addressed, stamped envelope.

In addition to asking the experts, Maron consults her collection of books and manuals on criminology, as well as a plethora of other reference books. "I have a handbook on poisoning; I have a handbook on guns; I have *Name Your Baby*, so I can find names. I have all kinds of dictionaries; I have a biographical dictionary; *Bartlett's Familiar Quotations*." She also has a world almanac, which she says is like having an updated encyclopedia on your desk. "I have polyglot reference books, law books, police organizations, criminalistic forensic science." She also likes the Howdunit Series published by Writer's Digest Books. "*Private Eyes*, *Police Procedurals*, *Deadly Doses*—I've got the whole set here on my shelf. I think they're very good, technical books." But the best book she's found is Vernon J. Geberth's *Practical Homicide*. "It's a textbook on tactics, procedures and forensic techniques," she says. "I know just enough law to get myself in trouble. When you don't know things, and you know you don't know things, you ask. But when you think you know stuff, and you don't ask, that's when you start getting yourself into trouble."

Maron's advice to new writers is simple: finish the book. "Talent is good, but perseverance is more important. I have read some very talented, some really beautiful first chapters and then, two or three years later, I meet this same beginning writer and they are still polishing that same first chapter." The main thing for a beginning writer, Maron says, "is to write and finish the work that you begin, send it out and start on something else. Don't be one of those who has a great first chapter and never gets beyond that. Finish a book. Look upon it as a learning process." Just as you didn't learn to ride a bicycle the first time you sat on one, Maron says, so it is with writing. You have to keep trying, keep practicing. "Most people seem to think all they have to do is start putting words on paper and, ergo, they're a writer. You have to serve an apprenticeship. You must think that maybe the first couple of books are just going to be learning experiences, proving you can finish a book. After that, it is perseverance and stick-to-itiveness, and all those dull, boring things your teachers have told you all your life."

NOVEL MARKETS

Marketing Your Mystery Novel

ROBIN GEE

Just as you wouldn't write a private eye novel set in Minneapolis without first researching the city and how private eyes operate there, you wouldn't want to send out that story without first finding which publishers are most likely to be interested in regional private eye novels. There's no substitute for a well-written, polished manuscript, but these days the savvy writer also devotes time and energy to researching the market to make the best of his or her efforts.

Marketing a mystery novel is in many ways the same as marketing any other form of commercial fiction. Yet, of all the various genres (romance, science fiction, westerns, etc.), mystery has the broadest range of markets. As with other categories of fiction, there are book publishers devoted solely to the genre and those with special lines set aside, but there seems to be room for at least a few mysteries on almost every publisher's list, including literary, religious and regional presses.

This is the good news in an area of publishing which remains very competitive. Developing a good marketing plan can give you a "leg up" on the competition. Each publishing house has its own particular focus or approach to the mystery field and finding those best suited to the kind of work you write is an essential first step on the road to publication. The market listings and in-depth interviews with editors in this book will help you target potential publishers.

Staying on top of changes and happenings in the mystery field is also essential to making the most of your marketing efforts. Become well-read in the genre, of course, but don't stop there. To really find out what's going on in the mystery field, start by visiting your local bookstore. Check out the shelves and talk to the bookseller if at all possible. These people are on the front lines—it's their business to keep track of what's selling and what different publishers are doing. There are hundreds of specialized mystery bookstores across the U.S. and Canada. Several are listed in the **Resources** section, beginning on page 395.

Networking is another way to keep on top of the mystery field. Try to attend one of the several annual mystery writers' conferences. Bouchercon travels to different locations each year and is considered one of the largest mystery events, but there are several regional conferences held across the country sponsored by Mystery Writer's of America, Private Eye Writers of America or other writing organizations. Meeting other writers, as well as editors, agents and publishers in the field, will lead you to first-hand knowledge of new markets, new mystery lines and developments in the field. We list conferences, writers' organizations and online services, another good route to meeting other writers, in the **Resources** section.

What Makes Mystery Publishing Different

While marketing a mystery is basically the same as marketing other types of novels, there are a few things unique about this publishing field. Although a certain degree of research is necessary for any well-written novel, authenticity and attention to detail is especially important in a mystery novel. Readers (and editors) have come to expect realistic depictions of settings, character occupations and crime scene investigations. If something presented as fact in a mystery novel doesn't ring true, the writer runs the risk of losing credibility. Successful mystery authors take time to visit libraries, interview police and other investigators and gather information to make their novels feel authentic.

Playing fair is another issue important to mystery readers and editors. Although the misleading clue or "red herring" is an acceptable device used in many mysteries, conclusions and solutions must come about through a logical sequence of events. Writers walk a fine line between playing fair and keeping things interesting. Editors look for writers whose solutions seem logical but who can keep the reader guessing until the end.

In general, the mystery field is made up of very distinct subgenres, although those lines are blurring. If your novel lies clearly within one of these subgenres, however, it's a good idea to label it accordingly when submitting to agents or publishers. See the **Glossary** starting on page 432 for definitions of the different subgenres.

One trend in mystery publishing that has affected almost all of the mystery subgenres is that today's mysteries explore a variety of different settings or cultures. Rather than New York, Chicago or Los Angeles, today's mysteries are set in small towns and non-traditional cities such as Seattle, Baton Rouge and Fairbanks. More and more novels feature detectives who are from different ethnic groups: Native American, Latin American, African American or Asian American. Women detectives remain popular, and books featuring gay or lesbian sleuths have made it onto mainstream publishers' lists, as well.

Quite a few mystery novels are set in ancient times and you'll find amateur detectives of all ages, backgrounds and careers. All this has brought a new level of excitement to the field and editors are clamoring for mysteries that will introduce readers to a variety of places and people.

One of the best ways to sell a mystery these days is to demonstrate the potential for a series. Keep in mind, however, that each book is bought on its own merits; so each novel must be complete in and of itself. For more on the ins and outs of developing and working in series, see "Writing a Series," on page 34.

About Mystery Publishers

Most mysteries are published in mass market paperback or hardcover form, although there is a growing number of trade paperbacks on the market. Traditionally, mysteries, like other category fiction, have been published in mass market paperback form; the paperbacks sold in grocery and chain store racks, as well as bookstores. Writers on all career levels are published in this format, but mass market is an especially good place for newer authors to start. Mysteries with broad appeal and mystery series do well as mass market titles. Today many publishers prefer hard/soft deals in which they contract to bring out a book in both hardcover and mass market paperback (softcover) form.

Many established authors are published first or simultaneously in hardcover, but in recent years publishers have been experimenting with bringing fairly new authors out in this form. Still, hardcover treatment is usually reserved for authors who have proven themselves in mass market or whose books have the potential to attract readers of mainstream fiction as well as hard-core mystery fans.

Trade paperbacks are larger paperbound books handled and sold in the same way as hardcover books. These are becoming a popular "midway" format for some publishers, enabling them to publish promising new authors and more of their established authors' backlists. Trade paperbacks are less expensive to produce than hardcover, but in terms of attention and prestige they are treated similarly to hardcover publication.

In addition to the large, commercial houses with lines devoted to mystery, there are several smaller publishers who incorporate a few mysteries into their regular fiction lists. Small and independent presses are usually very open to the work of talented new writers. The financial rewards may not be as great with a small or independent press, but writers say the personal attention and control they have over their books make these publishers very attractive. Writers whose work is considered too literary or experimental for most commercial houses may have a better chance at a small press.

While only a handful publish fiction, book packagers and producers can offer opportunities for mystery writers. Packagers produce books for other publishers. Either the publisher or the packager will come up with the idea for a book or series, but it is the packager who develops the book, hires the writer and artists, and produces the finished product. Most work done for packagers is work-for-hire—writers are paid a flat fee and the copyright belongs to the publisher. Quite often the writer will receive no credit for the book and will write under a pseudonym. New writers may find book packagers are a nice way to ease into publishing. The editors who work for packagers play an important role in the development of the book and provide writers with background information and other help along the way. Some of the popular young adult and children's mystery series, such as Mega Books's *Hardy Boys* and *Nancy Drew* series, have been published in this way.

About Agents

Not much more can be said about targeting publishers for your mystery manuscript without discussing agents. More and more commercial publishers are turning to agents as their sole source of submissions. The sheer volume of work, as well as cutbacks in many editorial staffs, has forced them to use agents as first-readers to screen out inappropriate submissions and unsuitable manuscripts.

Unfortunately for a new writer, getting an agent is almost as hard as getting published. Many writers try to market their first book themselves because it's much easier to find an agent once you have at least one published novel. Others try publication at magazines first to attract the attention of agents and publishers.

Many writers find their agents through networking. For new mystery writers especially, joining Mystery Writers of America, Private Eye Writers of America, Sisters in Crime or another professional mystery writers' organization can be a good career move. You can make important contacts, particularly with published mystery writers, who may be willing to refer you to an agent. These groups hold regular conferences and many offer opportunities to meet agents.

Approach agents as you would a publisher, with a query and sample chapters or a complete manuscript, depending on the agent's guidelines. It is generally acceptable to query more than one agent at a time, but avoid sending complete manuscripts to more than one agent for consideration. For more on finding and working with mystery agents, see "How to Find, and Keep, a Top-Notch Mystery Agent," by agent Donald Maass, beginning on page 277.

If you are interested in acquiring an agent, take a look at those listed in the **Agents** section of this book starting on page 291. This group of agents say they specialize in mystery manuscripts. Other agents may handle mystery on a case-by-case basis. For more agents, see the *Guide to Literary Agents*, published by Writer's Digest Books or the *Literary Market Place*, published by R. R. Bowker.

Above all, remember your agent is your business partner. Take your time when looking for an agent and do not hesitate to ask questions. A good agent will not only get you the best deal, but will also act as a business liaison between you and the publisher.

Approaching Book Publishers and Agents

After you have targeted a list of potential agents or publishers, find out exactly how they want to receive submissions. Some prefer query letters with sample chapters, while others prefer a complete manuscript. The listings in this book outline the preferences of different publishers and agents. Usually, you also can send a self-addressed, stamped envelope (SASE) to receive writers' guidelines.

Whether you approach an agent first or submit directly to a publisher, a professional presentation is essential. Granted, a poorly written manuscript will not make it out of a publisher's slush pile no matter how dazzling its presentation. But, a well-written piece may never be read if it's not presented properly. Editors are very busy and the competition is keen, so the best idea is to make your manuscript as easy to read and deal with as possible. As one publisher has said, "If it looks as though you don't care about your manuscript, why should I? I've got too many manuscripts to waste my time with one I can't read."

Ensure that your manuscript will be read and your talent has a fighting chance by making your manuscript easy to read. Here are a few manuscript do's and don'ts:

- Do type or computer print your manuscript on clean, white bond.
- Do make sure your submission is error-free and double-spaced with wide margins.
- Do use a new or dark, clean typewriter or computer printer ribbon.
- Don't use fancy or hard-to-read typefaces. Photocopies are fine as long as they are clear and always keep a copy for yourself.
- Don't fax queries, submissions or other correspondence unless you have cleared it with the publisher first. For the most part fax submissions are discouraged.

A word about computers and submissions: When sending a query with sample chapters or a complete manuscript, send a hard copy, not a disk. Unless otherwise noted, publishers do not want unsolicited disk or electronic mail submissions. If a publisher has requested a complete manuscript, check to find out if disk submissions are acceptable.

Always include a self-addressed, stamped envelope large enough (and with enough postage) to return your manuscript if you want it returned. Many writers send disposable copies of their manuscripts along with a self-addressed, stamped business-size envelope or postcard for a reply.

Queries, Cover Letters and Manuscript Formats

Some publishers ask for queries before you submit a complete manuscript. A query usually includes a whole package of material (also known as a proposal) including a query letter and samples of your writing—sample chapters, an outline and/or a summary of your story.

Keep your query letter to one page, preferably only a few paragraphs (see **Sample Query Letter**, page 57). Mention what type of mystery novel you've written and the approximate word count. You may want to start your letter with a hook, something interesting about your novel that will catch the editor's eye, but avoid too much hype—a clever capsule of the material is all you really need. Avoid telling the whole story, just give a few sentences that describe what the story is about. Since series are so popular with mystery readers and editors, if you think your book has series potential, mention this as well, but keep in mind each book must be sold on its own merits.

Personal information should be kept to a minimum. A rule of thumb is to include only the information that lends credibility to your writing. If your novel is a medical thriller set in a big city hospital and you are a doctor in a similar hospital, by all means mention it. If you, like your sleuth, happen to be an amateur rock climber, you may want to mention that, too. You can also briefly list previous publishing credits, especially if you have had mysteries or other fiction published in magazines or by other publishers. Just avoid personal details that have nothing to do with your story or your publishing history.

Often you will be asked to include a brief outline, a summary or a synopsis of your book. Unfortunately, these terms have sometimes been used interchangeably throughout the industry, so when in doubt about exactly what a publisher wants, check their guidelines. A synopsis is usually a brief summation of your story, a page or page and a half, single spaced. An outline generally follows the chapters in the book and can run from five to 20 pages depending on the depth and length of your book. List chapter headings and a few lines about what happens in each chapter. A summary can be a few paragraphs or a few pages—it depends on the particular publisher's definition of the term, so, again, check with the publisher if it seems unclear.

A proposal package may also include an author's biographical statement or "bio." Again, keep it brief—just a paragraph or two about your achievements and where you are from (see **Sample Bio**, page 58).

In fiction, queries or proposals are almost always accompanied by some example of your work, usually three sample chapters. Generally, publishers want the first three *consecutive* chapters. Editors want to know how your work flows from one chapter to the next.

When sending either a partial or a complete manuscript, include a title page (see **Sample Title Page**, page 59). Type your name, address and phone number in the upper left-hand corner and the word count on the right. Agented authors often leave the right-hand corner open so the agent can stamp or type in their name and address. Check with your agent about his or her preferences; some agents prefer that their address information be the only such material included on the title page. Center your title and byline about halfway down the page, and start your first chapter on the next page. If your chapter has a title, place it about a third of the way down the page. Be sure to number and include your last name on each page. Carry page numbers all the way to the end of the manuscript; do not start renumbering at the start of each chapter.

For complete manuscripts, include a cover letter (see **Sample Cover Letter**, page 60). Keep it brief as you would a query. Avoid retelling the story beyond one or two sentences since it's all there for the editor to read. For more information on how to set up a manuscript, cover letter, query letter or title page, see *The Writer's Digest Guide to Manuscript Formats*, by Dian Dincin Buchman and Seli Groves, or *Manuscript Submission*, by Scott Edelstein (both published by Writer's Digest Books). For more on submitting to publishers see *Novel & Short Story Writer's Market* or *Writer's Market* (also published by Writer's Digest Books).

More About Submitting to Publishers

Some mystery publishers will look at simultaneous queries—letters sent to more than one publisher at a time—but don't send a simultaneous manuscript submission unless the publisher has indicated a willingness to accept it. If you do send to more than one publisher at a time, however, it is common courtesy, if your work is accepted by one of them, to inform all the publishers who have been considering it.

Response time varies and agents in particular are known for having relatively slow response times. The times given in the listings and in writers' guidelines are estimates. Allow an additional three or four weeks beyond the stated reporting time before you check on the status of your submission. A follow-up letter should be courteous and brief and should include a SASE for reply.

As with any business, it's important to keep careful records. Record the date and nature of your submission as well as to whom it was made. When you receive a response, record the date. If accepted, keep track of when rewrites are due and any other deadlines you must meet. Some writers find it helpful to include information on rejections also—especially notes of encouragement. Not only does keeping records help you manage your submissions, but it can also help you make informed decisions when making future submissions.

The hardest part of the whole submission process is the waiting. Many established writers will tell you the best way to combat this "submission anxiety" is to start as soon as possible on your next writing project.

Bonnie Booth
1453 Nuance Blvd.
Norwood, OH 45212

April 12, 1996

Ms. Thelma Collins
Bradford House Publishing
187 72nd St., Fifth Floor
New York, NY 10101

Dear Ms. Collins:

I am a published mystery writer whose short stories have appeared in *Modern Mystery* and *Doyle's Mystery Magazine*. I am also a law student and professional hair designer and have brought these interests together in *Only Skin Deep*, my 60,000-word novel set in the glamorous world of beauty care, featuring hair designer to the stars and amateur detective Norma Haines.

In *Only Skin Deep* Haines is helping to put together the state's largest hair design show when she gets a call from a friend at the local police station. The body of famed designer Lynette LaSalle has been found in an Indianapolis motel room. She's been strangled and her legendary blonde mane has been shaved off. Later, when the bodies of two other designers are discovered also with shaven heads, it's clear their shared occupation is more than a coincidence.

Your successful series by Ann Smythe and the bestseller *The Gas Pump Murders*, by Marc Crawford, point to the continued popularity of amateur detectives. *Only Skin Deep* would make a strong addition to your line.

I look forward to hearing from you.

Sincerely,

Bonnie Booth
(513)555-5555

Encl.: three sample chapters
      synopsis
      SASE

Sample Query Letter

About the Author

Bonnie Booth

Bonnie Booth has been writing both fiction and nonfiction since 1990. Her mystery stories have appeared in *Modern Mystery, Doyle's Mystery Magazine* and *Mystery Zone Zine.* A professional hair designer, her nonfiction articles have been published in several trade journals including *Hairdressing News* and *Salons Today.*

Booth is also a student at Buckeye University's Marshall School of Law and plans to enter the field of corporate law.

Only Skin Deep is Booth's first full-length novel. She is currently working on a sequel, *Die Job,* featuring hair designer and amateur detective Norma Haines.

Booth operates The Cut Above salon in Covington, Kentucky, and lives in nearby Norwood, Ohio.

Sample Bio

Bonnie Booth   60,000 words
1453 Nuance Blvd.
Norwood, OH 45212

Only Skin Deep

by Bonnie Booth

Sample Title Page

Bonnie Booth
1453 Nuance Blvd.
Norwood, OH 45212

April 12, 1996

Ms. Thelma Collins
Bradford House Publishing
187 72nd St., Fifth Floor
New York, NY 10101

Dear Ms. Collins:

I am a published mystery writer whose short stories have appeared in *Modern Mystery* and *Doyle's Mystery Magazine*. I'm also a law student and professional hair designer and have brought these interests together in *Only Skin Deep*, my 60,000-word novel enclosed. *Only Skin Deep* is set in the glamorous world of beauty care, and features hair designer to the stars and amateur detective Norma Haines.

Your successful series by Ann Smythe and the bestseller *The Gas Pump Murders*, by Marc Crawford, point to the continued popularity of amateur detectives. *Only Skin Deep* would make a strong addition to your line.

I look forward to hearing from you.

Sincerely,

Bonnie Booth
(513)555-5555

Encl.: manuscript
       SASE

Sample Cover Letter

Primary Novel Markets

T he publishers listed in this section either publish mystery and crime fiction exclusively, have a strong mystery imprint, or maintain a strong mystery presence in their fiction lines. Since these are the primary markets for mystery novels, we've included in-depth interviews with senior editors at each of these companies.

We asked the editors about the history of their companies or mystery book lines. We've included information on how many books they publish each year, as well as how many of these are novels by authors who have not been published before. Editors gave us tips for writers submitting to their company, and a few general writing and marketing tips. They also told us what they like to read, what they've published recently and what they've published from their "slush" piles.

Before each profile, there is a brief list of subgenres that most interest the publisher. These will help you find the editors most receptive to the type of mystery you write. Read the interview and a few of the publisher's recent books, however, to get a more in-depth feel for the types of material they look for.

After the profile, you'll find a short listing outlining how to contact the publisher, including specifics on how to submit and how long it usually takes for the publisher to reply (the reporting time). Keep in mind that these times are estimates; give the publisher three or four weeks in addition to the stated reporting time before writing to check the status of your submission. Keep careful records in order to track when you sent your material and what responses you've received.

☀ ☀ ☀ ☀

BALLANTINE BOOKS

Established: 1952

Joe Blades, Executive Editor

CATEGORIES
Private Eye, Cozy, Suspense, Thrillers, Historical, Hardboiled Detective, Amateur Sleuth, Humorous Mystery, Urban Horror, Dark Mystery, Light Horror, Police Procedural, Malice Domestic, Psychological Suspense, Romantic Suspense, Surrealistic Mystery, Espionage, Courtroom/Trial

Ballantine, says Executive Editor Joe Blades, is a "general purpose, mass market purveyor of crime fiction. We do try to run the gamut—hardboiled and cozy or body-in-the-library are two ends of the spectrum." The company, he says, has a strong mystery publishing program, especially in the area of paperback originals and reprints. In the last few years, the publisher has turned its attention to publishing more hardcovers as well.

Along with his responsibilities as editor of a variety of general fiction and nonfiction titles, Blades is the primary editor responsible for Ballantine's mystery program which includes about fifteen paperbacks and six to seven hardcovers each year. He came to Ballantine from Avon in the mid-1980s, where he already had a reputation as an experienced mystery editor.

Although he is open to any type of mystery (and, indeed, you can find almost any of the various subgenres on the publisher's list), Blades says he doesn't find much fresh material in many of the hardboiled mysteries he sees. Admittedly, his tastes run toward cozies. "There's a richness in the cozy mystery. It seems to be a way for writers to explore professions and places that are far more diverse."

Regardless of subgenre, however, Blades says he's looking for strong, likable characters and fresh approaches to material. Well-written novels whose protagonists have interesting or unusual vocations and those set in locales outside the big cities like New York, Los Angeles or Chicago are most likely to catch his eye.

Ballantine's list is full of examples of mysteries that take a different approach to the classic mystery story. "I think it's good to get a mix of geography in our list. We do a number of series that involve specific professions like the priesthood or forensic anthropology and particular locales. We do several that could be called history mysteries. For example, we publish books by Lynda S. Robinson who is doing a series set in ancient Egypt in the court of King Tutankhamen."

One author whose work grabbed the editor's attention is Jeff Abbott, whose first book, *Do Unto Others*, could be categorized as a "nontraditional cozy." The book introduces a librarian as sleuth and is set in a small east Texas town.

"I like the author's fresh way of thinking, the interesting variations on themes he uses and even the new setting. Often these kinds of semicozy or malice domestic mysteries have been the province of women protagonists. Abbott's protagonist is a male, a former book editor in Boston, who has returned home to take care of his ailing mother. For extra income, he takes a job as a librarian at the local library. The setting is new to us too. East Texas is more in line with what I think of as the Southern tradition rather than the West, so that to me was exciting and new. While Abbott is traveling some familiar roads, he's also taking some nice detours I find very fresh and invigorating." (For advice from Jeff Abbott, see "Writing A Series," page 34.)

Blades says Mary Daheim is another Ballantine author whose work takes some different directions. "I think her books address a number of issues interesting to mystery readers today. She presents a particular piece of geography vividly and has very imaginative, colorful characters. Her protagonist is a newspaper editor in a small town in Washington state. This town existed once upon a time and for some reason disappeared around the time of WWII or shortly thereafter. She's reinvented the town and it has become a major character in her books as well."

Setting stories away from big urban centers and exploring small town life or "getting back to one's roots," says Blades is one way writers can find add a fresh perspective to their work. What makes Abbott's, Daheim's and other successful authors' work so popular with editors and readers, he says, is they are not just "pulling things out of the same old bag of tricks each time."

Having a good agent is also important for writers who want to break in, he says. As with most editors at large publishing houses, Blades does look at unagented submissions, but the last time he actually bought one was in 1991. That author has gone on to publish additional books with Ballantine, but now she has an agent.

Most new writers break in with paperback originals and these are often series books, but Blades says writers should be aware of a recent shift of interest to single books. "I think for the longest time the only sure-fire way to launch a career in crime fiction was through a series and particularly paperback originals, ultimately hoping to gain an audience and eventually becoming a hardback author. And it remains true that series are the bread and butter of the paperback originals market. Certainly mystery readers, myself included, love series because of the continuity they provide, but there has been a growing acceptance of writers who do nonseries books.

"Nonseries books were the way it used to be. Agatha Christie did some series, but then a lot of her books were one-shots. Patricia Highsmith had a few continuing characters, but most of her books were novels of suspense. There are a growing number of newer authors such as Laurie R. King and Minette Walters who have recently broken away from ongoing characters and their books have been big successes."

Others have started new series to give themselves a new challenge. Blades names Sharyn McCrumb, Joan Hess and Carolyn Hart as three authors who have started new series. This shift has been good for both readers and authors, says Blades. Taking a break from an ongoing series keeps authors from becoming bored or their work from becoming stale.

New writers also need to pay attention to the basics, he adds. "Neatness really does count. In this increasingly competitive time, it's increasingly important that the physical manuscript be impeccable." Keep your proposal succinct, he says. He'd rather see a short description with the manuscript than an elaborate 20 or 30-page outline. Beyond this, he says, "the opening pages really have to be grabbers. There needs to be an immediate impact and an avoidance of cliché. If the manuscript is coming in unsolicited, I think that's where the most polished writing has to come. Oddly enough, that is usually where the worst writing is."

Overall, freshness and quality writing can give writers the extra edge they need in what Blades concedes is a highly competitive market. He advises writers to "let loose and be experimental," to avoid copying others or paying too much attention to trends. Take a new route, a different road, and readers (and editors) will follow.

Address: Random House, 201 E. 50th St., New York, NY 10022
Phone: (212)751-2600
How To Contact: Submit a brief outline/synopsis and complete manuscript with SASE. Ballantine is a large commercial division of Random House and includes several imprints, including Ivy, Fawcett and Columbine. Publishes hardcover, trade paperback and mass market originals and reprints. Publishes 120 titles a year. ☼

BANTAM BOOKS

Established: 1945 • Mystery imprint: Crimeline

Kate Miciak, Associate Publisher

CATEGORIES
Private Eye, Cozy, Suspense, Crime, Thrillers, Historical, Hardboiled Detective, Amateur Sleuth, Humorous Mystery, Urban Horror, Juvenile, Light Horror, Police Procedural, Malice Domestic, Psychological Suspense, Romantic Suspense, Surrealistic Mystery, Espionage, Courtroom/Trial

"I just love the notion that you can actually change people's lives with books," Kate Miciak says, "and I love the notion that being editor—I know this sounds prim—but it's like being a midwife in many cases, with people's dreams. So I think the best editors are the ones who are most respectful of that."

Miciak entered the industry 14 years ago after becoming disheartened in her job as a magazine editor's assistant. Hunting for the right job took seven months, but she found it at one of the oldest paperback publishing houses in America, Bantam Books. In 1985, when Bantam's mystery editor left, the search for a successor led back to Miciak.

"At that point we were only publishing British mysteries from the thirties and forties and the authors were always dead," Miciak says. "I said I would agree to do the mystery list here, but only if we were publishing living authors, because the editorial dialogue is why I'm in the business. They figured I couldn't do too much damage, so they agreed to it and the monster was born."

Doubleday and Dell became Bantam's corporate sisters in 1989, and the following year Miciak was offered the post of associate publisher in addition to editing Bantam's suspense hardcovers and paperback originals. Opportunity knocked once more when Miciak's former publisher approached her and asked for help in revitalizing the Doubleday mystery list. Miciak jumped at the chance to give Bantam's paperback originals a hardcover home at Doubleday. The arrangement proved to be a smart one. "There was one year we had all five of the Edgar nominations for best paperback original," says Miciak. "The books were that strong."

As editor of Bantam Crimeline, as well as the one who oversees many Doubleday mysteries (senior editor Judy Kern is Miciak's counterpart at Doubleday), Miciak looks for manuscripts that are rich in voice, the main criterion she uses to gauge a book's potential. "I really do fall for voice," she says. "I've read books where I knew after reading the first paragraph that I would buy the book." Elizabeth George, who has been published by Miciak from the beginning, and Sue Grafton, whose first five or six books were published by Miciak, are prime examples. George's book, *Playing for the Ashes*, was a *New York Times* bestseller in 1994. Other examples are Laurie King's *A Grave Talent* (1994 Edgar winner for Best First Novel), Carolyn Hart's *Dead Man's Island* (1994 Agatha winner for Best Novel), Sandra West Prowell's *By Evil Means* (1994 nominee for both the Hammett and Shamus awards), Bob Crais's *Free Fall* (1994 Edgar nominee for Best Novel), and Mary Willis Walker's *The Red Scream* (1995 Edgar winner for Best Novel).

After a manuscript catches Miciak's attention through voice, the next hurdle is to show a lucid writing style and a high level of characterization, which Miciak considers more important than plot. "I know I can reinvent the plot and I can work with an author to fix anything that doesn't work," she says, "but I want to be convinced that these people are alive and I want to be convinced that I should care about them."

Bantam and Doubleday publish a wide range of mysteries, from hardboiled detective to romantic suspense, but it's the psychological suspense category that Miciak finds especially engrossing. "It's my favorite category to read, and I know it's what every editor in town is looking for at the moment," she says. Psychological suspense written by women mostly appeals to Miciak because "the kind of book I like is more frequently done by women." When it comes to the male action kind of suspense, Miciak admits to having a tin ear for it.

What has quickly become tiresome for Miciak is reading manuscripts in which the author "tries to invent a new body part to lop off" or is convinced the plot needs a number of murders to keep reader interest high. "I was re-reading an Agatha Christie mystery recently," Miciak says, "and I thought, whatever you think about Christie, she does manage to create a whole novel around generally one murder and it tends to keep your interest. You don't need to find the genitalia stuffed in the dead man's mouth to keep you reading. The psychotic-killer novel can really be overdone."

What kind of story should writers be putting on their pages to grab Miciak's attention? "Just write what you know and write what means something to you," Miciak advises. "Please don't study the market to see what's working. I don't give a damn that serial killer books are working right now. Virtually every editor is about five years ahead of the trend, and by the time it's at its peak in sales, most editors are thinking, if I see another serial killer book, I will *become* a serial killer. So do what you want to do and surprise me."

Miciak only reads agented manuscripts. "It only behooves an author," she says, "to have somebody representing him or her who knows what a book is worth in this market and who can read a manuscript and say, 'I know which editor at which house is going to be as crazy about this book as I am.' And I love those situations where the editor, the agent and the author can sit there and say, 'this scene doesn't work for me.' I think a third party to bounce ideas off is always useful."

Writers with a winning idea for a suspense novel who have not yet found an agent are encouraged to send the opening chapter along with a query letter, which Miciak responds to the day it's received. "I do read every query letter and I will on occasion be piqued enough to ask somebody to send something in," Miciak says. "It's not only the description of the book but also something unique in the author's credentials that convince me I should take a look at this. If I fall in love with the book, and I've done this many times before, I'll give the author five or six suggestions for agents he or she should speak with. I'll call those agents and say, I read this, I'm interested in acquiring it, if you want to meet with this author and read this material, I'd really appreciate it. So I will act as intermediary in that respect. I will not, however, buy a book directly from an author."

Not all query letters get a full reading, though. "What makes me so berserk I will not even read through the query letter," Miciak says, "is when a query letter tells me how much money we're going to make on this jointly, and then goes on to say: 'and enclosed are selected chapters,' because in my early days as a mass market editor I noticed we always got a collection of sex scenes, and it just makes me nuts that somebody would think that's what an editor would buy a book based on."

Authors can expect a close editorial relationship once they sign with Bantam. "Most of my authors have my home number," Miciak says, "and they know they can call me virtually anytime and say, this scene doesn't work, what do I do, or I love this scene, you have to hear it."

Developing characters for a mystery series is usually encouraged. While Miciak says this can be a bit of a crutch at times, she also believes the suspense market is very much dominated by the reader's sense of coming home. "When you read the second or third book in a series and you're once again in that universe that you were in in the first," she says, "there does seem to be that hook that pulls the reader in and it seems to be pretty much the way the market works."

Bantam is highly responsive to author concerns, says Miciak. In most cases, authors see the early sketches of the jacket covers for their work. "I don't think any author should walk into a bookstore and cringe every time they see their book," she says. "That's important to me. I want my authors involved, and I encourage my authors to send me greeting cards or ads that strike them as being effective and playing to their audience. I'll go through portfolios with my art director and we'll match up artists to what my sense of what the reader would like on the front of the book."

Regarding the visual elements of a hardcover and paperback, Miciak says the philosophy these days seems to be to keep the cover as clean as possible. "There was a point where covers were designed with what we would call key art, which is just one small logo," she says. "Bantam was one of the first, I think, with the Sue Grafton mass markets about ten years ago, to do very complicated covers that were fresh and different. The books stood out on the shelves and that worked for awhile, but the time has come, now that everybody is doing very complicated covers, to go to stark covers again."

Bantam publishes 25 hardcover and 60 to 75 paperbacks and Doubleday publishes nine to ten mystery hardcovers yearly, which includes the hardcovers Miciak buys from other publishing houses for paperback reprints at Bantam. Miciak is doing her first trade paperback reprint for a suspense book in 1996. The book is highly literary and the trade paper caters to a literary audience. But generally, she does not publish suspense in trade paper. Mystery buyers, she explains, are unwilling to spend $13 on a trade paper when they can buy a paperback for $4 to $7. Hardcover mystery bestsellers are born when readers aren't willing to wait a year for a book to come out in paperback, she says.

Miciak says it's sheer love of a book and not what the hottest sub-genre happens to be at the moment, that helps her decide what to publish. "As a baby editor, it was a revelation when a senior editor said to me, 'You can't look over your shoulder and try to figure out what's working or what everybody else has published. The only thing you should do is just presume that if you love it, somebody else will.' "

Miciak fell in love with the work of Elizabeth George, David Lindsey, Mary Willis Walker, Leslie Glass, and Carolyn Hart, among others. All exemplify Bantam's publishing philosophy, she says. Lindsey's book, *Mercy,* is "the quintessential serial killer book," and Hart "writes the closest thing to Christie in the nineties." Miciak is proud of the fact that she was the first reader and publisher of George's fiction. In 1994, Bantam published first-time novelist Stephen Collins, who made his book publishing debut with *Eye Contact.*

Advances for a mystery book at Bantam range from $10,000 to millions of dollars, Miciak says. "It's easy for certain beginning writers to get huge advances because of the publishing universe where marketing monies don't always seem to be effective in launching authors," she says. "Publishers tend to pay multi-million dollar advances for authors with no track record because that gets them a lot of advance publicity."

Writers can gain a thorough understanding of suspense publishing at the Bouchercon convention, which Miciak highly recommends as the most effective conference around. It is the only mystery conference Miciak willingly attends, mostly because of her heavy workload, but also because too much socializing makes her uneasy. "At my second or third convention I actually had a manuscript shoved under a toilet stall at me," Miciak says. "I would prefer authors not try that again. Otherwise I think I'm thoroughly accessible." Miciak also prefers that writers send a letter explaining why their book fits into the Bantam or Doubleday lines, rather than argue the issue with her at a conference.

Miciak knows the craziness and isolation of being a writer. In the seventies she wrote and published under pseudonyms. "I was writing gothics, mysteries with the most veritable smidgeon of romance thrown in, because my mother was reading 3,000 of them a week and I used to make fun of them," she says. "So I started by writing one for my mother as a Christmas present." Miciak stopped publishing shortly after college because "I knew that I'm crazy enough as I am. To be a full-time writer would make me a certifiable basket case. I don't have the courage it takes to be a writer. I did well writing, I was successful at it, but I guess I don't have a big enough ego for it." Miciak longed for a sense of collegiality where everyone works for a common goal, which she has found at Bantam. On occasion, Miciak, whose reading tastes are catholic, will receive a phone call from her mother. "She'll say, I can't believe you're publishing this, and I'll say, I love it."

Miciak encourages writers to view publishers as allies, not adversaries. "My colleagues and I seem to be spending more and more time trying to convince authors or soothing authors that we're not being malevolent in the way that we publish them," Miciak says. "Writers need to understand that in the way that a book is a special and individual thing for them, it is for a publisher as well. We do not publish books in order to not sell them." The problem, she says, stems from the fact that the bond of the thirties when publishers and writers stuck with each other through thick and thin no longer exists. "It's very much a money-oriented business," Miciak says. "We do have bean counters just like every other business." That may sound bleak to some writers, but a positive outlook can change that. Miciak urges writers to: "Just believe in what you write and work with your publishing house as much as you can to make it work."

Address: 1540 Broadway, New York, NY 10036

Phone: (212)782-9834

Fax: (212)782-9523

How To Contact: Does not accept unsolicited manuscripts. Accepts agented manuscripts only. Accepts faxed queries. Allows simultaneous submissions. Submissions on computer diskette should be formatted for IBM in ASCII. 99% of accepted manuscripts are submitted through agents. Responds to queries in 1 week. Reports on manuscripts in 2 months.

Terms: Purchases first serial, second serial, book club, storage & retrieval, translation rights. Manuscript is published 1 year after acceptance. Author reviews galleys, copyedited manuscript, jacket copy. Author receives biographical note on jacket or in book. 25 free copies of book go to author; additional copies available at 40% discount. ☀

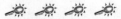

BERKLEY PUBLISHING GROUP

Mystery imprint: Berkley Prime Crime

Natalee Rosenstein, Senior Executive Editor

CATEGORIES
Private Eye, Cozy, Suspense, Crime, Young Adult, Thrillers, Historical, Hardboiled Detective, Amateur Sleuth, Humorous Mystery, Police Procedural, Malice Domestic, Psychological Suspense, Courtroom/Trial

A long-time mystery enthusiast, Natalee Rosenstein first came to the Berkley Publishing Group about 14 years ago as a freelance copywriter. Since then she's worked her way up to senior executive editor and head of the company's new mystery imprint, Berkley Prime Crime. "At Berkley, every editor can, has and will acquire mysteries, so our whole staff is involved in the program. I coordinate it overall and am certainly a part of the acquisition of every mystery in a sense. A book doesn't have to be brought in by me but I'll read it and give my opinion as to whether it belongs in the program."

Berkley has always included mysteries in its line, but it wasn't until 1994 that the publisher decided to create a separate imprint devoted to the category. "Based on the success of our mystery program we came to realize we were one of the major publishers in the mystery arena, but it took us awhile to recognize it," Rosenstein explains. "One of the reasons for this was that we were publishing mysteries in all of our different imprints—Berkley, Jove and Diamond.

"We decided to consolidate our mysteries into a separate mystery imprint, Berkley Prime Crime, and we launched our first list in March 1994. We thought this would give our program much greater visibility and enable us to give more support, promotion and attention in general to the mystery program."

The new imprint also has enabled Berkley to add a hardcover component to their mystery program. "This is something we haven't done before and it gives us a way to attract authors who in the past would have gone somewhere else because they wanted hardcover publication instead of paperback original. It also allows us to take authors from our paperback list who, based on their editorial merit and sales success, really deserve to be in hardcover initially. So we began the hardcover program in March 1994 as well."

Berkley intends to keep its hardcover list small (six or seven books a year) and flexible. The publisher launched three books in the first hardcover list, a cross section of authors including Hamilton Crane, current author of the best-selling Miss Seeton series; Dana Stabenow, whose book *A Cold Day for Murder* received an Edgar Award for best paperback original in 1993; and newcomer Earlene Fowler, whose first book, *Fool's Puzzle* was the first hardcover original published in the line.

On the paperback side, Prime Crime features three or four paperbacks a month, a mix of reprints and original titles. "Starting in June 1995, we also added a new program of trade paperback mysteries," Rosenstein says. "This is for authors who may not have the name recognition at this time to warrant hardcover treatment, but for their editorial merit and in terms of what we feel their stature is, we think breaking them out of the mass market original and giving them trade paperback is a way to get them more review attention. We'll probably do four to six trade paperbacks a year."

The company also plans some mystery anthologies in addition to the four-book paperback list. These are usually themed and may contain original stories or reprints from various mystery magazines such as *Alfred Hitchcock Mystery Magazine* and *Ellery Queen's Mystery Magazine*. "We brought out one to tie to Valentine's Day, a collection called *Crimes of the Heart* edited by Carolyn G. Hart. We've also done themes around Halloween, women private eyes and we even have one titled *Murder With a Southern Twist*." Berkley does not solicit stories for their anthologies. These are put together by outside anthologists, explains Rosenstein, but she may make suggestions on whom to include.

Looking at the overall program Rosenstein notes that, although most of Berkley's mysteries have been consolidated into Prime Crime, a few bestselling authors remain with their original imprints—folks like well-known author Lawrence Sanders and Lilian Jackson Braun, author of the "Cat Who" series. Braun was Rosenstein's first major acquisition as a new editor at Berkley.

Authors interested in the new imprint should note Berkley does not accept unagented manuscripts. Yet, Rosenstein says an unpublished author does have a good chance as long as the work is of top quality and offers a unique voice. "The main things I'm looking for are the voice, the specialness—how engaging the characters are, if there's some kind of internal hook—what makes this book different, what's special about it? Unfortunately, the problem is the wealth of material out there; it can't be just another well-written mystery."

Writers must be aware of what's out there, says Rosenstein, but should be careful not to get too hung up on trends. "Look at the rise of interest in the woman P.I. novel. It continues, but there are so many of them out there right now that the feedback we get from booksellers is that there just isn't any more room for these types of books on the shelves, unless it's really special.

"Throughout the industry the success of the genre has bred more and more competition, so it's even harder to get published today than it was a few years ago. Every publisher, every house is publishing mystery so now you really have to distinguish yourself, have something different. In purely business terms, I don't think any company can succeed doing the same old things over and over."

Rosenstein says to stay competitive publishers are looking for ways to distinguish their books from the hundreds of other titles on bookstore shelves. "We're looking for more diversity and I think that's reflected in terms of ethnicity, age (the whole phenomenon of the senior citizen sleuth) and geographic region as well as a growing interest in more serious mystery novels. Some of the top authors in our Prime Crime list—Stabenow, Peter Robinson, Deborah Crombie—are all really serious novelists who happen to write in the mystery genre. In the long run these are the people who are going to last."

Berkley also actively seeks books about people from a variety of different backgrounds. Rosenstein points to the success of Gar Anthony Haywood's books featuring an African-American couple, a retired police detective and his wife, who solve mysteries as they travel the country in an old Airstream trailer. Other books have a hook or special twist to make them different. For example, Rosenstein mentions one series revolving around a four-star gourmet restaurant; each book includes a recipe. Fowler's books are all named for American quilt patterns and folk crafts figure prominently into the stories.

"The main advice I would give anybody right now," says Rosenstein, "is to really find something that makes your mystery or series stand out. It doesn't have to be totally esoteric, but it does have to be distinctive."

Rosenstein sees the change in the marketplace for mysteries as a natural outgrowth of our changing society. "This diversity [in mysteries] reflects a diverse society. We're not a homogeneous group of people and we certainly don't all live in New York or L.A. I think people are interested in reading about the places they come from or about places that really fascinate them. Also there's a real explosion of people who want to be involved in writing mysteries and they come from all over. They're all different kinds of people and that's what their books reflect."

Address: 200 Madison Ave., New York, NY 10016
Phone: (212)951-8800
Fax: (212)545-8917
How To Contact: Does not accept unsolicited manuscripts. Accepts agented manuscripts only. Accepts faxed queries. Allows simultaneous submissions. Submissions on computer diskette should be formatted in ASCII. 100% of accepted manuscripts are submitted through agents. Responds to queries in 3 weeks. Reports on manuscripts in 8 weeks.
Terms: Manuscript is published 24-30 months after acceptance. Author receives biographical note on jacket or in book.

☼ ☼ ☼ ☼

Photo: Jeffrey Marks

DUTTON/SIGNET, A DIVISION OF PENGUIN USA

Established: 1852

Joseph Pittman, Editor

CATEGORIES
Young Adult, Juvenile

"We like to grow authors," says Joseph Pittman, editor at Dutton/ Signet, a division of Penguin USA. "We're particularly good at publishing new authors who we can really get behind. Our authors benefit from in-house enthusiasm."

That excitement shows in Pittman who's been a lifelong fan of mysteries and has always known he would be involved in publishing. "The summer I was 16 I read the entire set of Hercule Poirot novels, starting with *Murder on the Orient Express*. Christie started it all for me." He's achieved his goal of being involved in the genre by having worked at Bantam for three years and editing at Dutton/Signet for the past two.

His advice for a new author is to write from the heart and get an agent, in that order. "I only look at agented manuscripts. I do not have the time to read anything unagented. There just aren't enough hours in the day." Fellow Dutton Mystery Editor, Danielle Perez, and Editorial Director, Michaela Hamilton, only read agented manuscripts as well.

Perez feels that the mystery market is saturated at the moment, but adds, "women writers have an easier time getting published today than ten or 15 years ago." The recent flurry of mergers and buy-outs in the publishing field has contributed to the tight market. However, Perez is quick to note, "anyone who is truly good will always be noticed."

Despite the number of manuscripts being submitted, Pittman is enthusiastic about his new authors. "I have a book from a new author I acquired a few months ago, *Snow Angel*, which is a suspense thriller that we'll do this year at Dutton. The author's name is Thom Racina and he's written for television. Also Laura Coburn has written a suspense novel starring a female cop set in a suburb of Los Angeles which is also particularly well done. *A Desperate Call* comes out in paperback original from Onyx, one of our paperback lines. Both novels have the right combination of a strong hook along with being very well written. They have different styles, but there was something immediate in my reading I reacted to."

The two editors read all types of mysteries and an agent can submit an author's novel to either one. The weekly editorial meeting provides the opportunity for Perez and Pittman to mention books that appealed to them. The staff works closely together and knows who would enjoy a particular type of mystery for the second reading, including those editors who aren't involved in the genre. If this reader agrees on the quality of the novel, the editor approaches the publisher about acquiring the manuscript.

When reading a manuscript from an agent, Editorial Director Hamilton looks for a hook. "I look for suspense, something fresh with an original voice. I want a book that stands out among all the other mysteries being published. I'm looking for a reliable challenge. The author must have the creativity to handle the basics of the mystery novel while giving the reader something new, different, and puzzling." In terms of the author, she looks for someone who can continue to produce books at the same high level of writing because series characters are becoming a fact of life in the genre.

Dutton/Signet publishes three to five mysteries a month and approximately 25% of those are from first-time authors. The rest are writers who have published before with the company; Dutton/Signet likes to maintain long-term relationships with their authors. The Joan Hess Maggody novels and the Lawrence Block Burglar series are stars at Dutton, being mysteries which reach a larger audience.

Today Pittman's favorite authors include Anne Perry, Jeremiah Healy, Dick Francis, and Jonathan Kellerman. "I read so much that it's hard to point to one author as my favorite. I'm just finishing up the new Dean Koontz novel, *Dark Rivers of the Heart*. I read at least a book a week for pleasure which is something I think all editors should do." The half-hour commute to the publishing firm always finds him with a book.

Pittman edits as well as reads all kinds of mysteries. "I have a little bit of everything: cozies, private eye novels, capers, psychological suspense, and police procedurals. We publish a lot of different types of mysteries and we try to balance out the list each month with a cozy or a P.I or an anthology of stories."

In terms of mystery subgenres, Pittman enjoys private eye novels and historical mysteries. "I'm not a particular fan of the legal thriller these days, but it's the same thing that happened to me about five years ago when I got tired of the technothriller. I've seen so many manuscripts from so many lawyers who probably had a manuscript in the bottom drawer. However, I just acquired a courtroom thriller. I was not looking for one. I read the manuscript and I responded. I decided this should be published and I was able to acquire it. The publishing industry latches on to a particular genre which becomes popular suddenly and there's sort of a trend. Let's everyone publish this.

"I hate the word 'trends'. I really respond to a particular manuscript. I have to pay attention to what seems to be working in the marketplace, but I'm not necessarily going to rush out trying to find them myself."

Pittman sees a bright future for the mystery field. "Publishers are always hungry for someone very talented, but there's a bit of luck. The right author writing the right book reaching the right editor puts the odds against the author, but every once in a while, there's something shining at the bottom of the pile."

Address: 375 Hudson St., New York, NY 10014
Phone: (212)366-2000
How To Contact: Query first. SASE required for query and manuscript response. Simultaneous submissions are OK, but query first. Receives 500 unsolicited manuscripts each month. Reports on queries in 2 months and manuscripts in 2-3 months. Sometimes comments on manuscripts. Guidelines available with SASE. Catalog available; include a first-class stamp.
Terms: Pays advance and royalties. Buys English world rights.

DONALD I. FINE, INC.

Established: 1983

Jason Jacob Poston, Associate Editor

CATEGORIES
Private Eye, Cozy, Amateur Sleuth, Police Procedural, Malice Domestic, Romantic Suspense, Courtroom/Trial

"The success of a new writer is particularly gratifying," says Jason Jacob Poston, associate editor for Donald I. Fine, Inc. "It's a special joy that we feel to have the opportunity to take a chance on somebody—to make him or her into someone important and to get a bestseller out of that person. It's a relationship that sometimes lasts many years."

First novelists would do well to land themselves a book contract with publisher Donald I. Fine. Small enough to deliver the personalized, hands-on attention of a highly skilled editorial staff, yet large enough to compete with all the major publishing houses and be represented by agents around the world, DIF Inc. is really a "mini-major" in the publishing community.

Because of its small size, DIF Inc. insists that all submissions be agented. Poston says that if they accepted unsolicited manuscripts, they wouldn't be able to keep up with the volume. It is also company policy to return all unsolicited manuscripts unopened. Poston is one of three editors (including Donald Fine himself) who reads every manuscript. "Don ultimately reads everything," explains Poston. "He has the final decision and it's often a gut one. The slush pile is a difficult place to be."

One of the rare remaining independent trade book publishers in New York City, Don Fine, the eponymous founder and sole proprietor, has the reputation of being the consummate editor—one who seeks to foster long-term relationships with his writers while nurturing their talent. In the business nearly 40 years (he started at Western Printing in the 1950s), Fine first built Arbor House, publishing Ken Follet's *Eye of the Needle*, Gerald A. Brown's *11 Harrowhouse* and the murder-mysteries of Margaret Truman. Hearst Publishing bought Arbor House in 1978, and Fine worked for them until 1983, when he decided he wanted to be his own boss again. Losing a bid to buy back Arbor House, he then created Donald I. Fine, Inc.

Since their first catalog of Fall/Winter 1984, DIF Inc. has expanded to offer 45-60 fiction and non-fiction (biography, history, cooking) titles a year. Mysteries comprise approximately 25% of their list—of which two or three are usually first novels. Instead of searching for the next multi- million dollar bestseller, Fine tends to seek strong writers and novelists, gripping storytellers with whom he can build a long-term publishing relationship.

Poston mentions author John T. Lescroart (whose seventh novel, *A Certain Justice*, is a thriller set in the San Francisco police department) as a perfect example of a DIF Inc. success story. "The mystery/thriller aspect of his writing is very strong, but the bottom line is, he's a novelist. So the reader has a tendency to get involved and swept up in the world that he has created—which happens to include some wonderful characters like Dismas Hardy and his pal Abe Glitzky. It's a page turner in the best, traditional sense." Poston suspects that this dual nature in the writers they represent developed from Fine's expertise as a general publisher. Thus successful writers "deal not just in the mystery aspect of the book, but also in the character and the story."

According to Poston, DIF Inc. signed Lescroart as a relatively young writer and Fine worked with him to develop his writing, his style and ultimately, his career. "I think John Lescroart really came into his own with *The 13th Juror*. It's doing tremendously well and his advances have been increasing by multiples. This is extremely gratifying for an editor. It's what Don loves to do when he has the chance."

A theme running throughout Don Fine's career is "variety makes it interesting for people." In an interview with *Publishers Weekly* in 1989, he described how each of his staff members fulfills more than one role—a notion he picked up from Bennett Cerf at Random House. Editors work on several different genres of books and in effect become "minipublishers."

Variety and the ever-changing cast of characters seem to be what Poston loves the most about his work. His own experiences as a professional New York theater actor and as the son of actor Tom Poston (with whom he sometimes traveled) developed in him his lifelong interest in plays and a keen appreciation of character, setting and drama.

Poston fondly remembers venues on the road with his father where they would often meet and befriend local police chiefs. His enthusiasm for their stories and the badges he once collected carries over into his work today. Poston says he especially enjoys working on a good police procedural mystery such as *Summer's Reason*, where the author, Cherokee Paul McDonald, is a former Fort Lauderdale motorcycle patrol officer. "*Summer's Reason* is the type of book I find myself drawn to more and more, because the author has drawn on his own experience in creating it."

Similarly, but in the true crime subgenre, Poston is especially proud of the recent work he did on David James Smith's *Beyond All Reason*. Smith is a reporter and writes for *Esquire* and *The London Sunday Times*. He cites the author's consummate professionalism and lack of hype as key to the superior writing of this shocking account of the James Bulger murder by two English boys. Though originally published in England immediately after the trial, DIF Inc. picked it up a year later and worked with the author to develop an epilogue and delve more deeply into an objective analysis of the crime. Whether he's referring to a reporter of true crime or a writer of mystery fiction, Poston returns to the same major tenet he shares with Fine: "The success and value of a book eventually rest on the narrative drive and the characters who are involved."

A recent title at DIF Inc. that seems to embody another important characteristic both Fine and Poston strive for is *Tropical Depression* by Jeffry P. Lindsay. Billed as a classic detective story set in Key West, *Tropical Depression* stars Billy Knight, a former Los Angeles police officer who thinks to retire to an idyllic life along the Florida coast. Both author and main character "have endured a lot and have a tremendous amount of history behind them." Lindsay and veteran author Michael Collins (whose latest, *Cassandra in Red*, features Dan Fortune, the one-armed private investigator) are two authors Poston feels are talented at combining their own and their characters' past experiences, storytelling skills and narrative pace into captivating mystery novels.

One could say that Poston has really worked on all sides of the industry. He began his career in New York working at the bookstore Shakespeare & Co. It was his introduction there to New York's literati (both in front of and behind the counter) that sparked his interest in publishing. He then worked briefly for the New York agent Fifi Oscard, who counts among her former clients Orson Welles. And though Poston has "done a little writing" himself, the nature and vehicle of his work is as shrouded in mystery, he jokes, as one of his author's stories.

It was luck, Poston says, that in his search for a "superb, hands-on editor," he found his position with Don Fine. It was important for him to apprentice with a truly fine editor. "One of the things that we are known for is taking a book that is maybe not necessarily 100 percent and helping the author to make it not only marketable, but potentially a bestseller."

It is clear that Poston enjoys his work and finds the mystery genre the most challenging. "From our point of view, the best readers are mystery readers," he says. When pressed to explain why, he easily encapsulates the ingredients of a good thriller in his description of a good reader: "They read for the joy of it—the entertainment. And mystery readers are tough to pull a fast one on. You really have to give them a story that is not a only entertaining but fresh *and* revealing."

DIF Inc. considers all subgenres of mystery, from the cozies of Corinne Holt Sawyer (*Ho Ho Homicide*) to the hardboiled of *State Street* by Richard Wittingham (a *Chicago Tribune* bestseller).

Poston cautions against gimmickry of any sort and says that terrorism, as a story line, is quickly rejected. What he finds exciting is something like Curtis Gathje's first novel, *A Model Crime*. Gathje intersperses actual tabloid newspaper headlines and photographs of the day with a fictionalized retelling of a scandalous New York City murder trial from 1937. Gathje's real- life uncle, Stephen Butter, was suspected of the heinous crime, and the tale, by it's nature and telling, could be straight from the headlines of today.

So what's a new writer to do besides join forces with an agent and submit "one hell of a story" to DIF Inc.'s mystery editor? Poston says that the market is always tough, but not impenetrable, for new authors. He likes the old expression 'no tears in the writer's eyes, no tears in the reader's.' "If you enjoy your work, then chances are we will too."

Address: 19 W. 21st St., New York, NY 10010

Phone: (212)727-3270

How To Contact: Query only. Does not accept unsolicited manuscripts. Submit through agent only. 100% of accepted manuscripts are agented. Publishes manuscript 1 year after acceptance. Catalog available. Publishes 30 titles a year. All mysteries are hardcover.

Terms: Average advance varies. Pays royalties. Buys world rights, all languages. ☀

FORGE (AN IMPRINT OF TOR BOOKS)

Established: 1980

Camille Cline, Associate Editor

> **CATEGORIES**
> Private Eye, Cozy, Suspense, Crime, Thrillers, Historical, Amateur Sleuth,
> Urban Horror, Dark Mystery, Light Horror, Police Procedural, Malice
> Domestic, Psychological Suspense, Romantic Suspense, Surrealistic
> Mystery, Espionage, Courtroom/Trial

"I appreciate all different types of mysteries," says Camille Cline, associate editor for Forge Books. Although she read the Hardy Boys and Nancy Drew growing up, it was just a small part of her childhood reading experience. "I'm very interested in mysteries. I'm also interested in other things." That's what she likes about Forge; the editors have a lot of freedom to publish the things they enjoy. "Forge is not interested in doing just category mysteries," she says. There are no slots or quotas for cozies, or hardboiled, or procedurals. "As long as it's fresh and new, it could fit any category. Interesting writing with an interesting story, that's the main thing we are looking for."

Forge, an imprint of Tom Doherty Associates, was founded in September of 1993. Since Tom Doherty Associates's first imprint, Tor Books, is well established in the science fiction and fantasy genre, the Forge imprint allows the publication of different, more mainstream titles, which include mysteries. Some recent books that show what Forge is doing in the mystery area include *Play It Again* by Steven Humphrey Bogart (the son of Humphrey Bogart and Lauren Bacall), the Midnight Louie and Irene Adler series by Carole Nelson Douglas, and *Presumed Dead* by Hugh Holton. *Play It Again* is a solid, hardboiled noir thriller. The Midnight Louie and Irene Adler series, while not category cozies, are a bit more comfortable than hard-boiled, and *Presumed Dead* is somewhere between a police procedural and a police thriller. Cline edits the Columbo series for Forge, which are not novelizations, but original storylines with TV's Columbo as the main character. "Tor has proven itself with science fiction and fantasy," Cline says, "and we're on our way to proving ourselves with Forge."

Writers with a previous track record are especially encouraged to submit to Forge. Agented work is also recommended. Cline points out that at Forge, "We read a tremendous amount of unagented work, and we are apparently one of the last houses which really gives a lot of consideration to unagented work, but I must admit most of the novels which we buy are agented." Her advice for unagented submissions is to at least have someone else, "who is pretty critical" read the manuscript first. She also warns that since Forge "really pays attention" to unagented manuscripts it may take several months to hear back on submitted works.

Because of the volume of manuscripts received (hundreds per week) Cline uses several out-of-house readers to help her work through submissions. Her freelance readers are in magazine publishing or some other type of publishing besides books. "That makes them very qualified as readers," Cline says. "They're up on the trends and they're good critics of works." She meets with her readers informally. They chat about publishing, and discuss what to look for and what Cline is interested in. "I trust all of my readers. They're seasoned in this." Cline's readers provide a critique of the work, which she is quick to point out she doesn't just take at face value. "Because people have their own biases." But if a critique says it's not the type of thing for Forge, she will spend less time looking at the manuscript.

Although book publishing has been her goal since early in college, after graduation Cline found herself "on the magazine track." She went to work for *PC Magazine*, where she says she was thrown headfirst into the world of computers. She was a researcher and a reviewer there, and soon became consumed by her work. Sometimes she worked from 7:00 a.m. until 2:00 a.m. the next day. Cline moved to New York because of *PC Magazine*, but she sees it as a "natural conclusion" for her, "because publishing is so strong in New York, and the resources are here." She came to work for Forge from *PC Magazine*.

Cline doesn't get much chance to write for herself these days. She was published at *PC Magazine*, and she writes promotional copy for Tor.

She does write regularly in her journal, which she's kept since the third grade. "Authors need to be able to write as they wish," Cline says. As far as determining what might sell, she advises writers to "feel out what people are reading and what people want to read." The writer can do this themselves. "What the author wants to read is very important."

If a writer does produce a work that Forge is interested in publishing, how will the writer be treated? "Every author is promoted differently. There is no formula for that."

Although Cline doesn't get to write much, she is still able to enjoy reading. "I love to read reviews of other books," she says. "To see not only what people are writing, but what opinions come out of reading those works." She also likes talking to her authors. "I have such a great time talking to my authors all over the country," she says. "About what the weather is in Albuquerque, or how things are going in Wisconsin. I feel like I have these insights from all over the country. It's really a kick."

When writing for Forge in particular, writers might want to think about a series character. As Cline points out, "You're more inclined to pick up a book on someone you're familiar with." She also notes that the first paragraph in a book, and even the first line, are extremely important. As an editor, Cline has to consider things the way a reader would. That means reading the front and back cover of a book, the flaps, and the first page. "There's a bookstore nearby. I think I've read the first chapter of just about every book in the fiction section." She goes on to say, "Sales reps have less than eight seconds to sell a single book to a bookseller. Nobody likes that, but it's the nature of the business. It means you need something that will catch the booksellers' and readers' attention right away."

For some final advice on submitting to Forge, remember that diversity is valued. "We don't want to read things that are working hard to fill a niche," Cline warns. "We want to find something that's fresh and interesting. That's our primary goal." To achieve this, take Camille Cline's advice: "Don't limit yourself."

Address: 175 Fifth Ave., New York, NY 10001
Phone: (212)388-0100
How To Contact: Accepts unsolicited manuscripts. Receives 300 unsolicited manuscripts each month. Send query letter with 3 chapters. 98% of accepted manuscripts are submitted through agents. Responds to

queries in 3-4 months. Reports on manuscripts in 3-4 months. Send SASE for writer's guidelines.

Terms: Authors receive advance and royalties on list price. Purchases world rights. Manuscript is published 12-24 months after acceptance. Author receives biographical note on jacket or in book. 20 free copies of book go to author; additional copies available at 40% discount. ✺

FOUL PLAY PRESS

Established: 1973

Louis Kannenstine & Laura Jorstad, Editors

CATEGORIES
Private Eye, Cozy, Suspense, Crime, Hardboiled Detective, Amateur Sleuth, Humorous Mystery, Dark Mystery, Police Procedural, Psychological Suspense

Just as Victor Kiam liked a certain electric shaver so much he bought the company that made it, Louis Kannenstine, editor of Foul Play, liked Countryman Press enough to buy into the New England publishing house. Shortly thereafter, he and his partner, Peter Jennison, decided to start the Foul Play imprint. "We decided that we should have a separate imprint for the mysteries so we wouldn't feel that we would have to maintain our New England image," Kannenstine says. "We could branch out."

And branch out they did. One particularly long limb extends to England. "We've gotten a lot of attention for our U.S. editions of British mysteries," he says. "First U.S. hardcover editions of certain British authors like Bill James and, more recently, Russell James. We published all of Joyce Porter's Dover novels, both in paperback reprints and a couple of originals, and we'll be doing the collected Dover short stories."

But Kannenstine doesn't want Foul Play to be pigeon-holed as publishing only British mysteries. "We try to keep a balance on our list. We try to maintain a fairly equal weight between English and American novels in the various categories. I suppose the two extremes are the cozies and the hard-edged stuff. We publish both, but we really like to reach the various segments of the mystery market. We'd like to be known as a general publisher of literate mysteries, especially crime novels that are perhaps closer to mainstream fiction than a lot of mysteries."

As a result, Kannenstine is very particular about the type of manuscript he wants to see. Although it is possible for a new writer to sell a book to Foul Play over the transom, most of what Kannenstine acquires is submitted through agents. "We have published an occasional novel that has come to us unsolicited, but I think it is important for a beginning writer to have an agent. I think that we're not the only publisher that tends to look a little more seriously at books from an agent we know and whose judgement we trust."

One reason for this is that it takes a lot of work to launch a new writer, and Kannenstine has a very small staff. "There have been times when I have been pretty much a committee of one here," he says. In 1994, Laura Jorstad joined the staff to assist Kannenstine, but submissions are still very heavy and tend to back up. Launching a new writer, then, builds up the list but offers little immediate payoff. "We're apt not to do well on sales of the first book [by a new author] and have to wait for the second or third to really catch on. It's a lot of uphill work to try to establish an author, and we like to do it occasionally, when we find a good one, but it's not something we can do every season."

This has nothing to do with current developments at Foul Play, Kannenstine says. "Our list is fairly small; we generally can't do more than six hardcover books a year and maybe eight paperback reprints or something like that. Although it varies from season to season, we just can't take on that much material. And once we commit ourselves to a series, that leaves less room to try out new writers."

The obvious way for new writers to increase their chances is by submitting good writing. Specifically, Kannenstine is looking for "some sense of character, some sense of place. A story that you sense the author really wants to tell, or *needs* to tell. There has to be a feeling of involvement on the part of the author. You can usually tell pretty quickly if his or her heart is in it."

Much of what Foul Play receives is clearly an author's attempt to tie in with a trend, Kannenstine says. "I've spent more than enough time inside the minds of serial killers to last me for quite a while. Although I think there are some fine novels fitting that pattern, it's really a bit of overkill." Kannenstine is also tired of the excessive violence that is prevalent in the movies and in some crime fiction now, as well as "mysteries revolving around computers or the latest electronic innovations."

While he says he ignores trends for the most part, Kannenstine does note that "mystery readers are always looking for a mystery writer with a fresh new sense of place." The popularity of books with characters from smaller ethnic groups or regions of the country supports this. One of Foul Play's more popular series is B. Comfort's Tish McWhinny Vermont village mysteries (*The Cashmere Kid, Grave Consequences, Phoebe's Knees,* etc.). These mysteries feature septuagenarian detectives. "People enjoy them. They like the detective and I think Vermont's own mystique is part of the appeal, too," Kannenstine says.

You should not be ashamed of writing in the mystery genre, Kannenstine says. "A lot of people who write to us are almost apologetic for having written a mystery, as though it's still regarded as an inferior genre in a literary sense. There's a lot of good work in the field." And overall, Kannenstine feels writers should write what they believe in, regardless of trends. "I think they should not try to adapt themselves to some trend or what they think might be marketable. They should write from what they know about and what they really feel they have to say. They probably have a story to tell and they need to tell it, whether it fits any current trends or not."

Address: P.O. Box 175, Woodstock, VT 05091-0175
Phone: (802)457-1049
Fax: (802)457-3250
How To Contact: Does not accept unsolicited manuscripts. Query first before submitting manuscript. Send query letter with 3 chapters. Allows simultaneous submissions. 95% of accepted manuscripts are submitted through agents. Responds to queries in 2 weeks. Reports on manuscripts in 3 months. Send SASE for writer's guidelines.
Terms: Authors are paid in royalties of 5% minimum, 10% maximum, on list price. Average advance is $1,000. Purchases standard print (and sometimes other) rights. Manuscript is published 1 year after acceptance. Author receives biographical note on jacket or in book. 10 free copies of book go to author; additional copies available at 40% discount. 🔆

HARPERCOLLINS PUBLISHERS

Established: 1817

Eamon Dolan, Editor

> **CATEGORIES**
> Private Eye, Suspense, Thrillers, Historical, Amateur Sleuth, Humorous Mystery, Dark Mystery, Romantic Suspense, Courtroom/Trial

"I consciously look for something off the beaten path, something unusual, that there isn't another one like," says Eamon Dolan of HarperCollins. "I don't look for something that is gratuitously quirky, whose quirkiness is its only attribute, but if you look at our list you'll see that it's not like anybody else's."

A New York native (he grew up in the Bronx), Dolan ventured northward and graduated from Yale. His longtime ambition—to become an attorney—paled when the prospect of attending law school actually drew near. He realized that his ability to string words together, combined with "the lack of the sort of sustained creativity a real writer needs," might make him well-suited to editing. Dolan returned to New York, landing an entry-level position at the *New Yorker*. Spending a year performing one perfunctory task after another, he sought something more challenging. He found it. "I came to Harper and it was totally fortuitous." He's been with them eight years.

HarperCollins prides itself on adopting authors who aren't afraid to stray beyond the margins. "I think—because we focus on the unusual— we're well-placed to take advantage of what's going to be happening in the future, what I call Domestic Exotica. I'm certainly on the prowl for sleuths who are part of immigrant communities, whether they're Russian, Hispanic, Korean, whatever. I would love, for example, to have a mystery set in a Chinatown featuring an indigenous sleuth," he says.

"Mysteries have traditionally probed and prodded the boundaries of the culture. I'm very actively searching for that," says Dolan. And he keeps finding just that. Take, for example, HarperCollins's most noted mystery author, Tony Hillerman, the man who took the mystery out of coastal big cities and into the heart of the Southwest. Dolan calls Hillerman "our flagship, and he really is emblematic of our list as a whole."

A recent testament to HarperCollins's openness to adopt authors who stray off the beaten path is Batya Gur, who depicts life in present-day Israel. Dolan proudly states, "Who else is Batya Gur like? What other house is doing stuff like this? She indicates what we're good at: finding an odd niche and making a lot out of it. She's really turning into a big hit for us."

However eager Dolan is to capture the unconventional, he cannot gainsay that what matters most to him is an author's capacity to tap into a character's internal terrain. Any writer, inside the margins or out, who executes this well will appeal to Dolan. He confesses, "The mysteries that I buy are almost invariably character driven. I don't think plot is unimportant; the plot *must* succeed. I'm just more likely to buy a mystery with strong characterization. In thrillers, plot must come first, but in mysteries, character is wholly important."

While untraditional sleuths and settings are chief concerns at Harper-Collins, Dolan readily admits that interest in the unconventional permeates the genre at large. "Mystery, more than any other genre," says Dolan, "goes where no other fiction goes. It's definitely the most socially conscious of all fiction. It explores unknown frontiers before any other fiction does—take the ecothrillers of the late 1980s, or look at the female sleuth. The glass ceiling in mystery was broken before any other glass ceiling was broken, like when Marcia Mueller, Sue Grafton and Sara Paretsky were starting out."

Dolan attributes this cutting-edge success to mystery readers. "Part of why people read mysteries is to escape, but I don't think such readers are afraid to deal with real world issues. Mysteries deal with such issues, and people enjoy reading about them."

The mystery is also a great way for readers to learn about alternative lifestyles. Regarding the rise in the popularity of gay and lesbian mysteries, Dolan says: "Many people who read these aren't the target market. They're 55-year-olds living in the suburbs who are curious about this alternative lifestyle. Maybe their son has just come out, or a nephew or the daughter of the woman across the street. It's a great way for them to be introduced, to get acquainted with, to understand, this way of life."

Just because there are trends these days, Dolan urges new writers not to emulate a favorite best-selling author. When Hillerman began receiving notoriety, Dolan started finding way too many manuscripts entering his office that were set in the Southwest, dealing with Native Americans, and so on. "Out of all those, Judy Van Gieson is the only other New Mexico author I plucked out and decided to run with, but she's very very good and has been well worth the running."

Despite being the large publisher it is, HarperCollins has no slush pile. Dolan finds nearly all his authors through agents. "It is extremely important for a writer to have an agent," he says. "Publishing is an arcane business, and it's an agent's job to be in command of all the arcana, like who's at what house, which house would prefer a particular manuscript, things like that. A good agent is worth the commission. Agents aren't just sifters: If I get a call from an agent whose taste I respect, and she says, 'I've just gotten this manuscript and it really knocked my socks off,' I'm going to have her send it right over. If that same piece came in over the transom, well, I *might* get to it. An agent definitely helps."

Like publishers, agents are very busy. Keep this in mind, Dolan advises; show your writing strengths early. "You don't need to eat the whole egg to know if it's rotten," he warns. "The first 50 pages are so important. They must lure me. People don't have time to wait 150 pages for the book to kick in. I want the pages to turn themselves."

Mystery is a hard nut for a beginning writer to crack. Dolan knows this, and that's why he buys almost everything in series. "First books rarely do well. To make a successful mystery, you need a sequel. I always buy the author's first two books." So if you have a good idea for the first book, you'd better already have an even better idea for a second.

An expert in the industry, Dolan has one strong piece of advice for writers: "Don't quit your day job." He's serious. "It's rare, rare, rare, it's like winning the lottery, to actually make enough on your first, second, or even fifth book to live on. If you quit your day job before your royalty statement allows, the push behind the writing becomes financial, not inspirational. Writing is not about the bottom line; it's about the process. Plus we like our writers to be engaged in the real world, not just secluded

16 hours a day in front of a computer monitor."

Fully convinced of the merit of process over product, Dolan encourages struggling writers who haven't had publishing success to be proud of themselves. "Some people think only a novel that gets published is worthwhile. Not at all. Any novel you finish, any novel you start, is worthwhile. If you're not ultimately doing it to make yourself happy, if the process of writing doesn't drive you, then you fail."

Although he cannot guarantee that anyone who loves to write will eventually get published, he does emphasize perseverance. "You must be persistent in honing your craft. Continue to chisel away at the writer you are, that way you'll find the writer you'll become."

Address: 10 East 53rd St., New York, NY 10022

Phone: (212)207-7000

How To Contact: Does not accept unsolicited manuscripts. Accepts agented manuscripts only. Allows simultaneous submissions. 99% of accepted manuscripts are submitted through agents. Reports on manuscripts in 2 weeks. Occasionally comments on rejected manuscripts.

Terms: Authors are paid in royalties of 10% minimum, 15% maximum, on list price. Purchases hard/soft, book club, electronic rights. Manuscript is published about 1 year after acceptance. Author reviews galleys, copyedited manuscript, jacket copy. Author receives biographical note on jacket or in book. 25 free copies of book go to author; additional copies available at 50% discount.

KENSINGTON PUBLISHING CORP.

Established: 1975 • Mystery Imprint: Partners In Crime, Zebra

Sarah Gallick, Executive Editor

CATEGORIES
Cozy, Young Adult, Amateur Sleuth, Romantic Suspense

"I have always enjoyed mysteries because I always like a story with a resolution in the end," says Sarah Gallick, executive editor of Kensington Publishing Corp. "And the good thing about mystery is that it has to be well-plotted."

A love of mystery has been with Gallick throughout her life. She recalls having read the Nancy Drew books while growing up, as well as Ruth Rendell and Erle Stanley Gardner. Her enjoyment of reading has clearly been key to her career choice. "I read *My Years with Ross* when I was in college, and I knew I wanted to be like Harold Ross, who founded the *New Yorker*.

Gallick is a fourth-generation New Yorker who earned an English degree from Hofstra University. She came to Kensington in 1993, after working for publisher Donald I. Fine. She clarifies that Kensington is the hardcover book division, while Zebra and Pinnacle are the paperback imprints. Most mysteries, when released in paperback, are published under the Zebra Books imprint.

When asked what a typical day at work is like, she simply says, "it is a little pressured." But her appreciation of the written word is evident in her own writing. Under the pseudonym of Nellie Bly, she has written three unauthorized biographies, among them a best-seller entitled *Oprah! Up Close and Down Home* published by Zebra.

Gallick finds that many times, what celebrities fight so hard to conceal is "the stuff that makes them most endearing. And for someone who also writes fiction, it is always very interesting for character details." Her most recent work of fiction is entitled *Born to be Rich* by Pinnacle, which was published before she came to Kensington in 1993. Gallick also edited an "instant book" by Kensington entitled, *O.J. Simpson: American Hero, American Tragedy*. The book was a project initiated by Kensington's Chairman of the Board, Walter Zacharius, and remained on the best-seller list last summer for five weeks.

Kensington is "one of the few privately held companies currently in business," according to Gallick. "It was founded about 15 years ago by Walter Zacharius, who is still very much involved in the day to day activities here." Kensington was designed as a mass market paperback house which was begun as Zebra Books, and whose backbone was histor-ical romance. Gallick explains that Kensington is still very much in the romance business, but that mystery is the current trend; one which Ken-sington has successfully followed.

When asked if new writers must have agents, she responds with a vehement "No!" , emphasizing that an agent for an unknown writer has as much clout as the writer who has not yet been published. On the other hand, writers who want to submit their work should not be discouraged. "I can tell you one of our mystery writers actually came in the slush pile," Gallick says. That writer is Jay Dayne Lamb, the author of *Questionable Behavior*, and more recently, *A Question of Preference*.

The Partners in Crime series tends to be very strong on female amateur sleuths. For example, Susanna Reeves is the heroine of *Just Desserts* by G.A. McKevett. Reeves, Gallick says, is a "big-boned, size 14 ex-beauty queen who is investigating a murder in a picturesque southern California town, and when things go wrong, she tends to turn to the deep-dish pizza and chocolate cheesecake, so she's all-girl."

When submitting work for the Partners in Crime series, writers should know that the current character of choice is the amateur sleuth. "Region-alism," Gallick says, "seems to be important. All of our mysteries have a very strong sense of place." The editors at Kensington are seeking interesting, engaging, strong, contemporary characters. "Certainly with our series, we want characters that you want to meet again," Gallick says.

Another area of interest at Kensington is Z-Fave, a mass market paper-back imprint which features Young Adult and Middle Grade titles. The books in the Young Adult or 12-16 age group are rack-sized, while the books in the Middle Grade or 8-12 age group are digest-sized. Executive Editor Elise Donner says, "We have a variety of series, including a thriving horror line." Z-Fave also features mysteries and supernatural romance. Writers recently published by Z-Fave include Cameron Dokey, author of the *Mystery Date* series, and Wendy Corsi Staub, author of the *Spellbound* trilogy. Donner says she simply wants "good writing" and that she has found there are "tons of excellent writers out there."

No mystery genre is taboo, although the popularity of the serial killer story has faded in past years. Gallick says that the editors try to remain open even in unpopular categories. What is the principal turn off? "Typos and grammatical errors in the cover letter or first page. You know in your heart it's not going to get any better," Gallick says. Gallick encourages "hopefuls" to continue submitting their work, and to attend writers conferences. "We do attend most of the conferences," Gallick encourages, including the California Writers' Conference in June and the Philadelphia Mid-Atlantic Book Fair in November. "We are always actively looking for new writers." Gallick also suggests that those who write mystery and are interested in learning more about it might consider joining writing groups, such as Sisters in Crime or Mystery Writers of America.

Whether submitting work to Kensington or to Z-Fave, Gallick has precise advice for those who want to see their story or stories in print. "Know your subject, and read what is selling," she says. "Write a story that you want to read."

Address: 830 Third Ave., New York, NY 10022
Phone: (212)407-1599
Fax: (212)935-0699
How To Contact: Query with a 3-5 page outline/synopis and sample chapters, or send complete manuscript with SASE. Accepts simultaneous submissions. 50% of accepted manuscripts are agented. Guidelines available with SASE. Catalog available. Publishes 400 books a year. ☀

MYSTERIOUS PRESS

Established: 1976

Sara Ann Freed, Executive Editor

CATEGORIES
Private Eye, Cozy, Hardboiled Detective, Amateur Sleuth, Police Procedural, Malice Domestic

"I have one of those lucky jobs where I really love coming to work in the morning," says Sara Ann Freed of Mysterious Press. She got involved in editing as a fan, starting out at a New York children's book publisher in the business department and in subsidiary rights for a number of years. It wasn't until she took a job at Walker and Company, however, that she started editing mysteries. "They knew I loved reading mystery novels, and asked me to edit their mystery line. It was a dream job!"

Mysterious Press was established in 1976 by Otto Penzler as an extension of his renowned bookstore, the Mysterious Bookshop. He began a distribution agreement with Warner Books in 1985, and sold the press outright to Warner in 1990. Freed started working for the company during the 1985 expansion, while also editing westerns for M. Evans and Company. "My colleague, William Malloy, was the other editor at Mysterious Press," she says, "and he is now the editor-in-chief. We've been working together at Mysterious Press for ten years."

Freed still reads many mysteries, but enjoys exploring other fields, as well. "I also like to read biography and contemporary fiction with a woman's slant, like Barbara Kingsolver and Carolyn See," she says. "I grew up reading Josephine Tey, Margery Allingham, Agatha Christie, Raymond Chandler. I also read Edith Pargeter, who I now work with. She writes as Ellis Peters these days, and her Cadfael novels are published by Mysterious. But I grew up reading her Edith Pargeter books."

The mysteries Freed reads now are mostly Mysterious Press authors, but she says she always read P.D. James and Ruth Rendell, and also likes the new writers Minette Walters and Nevada Barr. "In terms of what subgenres interest me personally, I've always liked regional novels," Freed says. "I suppose that has to do with growing up on a farm and feeling kind of isolated and wanting to know about other people's lives. I've always loved Tony Hillerman's books, and like Rudolph Anaya, who's not strictly a mystery writer, but he has a lot of suspense in his novels. He writes about contemporary New Mexico."

The editors of Mysterious Press pride themselves on maintaining a very diverse list of authors, Freed says. They publish established writers such as Margaret Yorke, Ellis Peters, Donald Westlake and Peter Dickinson, as well as the newer voices of Jack O'Connell and Abigail Padgett. "They all have different perspectives."

One such voice belongs to Margaret Maron, whose novel *Bootlegger's Daughter* won the Anthony, the Agatha, the Edgar and the Macavity Awards for best novel of 1993. Freed was one of the people who encouraged Maron to write that novel. "Margaret has been writing a series set in New York, but she grew up in North Carolina and had a very interesting Southern storytelling style. Her stories came out of the rich North Carolina soil and I thought she should be using that voice." (For more about Margaret Maron, see page 43.)

Freed and her colleagues sometimes meet new authors at conventions, but for the most part, new writers come to them through agents. Having an agent, Freed says, is "absolutely vital, of the utmost importance. There are very, very few houses that read unsolicited manuscripts. Houses just don't have the staff anymore. Most houses don't employ full-time readers, so we need some of that pre-selecting that good agents do." An agent also saves a writer time, money and unnecessary rejection. "There are so many things that are submitted to us that are good books, but they're just wrong for our list. They're not books that we do or not books that make any sense to do. People think we do a lot of mystical books because our name is Mysterious Press, so they waste a lot of time sending us books we can't do."

While an agent will get your manuscript read by Mysterious Press, only good writing will get it purchased. Freed looks for interesting characters and fresh prose initially, but says that even if a novel starts out great, it has to stay great until the end. "It has to have a good plot, there has to be some resolution, because that's what mystery fiction is all about. But a good novel always sustains the initial promise. What turns me away from manuscripts are cardboard characters, lackluster prose and 'copycatism.' There are a lot of writers that say, 'Oh, I think I'll write a mystery.' And they'll go to the shelf and copy whomever they think is in favor that day." Such an approach will not sell to Mysterious Press.

Although Freed says there are no topics she considers taboo, some have been so overdone that they would require a very unique approach in order to be considered. "I think we're all tired of seeing drug plots that happen just because the author couldn't figure out any way of solving the plot other than making it a crime involving drugs," she says. "Sex abuse has become a very tiresome plot thread. And we're seeing too many run-of-the-mill courtroom thrillers." She also dislikes gratuitous sex and violence.

Authors who represent what Freed and her colleagues are looking for are Marcia Muller and Ross Thomas. Both are writers that have been publishing with Mysterious Press for a long time and represent the house's best.

As a new writer, Freed feels you should not get discouraged with rejections. "All publishers have full schedules and little room for new authors. If you believe you've written the best book you have in you, keep submitting it and don't forget small, regional presses." Small presses, she says, are often more open to new writers than the larger houses.

"Find your own voice," says Freed. "Explore new territory and write the best novel that you have in your heart, soul and mind."

Address: Warner Books, 1271 Avenue of the Americas, New York, NY 10020

Phone: (212)522-5144

Fax: (212)522-7991

How To Contact: Query first with SASE. Accepts simultaneous submissions. Receives 20-50 unsolicited manuscripts per month. 95-100% of accepted manuscripts are agented. Reports on queries in 6-8 weeks. Sometimes comments on manuscripts. Publishes both hardcover and paperback originals. Publishes 40-60 titles a year; 1-3 first novels a year.

THE NAIAD PRESS INC.

Established: 1973

Barbara Grier, Editor

CATEGORIES
Private Eye, Cozy, Suspense, Crime, Thrillers, Hardboiled Detective, Amateur Sleuth, Humorous Mystery, Dark Mystery, Light Horror, Police Procedural, Psychological Suspense, Romantic Suspense, Espionage, Courtroom/Trial

"As a result of writing badly, I long ago thought the fun thing in life would be to surround myself with authors," Barbara Grier admits. As the co-founder of Naiad Press, she has done that quite well. From its humble beginnings in 1973, Naiad Press has grown to employ eight full time workers and publish 24 books a year. Around half of the books are mysteries and up to a quarter are by new authors.

Be aware that Naiad is a specialized press: Naiad only publishes lesbian fiction. Not cosmetic lesbian fiction (where the author mentions the heroine's sexual preferences once then makes her asexual throughout the novel) but lesbian fiction with actual living breathing, humans who have wants, desires, and needs.

New authors are in good hands at Naiad, which offers both strong editors and an extremely fair weeding process. Besides Grier, who gets less time than she likes to read new manuscripts, Christine Cassidy is an editor at Naiad. Cassidy, a poet as well as an editor, possesses what Grier feels is a rare talent. "Editing mysteries requires a unique skill, and Christine does an excellent job."

Before Cassidy or Grier sees a manuscript it is sent to one of fifteen volunteers, scattered throughout the United States, who give a first and a second reading to a potential novel. Grier favors the idea of a second reader because she understands anyone can have a bad day. If the first reader "had a fight with a lover, got bitten by a dog, lost her job, fell out of bed, or was somehow rendered unfit to read a book," there is always a second reader to offer a different perspective. If both readers reject a manuscript, it is sent back to the author. If one or both recommend a manuscript, it is read by an editor. Occasionally, a rejected manuscript will be accompanied by a critique.

A writer is expected to query first, with a one page outline of her novel and a brief biography that lists pertinent facts. Queries are usually responded to within one week. An agent is not necessary: none of Naiad's books are submitted through agents. Though they publish almost every sub-genre of mystery, from cozy to hard-boiled, series characters are in demand.

Because of Naiad's specialized focus, Naiad does not publish men. Over 300 queries and manuscripts a year are weeded out of the submissions based upon gender. Grier says many people are surprised, but men can write realistic women protagonists. Male writers are not published by Naiad because they are not what Naiad's audience expects, nor necessarily wants. Nor does Naiad publish stories featuring incest, abuse, exploitation, S&M fantasies, or an unremittingly bleak picture of lesbian life.

"It's easy to go through life like a teenager with forearm to brow, saying 'woe is me,' easy and sensationalistic. It's not necessarily realistic, though. I know thousands of lesbians who live happy lives," Grier said. Naiad is looking for uplifting, positive fiction with a lesbian protagonist or protagonists.

Barbara Grier knows her field and her readers well. Despite her protestations that she writes badly, Grier worked as a columnist for a lesbian magazine, *The Ladder*, in the sixties. She moved up through the ranks to become an editor and eventually publisher, before the magazine folded in 1972. Having tasted publishing and having seen an opening in the field, she and Donna McBride started Naiad in 1973.

Recent mysteries that Naiad has published include *A Rage of Maidens* by Lauren Wright Douglas, *Second Guess* by Rose Beecham, and *Crosswords* by Penny Sumner. Katherine V. Forrest's novels, *Beverly Malibu* and *Murder By Tradition*, both won Lambda Literary Awards for best lesbian mystery novel, and her *Murder at the Nightwood Bar* has been optioned for film. Lauren Wright Douglas has also won a Lammy, as has Jaye Maiman for *Crazy for Loving.*

Even after 30 years in the business, Grier still speaks of seventeen hour workdays, of attending conventions, of visiting bookstores to talk to customers. She remembers one visit to a book store when she noticed a woman holding a Naiad book, running her finger along the page as she struggled to read. "That young woman is one of my most important readers," Grier says. "If she keeps it up, after three of four years, she won't need the finger [to read] anymore." Grier envisions the woman interested enough in the works to keep reading them until she works her way up to more difficult, perhaps more literary, writers.

Grier goes on to discuss how Naiad publishes for a wide spectrum of literary levels, hoping to appeal to struggling readers, like the young woman at the bookstore, as well as people like herself who can easily switch from Shakespeare quotations to citations of Theodore Sturgeon to poking gentle fun at Sara Paretsky's V.I. Warshawski.

Not surprisingly, the best advice Grier has to give any potential writer is "know your genre, your field, and the publisher." In other words: Read. It's often repeated advice, but essential. Before submitting to Naiad, read over authors Katherine V. Forrest, Claire McNab, Lauren Wright Douglas, Jaye Maiman, Rose Beecham, and other lesbian mystery writers. Grier also suggests Ruth Rendell, Sara Paretsky, Sue Grafton, and other writers who feature strong female protagonists.

Address: P.O. Box 10543, Tallahassee, FL 32302
Phone: (904)539-5965
Fax: (904)539-9731
How To Contact: Does not accept unsolicited manuscripts. Query first before submitting manuscript. Responds to queries in 1 week. Reports on manuscripts in 10 weeks. Send SASE for writer's guidelines.
Terms: "We have over 200 varying contracts." Purchases world rights. Manuscript is published 1-2 years after acceptance. Author receives biographical note on jacket or in book. 20 free copies of book go to author; additional copies available at 40% discount.

☀ ☀ ☀ ☀

RANDOM HOUSE, INC.

Established: 1925

Elisa Wares, Senior Editor

CATEGORIES
Private Eye, Cozy, Suspense, Crime, Young Adult, Thrillers, Historical, Hardboiled Detective, Amateur Sleuth, Humorous Mystery, Urban Horror, Juvenile, Dark Mystery, Light Horror, Police Procedural, Malice Domestic, Psychological Suspense, Romantic Suspense, Surrealistic Mystery, Espionage, Courtroom/Trial

---

"We are *the* publisher in mysteries," says Elisa Wares, senior editor for Fawcett/Ivy, a division of Random House, Inc. "We are not limited by subgenres—we will buy anything."

Wares's fellow editors at Fawcett/Ivy include Leona Nevler, Editor-in-Chief; Daniel Zitin, Executive Editor; Barbara Dicks, Executive Editor; and Susan Randol, Senior Editor. As a team, these four and Wares are responsible for the editorial philosophy of four imprints in the larger Ballantine Group: Fawcett Columbine, Fawcett Crest, Fawcett Gold Medal, and Ivy Books. The first three were founded in the 1950s. Fawcett Columbine does mostly hardcovers, usually on the order of six mysteries per year. Fawcett Crest and Fawcett Gold Medal are mass market, and each publishes around twelve mass market mystery titles per year, the former mostly reprints and the latter predominantly originals. Ivy is the relative newcomer, started in 1988 and publishing 12 mass market reprints per year.

The imprints are not particularly differentiated by subject matter; books are placed into the list as room permits. Fawcett/Ivy publishes such big names as Sue Grafton, Dick Francis, Anne Perry and Martha Grimes, either as hardcover originals or in paperback reprints.

"We like series and stay away from one-shots," says Wares. "We like ordinary people who use their heads more than their arms. And we want more than a routine mystery—we like to see novels. Our books are not just mysteries; they address other issues like gay and lesbian themes, or environmental concerns. We do not like excessive violence and blood spurting, especially brutality against women."

Though Wares published no first novels in 1994, she and her fellow editors are always open to first-time authors. "It's better to bring in a new person, almost, to fill our slots in mass market originals. We like fresh faces in our paperback lines." Fawcett/Ivy has an impressive record of mid-list authors who started out publishing in paperback and have recently graduated to hardcover as they've established a reputation. "We like to have long-term relationships with our authors," Wares says. Some examples include Julie Smith, who recently appeared in hardcover with *New Orleans Beat*, part of "a great New Orleans mystery series. New Orleans is very atmospheric, and there are so many social levels. You can place the same character in different areas of this city and have a different kind of book each time." Janet Dawson also recently appeared in hardcover with *Don't Turn Your Back on the Ocean*. Paul Mann also had his most recent title, *Season of the Monsoon*, a mystery set in India, come out in hardback after several novels in mass market editions.

"I prefer receiving submissions from agents," says Wares. "They know how to target the most appropriate publishing houses and even the most suitable editors." Fawcett/Ivy does, however, accept unsolicited manuscripts and prefers to see an outline and three chapters. Editorial assistants generally go through the slush pile, forwarding the best manuscripts. "Everything is looked at— though it may take six months!"

"I'm excited by the trends I see in mystery publishing," says Wares. "It seems to be moving away from the standard hardboiled fiction to broader themes. Women P.I.s are so hot now, as are mysteries with ethnic elements—Hispanic or African-American detectives for example. Also, mysteries are becoming more international. In fact, I'd like to see one set in Hong Kong; I haven't seen this yet."

Wares knows whereof she speaks. She's been reading mysteries all her life, from Agatha Christie and John D. McDonald to romantic suspense writers like Phyllis Whitney. "I'd like to do more well-written romantic suspense, but there's always such a problem with bookstores filing them in the romance section." Wares has been with Fawcett/Ivy all 10 years of her professional life. "Though my main focus has always been in mystery, I've also dabbled in romance, true medicine and true crime— my interest is in good writing."

Her advice to writers is to read as many mysteries as possible. "See what's out there, see what the trends are. Have some fun with the sleuth. Find a good profession, and make it a real person. Keep going over it. If you don't have an agent or a reading group, make sure you go over it until everything is really precise. And surprise yourself."

Address: 201 E. 5th St., New York, NY 10022
Phone: (212)751-2600
How To Contact: Query with outline/synopsis and 3 sample chapters. SASE required for response. Agented manuscripts recommended.
Terms: Pays advance and royalties. ☼

ST. MARTIN'S PRESS

Established: 1952 • Mystery Imprint: Dead Letter Mysteries

Keith Kahla, Editor

CATEGORIES
Private Eye, Cozy, Suspense, Crime, Thrillers, Historical, Hardboiled
Detective, Amateur Sleuth, Humorous Mystery, Juvenile, Light Horror,
Police Procedural, Malice Domestic, Psychological Suspense, Espionage,
Courtroom/Trial

"Like most editors, my involvement in editing came out of a long term
interest in books," says Keith Kahla. "First as a reader (I have been a
voracious reader for most of my life), then, later, as a bookseller." Kahla
began his career as a manager/buyer at the University of Texas at Austin's
University Co-op Bookstore. After dealing with sales reps and viewing
books in catalogs for six years, Kahla decided he could do better himself.
So he moved to New York determined to land a job in publishing. "What
comes first is a desire to work on books, to shape and develop them, and
then comes the search for a means to do that," says Kahla.

Kahla's first job in New York was in the rights department of a major
publishing house. Unhappy with the corporate philosophy and the books
published, he left that position and joined St. Martin's Press as assistant
to an editor he admired, Michael Denneny (currently at Crown Books).
Kahla is now an editor with St. Martin's and works on a wide range of
books from popular science to nonfiction to mysteries.

St. Martin's has a successful mystery program that is very open to
first-time writers. Kahla has recently published first-time mystery writers
Abbey Pen Baker, Wendi Lee, S.J. Rozan and Randye Lordon. "St. Martin's has for decades been the publisher of more first mysteries than any
other publisher, and our interest and commitment to them continue,"

he says. Although an agent is not necessary to submit manuscripts to St. Martin's, he suggests having one may gain a writer access. "A good agent knows which editors are acquiring what types of books and can get a response to a submission faster than can writers working on their own. However, it is very rare (at St. Martin's, anyway) that having an agent will get a larger advance or print run for an author."

Kahla reads his own slush pile and is attracted to manuscripts with the basics: good writing, well-developed characters and established settings. His personal favorites are historical and ethnic mysteries. "The only way this affects my reading is that I'm likely to give these types of manuscripts a bit more of the benefit of doubt." Kahla believes a good mystery "comes from a talented writer who knows the genre and is in control of the material. What makes a bad mystery is a writer who is trying to write a book just like some other writer's work or is trying to capitalize on a trend." Once a manuscript piques Kahla's interest, it may be passed on to others. The final decision to publish is made during a weekly editorial meeting headed by the company's editorial director.

Neither Kahla nor St. Martin's limit themselves to a particular niche in the mystery market. "Since we publish about 100 mysteries a year in hardcover, we can't afford to focus on one particular niche. For most of St. Martin's history, we have concentrated on publishing hardcover books. So the basic criteria have been books that the editor feels will appeal to the buying audience as well as the ever-shrinking library market. In the last year alone, I've published traditional, P.I., gay/lesbian, Sherlockian, soft-boiled and historical mysteries. All of which I published because they were, in my opinion, good books." St. Martin's recently launched a mass market mystery program, **Dead Letter**, which is designed to compliment the hardcover program and address the specific concerns of mass market.

When it comes to their whole mystery line, St. Martin's publishing goals are fairly basic. "We try to publish the very best mystery fiction available without regard to specific type or sub-genre within the field. As a rule, we don't chase trends. We rely on the talent of the author to carve himself a place in the mystery market."

Kahla adheres to a general guiding principal for promoting established and first-time authors. "The publicity should fit the expectations for the book and it should generate sales. Doing a reading tour for a first-time author makes very little sense because they have no established audience and are very unlikely to draw an audience who will buy the book. Most, if not all, of the sales for first-time authors are acquired by reviews and word of mouth and the publicity effort should be focused on generating those. However, a truly good book is an end in and of itself. The only proven way to create interest in any book is by getting other people inside and outside the publishing house to read it."

A recently published book that typifies St. Martin's Press is *The Apothecary Rose* by Candace Robb, the first in an historical series set in 14th century York. "Why it is 'typical' of St. Martin's (if any one book could be typical of a program the size of ours) is that it was a wonderfully written, exhaustively researched book by a beginning writer," says Kahla. "What we concentrated on when publishing it was getting the right package (i.e. cover and design), getting it reviewed, getting advance comments from other writers, and providing advance galleys to mystery bookstore owners to generate positive advance word. The result was a very successful publication both in cloth, and later, in mass market."

As a final piece of "reasonable" advice, Kahla says to "write the book that they want to write and don't try and second-guess the market. No one knows what will be 'popular' when your book is finished. When deciding where to submit your book, take a bit of time to investigate which publishing house has what kind of mystery program so that you aren't wasting your time or the editor's."

Address: 175 5th Ave., New York, NY 10010
Phone: (212)674-5151
Fax: (212)420-9314
How To Contact: Accepts unsolicited manuscripts. Receives 20-25 unsolicited manuscripts each month. Send query letter with 3 chapters. Accepts faxed queries. Allows simultaneous submissions. 75% of accepted manuscripts are submitted through agents. Responds to queries in 2 months. Reports on manuscripts in 2 months.
Terms: Authors are paid in royalties of 10% minimum, 15% maximum, on list price. Purchases mass market, book club, second serial, merchandising, and other rights. Author reviews galleys, copyedited manuscript, jacket copy. Author receives biographical note on jacket or in book. 104 free copies of book go to author; additional copies available at 40% discount. ☀

Photo: Jane Jewell

WALKER & COMPANY

Established: 1959

Michael Seidman, Editor

CATEGORIES
Private Eye, Cozy, Suspense, Crime, Historical, Hardboiled Detective, Amateur Sleuth, Humorous Mystery, Dark Mystery, Police Procedural, Malice Domestic, Psychological Suspense, Surrealistic Mystery

Walker & Company is a publisher known for its willingness to take a chance on a new writer, according to mystery editor Michael Seidman. This reputation is not founded on altruism or on devotion to the dreams of novices so much as on dollars and cents. A small, family-owned company, Walker, especially in its early years, simply didn't have the bucks to compete with bigger publishers for top-name writers.

Although the company has grown since it was founded in 1959, it is still small and still very much open to new writers. Seidman, who began editing mysteries for Walker in 1991, takes pride in the company's reputation for openness. "Julie Smith, Jeremiah Healy, dozens of writers who are now among the more popular in the genre, got their start here," he says.

Many of those writers, however, are still at Walker and are working on continuing series—not exactly good news for aspirants. The company's small list doesn't have many openings. But Seidman says, "The upside is in our willingness to take risks, and that willingness extends not only to new writers but to those who've established themselves but want to try something new, something their own publishers might bridle against or even their agents might suggest forgetting about." He sums up his editorial philosophy this way: "Publishing is, almost by definition, a risk, but I've been given enough rope and haven't hanged myself yet."

Since taking over the mystery line, Seidman has orchestrated some changes in Walker's niche. For years, it has been known primarily as a publisher of British mysteries. They were, in fact, John Le Carré's first publisher. But now the line features many more American writers, mostly as a result of Seidman's influence. "A touch of chauvenism," he admits, "but so what?" He has added a number of "name" writers to the Walker list, such as Rex Burns, Bill Pronzini, and Bill DeAndrea, among others.

His personal tastes run "to the harder-boiled, the noir, the dark side—with a touch of humor just so things don't get too grim," he says. But the manuscripts he selects are not limited to this type. Walker publishes a wide range of subcategories, from cozies to police procedurals to classic puzzles. "One of the challenges I face is making certain the list reflects a knowledge of the marketplace and the reader's needs, even if I don't have sympathy for the subcategory," he says.

Above all, he looks for excellent writing and compelling characters. "I'm always looking for something somehow *better*," he explains. "I'm looking for broader canvases, stories that start with characters who are proactive rather than reactive and that are written first for the story, not the market." Writers, he contends, who write to follow perceived trends in the marketplace usually will not get his attention. Their lack of engagement in the story and the characters will bleed through the narrative. He has been in publishing for nearly thirty years and can quickly spot a put-up job. "I look for something I haven't seen before," he says.

He advises writers to undertake a novel "because it means something, not because it seems the easiest way to make a buck." An original voice and a unique vision will make a manuscript leap from the slush pile, and these ingredients simply can't be forced. Seidman especially dislikes "copycat" manuscripts that are slavish to current trends and those manuscripts that try to exploit events in the headlines.

One more piece of advice: get an agent. "As publishers, we've slammed the transoms shut," he explains, although Walker, itself, still accepts unsolicited materials. Seidman receives approximately 100 submissions per week and publishes only 20 books per year. And he is the only full-time reader. So, while you can still get a fair, though perhaps slower, reading at Walker, Seidman admits that generally writers who send unsolicited, unrepresented manuscripts face excruciating odds. He laments the situation, knowing that agents, too, are not easy to find. But the volume of submissions seems to dictate the need for representation.

If you want still more advice from Seidman on writing and the writing life, you can find it in the books he's written on the subject: *Living the Dream* and *From Printout to Published*, both from Carroll & Graf. He regularly offers guidance through his syndicated column "Ask Michael" and as a frequent contributor to the "Ask the Experts" feature in *Writer's Digest* magazine. And he tells you why and how he bought Richard Barre's novel, *The Innocents*, in the "Editors at Work" chapter (see page 340).

Seidman also writes fiction. He has published a number of mainstream short stories and hopes to write more. In fact, though his reading is "broadly based," he prefers mainstream fiction, especially short stories. His favorite authors include Alice Hoffman, Joyce Carol Oates, Frederick Busch and Robertson Davies.

Walker & Company has published *Satan's Lambs* by Lynn Hightower (which won the 1994 Shamus Award for best first P.I. novel), *World of Hurt* by Edgar winner Richard Rosen, *The Killing of Monday Brown* by Sandra West Prowell, and *Murder at the God's Gate* by Lynda S. Robinson. Seidman declines to name favorite mystery writers, afraid of inadvertently leaving someone off the list, though he admits to preferring less traditional writers, such as James Sallis. He's a mystery reader (and editor) who doesn't much care whodunit. What he wants is a character to care about and writing that dazzles.

He is equally politic about discussing authors and books that he has worked with through the years. He explains, "I suppose I have favorites among them, books that were somehow special, authors who've touched my life above and beyond the usual, but, well, which of your kids do you love best?"

That statement provides a good view of the man behind the editor's desk at Walker: diplomatic, pragmatic, with a fine sense of humor.

Address: 435 Hudson St., New York, NY 10014
Phone: (212)727-8300
Fax: (212)727-0984
How To Contact: Accepts unsolicited manuscripts. Receives 300 unsolicited submissions each month. Send query letter with 3 chapters. Allows simultaneous submissions. 75% of accepted manuscripts are submitted through agents. Responds to queries in 4 weeks. Reports on manuscripts in 6 months. Send SASE for writer's guidelines.

Terms: Authors receive advances, royalties and rights purchased vary. Manuscript is published 12-18 months after acceptance. Author receives biographical note on jacket or in book. 10 free copies of book go to author; additional copies available at 40% discount. ☼

Secondary & Foreign Novel Markets

ACADEMY CHICAGO

Established: 1975

Editor: Anita Miller

CATEGORIES
Private Eye, Cozy, Suspense, Crime, Young Adult, Thrillers, Historical, Hardboiled Detective, Amateur Sleuth, Humorous Mystery, Urban Horror, Juvenile, Dark Mystery, Light Horror, Police Procedural, Malice Domestic, Psychological Suspense, Romantic Suspense, Surrealistic Mystery, Espionage, Courtroom/Trial

Publishes few first novels per year.

Address: 363 West Erie, Chicago, IL 60610-3125
Phone: (312)751-7300
Fax: (312)751-7306
How To Contact: Accepts unsolicited manuscripts. Query first before submitting manuscript. Send query letter with 3 chapters. 30% of accepted manuscripts are submitted through agents. Responds to queries in 6 months. Reports on manuscripts in 6 months. Send SASE for writer's guidelines.
Terms: Purchases world rights. Manuscript is published 18 months to 2 years after acceptance. Author receives biographical note on jacket or in book.Varying number of free copies of book go to author.

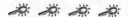

ACCORD COMMUNICATIONS

Established: 1986 • Mystery imprint: aka Seattle

Editor: Karen Duncan

CATEGORIES
Cozy, Amateur Sleuth, Humorous Mystery, Malice Domestic

Accord Communications is not currently accepting submissions.

Address: 18002 15th Ave. NE, Suite B, Seattle, WA 98155
Phone: (206)368-8157
How To Contact: Does not accept unsolicited manuscripts.

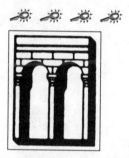

ARCADE PUBLISHING

Established: 1988

Editors: Richard Seaver, Jeannette Seaver, Cal Barksdale, Tim Bent, David Szanto

CATEGORIES
Private Eye, Suspense, Crime, Thrillers, Police Procedural, Psychological Suspense, Espionage

"We're starting a new series: An Arcade Mystery."
Arcade Publishing has recently published *Death by Publication* by J. J. Fiechter and *Murder Chez Proust* by Estelle Monbrun.
Publishes 20-25 hardcovers per year. Publishes 2-4 first novels per year; average print run is 5,000-10,000.

Address: 141 Fifth Avenue, New York, NY 10010
Phone: (212)475-2633
Fax: (212)353-8148
How To Contact: Accepts agented manuscripts only. Allows simultaneous submissions. Submissions on computer diskette should be formatted for for MS Word (Mac) and accompanied by a printed copy. 100% of accepted manuscripts are submitted through agents. Reports on manuscripts in 8-12 weeks.
Terms: Purchases world or world English rights. Manuscript is published within 18 months after acceptance. Author receives biographical note on jacket or in book. 10 free copies of book go to author; additional copies available at 40% discount.

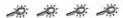

ATHENEUM BOOKS FOR YOUNG READERS

Vice President & Editorial Director: Jonathan J. Lanman

> **CATEGORIES**
> Young Adult, Amateur Sleuth, Juvenile

Publishes 8-12 hardcovers per year. Publishes 20% first novels per year; average print run is 5,000-6,000.

Address: 866 Third Ave., New York, NY 10022-6299
Phone: (212)702-7894
How To Contact: Accepts unsolicited manuscripts. Receives 800 unsolicited manuscripts each month. Query first before submitting manuscript. Allows simultaneous submissions. 20% of accepted manuscripts are submitted through agents. Responds to queries in 3 weeks. Send SASE for writer's guidelines.
Terms: Purchases world rights. Manuscript is published 12-16 months after acceptance. Author receives biographical note on jacket or in book. 15 free copies of book go to author; additional copies available at 50% discount.

AVALON BOOKS

Established: 1961

Editor: Marcia Markland

CATEGORIES
Private Eye, Cozy, Suspense, Crime, Thrillers, Hardboiled Detective, Amateur Sleuth, Police Procedural, Malice Domestic, Psychological Suspense, Romantic Suspense, Courtroom/Trial

Marcia Markland, the publisher, used to be the editor of **The Mystery Guild**. Markland says that private detective agencies are overused. She would like to see more ethnic mysteries.

Avalon Books has recently published *The Curious Cape Cod Skull* and *The Body in the Red Velvet Robe*.

Publishes 12 hardcovers per year.

Address: 401 Lafayette St., New York, NY 10010

Phone: (212)598-0222

How To Contact: Does not accept unsolicited manuscripts. Send query letter with 3 chapters. Allows simultaneous submissions. 10% of accepted manuscripts are submitted through agents. Responds to queries in 3 months. Reports on manuscripts in 3 months. Send SASE for writer's guidelines.

Terms: Purchases world rights. Manuscript is published 6 months to a year after acceptance. Author receives biographical note on jacket or in book. 10 free copies of book go to author; additional copies available at 50% discount.

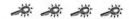

AVON FLARE BOOKS

Established: 1945

Editors: Gwen Montgomery, Editorial Director & Juvenile Books Editor; Tom Colgan and Carrie Ferron, Adult Books Editors

CATEGORIES
Private Eye, Cozy, Suspense, Crime, Young Adult, Thrillers, Historical, Hardboiled Detective, Amateur Sleuth, Humorous Mystery, Urban Horror, Juvenile, Dark Mystery, Light Horror, Police Procedural, Malice Domestic, Psychological Suspense, Romantic Suspense, Surrealistic Mystery, Espionage, Courtroom/Trial

Avon Flare is always looking for more mature novels. They would like especially to see female mysteries and mysteries geared toward 8 to 12 year-olds.

Receives 250 adult and 100 juvenile manuscripts per month. Most adult manuscripts are submitted through agents, but only 50% of juvenile manuscripts are agented.

Publishes 52 mass market paperbacks per year. Publishes 15 juvenile first novels per year; average print run is 25,000.

Address: 1350 Avenue of the Americas, New York, NY 10019
Phone: (212)261-6817
How To Contact: Accepts unsolicited manuscripts. Receives 250 adult unsolicited manuscripts each month. Send query letter with 3 chapters. Allows simultaneous submissions. 50% of accepted manuscripts are submitted through agents. Responds to queries in 3 months. Reports on manuscripts in 3 months. Send SASE for writer's guidelines.
Terms: Advances and royalties are negotiable. Manuscript is published 18-24 months after acceptance. Author receives biographical note on jacket or in book.

☼ ☼ ☼ ☼

BAKER BOOK HOUSE COMPANY

Assistant to Director of Publications: Jane Schrier

CATEGORIES
Cozy, Amateur Sleuth, Malice Domestic

All manuscripts submitted to Baker Book House should have an Evangelical or Christian perspective, but they do not want preachy fiction or fiction that just serves as a vehicle to make a moral point about an issue. Do not submit historical, romance or adventure plots. Baker is looking for contemporary and traditional mysteries.

Publishes 1-2 trade paperbacks per year.

Address: PO Box 6287, Grand Rapids, MI 49516-6287
Phone: (616)676-9185
Fax: (616)676-9573
How To Contact: Does not accept unsolicited manuscripts. Send query letter with 3 chapters. 7.5% of accepted manuscripts are submitted through agents. Responds to queries in 3 weeks. Reports on manuscripts in 2 months. Send SASE for writer's guidelines.
Terms: Authors are paid in royalties of 14% average, on net price. Purchases world rights. Manuscript is published 1 year after acceptance. Author receives biographical note on jacket or in book. 10 free copies of book go to author; additional copies available at 50% discount.

BEPUZZLED

Established: 1986

Editor: MaryAnn Lombard

CATEGORIES
Private Eye, Cozy, Suspense, Crime, Hardboiled Detective, Amateur Sleuth, Humorous Mystery, Juvenile, Malice Domestic

BePuzzled publishes mystery jigsaw puzzles which are a mix of written and visual clues. They publish 4-6 adult and 6-8 children's puzzles per year. Stories must be previously unpublished and should incorporate six written clues and six visual. Adult stories should run between 3,000 and 6,000 words, while children's should be 3,000 to 4,000 words. Do not submit stories involving war, graphic violence, gore, sex, profanity, drugs or child custody.

Address: 22 E. Newberry Rd., Bloomfield, CT 06002
Phone: (203)242-0735
Fax: (203)286-8710
How To Contact: Accepts unsolicited manuscripts. Query first before submitting manuscript. Accepts faxed queries. Send e-mail to malbepuzz-d@aol.com. Responds to queries in 2 weeks. Reads all submissions. Reports on manuscripts in 4 weeks. Send SASE for writer's guidelines.
Terms: Pays a flat, one-time fee. Purchases world rights. Manuscript is published within a year after acceptance. 12 free copies of book go to author.

BETHEL PUBLISHING

Established: 1909

Contact: Senior Editor

CATEGORIES
Private Eye, Cozy, Suspense, Crime, Young Adult, Thrillers, Historical, Hardboiled Detective, Amateur Sleuth, Humorous Mystery, Juvenile, Police Procedural, Malice Domestic, Romantic Suspense, Courtroom/Trial

Bethel Publishing is a Christian book publisher, so all stories should have a Christian emphasis. Do not send occult or new age stories.

Publishes 3 trade paperbacks per year. Publishes 10% first novels per year; average print run is 10,000.

Address: 1819 S. Main St., Elkhart, IN 46516-4299

Phone: (219)293-8585

Fax: (800)230-8271

How To Contact: Accepts unsolicited manuscripts. Receives 200 unsolicited manuscripts each month. Query first before submitting manuscript. Accepts faxed queries. Allows simultaneous submissions. Less than 10% of accepted manuscripts are submitted through agents. Responds to queries in 1 month. Reports on manuscripts in 3 months. Occasionally comments on rejected manuscripts. Send SASE for writer's guidelines.

Terms: Authors are paid in royalties of 5% minimum, 10% maximum, on list price. Purchases all rights. Manuscript is published 1 year after acceptance. Author reviews galleys, copyedited manuscript, jacket copy. Author receives biographical note on jacket or in book. 24 free copies of book go to author; additional copies available at 40% discount.

CEDAR BAY PRESS

Established: 1970

Editor: Susan L. Roberts

CATEGORIES

Private Eye, Cozy, Suspense, Crime, Young Adult, Thrillers, Hardboiled Detective, Amateur Sleuth, Humorous Mystery, Juvenile, Dark Mystery, Light Horror, Psychological Suspense, Romantic Suspense, Surrealistic Mystery, Espionage

"We are moving toward electronic publishing on disc, audio, and CD formats." Does not want to see plots involving drugs in Miami.

Cedar Bay Press has recently published *Babes From Venus, Beyond the Bamboo Curtain* and *In A Heart Beat.*

Publishes 6 hardcovers and 6 mass market paperbacks per year. Publishes 6 first novels per year; average print run is 50,000.

Address: P.O. Box 751, Beaverton, OR 97075-0751
Phone: (503)644-8223
How To Contact: Accepts unsolicited manuscripts. Receives 48-60 unsolicited manuscripts each month. Query first before submitting manuscript. Send e-mail queries to cbp@nwcs.org. Allows simultaneous submissions. Submissions on computer diskette should be formatted in ASCII. 5% of accepted manuscripts are submitted through agents. Responds to queries in 3 weeks. Reports on manuscripts in 4 weeks. Occasionally comments on rejected manuscripts.
Terms: Authors are paid in royalties of 10% minimum, 20% maximum, on list price. Purchases electronic (digital), all languages, worldwide rights. Manuscript is published 3-6 months after acceptance. Author receives biographical note on jacket or in book. 1 free copy of book goes to author; additional copies available at 50% discount.

MANUSCRIPT PRESENTATION

No matter which publisher you are submitting your work to, it pays to be professional. Be sure to read Robin Gee's "Marketing Your Mystery Novel" on page 49 for tips on how to write and format expert query letters, cover letters and manuscripts. You'll also learn valuable techniques for approaching editors and agents.

COMICART PUBLISHING COMPANY

Established: 1992

Contact: Joan Harryman

CATEGORIES
Private Eye, Crime, Young Adult, Historical, Espionage

Publishes 6 trade paperbacks per year.

Address: 329 Harvey Dr., Suite 400, Glendale, CA 91206
Phone: (818)551-0077
Fax: (408)338-9861
How To Contact: Accepts unsolicited manuscripts. Receives 20 unsolicited manuscripts each month. Send query letter with 3 chapters. Accepts faxed queries. Allows simultaneous submissions. Submissions on computer diskette should be formatted for Macintosh. 2.5% of accepted manuscripts are submitted through agents. Responds to queries in 2 months. Send SASE for writer's guidelines.
Terms: Authors are paid in royalties of 5% minimum, 10% maximum, on net price. Purchases first North American serial rights. Manuscript is published 3-4 months after acceptance. Author receives biographical note on jacket or in book. 100 free copies of book go to author; additional copies available at 40% discount.

CREATIVE ARTS BOOK COMPANY

Established: 1976 • Mystery imprint: Saturday Night Specials

Editor: George Samsa

CATEGORIES
Suspense, Crime, Hardboiled Detective, Dark Mystery

Publishes 5 trade paperbacks per year and 5 first novels per year; average print run of a first novel is 5,000 copies.

Address: 833 Bancroft Way, Berkeley, CA 94710
Phone: (510)848-4777
Fax: (510)848-4844
How To Contact: Accepts unsolicited manuscripts. Receives 100 unsolicited manuscripts each month. Send query letter with 2 chapters. Accepts faxed queries. Allows simultaneous submissions. 10% of accepted manuscripts are submitted through agents. Responds to queries in 8 weeks. Reports on manuscripts in 8 weeks. Send SASE for writer's guidelines.
Terms: Authors are paid in royalties of 5% minimum, 15% maximum, on net price. Average advance is $1,000. Purchases all rights. Manuscript is published 12-18 months after acceptance. Author reviews galleys, copyedited manuscript, jacket copy. Author receives biographical note on jacket or in book. 20 free copies of book go to author; additional copies available at 40% discount.

CROSSWAY BOOKS

Established: 1938

Contact: Leonard G. Goss

CATEGORIES
Private Eye, Cozy, Suspense, Crime, Young Adult, Thrillers, Historical, Hardboiled Detective, Amateur Sleuth, Humorous Mystery, Urban Horror, Juvenile, Dark Mystery, Light Horror, Police Procedural, Malice Domestic, Psychological Suspense, Romantic Suspense, Surrealistic Mystery, Espionage, Courtroom/Trial

---

Crossway Books advises writers to "know about our company first. No blind submissions."

Publishes 6-10 trade paperbacks per year. Publishes 6 first novels per year; average print run is 5,000-7,000.

Address: 1300 Crescent St., Wheaton, IL 60187

Phone: (708)682-4300

Fax: (708)682-4785

How To Contact: Accepts unsolicited manuscripts. Receives 250-300 unsolicited manuscripts each month. Query first before submitting manuscript. Accepts faxed queries. 20% of accepted manuscripts are submitted through agents. Responds to queries in 8 weeks. Reports on manuscripts in 8 weeks. Send SASE for writer's guidelines.

Terms: Authors receive advance and royalties on net price. Purchases all rights. Manuscript is published 7-9 months after acceptance. Author receives biographical note on jacket or in book.

DANCING JESTER PRESS

Established: 1994 • Mystery imprint: Dancing Dagger Publications

Publisher: Glenda Daniel; Editor: L.D. Gilbert

CATEGORIES
Private Eye, Suspense, Crime, Young Adult, Thrillers, Historical, Hardboiled Detective, Amateur Sleuth, Humorous Mystery, Juvenile, Police Procedural, Malice Domestic, Psychological Suspense, Espionage, Courtroom/Trial

"My advice to a beginning writer is to consider what small independent publishers have to offer," says Glenda Daniel. "We are a small publishing company and this can be advantageous for the author for at least three reasons. The author is considered a partner in the packaging. No aspect of production is done without the author's whole-hearted approval. Secondly, since we are promoting a very small number of books, we do so aggressively, and possibly longer than other larger publishing concerns. Finally, we might consider keeping a book in print possibly longer than a larger publisher.

"We prefer strong women characters, no sexism, good writing, characterization, and an exciting story line," she says, but adds "I would not be comfortable censoring anyone's concepts by listing 'taboo' topics. What has been done and done and done to death can always suddenly be done again better than ever and in a completely original way. No theme is ever completely overused nor any subject taboo. Intention and execution are all."

Dancing Jester Press has recently published *Driver Without Brakes, Driver Without Malice, Driver Without Distractions*, all published as both trade paperbacks and audio books.

Publishes 3 hardcovers per year.

Address: 3411 Garth Rd., Baytown, TX 77521
Phone: (713)427-9560
Fax: (713)428-8685
How To Contact: Accepts unsolicited manuscripts. Receives up to 100 unsolicited manuscripts each month. Send query letter with 3 chapters. Allows simultaneous submissions. Responds to queries in 3 weeks. Reports on manuscripts in 2 months. Send SASE for writer's guidelines.
Terms: Authors are paid in royalties of 7% minimum, 10% maximum, on list price. Manuscript is published 12 months after acceptance. Author reviews galleys, copyedited manuscript, jacket copy. Author receives a photo and biographical note on jacket or in book. 10 free copies of book go to author; additional copies available at 45% discount.

DARE TO DREAM BOOKS

Established: 1992

Editors: Maria Williams, Tony McCawley

CATEGORIES
Private Eye, Suspense, Thrillers, Hardboiled Detective, Amateur Sleuth, Humorous Mystery

"Our most current needs are non-romance, non-murder whodunit mysteries and adventure for adults." Dare To Dream Books's guidelines are very specific, and you should definitely send for them before submitting. Send #10 SASE for guidelines. They publish personalized books. "We personalize characters in our books. The main character's picture and name are printed on the book cover. Supporting characters in books are personalized with names of friends or loved ones of the main character."

Publishes 3 mass market paperbacks per year. Publishes 6 first novels per year.

Address: 5062 S. 108th St. #112, Omaha, NE 68137
Phone: (402)455-4946
How To Contact: Accepts unsolicited manuscripts. Receives 18 unsolicited manuscripts each month. Send query letter with first 3 chapters and synopsis of entire book. If you'd like your manuscript returned, enclose SASE with sufficient postage. Allows simultaneous submissions. Submissions on computer diskette should be formatted for IBM. 5% of accepted manuscripts are submitted through agents. Responds to queries in 3 weeks. Reports on manuscripts in 2 months. Send SASE for writer's guidelines.
Terms: Authors receive $1,000-$1,500 payment plus a certain amount per copy. Purchases 3 years minimum publishing rights. Manuscript is published 6 months after acceptance. 3 free copies of book go to author.

DARK HORSE COMICS

Established: 1986

Submissions Editor: Jamie S. Rich

CATEGORIES
Suspense, Crime, Thrillers, Hardboiled Detective, Urban Horror, Juvenile, Dark Mystery, Light Horror, Psychological Suspense

Dark Horse says, "Largely, we want to see stories that are geared to comic books. We would like the writer to understand the language and conventions of the medium; at the same time, we don't want the writer to be restricted by the stereotypical perception of comic books. It's wide open for creativity. The fact that Dark Horse is a comic book publisher sets us apart from most other avenues. Our goal is to expand the art form by exploring genres that are not currently widely used in comics."

No subjects are taboo. "If the story is good and told in a fresh manner, it has a shot at Dark Horse. The only restriction we have is that creators must stick to their own concepts and creations. We do not accept unsolicited manuscripts based on or featuring licensed properties we currently publish." Dark Horse advises writers to "be creative, be bold and above all, *know comics!*"

Dark Horse Comics has recently published *Sin City* by Frank Miller (a former Eisner winner), *Hellboy* by Mike Mignola, *James Bond 007* (with Acme Comics), *Aliens & Predator* (with 20th Century Fox), and *Ghost* (part of Dark Horse Heroes line).

Publishes 1-2 hardcovers and 2-5 trade paperbacks per year. Stories are normally serialized or published as comic book series first.

Address: 10956 SE Main St., Milwaukie, OR 97222

Phone: (503)652-8815

Fax: (503)654-9440

How To Contact: Accepts unsolicited manuscripts. Will not respond to phone or fax inquiries. Receives 200+ unsolicited manuscripts each month. Query by mail first before submitting manuscript. Allows simultaneous submissions. 1% of accepted manuscripts are submitted through agents. Responds to queries in 2 weeks. Reports on manuscripts in 10 weeks. Send SASE for writer's guidelines.

Terms: Authors receive initial comic book page rate, followed by royalties based on sales. Varies depending on project. Purchases various rights. Manuscript is published 9 months to 1 year after acceptance. 10-25 free copies of book go to author; additional copies available at 40% discount.

DOUBLEDAY

Editor: Judy Kern

CATEGORIES

Private Eye, Cozy, Suspense, Crime, Thrillers, Historical, Hardboiled Detective, Amateur Sleuth, Humorous Mystery, Urban Horror, Dark Mystery, Light Horror, Police Procedural, Malice Domestic, Psychological Suspense, Romantic Suspense, Surrealistic Mystery, Espionage, Courtroom/ Trial

---

Doubleday is not currently seeking new writers.

Address: 1540 Broadway, New York, NY 10036

Phone: (212)354-6500

Fax: (212)782-9700

How To Contact: Does not accept unsolicited manuscripts. Accepts agented manuscripts only. 100% of accepted manuscripts are submitted through agents. Responds to queries in 1 month. Reports on manuscripts in 1 month. Occasionally comments on rejected manuscripts.

Terms: Authors receive advance and royalties. Purchases various rights. Author receives biographical note on jacket or in book.

FAWCETT

Executive Editor: Barbara Dicks

CATEGORIES
Cozy, Crime, Young Adult, Thrillers, Historical, Amateur Sleuth, Humorous Mystery, Police Procedural, Courtroom/Trial

Publisher has a slow turn around due to their high volume of submissions.

Publishes 5 hardcovers and 24 mass market paperbacks per year. Publishes 2-3 first novels per year; average print run is 15,000.

Address: 201 E. 50th St., New York, NY 10022
Phone: (212)751-2600
Fax: (212)572-4912
How To Contact: Accepts unsolicited manuscripts. Receives 100 unsolicited manuscripts each month. Send query letter with 50 pages. Allows simultaneous submissions. 99% of accepted manuscripts are submitted through agents. Responds to queries in 3 months. Reports on manuscripts in 3 months.
Terms: Authors receive advance and royalties. Purchases US-Canada open market and world rights. Manuscript is published 1 year after acceptance. Author receives biographical note on jacket or in book. 10 free copies of book go to author; additional copies available at 40% discount.

GASOGENE PRESS LTD.

Established: 1988

Contact: David Hammer

CATEGORIES
Private Eye

Gasogene publishes only Sherlock Holmes mysteries.
Publishes 3 trade paperbacks and 2 first novels per year.

Address: Box 1041, Dubuque, IA 52001-1041

Phone: (319)583-3730

Fax: (319)583-3402

How To Contact: Accepts unsolicited manuscripts. Send query letter with 3 chapters or submit full manuscript. Accepts faxed queries. Allows simultaneous submissions. Responds to queries in 6 weeks. Reports on manuscripts in 6-10 weeks. Occasionally comments on rejected manuscripts.

Terms: Authors receive royalties. Manuscript is published 8 months to 1 year after acceptance. Author receives biographical note on jacket or in book. 5 free copies of book go to author.

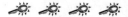

GRYPHON PUBLICATIONS

Established: 1985

Editor: Gary Lovisi

> **CATEGORIES**
> Private Eye, Suspense, Crime, Hardboiled Detective, Urban Horror, Police Procedural, Psychological Suspense

Lovisi is looking for "hard, cutting-edge crime fiction with *impact.* Also new ways of telling these stories, new ways of showing how the private eye or detective has changed and grown in the 90's. I'm publishing simply the best crime and hardboiled fiction being done today, in my magazine *HARDBOILED*(see profile, page 187) and with some of the books, also."

Lovisi doesn't want to see "Chandler clones, serial killers hunting women at single's bars and lots of cliches and pastiche."

Gryphon Publications has recently published *Man Alone* by William Campbell Gault, *Difficult Lives* by James Sallis, *Hammett & Chandler in Paperback* by Gary Lovisi.

Publishes 1-2 hardcovers and 3-4 trade paperbacks per year. Publishes 2 first novels per year.

Address: P.O. Box 209, Brooklyn, NY 11228-0209

How To Contact: Does not accept unsolicited manuscripts. Query first before submitting manuscript. Submissions on computer diskette should accompanied by a printed copy. 5% of accepted manuscripts are submitted through agents. Responds to queries in 2 weeks. Reports on manuscripts in 6 weeks.

Terms: Authors receive nominal cash payment upon publication and 2 copies. Purchases one-time first North American rights. Manuscript is published 6-18 months after acceptance. Author receives biographical note on jacket or in book.

HENRY HOLT & COMPANY

Established: 1866

CATEGORIES
Private Eye, Cozy, Suspense, Crime, Young Adult, Thrillers, Historical, Hardboiled Detective, Amateur Sleuth, Humorous Mystery, Juvenile, Dark Mystery, Police Procedural, Malice Domestic, Psychological Suspense, Romantic Suspense, Surrealistic Mystery, Espionage, Courtroom/Trial

---

Publishes 15-20 hardcovers, 15-20 trade paperbacks and 2-3 mass market paperbacks per year. Publishes 5 first novels per year.

Address: 6th Floor, 115 W. 18th St., New York, NY 10011
Phone: (212)886-9200
Fax: (212)645-2610
How To Contact: Accepts unsolicited manuscripts. Send query letter with 1 chapter. Accepts agented manuscripts only. 90% of accepted manuscripts are submitted through agents. Send SASE for writer's guidelines.
Terms: Authors receive advance and royalties. Purchases various rights. Author reviews galleys, copyedited manuscript, jacket copy. Author

receives biographical note on jacket or in book. 15 free copies of book go to author; additional copies available at 50% discount.

INTERCONTINENTAL PUBLISHING

Established: 1991

Editor: H.G. Smittenaar

CATEGORIES
Suspense, Crime, Thrillers, Police Procedural

Has a very wide readership.

Intercontinental Publishing has recently published *Dekok* Series (in *Reader's Digest* and *Vengeance* (Winner of Golden Noose)

Publishes 6-12 trade paperbacks per year. Publishes 6-12 first novels per year; average print run is 5,000.

Address: 6451 Steeple Chase Ln., Manassas, VA 22111
Phone: (703)369-4992
Fax: (202)293-1376
How To Contact: Accepts unsolicited manuscripts. Receives 4 unsolicited manuscripts each month. Allows simultaneous submissions. Submissions on computer diskette should be formatted for WordPerfect 5.1 only. Responds to queries in 3 weeks. Reports on manuscripts in 3 months.
Terms: Manuscript is published 6-8 months after acceptance. Author receives biographical note on jacket or in book. 6 free copies of book go to author; additional copies available at 40% discount.

KITCHEN SINK PRESS

Established: 1969

Editors: Philip D. Amara, Chris Couch

CATEGORIES
Historical, Humorous Mystery, Urban Horror, Dark Mystery,
Psychological Suspense, Surrealistic Mystery

Kitchen Sink Press says: "Since we are a publisher of comic books and graphic novels, we like to see manuscripts accompanied by a sampling of illustrations. The author does not have to also be the artist. A writer/artist team is acceptable, but we often do have a sole creator who is producing the script and art. It should also be noted that we expect sequential art, art in a 'comic book' form that carries the story throughout, not simply spot illustrations to complement full text pages.

"Our mystery books are currently a minority genre. The mystery aspect that makes us outstanding is that we publish mysteries in graphic novel form, which adds a new dimension to the genre. While we are not aggressively seeking out mysteries, we are always receptive to them.

"Our products and books run the gamut of subject matter. For a better idea of what we publish, please obtain a copy of our catalog. We are not necessarily concerned with overused themes, but rather with what new elements an author can bring to add sparkle to the usual mystery cliches."

Their advice to new writers is to start submitting your work. "It's never too soon to send material to a publishing house and make contacts. Be prepared and professional enough to handle early-career rejections. Attend conventions and conferences. Follow your own vision and temper persistence with patience. Be creative when sending your proposal or manuscript. Make your package stand out."

Kitchen Sink Press has recently published *From Hell* (1994 Harvey Nominee and Eisner Winner) by Alan Moore & Eddie Campbell, *The Acid Bath Case* by Kellie Strom and Stephen Walsh, *Black Cat Crossing* and *Hypnotic Tales* (Harvey Nominee) by Richard Sala.

Publishes approximately 6 trade mystery-related paperbacks per year. Publishes at least 20 original works per year; average first print run is 5,000.

Address: 320 Riverside Drive, Northampton, MA 01060
Phone: (413)586-9525
Fax: (413)586-7040
How To Contact: Accepts unsolicited manuscripts. Receives 75-100 unsolicited manuscripts each month. Send query letter with synopsis, sample art and 1 chapter. Send e-mail queries to jamieks@aol.com. Allows simultaneous submissions. 1% of accepted manuscripts are submitted through agents. Responds to queries in 2 months. Reports on manuscripts in 3 months. Occasionally comments on rejected manuscripts. Send SASE for writer's guidelines.
Terms: Purchases all rights. Manuscript is published 6-24 months after acceptance. Author receives biographical note on jacket or in book. 25 free copies of book go to author; additional copies available at 60% discount.

LITTLE, BROWN AND COMPANY, INC. CHILDREN'S DIVISION

Editorial Assistant: Erica Lombard

CATEGORIES
Young Adult, Juvenile

Only accepts manuscripts from published authors and literary agents. Query should be sent with three sample chapters or an outline. Any submission needs to be sent along with a list of credits. Publisher is looking for strong character and plot development. Young children witnessing a crime and/or solving it is an overused and unwanted plot.

Publishes 3-4 hardcovers per year. Publishes 3-4 first novels per year; average print run is 5,000-6,000.

Address: 34 Beacon St., Boston, MA 02108
Phone: (617)227-0730
Fax: (617)227-8344
How To Contact: Accepts manuscripts submitted by published authors or agents only. Accepts faxed queries. Allows simultaneous submissions. 65% of accepted manuscripts are submitted through agents. Responds to queries in 1 month. Reports on manuscripts in 3 months. Send SASE for writer's guidelines.
Terms: Authors receive advance and royalties. Purchases world rights. Manuscript is published 18 months after acceptance. Author receives biographical note on jacket or in book. 10 free copies of book go to author; additional copies available at 40% discount.

LITTLE, BROWN AND COMPANY, INC.

CATEGORIES
Private Eye, Suspense, Crime, Thrillers, Historical, Hardboiled Detective, Amateur Sleuth, Humorous Mystery, Dark Mystery, Police Procedural, Malice Domestic, Psychological Suspense, Romantic Suspense, Surrealistic Mystery, Espionage, Courtroom/Trial

Publishes 3-4 hardcovers per year. Publishes 4 first novels per year; average print run varies.

Address: 1271 Avenue of the Americas, New York, NY 10020
Phone: (212)522-8700
Fax: (212)522-2067
How To Contact: Accepts agented manuscripts only. Allows simultaneous submissions. 100% of accepted manuscripts are submitted through agents. Responds to queries in 4 months. Reports on manuscripts in 4 months. Occasionally comments on rejected manuscripts.
Terms: Authors receive advance and royalties. Purchases various rights. Manuscript is published 1-2 years after acceptance. Author receives biographical note on jacket or in book.

LONGMEADOW PRESS

Established: 1980

Executive Editor: Nancy Starr

CATEGORIES
Private Eye, Suspense, Thrillers, Urban Horror, Light Horror, Police Procedural, Malice Domestic, Psychological Suspense, Espionage, Courtroom/Trial

Publishes 2 hardcovers per year.

Address: Box 10218, 201 High Ridge Rd., Stamford, CT 06904
Phone: (203)552-2648
How To Contact: Accepts unsolicited manuscripts. Receives "lots" of unsolicited manuscripts each month. Send query letter with 2 chapters.

Allows simultaneous submissions. Submissions on computer diskette should be formatted for Macintosh or IBM. 99% of accepted manuscripts are submitted through agents. Responds to queries in 6 months. Reports on manuscripts in 6 months. Send SASE for writer's guidelines.

Terms: Authors receive advance and royalties. Purchases all rights. Manuscript is published 1 year after acceptance. Author receives biographical note on jacket or in book.

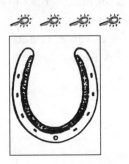

LUCKY BOOKS

Established: 1989

Contact: Donna Rutherford

CATEGORIES
Private Eye, Cozy, Suspense, Crime, Young Adult, Thrillers, Historical, Hardboiled Detective, Amateur Sleuth, Humorous Mystery, Urban Horror, Juvenile, Dark Mystery, Light Horror, Police Procedural, Malice Domestic, Psychological Suspense, Romantic Suspense, Surrealistic Mystery, Espionage, Courtroom/Trial

Lucky Books would like to see more historical mysteries, and does not accept pornography, sex and violence.

Publishes 4 trade paperbacks per year. Publishes 5 first novels per year; average print run is 2,000.

Address: Box 1415, Winchester, VA 22604
Phone: (703)662-3424
How To Contact: Accepts unsolicited manuscripts. Receives 300 unsolicited manuscripts each month. Submit full manuscript. Allows simulta-

neous submissions. 1% of accepted manuscripts are submitted through agents. Reports on manuscripts in 9 months. Occasionally comments on rejected manuscripts.

Terms: Authors are paid in royalties of 3% minimum, 5% maximum, on net price. Manuscript is published 6 months after acceptance. Author receives biographical note on jacket or in book. 100 free copies of book go to author; additional copies available at 75% discount.

MADWOMAN PRESS, INC.

Established: 1991

Editor: Diane Benison

CATEGORIES
Private Eye, Cozy, Suspense, Crime, Thrillers, Hardboiled Detective, Amateur Sleuth, Humorous Mystery, Police Procedural, Romantic Suspense, Courtroom/Trial

---

Madwoman Press says, "Our stories have lesbian protagonists." Their advice to new writers is to "join a writer's group and resist the urge to tell your editor or publisher 'but all my friends say it's wonderful.' "

Madwoman Press, Inc. has recently published *Fool Me Once* by Katherine E. Kreuter, *The Burnton Widows* by Vicki P. McConnell, *Sinister Paradise* by Becky Bohan

Publishes 1-2 trade paperbacks per year. Publishes 1-2 first novels per year; average print run is 4,000.

Address: P.O. Box 690, Northboro, MA 01532-0690
Phone: (508)393-3447
Fax: (508)393-8305
How To Contact: Accepts unsolicited manuscripts. Receives 4-5 unsolicited manuscripts each month. Query first before submitting manuscript. Send e-mail queries to 76620.460@compuserve.com. Allows simultaneous submissions. 1% of accepted manuscripts are submitted through agents. Responds to queries in 8-12 weeks. Reports on manuscripts in 6 months. Send SASE for writer's guidelines.
Terms: Authors receive 15% of collected receipts after print costs. Pur-

chases all rights. Manuscript is published 18-24 months after acceptance. Author receives biographical note on jacket or in book. 20 free copies of book go to author; additional copies available at 40% discount.

MARGARET K. McELDERRY BOOKS

Established: 1971

Contact: Emma Dryden

> **CATEGORIES**
> Suspense, Young Adult, Historical, Humorous Mystery, Juvenile, Dark Mystery, Psychological Suspense

Publishes over 25 hardcovers per year. Publishes 3-4 first novels per year; average print run is 5,000-6,000.

Address: 866 Third Ave., New York, NY 10022
Phone: (212)702-2000
How To Contact: Accepts unsolicited manuscripts. Receives 60-75 unsolicited manuscripts each month. Send query letter with 3 chapters. Allows simultaneous submissions. 5% of accepted manuscripts are submitted through agents. Responds to queries in 1 month. Reports on manuscripts in 4 months. Send SASE for writer's guidelines.
Terms: Authors receive advance and royalties. Purchases all rights. Manuscript is published 18 months after acceptance. Author reviews galleys, copyedited manuscript, jacket copy. Author receives biographical note on jacket or in book. 10 free copies of book go to author; additional copies available at 50% discount.

MEGA-BOOKS

Established: 1983

Editor: Carol Gilbert

CATEGORIES
Private Eye, Cozy, Suspense, Crime, Young Adult, Thrillers, Historical, Hardboiled Detective, Amateur Sleuth, Humorous Mystery, Urban Horror, Juvenile, Dark Mystery, Light Horror, Police Procedural, Malice Domestic, Psychological Suspense, Romantic Suspense, Surrealistic Mystery, Espionage, Courtroom/Trial

Mega-Books is a book packager producing trade and mass market originals, including mystery and mystery series. Produces 95 books a year.

Address: 116 E. 19th St., New York, NY 10003
Phone: (212)598-0909
Fax: (212)979-5074
How To Contact: Does not accept unsolicited manuscripts. Write for writer's guidelines before submitting. Submit resume, publishing history and writing samples. 25% of accepted manuscripts are agented. Guidelines are free.
Terms: Negotiable.

NEW READERS PRESS

Established: 1969 • Mystery imprint: Signal Hill Publications

Publisher: Marianne Ralbovsky

CATEGORIES
Private Eye, Cozy, Suspense, Crime, Young Adult, Thrillers, Historical, Hardboiled Detective, Amateur Sleuth, Humorous Mystery, Urban Horror, Juvenile, Dark Mystery, Light Horror, Police Procedural, Malice Domestic, Psychological Suspense, Romantic Suspense, Surrealistic Mystery, Espionage, Courtroom/Trial

All submissions need to be written at the third and fourth grade reading levels for adults learning to read. No explicit sex or violence is accepted.

Address: 1320 Jamesville Ave., Box 131, Syracuse, NY 13210
Phone: (315)422-9121
Fax: (315)422-6369
How To Contact: Accepts unsolicited manuscripts. Receives 50 unsolicited manuscripts each month. Query first before submitting manuscript. Send query letter with 3 chapters. Accepts faxed queries. Allows simultaneous submissions. Submissions on computer diskette should be formatted for for WordPerfect 5.1. 5% of accepted manuscripts are submitted through agents. Responds to queries in 2 months. Reports on manuscripts in 2 months. Send SASE for writer's guidelines.
Terms: Authors receive flat fee or royalties—percentage negotiable. Purchases world rights. Manuscript is published 2 years after acceptance. Author receives biographical note on jacket or in book. 10 free copies of book go to author.

NEW VICTORIA PUBLISHERS, INC.

Established: 1977

Editor: Rebecca Beguin

CATEGORIES
Private Eye, Crime, Historical, Amateur Sleuth, Humorous Mystery, Romantic Suspense

New Victoria would like to see more humorous and suspenseful plots. "We publish mysteries with primarily lesbian protagonists. New Victoria

Publishers is interested in fiction with a clear narrative story line. We are looking for well-written romance, adventure or mystery novels, science fiction (speculative fiction) or fantasy with lesbian and/or strong feminist protagonists. We like well-drawn characters dealing with issues pertinent to the lesbian community whether emotional or intimate, or societal and political. We have found humor and eroticism to be important ingredients."

New Victoria has recently published *Other World, Tell Me What You Like* and *Nun in the Closet*

Publishes 8 trade paperbacks per year. Publishes 3 first novels per year; average print run is 5,000.

Address: P.O. Box 27, Norwich, VT 15055
Phone: (802)649-5297
Fax: (802)649-5297
How To Contact: Accepts unsolicited manuscripts. Receives 30 unsolicited manuscripts each month. Query first. Accepts faxed queries. Send e-mail queries to bethd0655@aol.com. Allows simultaneous submissions. 5% of accepted manuscripts are submitted through agents. Responds to queries in 3 weeks. Reports on manuscripts in 2 months. Send SASE for writer's guidelines.
Terms: Authors are paid in royalties of 10% minimum on net price. Manuscript is published 1-2 years after acceptance. Author reviews galleys, copyedited manuscript, jacket copy. Author receives biographical note on jacket or in book. 15 free copies of book go to author; additional copies available at 40% discount.

PERMANENT PRESS

Established: 1977

Editor: Judith Shepard

CATEGORIES
Suspense, Crime

Wants truly engaging plots, compelling characters and good writing. "We've had a finalist for the Hammett Prize, and specialize in non-genre, well written fiction." Doesn't like serial killers and explicit sex crimes with no characters to back them up.

Advice to writers is "don't concentrate on the movie deal before the book is written."

Permanent Press has recently published *An Occassional Hell* (Hammett Prize Finalist), *Protocol for Murder*, *Curse of the Montrolfes*.

Publishes 12 hardcovers per year.

Address: Rd 2, Noyac Road, Sag Harbor, NY 11963
Phone: (516)725-1101
How To Contact: Accepts unsolicited manuscripts. Receives 500 unsolicited manuscripts each month. Query first before submitting manuscript. Send query letter with 1 chapter. Allows simultaneous submissions. 30% of accepted manuscripts are submitted through agents. Responds to queries in 4 weeks. Reports on manuscripts in 6 months. Send SASE for writer's guidelines.

Terms: Authors are paid in royalties of 10% minimum, 20% maximum, on list price. Average advance is $1,000. Purchases world and film industry rights. Manuscript is published 1-2 years after acceptance. Author reviews galleys, copyedited manuscript, jacket copy. Author receives biographical note on jacket or in book. 10 free copies of book go to author; additional copies available at 50% discount.

PLAYERS PRESS INC.

Established: 1965 • Mystery imprint: Ian Henry Books

Editor: R.W. Gordon

CATEGORIES
Private Eye

Only publishes Sherlock Holmes.

Players Press Inc. has recently published *Sherlock Holmes and the Earthquake Machine*, *Sherlock Holmes and the Somerset Hunt*, *Singular Case of the Duplicate Holmes*, all by the London Society of S. Holmes.

Publishes 3-5 hardcovers and 1-3 trade paperbacks per year. Publishes 0-2 first novels per year; average print run is 5,000.

Address: P.O. Box 1132, Studio City, CA 91614

Phone: (818)789-4880

How To Contact: Does not accept unsolicited manuscripts. Query first before submitting manuscript. 25% of accepted manuscripts are submitted through agents. Responds to queries in 2 weeks. Reports on manuscripts in 2 months.

Terms: Authors are paid in royalties of 6% minimum, 10% maximum, on net price. Purchases world rights. Manuscript is published 6-24 months after acceptance. Author reviews galleys, copyedited manuscript, jacket copy. Author receives biographical note on jacket or in book. 10 free copies of book go to author; additional copies available at 20% discount.

PRESIDIO PRESS

Established: 1977

Editor: E.J. McCarthy

CATEGORIES
Private Eye, Thrillers, Hardboiled Detective, Police Procedural

Racial and Soviet Union themes are not welcome. "We're really looking for something original. Keep your plots simple and limit the number of characters you use."

Presidio Press has recently published *Nantucket Revenge.*

Publishes 1-2 mystery hardcovers per year. Publishes 6-8 first novels per year; average print run is 5,000.

Address: 505B San Marin Drive, Suite 300, Novato, CA 94945

Phone: (415)898-1081

How To Contact: Accepts unsolicited manuscripts. Receives 150 unsolicited manuscripts each month. Send query letter with outline and 3 chapters. Allows simultaneous submissions. 65% of accepted manuscripts are submitted through agents. Responds to queries in 2 weeks. Reports on manuscripts in 6 months. Send SASE for writer's guidelines.

Terms: Authors are paid in royalties of 15% minimum, 20% maximum, on net income. Purchases all rights. Manuscript is published 9-18 months after acceptance. Author receives biographical note on jacket or in book. 10 free copies of book go to author; additional copies available at 40% discount.

RED CRANE BOOKS

Established: 1989

Contact: Marianne O'Shaughnessy

CATEGORIES

Private Eye, Cozy, Suspense, Crime, Young Adult, Thrillers, Historical, Hardboiled Detective, Amateur Sleuth, Humorous Mystery, Urban Horror, Juvenile, Dark Mystery, Light Horror, Police Procedural, Malice Domestic, Psychological Suspense, Romantic Suspense, Surrealistic Mystery, Espionage, Courtroom/Trial

Seeks novels that have "identification with place & integration of the mystery with the story."
Publishes 2-3 hardcovers and 7-10 trade paperbacks per year. Publishes 2-3 first novels per year; average print run is 7,000.

Address: 2008 Rosina St., Suite B, Santa Fe, NM 87505
Phone: (505)988-7070
Fax: (505)989-7476
How To Contact: Does not accept unsolicited manuscripts. Query first before submitting manuscript. Accepts faxed queries. Allows simultaneous submissions. Submissions on computer diskette should be formatted for IBM WordPerfect 5.1. A low percentage of accepted manuscripts are submitted through agents. Responds to queries in 1 month.

Reports on manuscripts in 6 months. Send SASE for writer's guidelines.

Terms: Authors receive advance and royalties. Purchases all rights. Manuscript is published 1 year after acceptance. Author receives biographical note on jacket or in book.

RISING TIDE PRESS

Established: 1991

Editor: Lee Boojamra

CATEGORIES

Private Eye, Cozy, Suspense, Crime, Thrillers, Historical, Hardboiled Detective, Amateur Sleuth, Humorous Mystery, Urban Horror, Dark Mystery, Light Horror, Police Procedural, Malice Domestic, Psychological Suspense, Romantic Suspense, Surrealistic Mystery, Espionage, Courtroom/ Trial

---

Rising Tide would like to see better research being done. "Study the mystery novel format before you begin writing. Build a unique plot around memorable characters. Write what you know about."

"We only publish mysteries for, by and about lesbians. We want mysteries that have a lesbian perspective."

Rising Tide Press has recently published *Deadly Rendezvous* by Diane Davidson, *Danger Crosscurrents* and *Danger in High Places* by Sharon Gilligan, *Corners of The Heart* by Leslie Grey.

Publishes 5-8 trade paperbacks per year. Publishes 3-5 first novels per year; average print run is 5,000.

Address: 5 Kivy St., Huntington Station, NY 11746

Phone: (516)427-1289

How To Contact: Accepts unsolicited manuscripts. Receives 20-25 unsolicited manuscripts each month. Query first before submitting manuscript. Responds to queries in 1 week. Reports on manuscripts in 2 months. Occasionally comments on rejected manuscripts. Send SASE for writer's guidelines.

Terms: Authors are paid in royalties of 10% minimum, 15% maximum, on list price. Manuscript is published 6-18 months after acceptance. Author receives biographical note on jacket or in book. 15 free copies of book go to author; additional copies available at 40% discount.

ROYAL FIREWORKS PRESS

Established: 1991

Editor: Charles Morgan

CATEGORIES
Young Adult, Juvenile

Wants clean language geared toward the middle school age group.
Royal Fireworks Press has recently published *The Death of Old Man Hanson* and *Grandfather Webster's Strange Will.*

Publishes 100 hardcovers and 100 trade paperbacks per year. Publishes 50 first novels per year; average print run is 1,000.

Address: 1 First Ave., Unionville, NY 10988

Fax: (207)726-3824

How To Contact: Accepts unsolicited manuscripts. Receives 200 unsolicited manuscripts each month. Query first before submitting manuscript. Accepts faxed queries. Small percentage of accepted manuscripts are submitted through agents. Responds to queries in 2-3 days. Reports on manuscripts in 2 weeks. Send SASE for writer's guidelines. **Terms:** Authors are paid in royalties of 5% on net price. Purchases all rights. Manuscript is published 12 months or less after acceptance. Author receives biographical note on jacket or in book. 5 free copies of book go to author; additional copies available at 40% discount.

SCRIBNER CRIME NOVELS

CATEGORIES
Suspense, Crime

Overstocked. Accepts agented submissions only.

Address: 1230 Avenue of the Americas, New York, NY 10020
How To Contact: Does not accept unsolicited manuscripts.

SINGER MEDIA CORP.

Established: 1940

Editor: Janis Hawkridge

CATEGORIES
Private Eye, Suspense, Crime, Young Adult, Thrillers, Hardboiled Detective, Amateur Sleuth, Urban Horror, Dark Mystery, Light Horror, Police Procedural, Psychological Suspense, Romantic Suspense, Espionage, Courtroom/Trial

Would like to see more books with international flavor that "can be sold in the USA but also translated into foreign languages. Will it be equally interesting to Finland, Japan, England and Singapore?" Tired of mysteries being mixed with horror, romance, political crusades, sex and those that are historically inaccurate. "Read. Read. Read. Read the mystery classics and modern masters."

Singer Media Corp. has recently published Dan Ross, W.E.D. Ross, Marilyn Ross, Dana Ross—all these are one author who published 326 titles.

Publishes 6 hardcovers and 35 mass market paperbacks per year.

Address: Seaview Business Park, 1030 Calle Cordellia #106, San Clemente, CA 92673

Phone: (714)498-7227

Fax: (714)498-2162

How To Contact: Does not accept unsolicited manuscripts. Query first before submitting manuscript. Accepts faxed queries. Allows simultaneous submissions. 30% of accepted manuscripts are submitted through agents. Responds to queries in 3 weeks. Reports on manuscripts in 2 months. Occasionally comments on rejected manuscripts. Send SASE and $2 for writer's guidelines.

Terms: Authors are paid in royalties of 5% minimum, 12% maximum, on list price. Average advance is $1,500, but some authors receive $3,000 to $20,000 advances. Purchases world rights and press rights. Manuscript is published 1-18 months after acceptance. 6 free copies of book go to author; additional copies available at 50% discount.

SOHO PRESS INC.

Established: 1986

Editor: Juris Jurjevics

CATEGORIES

Private Eye, Suspense, Thrillers, Historical, Hardboiled Detective, Amateur Sleuth, Humorous Mystery, Police Procedural, Malice Domestic, Espionage, Courtroom/Trial

Desires good writing with "authenticity of setting and situations." Drug trade and alcoholic sleuths are overused.

Soho Press Inc. has recently published *The Woman Who Married a Bear* by John Straley (Shamus Award Winner for Best First Novel) Publishes 2-4 hardcovers and 2-4 trade paperbacks per year.

Address: 853 Broadway, New York, NY 10003

Phone: (212)260-1900

How To Contact: Accepts unsolicited manuscripts. Receives 400 unsolicited manuscripts each month. Send query letter with 3 chapters. Allows simultaneous submissions. 50% of accepted manuscripts are submitted through agents. Responds to queries in 6 weeks. Reports on manuscripts in 6 weeks.

Terms: Authors are paid in royalties of 10% minimum, 15% maximum, on list price. Purchases world rights. Manuscript is published 18 months after acceptance. Author receives biographical note on jacket or in book. 20 free copies of book go to author; additional copies available at 50% discount.

SPINSTERS INK

Established: 1978

Editor: Kelly Kager

CATEGORIES
Private Eye, Cozy, Amateur Sleuth, Police Procedural

"We are a feminist press," says Spinsters Ink, "therefore we only publish women authors who write from a feminist perspective. Any manuscripts where women are only secondary characters are rejected.

"Do your homework before submitting a manuscript. Don't waste your time by sending something that does not match the guidelines."

Wants manuscripts with solid writing.

Spinsters Ink has recently published *The Two-Bit Tango* by Elizabeth Pincus (1993 Lesbian Mystery Lambda Literary Award Winner), *The Other Side of Silence* by Joan Drury, *The Lessons* by Melanie McAllester, *The Solitary Twist* by Elizabeth Pincus.

Publishes 4-6 trade paperbacks per year. Publishes 1-2 first novels per year; average print run is 5,000.

Address: 32 E. 1st St., #330, Duluth, MN 55802
Phone: (218)727-3222
Fax: (218)727-3119
How To Contact: Send queries to Claire Kirch. Does not accept unsolicited manuscripts. Query first before submitting manuscript. Accepts faxed queries. Allows simultaneous submissions. Responds to queries in 2 months. Reports on manuscripts in 4 months. Send SASE for writer's guidelines.
Terms: Authors are paid in royalties of 7% minimum on list price. Purchases English language rights. Manuscript is published 1-2 years after acceptance. Author reviews galleys, copyedited manuscript, jacket copy. Author receives biographical note on jacket or in book. 10 free copies of book go to author; additional copies available at 40% discount.

THIRD SIDE PRESS

Established: 1991

Contact: Midge Stocker

CATEGORIES

Private Eye, Cozy, Historical, Amateur Sleuth, Humorous Mystery, Malice Domestic, Psychological Suspense, Romantic Suspense, Surrealistic Mystery, Espionage, Courtroom/Trial

Third Side Press publishes only lesbian mysteries and is looking for manuscripts with more political & social awareness, dramatic tension, and creative use of the language.

Publishes 5-8 trade paperbacks per year. Publishes 1-2 first novels per year; average print run is 3,000.

Address: 2250 W. Farragut, Chicago, IL 60625-1802

How To Contact: Accepts unsolicited manuscripts, but prefers writers to query first before submitting. Allows simultaneous submissions. Responds to queries in 2 weeks. Reports on manuscripts in 4 months. Occasionally comments on rejected manuscripts. Send SASE for writer's guidelines.

Terms: Authors receive royalties on net price. Purchases all rights. Manuscript is published 18 months after acceptance. Author receives biographical note on jacket or in book.

☀ ☀ ☀ ☀

VISTA PUBLISHING, INC.

Established: 1991

Editors: Caroyln Zagury, David Zagury

CATEGORIES

Private Eye, Suspense, Thrillers, Historical, Hardboiled Detective, Amateur Sleuth, Humorous Mystery, Police Procedural, Psychological Suspense, Romantic Suspense, Espionage, Courtroom/Trial

Prefers medical/nursing themes. "We're a nurse-owned company specializing in nurse authors." No cops and robbers type mysteries. Advises writers to "write from your knowledge and from your heart and believe in your work."

Vista Publishing, Inc. has recently published *Deadlier than Death, Dangerous Alibis, The Enemy Within* and *The Nurse Wore Black*

Publishes 2-3 softcovers per year. Publishes 2-3 first novels per year; average print run is 1,000.

Address: 473 Broadway, Long Branch, NJ 07740
Phone: (908)229-6500
Fax: (908)229-9647
How To Contact: Accepts unsolicited manuscripts. Receives 20-25 unsolicited manuscripts each month. Submit full manuscript. Allows simultaneous submissions. Responds to queries in 12 weeks. Reports on manuscripts in 2 months. Send SASE for writer's guidelines.
Terms: Authors receive a percentage of profit. Author receives biographical note on jacket or in book. 10 free copies of book go to author; additional copies available at a discount.

WINDSWEPT HOUSE PUBLISHERS

Established: 1980

Contact: Jane Weinberger

CATEGORIES
Cozy, Young Adult, Amateur Sleuth, Juvenile, Romantic Suspense

Publishes 2 hardcovers, 6 trade paperbacks and 8 mass market paperbacks per year. Publishes 2 first novels per year; average print run is 1,000.

Address: Rte 3 198, Mount Desert, ME 04660-0159
Phone: (207)244-7149
Fax: (207)244-3369
How To Contact: Does not accept unsolicited manuscripts. Query first before submitting manuscript. Accepts faxed queries. Allows simulta-

neous submissions. Submissions on computer diskette should be formatted for IBM WordPerfect. Responds to queries in 2-3 days. Reports on manuscripts in 1 week. Send SASE for writer's guidelines.

Terms: Purchases all rights. Manuscript is published 2 months after acceptance. Author receives biographical note on jacket or in book. 10-12% royalties paid quarterly. 10 free copies of book go to author; additional copies available at 40% discount.

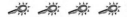

WRITE WAY PUBLISHING

Established: 1993

Editor: Dorrie O'Brien

CATEGORIES
Private Eye, Cozy, Suspense, Crime, Thrillers, Historical, Hardboiled Detective, Amateur Sleuth, Humorous Mystery, Urban Horror, Dark Mystery, Light Horror, Police Procedural, Malice Domestic, Psychological Suspense, Romantic Suspense, Surrealistic Mystery, Espionage, Courtroom/Trial

---

Does not want to see stories that are grossly sexual or bloody. "Intricate plotting and leaving clues at just the right moment is far more important than heavy characterization, setting or moralizing."

Write Way Publishing has recently published *All the Old Lions* by Carol Caverly, and *St. John's Bestiary* by William Babula.

Publishes 5-7 hardcovers per year. Publishes 3-5 first novels per year; average print run is 1,000.

Address: 3806 S. Fraser, Aurora, CO 80014
Phone: (800)680-1493
Fax: (303)680-2181
How To Contact: Accepts unsolicited manuscripts. Receives 10-50 unsolicited manuscripts each month. Query first before submitting manuscript. Send query letter with 2 chapters. Accepts faxed queries. Allows simultaneous submissions. 10% of accepted manuscripts are submitted through agents. Responds to queries in 4 weeks. Reports on manuscripts in 8 months. Send SASE for writer's guidelines.

Terms: Authors are paid in royalties of 8% minimum, 10% maximum, on net price. Manuscript is published 1-3 years after acceptance. Author receives biographical note on jacket or in book. 10 free copies of book go to author; additional copies available at 40% discount.

INTERNATIONAL MAIL

When enclosing a self-addressed envelope for the return of your query or manuscript from a publisher outside the U.S., you must include International Reply Coupons (IRCs). IRCs are available at your local post office and can be redeemed for stamps of any country. You can cut a substantial portion of your international mailing expenses by sending out disposable proposals and manuscripts (i.e., photocopies or computer printouts which the recipient can simply throw away if he or she is not interested), instead of paying postage for the return of the rejected material.

CANADA

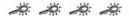

SIMON & PIERRE PUBLISHING CO. LTD.

Established: 1972

Editor: Jean Paton

CATEGORIES
Cozy, Crime, Historical, Amateur Sleuth, Humorous Mystery

"We want stories with Sherlockian connections and/or Canadian settings. Be sure to research a publisher to ensure the manuscript fits the publisher's list. A lot of money is wasted when writers do not send appropriate material. Cover letter or resume should indicate the writer's expertise if such is necessary for the story—e.g., if set on campus, writer is a professor or student; if a police prodecural, writer has 20 years' experience in the NYPD etc."

Simon & Pierre Publishing Co. Ltd. has recently published *Found: A Body* by Betsy Struthers (shortlisted for the Arthur Ellis Award of the Crime Writers of Canada), *Crime in Cold Climate* by David Skene-Melvin, an anthology of 1930's and 40's crime writings, and *Sherlock Holmes: Travels in the Canadian West* by Ronald Weyman

Publishes 1-2 trade paperbacks per year. Publishes 1 first novel per year; average print run is 2,000.

Address: 2181 Queen St. E. Ste. 301, Toronto, Ontario, Canada, M4E 1E5
Phone: (416)698-0454
Fax: (416)698-1102
How To Contact: Accepts unsolicited manuscripts. Canadian authors only at this time. Receives 15 unsolicited manuscripts each month. Send query letter with 2 chapters. Accepts faxed queries. Allows simultaneous submissions. Responds to queries in 3 weeks. Reports on manuscripts in 3 months. Send SASE for writer's guidelines.
Terms: Authors are paid in royalties of 10% on list price. Average advance is $750. Purchases all rights. Manuscript is published 1 year after acceptance. Author reviews galleys, copyedited manuscript,

jacket copy. Author receives biographical note on jacket or in book. 10 free copies of book go to author; additional copies available at 40% discount.

TURNSTONE PRESS

Established: 1976

Editor: James Hutchison

CATEGORIES
Private Eye, Crime, Humorous Mystery

Wants high standard of writing, unusual characterization and plot, contemporary setting and work that is outside of the mainstream. **Only publishes Canadian writers.**
Publishes 2-3 first novels per year; average print run is 1,500.

Address: 607-100 Arthur St., Winnipeg, Manitoba, Canada, R3B 1H3
Phone: (204)947-1555
Fax: (204)942-1555
How To Contact: Accepts unsolicited manuscripts. Receives 100 unsolicited manuscripts each month. Send query letter with 1 chapter. Accepts faxed queries. E-mail queries to editor@turnstonepress.mb.ca. Allows simultaneous submissions. 15% of accepted manuscripts are submitted through agents. Responds to queries in 8 weeks. Reports on manuscripts in 12 weeks. Send SASE for writer's guidelines.
Terms: Authors are paid in royalties of 10% on net price. Authors receive advance of 10% to 40% of advance print run. Purchases world rights. Manuscript is published 6-18 months after acceptance. Author reviews galleys, copyedited manuscript, jacket copy. Author receives biographical note on jacket or in book. 10 free copies of book go to author; additional copies available at 40% discount.

VESTA PUBLICATIONS, LTD.

Established: 1974

Contact: Stephen Gill

CATEGORIES
Private Eye, Cozy, Suspense, Crime, Young Adult, Thrillers, Historical, Hardboiled Detective, Amateur Sleuth, Humorous Mystery, Urban Horror, Dark Mystery, Light Horror, Police Procedural, Malice Domestic, Psychological Suspense, Romantic Suspense, Surrealistic Mystery, Espionage, Courtroom/Trial

Publisher is looking for stories that are "in good taste"—no pornography, terror or bloodshed.

Publishes 8-10 trade paperbacks per year. Publishes 8-10 first novels per year; average print run is 5,000.

Address: Box 1641, Cornwall, Ontario, Canada, K6H 5V6
Phone: (613)932-2135
Fax: (613)932-7735
How To Contact: Does not accept unsolicited manuscripts. Query first before submitting manuscript. Send query letter with 1 chapter. Accepts faxed queries. Allows simultaneous submissions. Submissions on computer diskette should be formatted for IBM WordPerfect. Responds to queries in 8 weeks. Reports on manuscripts in 10 weeks.
Terms: Purchases all rights. Manuscript is published 1 year after acceptance. Author receives biographical note on jacket or in book.

FRANCE

10/18 (AN IMPRINT OF UGE)

Established: 1962 • Mystery imprint: Grauds Detectives

Editor-in-Chief: Mr. Zylberstein

CATEGORIES
Historical, Amateur Sleuth, Police Procedural

Thinks noir and private eye novels are overused; encourages writers to "go historical, go exotic" if they want to sell a manuscript. Has a very strong reputation for publishing genre novels.

Publishes 40 mass market paperbacks per year. Publishes 2 first novels per year; average print run is 10,000 copies.

Address: 12 Avenue d'Italie, Paris, France 75013
Phone: (441)606-08
Fax: (435)481-08
How To Contact: Does not accept unsolicited manuscripts. Query first before submitting manuscript. 90% of accepted manuscripts are submitted through agents. Responds to queries in 3 weeks. Reports on manuscripts in 3 months. Occasionally comments on rejected manuscripts.
Terms: Authors are paid in royalties of 5.00% minimum, 6.00% maximum, on list price. Average advance is $3,000. Purchases French language rights. Manuscript is published 6 months after acceptance. Author receives biographical note on jacket or in book. 10 free copies of book go to author; additional copies available at 10% discount.

GERMANY

☼ ☼ ☼ ☼

BUEST VERLAG

Established: 1993

Publisher: Joachim Von Beust; Managing Editor: Gerd Simon,

> **CATEGORIES**
> Private Eye, Thrillers

"We are interested in well-crafted literary novels, those with cultivated eroticism and avant-gard topics." Publishes 4-6 first novels per year; average print run is 6,000.

Address: Fraunhoferstr. 13, Munchen, Germany D-80469
Phone: (089)266-431
Fax: (089)266-471

How To Contact: Does not accept unsolicited manuscripts. Send query letter with 1 chapter. Accepts faxed queries. Submissions on computer diskette should be formatted for MS Word for Macintosh. 50% of accepted manuscripts are submitted through agents. Responds to queries in 6 weeks. Reports on manuscripts in 6 weeks.

Terms: Authors are paid in royalties of 8.00% minimum. Average advance is $1,500. Purchases volume rights. 10 free copies of book go to author; additional copies available at 40% discount.

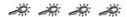

EICHBORN VERLAG

Established: 1982

Editor: Doris Engelke

CATEGORIES
Private Eye, Suspense, Historical, Amateur Sleuth, Humorous Mystery, Urban Horror, Psychological Suspense

"We want less horror and more psychological suspense. We're not into blood-dripping murders."

Publishes 4-6 hardcovers per year. Publishes 2-4 first novels per year; average print run is 4,000.

Address: Kaiser St. 66, Frankfurt, Germany 60318
Phone: (069)593-518
Fax: (069)596-1380
How To Contact: Does not accept unsolicited manuscripts. Send query letter with 2 chapters. Allows simultaneous submissions. 70% of accepted manuscripts are submitted through agents. Responds to queries in 2 months. Reports on manuscripts in 2 months.

Terms: Authors are paid in royalties of 5.00% minimum, 10.00% maximum, on net price. Average advance is $1,000. Manuscript is published 10 months after acceptance. Author receives biographical note on jacket or in book. 10 free copies of book go to author; additional copies available at 45% discount.

KBV - KLEIN & BLECHINGER VERLAG GMBH

Established: 1989

Editors: Mr. Klein, Mr. Gruch

CATEGORIES
Private Eye, Suspense, Crime, Hardboiled Detective, Amateur Sleuth

"We are specialized in crime fiction with local connections, related to contempary history and politics; we prefer good female authors."
Publishes 4-6 hardcovers per year. Publishes 6-8 first novels per year; average print run is 3,000.

Address: Postfach 1244; Mittelstr. 65, Elsdorf, Germany D-50189
Phone: (022)74-4029
Fax: (022)748-1108
How To Contact: Accepts unsolicited manuscripts. Receives 10-15 unsolicited manuscripts each month. Send query letter with 5 chapters. Submit full manuscript. Accepts faxed queries. Submissions on computer diskette should be formatted for either IBM or Macintosh. 5% of accepted manuscripts are submitted through agents. Responds to queries in 4 weeks. Reports on manuscripts in 2 months. Occasionally comments on rejected manuscripts.
Terms: Authors are paid in royalties of 8.00% minimum, 8.00% maximum, on list price. Purchases publication, translation, publication in journals, CD-ROM, paperback and theatrical rights. Manuscript is published 1-1½ years after acceptance. Author receives biographical note on jacket or in book. 20 free copies of book go to author; additional copies available at 40% discount.

VERLAGSBURO SIMON & MAGIERA

Editor: Gerd Simon

CATEGORIES
Private Eye, Thrillers

Publishes 4-6 first novels per year; average print run is 6,000.

Address: PF431062, Munchen, Germany D-80740
Phone: (089)39-5294
Fax: (089)39-5294
How To Contact: Does not accept unsolicited manuscripts. Send query letter with 1 chapter. Accepts faxed queries. Submissions on computer diskette should be formatted for MS Word for Macintosh. 50% of accepted manuscripts are submitted through agents. Responds to queries in 6 weeks. Reports on manuscripts in 6 weeks.
Terms: Authors are paid in royalties of 8.00% minimum. Average advance is $1,500. Purchases volume rights. 10 free copies of book go to author; additional copies available at 40% discount.

SPAIN

MUNOZ MOYA EDITORES SA

Established: 1984

Editor: Mr. Munoz

CATEGORIES
Private Eye, Suspense

Publishes 2-4 hardcovers per year. Publishes 1 first novel per year.

Address: 28 De Febrero, 6, Brenes (Sevilla), Spain 41310
Phone: (345)479-7251
Fax: (345)479-6650
How To Contact: Accepts unsolicited manuscripts. Receives numerous unsolicited manuscripts each month. Submit full manuscript. Allows simultaneous submissions. 10% of accepted manuscripts are submitted through agents. Responds to queries in 2 months. Reports on manuscripts in 3 months.
Terms: Manuscript is published 6-12 months after acceptance. Author receives biographical note on jacket or in book. 25 free copies of book go to author; additional copies available at 15% discount.

UNITED KINGDOM

ALLISON & BUSBY CRIME

Established: 1968

Publisher: Peter Day

CATEGORIES
Private Eye, Hardboiled Detective, Police Procedural, Malice Domestic

Allison & Busby is a newly independent publisher. Publishes 30 books per year, seven of which are mystery. Publishes 3 first novels per year. Average print run: hardcover, 2,000; trade paperback, 3,000; mass market paperback, 6,000.

Address: The Lodge, Richmond Way, London W12 8LW England
Phone: (081)749-9441/3254
Fax: (081)749-9496
How To Contact: Submit outline and sample chapters. SASE required for query and manuscript response. Fax queries and simultaneous submissions are OK. Receives 100 unsolicited manuscripts/month. 80% of accepted manuscripts are agented. Reports in 1 week. Guidelines available. Free catalog available.
Terms: Average advance £1,500. Average royalty 10% hardcover; 1½% paper. Author receives 12 hardcover, 20 paper copies of printed book. Buys world rights if possible; always buys U.S. and United Kingdom rights. Publishes manuscripts 1 year after acceptance. Average time to write book after contract signing is 1 year. Author receives galleys and copyedited manuscript and reviews jacket copy. Author gets bio note.

CENTURY BOOKS

Established: 1982

Publisher: Oliver Johnson

CATEGORIES
Private Eye, Hardboiled Detective, Police Procedural, Historical

Century Books publishes hardcovers, trade paperbacks and mass market paperbacks. Publishes 2-3 first novels per year.

Address: Random Century Group, 20 Vauxhall Bridge Rd., London SW1V 2SA England
Phone: (071)973-9000
Fax: (071)233-6115
How To Contact: Submit through agent only. Fax queries and simultaneous submissions are OK. Receives 20 unsolicited manuscripts/month. 99% of accepted manuscripts are agented. Reports on queries in 1-2 weeks; manuscripts in 1-2 months.
Terms: Average royalty 10% minimum. Author receives 6 copies of printed book. Buys English language world rights. Publishes manuscripts 1 year after acceptance. Average time to write book after contract signing is 1 year. Author receives galleys and copyedited manuscript and reviews jacket copy. Author receives bio note.

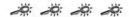

CONSTABLE & CO., LTD.

Established: 1790

CATEGORIES
Private Eye, Hardboiled Detective, Police Procedural, Cozy, Malice Domestic

Constable & Company publishes 75 books per year. Average print run in hardcover is 1,750. Publishes 4 first novels per year.

Address: 3, The Lancesters, 162 Fulham Palace Rd., London W6 9ER England
Phone: (081)748-7562
How To Contact: Submit outline and sample chapters. Reports in 1 month. E-mail and fax queries are OK. Receives 30 unsolicited manuscripts/month. 90% of accepted manuscripts are agented. Sometimes

comments on manuscripts. Catalog available for adequate return post-age in IRCs.

Terms: Average advance £1,500. Average royalty 10%. Author receives 10 copies of printed book. Buys United Kingdom and commonwealth rights. Publishes mansucripts 9 months after acceptance. Average time to write book after contract signing is 3 months. Author receives galleys and copyedited manuscript and reviews jacket copy. Author gets bio note.

THE CRIME CLUB

Established: 1930

Elizabeth Walter, Editor

CATEGORIES
Private Eye, Police Procedural, Cozy, Amateur Sleuth, Malice Domestic

The Crime Club is the mystery imprint of HarperCollins and publishes 1-6 first novels per year.

Address: HarperCollins Publishers Ltd., 77-85 Fulham Palace Rd., Hammersmith, London W6 8JB England
Phone: (081)741-7070
Fax: (081)307-4440
How To Contact: Query with outline and sample chapters. SASE required for manuscript response. 65% of accepted manuscripts are agented. Reports on queries in 2 weeks; manuscripts in 2 months. Sometimes comments on manuscripts.
Terms: Pays advance and royalty. Author receives 10 copies of book. Buys world rights, all languages. Publishes manuscript 9-10 months after acceptance. Author receives galleys and reviews jacket copy. Author gets bio note.

VICTOR GOLLANCZ, LTD.

Established: 1929

CATEGORIES
Private Eye, Young Adult, Juvenile, Hardboiled Detective, Police Procedural, Cozy, Amateur Sleuth, Malice Domestic, Romantic Suspense

Publishes 200 books per year, usually 1-2 first novels.

Address: 14 Henrietta St., Covent Garden, London WC2E 8QJ England
Phone: (071)836-2006
Fax: (071)379-0934
How To Contact: Submit outline and sample chapters. SASE required for query and manuscript response. Fax queries are OK. Receives 20 unsolicited manuscripts/month. 95% of accepted manuscripts are agented. Reports on queries in 1-2 months; manuscripts in 2 months. Sometimes comments on manuscripts. Catalog available.
Terms: Payment terms not disclosed. Author receives galleys and copyedited manuscript. Author gets bio note.

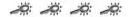

HEADLINE BOOK PUBLISHING PLC

Established: 1986

Editor: Susan J. Fletcher

CATEGORIES
Private Eye, Police Procedural, Cozy, Amateur Sleuth, Malice Domestic

Headline Book Publishing PLC is a mainstream publisher of popular fiction and nonfiction. Publishes 300-400 titles per year, including hardcovers, trade paperbacks and mass market paperbacks. Publishes 3 first novels per year.

Address: 79 Great Titchfield St., London W1P 7FN England
Phone: (071)631-1687
Fax: (071)436-4220
How To Contact: Submit outline and first 100 pages. SASE required for query and manuscript response. E-mail and fax queries and simultaneous submissions are OK. Receives 300 unsolicited manuscripts/month.

98% of accepted manuscripts are agented. Reports in 1 month. Comments on mansucripts. Catalog available for adequate return postage in IRCs.

Terms: Average advance and royalty varies. Author receives 6 hardcover and 10 paper copies of printed book. Rights purchased vary. Publishes manuscript 9 months after acceptance. Average time to write book after contract signing is 6-12 months. Author receives galleys and copyedited manuscript and reviews jacket copy. Author gets bio note.

HODDER & STOUGHTON, LTD.

Established: 1868 • Imprint: Coronet

Editor: Mrs. Ornsby

CATEGORIES
Hardboiled Detective, Private Eye, Police Procedural, Malice Domestic

Publishes over 1,000 books per year, including 10 mystery hardcovers and 15-20 mystery mass market paperbacks. Publishes "a few" first novels each year.

Address: Mill Road, Dunton Green, Sevenoaks, Kent TN13 2YA England
Phone: (071)636-9851
Fax: (071)631-5248
How To Contact: Submit query letter only. SASE required for query and manuscript response. No sumultaneous submissions. Receives "many" unsolicited manuscripts/month. "Nearly all" accepted manuscripts are agented. Reports in 3 months. Sometimes comments on manuscripts.
Terms: Pays advance and royalties. Author receives 12 hardcover copies of printed book. Buys world rights. Publishes manuscript about 9 months after acceptance (varies). Author reviews galleys, copyedited manuscript and jacket copy. Author usually gets bio note.

MACMILLAN CRIME CASE

Established: early 1970s

Editor: Maria Rejt

CATEGORIES
Hardboiled Detective, Private Eye, Police Procedural, Cozy, Amateur
Sleuth, Malice Domestic, Romantic Suspense, Psychological Suspense

MacMillan Crime Case is an imprint of the large international publisher, Pan MacMillan. Publishes hardback books, usually 2-4 first novels per year. Says editor Rejt, "A fresh, original voice stands out to us. Use original, yet believable, characters and an ingenious plot. We're specifically interested in medical/hospital whodunits and forensic backgrounds. I am willing to publish in every category that comes under the broad umbrella of crime fiction, but I do have a preference for contemporary whodunits and psychological suspense, and strong series characters. We don't need any private eyes with drinking problems or violence that is excessive for the dynamics of the plot, especially involving children."

Address: Pan MacMillan Ltd., 18-21 Cavaye Place, London SW10 9PG
England
Phone: (071)373-6070
Fax: (071)370-0746
How To Contact: Query first, then submit sample material. "It is not necessary to acquire an agent before contacting editor." Fax queries and simultaneous submissions are OK. Receives 10-20 unsolicited manuscripts/month. 90% of accepted manuscripts are agented. Reports on queries in 2 weeks; manuscripts in 6 weeks. Sometimes comments on manuscripts. Catalog available for large, self-addressed envelope and IRC's.
Terms: Average advance varies. Average royalty 10%/12½%/15%. Author receives 6 copies of printed book. Buys all rights. Publishes manuscript 9-12 months after acceptance. Average time to write book after contract signing is 1 year. Author receives galleys and copyedited manuscript and reviews jacket copy. Author gets bio note.

SEVERN HOUSE PUBLISHERS, LTD.

Established: 1974

CATEGORIES
Hardboiled Detective, Private Eye, Police Procedural, Amateur Sleuth, Malice Domestic, Romantic Suspense

Severn House is a "small publisher specializing in new hardcover fiction (including reprints) for the library market." Publishes about 120 books per year, 10-50 of which are mystery hardcovers. Average print run is 1,500. "A well-thought-out plot, essential characters, and a good twist in the end" are appealing to the editors at Severn House. Will be concentrating on crime trade paperbacks in the near future.

Address: 9-15 Hight St., Sutton, Surrey England
Phone: (081)770-3830
Fax: (081)770-3850
How To Contact: Submit through agent only. Reports on queries in 2-3 weeks; mansucripts in 2 months. Sometimes comments on manuscripts. Catalog for self-addressed envelope with 1 U.K. or 3 U.S. first-class stamps.
Terms: Average royalty 10-15%. Author receives 6 hardcover copies of printed book. Buys world rights, if possible. Publishes manuscript 6-7 months after acceptance. Author receives copyedited manuscript. Author gets bio note.

VIRAGO PRESS, LTD.

Established: 1973

Melanie Silgardo, Editor

CATEGORIES
Private Eye, Amateur Sleuth, Psychological Thriller

Virago publishes about 110-120 books a year, 2 or so of which are first novels. Average hardcover print run is 1,000-2,000; trade paperback

5,000; mass market paperback 7,000. "We look for a manuscript with intelligent, lively writing and well-researched subject matter, a sleuth who is quirky, engaging and well-thought-out as a personality, and obviously, a plot with plenty of suspense and psychological twists. We are looking for good British crime and mystery fiction, which there seems to be a dearth of. We welcome American submissions."

Address: Centro House, 20-23 Mandela St., London NW1 0HQ England
Phone: (071)383-5150
Fax: (071)383-4892
How To Contact: Submit outline and sample chapters. SASE required for query and manuscript response. E-mail and fax queries and simultaneous submissions are OK. Receives 10-12 unsolicited manuscripts/ month. 90% of accepted manuscripts are agented. Reports in 2 months. Comments on manuscirpts. Catalog available.
Terms: Average advance is confidential. Average royalty 10% hardcover; 7.5% paper. Author receives 6 copies of printed book. Buys world rights, all languages. Publishes manuscripts 8-12 months after acceptance. Average time to write book after contract signing is 1 year. Author receives galleys and copyedited manuscript and reviews jacket copy.

MAGAZINE MARKETS

Marketing Your Mystery Short Story

ROBIN GEE

Some say the first recorded murder story could have been that of Cain and Abel, but most put the beginning of the modern detective story at 1841, the year Edgar Allan Poe published "The Murders in the Rue Morgue" in his magazine, *Graham's*. About 40 years later came Sir Arthur Conan Doyle's Sherlock Holmes stories, but it wasn't until the pulp magazine era of the late 1920s to the early 1950s that mystery short stories hit their "golden age."

With names like *Black Mask, Dime Detective, The Strand, Popular Detective* and *Detective Story*, dozens of magazines featuring short stories of murder and detection flourished and the writers they published became household names—Ellery Queen, Erle Stanley Gardner, Dashiell Hammett, Dorothy L. Sayers, John Dickson Carr and many others. Yet, by the 1960s, almost all these magazines had ceased publication.

Although the market for short mystery fiction has never been as big as it was during the "golden age," there have always been a few very strong markets and the last few years have seen a small, but steady growth in the field. Two major mystery magazines published by Dell, *Ellery Queen's Mystery Magazine* and *Alfred Hitchcock Mystery Magazine*, have survived and continue to dominate the field. In fact, if you look at lists of award-winning stories from the 1970s, 1980s and even 1990s, most of those winners and those nominated for awards were published in *EQMM* or *AHMM*. Publication in either magazine brings a certain prestige, as well as attention in the field.

Although the Dell magazines publish a variety of mystery material, several publications have emerged in the last few years devoted to less-traditional mysteries, such as *New Mystery, Dark Kiss* and *Hardboiled*. Publication in any of the commercial mystery magazines has proven a good inroad to book publication. Almost all mystery magazines devote special attention to new writers, and book publishers frequently mine them for new talent.

In addition to the magazines devoted solely to mystery, a few large, commercial publications also publish mystery short stories. Even some city and regional publications like a good mystery every now and then, especially if the setting is within their city or region.

Smaller magazines also publish mysteries and are a good place for new writers to start. Some are devoted entirely to mystery and some are considered "fanzines," with stories based on the characters or works of a particular author. On occasion literary journals will publish mystery stories, if the writing is literary—cozies seem to have the best chance with many of these.

Anthologies

Many magazines and most of the book publishers with large mystery lines publish anthologies. Most are themed either by type of mystery, such as malice domestic, cozy or hardboiled detective, by location of setting, or by a certain characteristic, such as holiday tales, cat stories or stories featuring older sleuths.

Most publishers use outside editors to help screen and select stories. Anthologists often find mystery magazines to be excellent sources of material for various compilations and collections. There are more reprint anthologies (using material previously published in magazines) than original anthologies, but most are a mix.

Publishing first in commercial fiction magazines seems the best route to anthologies, but savvy writers can sometimes find out about projects through word-of-mouth. While many of these projects are invitation-only affairs, some are open to submissions. To avoid being deluged with inappropriate manuscripts, however, editors spread the word through the outlets most likely to reach professional writers. Conferences such as Bouchercon and the various Mystery Writers of America events offer writers a good opportunity to meet anthologists and editors, as well as other writers, and to learn about upcoming projects. Mystery organizations such as the Mystery Writers of America, Sisters in Crime and the Private Eye Writers of America publish newsletters which may list anthology projects. Online services for writers, too, may include announcements for upcoming anthologies.

A word of caution about the grapevine—make sure you check all the details. If you learn of an anthology and think you have a story suitable for the theme or focus, ask the editor for guidelines. If it is a later edition of an established anthology, read earlier editions to get a feel for the type of work included.

Keeping up with the market

Any magazine editor will tell you the best way to keep up with the market is to read mystery magazines. Read also some of the various anthologies. The anthologies compiled from work previously published in magazines will give you a good feel for the type of material accepted in those magazines. Beyond this there are several trade journals devoted to mystery writing. Check out issues of *Mystery Scene*, *The Armchair Detective* or other magazines listed under "Nonfiction Short Markets" (page 244) and "References" (page 390). These supply news and information about the mystery field including new markets for mystery fiction.

Networking can also lead you to information on new magazines and changes in the field. The aforementioned mystery writer's organizations provide their members with newsletters and hold regional and national conferences. The news you pick up at conferences can be especially fresh, since you may hear it from an editor before it hits any printed publication.

If you own a computer, you can also network with other writers online and pick up information on new markets. See "Online Resources" in the **Resources** section (page 382) for more about what these services can offer mystery writers.

Approaching magazine editors

When submitting short fiction to magazines, professional presentation is important. Editors at magazines can receive hundreds of submissions, and most magazines only publish one or a handful of short stories in each issue. No matter how well-written your story, editors simply do not have time to deal with work that is difficult to read.

Before submitting, read several recent issues of the magazine to make sure your work is a good fit. Study the listings and read the interviews in this book to get a feel for the publication and its editor's needs. Pay special attention to submission guidelines. You can also write the magazine to obtain writer's guidelines if available. Most editors will send them if given a self-addressed, stamped envelope. Some magazines will accept a simultaneous submission, but be sure to let other editors considering your manuscript know if your story has been accepted and is no longer available for consideration.

Almost all magazines want to see the complete short story manuscript. Send it along with a brief cover letter (no longer than one page) and a self-addressed, stamped envelope large enough to fit your manuscript if you want it returned. Many writers prefer to send a disposable manuscript and a #10 SASE or stamped postcard for a reply.

If the magazine accepts disk or online submissions, check with them about format and how to submit. Always include a hard copy with your disk submission.

In your cover letter, you may want to include a few short sentences about your story, but avoid retelling it—after all, the editor has it in his or her hands. Include only the personal information that lends credibility to your story. If your story is set in Mexico, for example, and you lived in Mexico for two years, you might want to mention this fact. If you've written a medical thriller and you are a doctor, such information would be important. A brief list of your publishing credits (one or two sentences) can also be included. Most editors appreciate an estimated word-count as well. See our "Sample Short Story Cover Letter" on page 177.

Payment for short stories can vary from only a contributor's copy to more than $1,000. Newer writers often feel a publishing credit is payment enough, and publication in nonpaying markets can help you gain exposure and experience.

Bonnie Booth
1453 Nuance Blvd.
Norwood, OH 45212

December 6, 1996

Janet Smythe
Modern Mystery
452 W. 50th St.
Brookside Park, IL 60633

Dear Ms. Smythe:

Enclosed is my short story, "Permanent Solution," for your consideration. The story is set in the world of high fashion hair design. In the weeks before a major hair design show, three of the state's top hair designers are missing. When their bodies turn up with shaven heads, it is clear their shared occupation is more than just a coincidence.

I was happy to discover your new magazine on the newsstand in September and was very pleased to find you are committed to publishing the work of new mystery writers. This is my first mystery story. I have published a few nonfiction pieces in *Hairdressing News* and *Salons Today*.

As a professional hair designer and part-time law student, I am intimately familiar with inner workings of the hair design industry and the hair show circuit. The story is 2,000 words and would fit well into your "Occupational Hazards" short story feature.

I look forward to your reply. I've enclosed a SASE for your convenience. Thank you for your consideration.

Sincerely,

Bonnie Booth
(513)555-5555
Encl: manuscript
SASE

Sample Short Story Cover Letter

Primary Short Fiction Markets

L isted in this section are the commercial magazines that publish mystery and crime fiction. Some are devoted entirely to fiction, while others publish one or two stories in each issue but have become known for publishing the best in the field. We've also included some of the promising, professional-looking newcomers in the field.

The markets in this section include detailed interviews with the editors and examine their philosophies and how they approach their work. We asked the editors about the history of their magazines and how they came to work for them. The editors told us a little about their own influences and what authors or books got them hooked on mysteries. Knowing this "inside" information can help you determine exactly which editors to target with *your* manuscript.

From there we asked about what they look for in a manuscript, what to avoid and what advice they had for new writers. To help you choose which editor will be most receptive to your work, each interview includes a detailed description of the publication and the type of mystery and crime fiction within its pages.

Before each interview, we've included a list of the subgenres (categories) that interest the editor to help you identify those magazines most likely to be interested in the type of mystery you write. We've also included brief information on the magazine's date of establishment, circulation, frequency of publication, size and number of pages. This data will help you get a feel for the audience and prestige of the magazine. For example, newer magazines are often the most receptive to the work of new writers. More established magazines with large circulations have more prestige (and more money to spend on manuscripts), but it may be harder for the new writer to break in there.

After the profile, you'll find specific pointers on how to contact the magazine and how to submit your short story. If a magazine is open to simultaneous submissions, we've noted it. We've also indicated if electronic submissions are acceptable, and the format for electronic submissions. Be sure with all such submissions, however, to include a printed copy.

Reporting times are given, but keep in mind that these are estimates. Allow an additional three or four weeks before checking on the status of your submission, and include a self-addressed, stamped envelope for a reply or your story's return. If you are sending to a magazine published in a country other than your own, include International Reply Coupons (IRCs) instead of stamps. These are available at most main post office branches.

Following this section are secondary short fiction markets, overseas short fiction markets, and markets for mystery and crime nonfiction.

Cover: Ron Finger

ALFRED HITCHCOCK MYSTERY MAGAZINE

Established: 1956 • Circulation: 215,000 copies; estimated 615,000 readers • Published: 13 times a year • Number of Pages: 160-288 • Size: 5¹⁄₁₆ × 7³⁄₈

Cathleen Jordan, Editor

CATEGORIES
Private Eye, Cozy, Suspense, Historical, Hardboiled Detective, Amateur Sleuth, Humorous Mystery, Police Procedural, Espionage, Courtroom/Trial

Although Cathleen Jordan has been editor of *Alfred Hitchcock Mystery Magazine* for 14 years, she says her criterion for what makes a good mystery story has not changed much over the years. "It's always a matter of the quality of the writing. One can tell very quickly whether the author is in control. However interesting a story might be, it's useless to us if the writing is not good. On the other hand, although we don't take stories that need a lot of revision, a first-rate writer might be able to work on the plot of a story to improve it."

In addition to overall quality, Jordan tries to include a mix of different mystery subgenres. "There's always been considerable variety in the short fiction market," she says. "At *Hitchcock* we are interested in all subgenres, every possible type of mystery and crime story, even some with supernatural, occult or science fiction overtones.

"I'd really like to see more classic whodunits featuring amateur detectives. I'd like to see more memorable characters like Miss Marple or Lord Peter. These are very hard to do well and we get fewer of them than I'd like. I'd love to publish more."

Although Jordan has no absolute taboos, one mistake writers make is in thinking mystery short stories must have surprise or trick endings.

"A good surprise ending is very difficult to do. A lot of writers get so excited about getting to the surprise at the end that they neglect the rest of the story. There's more to it than a punch line.

"On the other hand, I do look for a strong ending. This is the place a lot of writers have trouble. They must pay particular attention to fulfilling their readers' expectations. Mystery readers want a satisfying ending."

Short stories, says Jordan, offer new writers opportunities to break into the mystery market, but only if their writing is of the same high quality expected in novels. "I'm convinced everything you can find in a novel, you can find in a short story." While she admits the short story presents certain challenges simply because of its brevity, she says "It is possible, even if it is in miniature, to have fully realized characters and a complicated plot."

In discussing the market for mystery fiction, Jordan says the biggest change she's noticed has been the increased interest by book publishers in publishing anthologies of original short fiction. Before coming to the magazine, she edited a few mystery novels for Doubleday for what was then called the Crime Club line. "When I was at Doubleday the conventional wisdom was that short story collections did not sell very well, so I wasn't aware of the market for mystery stories. When I came here I found the short story market was much more alive than I thought."

In recent years mystery anthologies, whether original or reprint material, have been doing very well, she says, and this fact has not been lost on Dell Magazines, the publisher of both *Hitchcock* and its sibling publication, *Ellery Queen's Mystery Magazine*. This has been a bonus for writers, especially those whose work is new or not widely known. Anthologies of stories published in the magazines offer writers increased exposure and a longer shelf-life for their work in bookstores. Included as part of the Dell Magazines' publishing contracts, all stories accepted for publication in *Hitchcock* may be considered for an anthology.

Although the company does not stick to a set number or schedule, its anthology program is active and ongoing, Jordan says. The anthologies are usually themed in some way and may include stories first published in either magazine. Jordan, *Queen's* Editor Janet Hutchings, and Cynthia Manson, vice president of marketing and subsidiary rights, divide up the anthology workload.

Writers interested in finding out more about what the different magazines publish may want to take a look at some of the various anthologies. Each one is packaged by the magazine and published by different book publishers. Recent titles include a collection of medical-related mysteries, *Murder Most Medical*, published in June 1995 by Caroll & Graf, and the second in a series of anthologies featuring women protagonists, *Women of Mystery II*, published in 1994 in hardback by Caroll & Graf and in 1995 in paperback by Berkley. Others include *Alfred Hitchcock's Tales of the Supernatural and the Fantastic*, published by Smithmark in 1993 and *Murder on Main Street*, a collection of about 40 stories from *Hitchcock*, published by Barnes & Noble Books. Jordan says other anthologies include a wide array of themes from cat stories to Halloween and Christmas mysteries.

Jordan's simple requirement for quality has worked well for the magazine. *Hitchcock* and *Queen* have long been known as the two strongest outlets in the small, highly competitive market for short mystery fiction. And, although her magazine has a history of publishing some of the top names in the mystery field, Jordan is particularly proud of the number of new writers she's published. "Many of our stories have received the Robert L. Fish Memorial Award from Mystery Writers of America for best first mystery short story. As many as twenty stories a year have been first publications."

Still, competition is keen. Jordan and one assistant read all submissions to the magazine, selecting about 100 for publication each year out of some 3,800 submissions. Yet, says Jordan, talented new writers have an excellent chance at being published. "It's not as though all the slots are filled. We have a number of established writers who have been writing for our magazine for awhile, but we even turn them down once in a while. There's a very real market here."

Address: 1540 Broadway, New York, NY 10036
How To Contact: Send complete manuscript and SASE. Send a business-sized SASE to obtain writing guidelines. Receives 300 unsolicited fiction submissions each month. Purchases 7-8 fiction manuscripts per issue. Responds to author submissions in 2 months. 85% of magazine is mystery/crime fiction. A sample copy is available for $3. Subscription cost is $34.97 for 13 issues.
Payment: Pays approximately 8 cents per word.
Terms: Acquires first North American and foreign serial rights.

ELLERY QUEEN'S MYSTERY MAGAZINE

Established: 1941 • Circulation: 500,000 readers • Published: 13 times a year, including 2 double issues • Number of Pages: 160-288 • Size: 5$\frac{1}{16}$ × 7$\frac{3}{8}$

Janet Hutchings, Editor

CATEGORIES

Private Eye, Cozy, Suspense, Crime, Thrillers, Historical, Hardboiled Detective, Amateur Sleuth, Humorous Mystery, Dark Mystery, Police Procedural, Malice Domestic, Psychological Suspense, Romantic Suspense, Espionage, Courtroom/Trial

"If you write well and can draw convincing characters, you can probably interest me no matter what the subject of your story is," says Janet Hutchings, editor-in-chief of *Ellery Queen's Mystery Magazine*. "We publish the top authors in the genre and try to reflect the great diversity of the field in our selection of stories. From the magazine's beginning, however, the door has been open to new writers and ideas."

The beginning that Hutchings refers to came in the fall of 1941, when Lawrence E. Spivak and Mercury Press launched *EQMM* under the editorship of "Ellery Queen"—which was actually the two-man writing team of cousins Frederic Dannay and Manfred Lee. From the outset, the magazine was, as Dannay said in his manifesto, "devoted to all types of detective crime stories, in which consistently good writing would be as important as original ideas, excitement and craftsmanship."

"The response of readers exceeded all their expectations," Hutchings says, "so that by January of 1946, the magazine had gone from bimonthly publication, which it began in May of 1942, to monthly publication. After a short time, Fred Dannay took over completely the editing of the magazine, and his cousin Mandfred Lee concentrated his efforts entirely on the novels and short stories that they continued to write together."

Hutchings says that Dannay and Lee started the magazine because there was virtually no market in America in the 20s and 30s for short mystery fiction. "Dannay conceived *EQMM* as a remedy to that. And his knowledge of the history of the mystery short story made the magazine a treasure house of the best pieces ever written in the genre. In the beginning, reprints of classic works featured heavily in the magazine's lineup."

Dannay died in 1982 and was succeeded by his longtime associate, Eleanor Sullivan. She ran the magazine for almost ten years, until her death in 1991, at which point Hutchings took it over. "One day I got a call from Eleanor Sullivan, who was aware that her health was failing," says Hutchings, who was then the mystery editor at Walker & Company. "She invited several editors, including me, to interview for the job, and things happened fast. It wasn't anything I ever expected."

Although Hutchings grew up reading Agatha Christie and Ngaio Marsh, she wasn't really immersed in the genre until she went to work for the Mystery Guild. "That was one of my first jobs in publishing, and it was a great place to get a background in the genre. I read everything that was being published, because the book clubs get submissions from all the publishers. The publishers love to get that sale. It can be a lot of money and it's also great publicity for their book." Such a position at a book club, she says, "is a marvelous way to get to know the field. You're reading everything that's being published and also some classics."

Hutchings enjoys all types of mysteries, from the police procedural and American P.I. to the more traditional mysteries like the British cozies. "But I do have a particular liking for the historicals, when they're well-researched and well-written," she admits, "and also for psychological suspense. That's not to say that I don't like the other subgenres, though, because I find the whole field intriguing." When she's not wading through the sea of submissions to Ellery Queen's Mystery Magazine, Hutchings tries to read the books of *EQMM* writers, "particularly Ruth Rendell, Peter Lovesey, Joyce Carol Oates and Kate Wilhelm." That sea, however, keeps her very busy.

"Recently, our submissions have actually been somewhat lighter," Hutchings says. "In the almost four years I've been here, they have never exceeded a hundred per week, but there have been many weeks in a row when we've gotten up to one hundred. My assistant reads them first, and she reads them more thoroughly than I do, but I do try to take a look, at least, at every single submission that comes in. It's impossible for me to read all of them, or the magazine would never get to the printer, but I do at least look at them." The high volume of submissions may make it seem like you must hook the editor on the first page, but Hutchings says that's not the case. "I think an experienced editor knows when reading on is going to be worthwhile. They get a very good reading here, because there are two people looking at their work."

Another misconception might be that *EQMM* receives more good stories than they can publish. Hutchings says no. "We really don't ever have enough well-written stories that provide something fresh and suspenseful in characterization and plot. As a result, we very rarely turn away stories simply because we've enough in inventory. If it happens to be a time when I do have a lot of inventory, I usually buy the story and hold it. We'll save it until we have space."

No matter how many submissions she receives from established writers, Hutchings always tries to print one story by a new writer in each issue's "Department of First Stories." Started in 1949 by Fred Dannay, the Department of First Stories has published beginning fiction from many now-established writers such as Harry Kemelman, Stanley Ellin, Jack Finney, Nancy Pickard and Susan Dunlap. "There are lots of others," Hutchings says. "We're always looking for good candidates. It's actually a little easier to sell a first story to us than a second or third story, because we like to try to feature at least one first story per issue. If I can't do that, then I'll try to catch it up in later issues so that we end up with at least thirteen per year."

In addition to publishing many first stories, *EQMM* publishes a lot of award-winning stories. Both "The Gentleman in the Lake" by Robert Barnard (June, 1994) and "The Necessary Brother" by Brendan DuBois (May, 1994) were nominated for Edgars in 1995, and "Me and Mr. Harry" by Batya Swift Yasgur, won the 1995 Robert L. Fish Award for best first short story by an American author (see "Anatomy of a Sale", page 329). And *EQMM* has a long history of other award-winners, and in fact took the Edgar for best short story the first year it was offered, in 1948. Stories from *EQMM* have won or been nominated almost every year since.

Hutchings' advice to those wishing to be published in *EQMM* is

"Write what you want to write and not what you think will sell, or what you think a mystery story should be. I think too many people come to it with an idea of what the editor is going to want and what a mystery story is, and they end up delivering something quite formulaic. I'm not interested in that." She also cautions to avoid trendy subjects or rehashing current news stories. "I am tired of the kinds of subjects that are constantly reported in the media. Child abuse, battered wives, the drug trade, gangs. Those are all things you see when you turn on the nightly news, and I don't want to read about it when I get to work and for pleasure. I also don't much like plot lines that are taken from real events. Some news stories get such enormous press that a lot of writers pick up on them and use that material in their fiction. I tend not to like that. I prefer a plot that comes entirely from imagination, unless it's an historical mystery, in which case it's fine to draw from real events."

"Learn to create believable characters," Hutchings says, "and if you can do that, and your prose is strong, then I guarantee you'll be published."

Address: 1540 Broadway, New York, NY 10036
Phone: (212)782-8546
Fax: (212)782-8309
How To Contact: Fiction submissions should be sent to Janet Hutchings, Editor. Make initial contact by sending brief cover letter with manuscript and SASE. Send a business-sized SASE to obtain writing guidelines. Receives 300-400 unsolicited fiction submissions each month. Purchases 11-18 fiction manuscripts per issue. Occasionally comments on rejected manuscripts. Responds to author submissions in 3 months. Preferred length for fiction manuscripts is 2,000-8,000 words. Allows simultaneous submissions. 95% of magazine is mystery/crime fiction. A sample copy is available for $2.50 plus SASE. Subscription cost is $34.97 for 13 issues.
Payment: Pays approximately 3-8 cents per word.
Terms: Acquires first serial and non-exlusive anthology rights.

HARDBOILED MAGAZINE

Established: 1988 • Circulation: 1,000 • Published: Quarterly • Number of Pages: 100 • Size: 5 × 8

Gary Lovisi, Editor

CATEGORIES
Private Eye, Suspense, Crime, Thrillers, Hardboiled Detective, Urban Horror, Dark Mystery, Police Procedural, Psychological Suspense, Surrealistic Mystery, Espionage, Courtroom/Trial

Hardboiled detective mystery fiction is a lot different today than it was when Raymond Chandler and Dashiell Hammett were writing, says Gary Lovisi, editor of *Hardboiled* magazine. "They were writing in the 1920s and 1930s and it was very interesting for that time. But today the tough guy detective sitting in his seedy office with a bottle in his desk drawer is such an incredible cliché it's in the same domain as Sherlock Holmes. When Doyle was writing Holmes it was cutting-edge stuff, but now it's considered nostalgic fiction.

"In the 1990s it's a whole new world, a whole different situation—more brutal, more violent, more ugly. Social issues, political issues and crime are all meshed together with money, violence, drugs. Stories today have to address many of these things in a way that is thoughtful, honest and with some impact on the reader."

On a personal level, Lovisi is a big fan of both modern and old-style hardboiled fiction. An avid collector of vintage paperbacks, he also edits *Paperback Parade*, a magazine devoted to paperback book collecting. He writes regularly about the subject for magazines such as *The Armchair Detective* and holds an annual book collecting show in New York each September. With the show he's been able to have as guests many authors whose books were popular in the 1950s and 1960s, as well as authors writing today.

Lovisi also writes short mystery fiction and his stories have been published in several anthologies and magazines, including *Dark Crimes II*, an anthology edited by Ed Gorman and published by Carroll and Graf, and magazines such as *Mean Streets, Dark Kiss* and *Naked Kiss*. At press time, his first novel, *Hellbent on Homicide* was about to be published by Scarlet Press.

All his interest and involvement in the field made Lovisi a natural choice to take over the helm at *Hardboiled* in 1991. A friend of Lovisi's, mystery author Wayne Dundee, started the magazine in the mid 1980s. When his career took off, he asked Lovisi to take over the magazine. "I had been doing *Detective Story* magazine at the time and wanted to use harder, more up-to-date, cutting-edge material. *Hardboiled* was really on the edge of the modern crime genre."

Dundee, whose Joe Hannibal series is published by Dell, still does a column for the magazine and is given free reign to write about anything related to crime and crime fiction. Another contributor, Mike Black, does a column on true crime and several other columnists and critics review books and movies related to the genre. Lovisi also includes interviews with well-known authors. "The nonfiction augments the fiction; it compliments it," he says. Fiction is still the heart of the magazine, however, and Lovisi publishes 10 to 12 stories each issue. He reads all submissions himself, anywhere from 10 to 50 manuscripts per week. Along with several newer writers, Lovisi's list of well-known contributors is impressive. "I've published Andrew Vachss, Eugene Izzi, Joe Lansdale, William Campbell Gault, Lawrence Block, Bill Pronzini . . . there are so many."

When asked to name a few new writers published in the magazine, Lovisi is quick to mention Cindy Rosmus, Ardath Mayhar, Rose Dawn Bradford and Billie Sue Mosiman, purposely listing women writers. "When I first started publishing most of my subscribers and writers were men and it seemed the whole genre appealed more to men than women. Over the years a lot more women have become involved and I think its great. Some of them are doing incredible things. Billie Sue Mosiman, for example, is a 60-year-old grandmother from Texas who writes stuff that is so hot it seems like it's coming out of a blast furnace. I think some of these women, along with some new male writers, are going to be the next new wave of writers in this field."

Thanks to movies like "Pulp Fiction" and several new anthology series coming out, Lovisi says he expects the market for authentic hardboiled crime fiction to grow. "I think hardboiled fiction will have to be looked at a lot more by editors and publishers. You'll still have the traditional, cozy mystery, which appeals to different people, but [the market for] hardboiled short fiction and novels is going to explode over the next five years. The people who are writing for me now may be in the center of that explosion."

For longer fiction, Lovisi also publishes Gryphon Doubles. These are two novellas (up to 25,000 words) published in one volume, back to back, similar to the Ace doubles popular a few decades ago. "They're really fun to do. I've done about nine of them so far, some new material, some reprints. I've published work by Jesse Sublett, Richard Prather, Mike Avallone. I even did a Sherlock Holmes double. I've got some really good artists working with me and it's a nice way to showcase longer works.

"Longer works must be of the quality to warrant the extra space," he says. "Right now I'm seeing a lot of padding in stories where it's not necessary and actually weakens the story. My advice to writers would be to keep it lean, keep it cut to the bone. Cut out all the excess that isn't really important and sometimes distorts from making a point. I think a short story should really try to make one specific point."

Lovisi says he feels very strongly that violence for violence's sake is not what he wants for *Hardboiled*. "There's a lot of blatantly sexist stuff out there and a lot of garbage I call retro pulp—blood, guts and gore—just cutting people up like it's a slasher film, but that's not what I'm after. I want work that has meaning. Yes, it's got to be truthful and, yes, there's violence and pain. That's what's going on in our society and it's mirrored in fiction. But, with a lot of the work I publish, there's a kind of justice in it. A story may have a hard-edged, kick-ass attitude, but I want the good guys to win."

Address: P.O. Box 209, Brooklyn, NY 11228-0209
How To Contact: Fiction submissions should be sent to Gary Lovisi, Editor. Make initial contact by sending query letter. Send a business-sized SASE to obtain writing guidelines. Receives 200 unsolicited fiction submissions each month. Purchases 10-12 fiction manuscripts per issue. Occasionally comments on rejected manuscripts. Responds to

author submissions in 2-4 weeks. Manuscripts are published 6-18 months after acceptance. Preferred length for fiction manuscripts is 3,000 words. 50-70% of magazine is mystery/crime fiction. A sample copy is available for $6. Subscription cost is $30 for 6 issues.
Payment: Pays approximately $5-50 plus 2 free copies.
Terms: Acquires one time first North American rights.

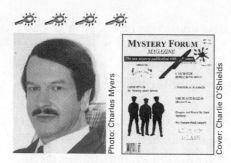

Photo: Charles Myers

Cover: Charlie O'Shields

MYSTERY FORUM MAGAZINE

Established: 1992 • Circulation: 600 + • Published: 6 times a year •
Number of Pages: 48 • Size: 8½ × 11

Bob Myers, Editor

CATEGORIES
Private Eye, Cozy, Suspense, Crime, Young Adult, Thrillers, Historical,
Hardboiled Detective, Amateur Sleuth, Humorous Mystery, Urban Horror,
Juvenile, Dark Mystery, Light Horror, Police Procedural, Malice Domestic,
Psychological Suspense, Romantic Suspense, Surrealistic Mystery,
Espionage, Courtroom/Trial

The life of Bob Myers has been one mystery after another. "I began
my career as a job jumper in public welfare but soon ventured into such
fields as private enterprise and security. I finally settled down to spend
four years as a probation and parole officer for the state of Missouri,
which is what really acquainted me with those involved in crime," says
Myers. "I wasn't just reading about mysterious crimes, I was witnessing
them." Although no longer a parole officer, Myers still solves mysteries
as a civil rights investigator.

In addition, he's founder and editor of *Mystery Forum*, a bimonthly
magazine geared toward today's mystery writer. "People who buy our
magazine are people who are doing the writing. Our magazine is for
mystery writers, not just casual mystery readers," he says. "There's
enough reading material out there for your average mystery reader, but
what is lacking in the genre is a source for writers, a place where they
can go to get the latest on what's going on in the field, besides who's hot
and who's not."

The magazine balances fiction and nonfiction. The first half of each
issue contains four or five short stories and one excerpt from a serialized

novel. The last half consists of five to six nonfiction pieces, such as *"Mystery Forum* Interviews Jim Lehrer," "The Legacy of Charles Dickens," "Famous Crimes of Yesteryear: The Lizzie Borden Murder Case," "Manuscript Mechanics" and "Disposing of the Body: How Murderers Conceal the Evidence."

Because he doesn't want *Mystery Forum* to be just another mystery magazine, Myers is eager to receive more nonfiction submissions. "We get 95 fiction submissions for every nonfiction submission we receive. We are definitely looking for more nonfiction pieces, more informative material about the genre."

Although *Mystery Forum*'s target audience is the mystery writer, the magazine has no specific theme or agenda. Says Myers, "We are generalists; we give attention to all subjects and themes within the vast mystery field. We have no bounds." Indeed, accessibility is one of *Mystery Forum*'s greatest attributes, which is good news for new writers, or writers who want to try something new. "We love to work with new, unpublished authors. We ignore authors' names and take the material on its own merit."

Myers notes four characteristics that make his magazine unique. First, *Mystery Forum* publishes serialized novels, which is highly unusual for the mystery field in the '90s. Thus far, the magazine has been running only one serialized novel per issue, but Myers is flexible. "We're not averse to having two serial pieces in the same issue." Second, in each issue Myers incorporates some historical material, relevant bits of information from the past that can be of great importance today. Third, the magazine tries to provide regular updates on mystery bookstores throughout the country. Fourth, *Mystery Forum* offers current scientific information helpful to the crime writer, such as the latest technology in DNA analysis, forensic science and arson. Myers works with a specialist who keeps him up to date on any scientific changes or breakthroughs.

Some may consider it strange for a mystery magazine to include science news, but Myers thinks it's an appropriate resource for mystery writers. "We feel that if you're going to write in this genre, you don't want to come up with this great ending only to find that it is technologically out of date. Working with our magazine can give you recent information on the technology that's important to crime stories."

Myers exercises patience when considering a submission. He doesn't determine its merit after reading just a few pages of the text. "Although

I like a catchy beginning, I've learned that I cannot tell on page one if a story is worth publishing." One reason Myers reads most submissions to the end is because, as he says, "I love surprise endings. You won't get that surprise if you put something down only minutes after you pick it up."

While Myers prides himself on his openness to publish almost anything of quality and appeal, he has standards. "We will not publish hate pieces," he warns. "There is no excuse for excessive violence, gore or obscenity. We're open on sexual content; we'll publish gay stories. But no violence against women and children. We're not into violence for the sake of violence."

Myers prefers to bypass agents and work directly with writers. "The writer wrote the piece, and I'd much rather deal with him or her than go through an agent. Plus, we pay only $30 per article, so it doesn't really make sense for a writer to foot an agent ten percent of that." If you do have an agent, don't fret: Myers doesn't refuse agented submissions; he just doesn't give them any leverage.

Myers encourages beginning writers to "try something new, a new approach, a new twist. If it gets rejected try something else. We realize a lot of folks get rejected if they do stuff outside the mainstream. These people should not give up. Send it to us; we'll at least look at it."

Although a relatively new kid on the block in the magazine industry (*Mystery Forum* began in 1992), Myers feels the market is getting stronger. "I think the mystery magazine market is growing," he says. "There are a lot more small publications out there." One problem with so many small publications—they don't pay much. But Myers doesn't think that's such a big deal. "Writers might not make lots of money from these publications, but they'll get to see their name in print." Often, seeing their byline tagged on a piece in a publication—however small— is gratifying enough to many writers. Myers knows: he receives around 70 submissions for each issue. Such exposure establishes your credibility, too. Once you're published, you greatly improve your chances of making subsequent sales.

Still, there aren't enough publications to tailor to the needs of every writer. You will get rejected. Yet Myers doesn't necessarily consider rejection as a commentary on one's writing: "Lots of good writing gets rejected. Just don't give up. If your feelings bruise easily, you're not in the right field. If you write for the fun of writing, you'll be better off—

and you may be surprised at what can happen once you embrace this attitude.

"Do not give up because you've just received your forty-fifth rejection. Who knows how that forty-sixth person will respond," says Myers. "Just send it, no matter how unconfident you feel. It could always land in the right, appreciative hands."

Address: 16503 3rd St. North, Independence, MO 64056
Phone: (816)257-0011
How To Contact: Fiction submissions should be sent to Bob Myers, Editor. Make initial contact by sending cover letter with short bio and manuscript. Send a business-sized SASE to obtain writing guidelines. Receives 30-40 unsolicited fiction submissions each month. Purchases 4 fiction manuscripts per issue. Occasionally comments on rejected manuscripts. Responds to author submissions in 60 days. Manuscripts are published 2-6 months after acceptance. Preferred length for fiction manuscripts is 2,000-5,000 words. Allows simultaneous submissions. Will print reprints. Submissions on computer diskette should be formatted for WordPerfect, MS Word or ASCII. 50% of magazine is mystery/crime fiction. A sample copy is available for $6. Subscription cost is $18 for 6 issues.
Payment: Pays approximately $30 per story or article.
Terms: Acquires first North American and reprint rights.

Photo: Beth Raisch

Cover: Dana Irwin

NEW MYSTERY MAGAZINE

Established: 1989 • Circulation: 90,000 • Published: Quarterly • Number of Pages: 96 • Size: 8½ × 11

Charles Raisch, Editor

CATEGORIES

Private Eye, Cozy, Suspense, Crime, Thrillers, Hardboiled Detective, Amateur Sleuth, Humorous Mystery, Police Procedural, Malice Domestic, Psychological Suspense, Romantic Suspense, Espionage

---

"In the 1920s and 1930s there were hundreds of magazines published in the United States that were printing short stories," says Charles Raisch, editor of *New Mystery* magazine. "All the major magazines were full of fiction. It hasn't really died out in other parts of the planet, just here in the U.S. and I think that's such a shame."

The lack of markets for short fiction, and, especially for mystery fiction, prompted Raisch and his friends to start their own magazine, one they hoped would showcase the work of both new and established writers from all over the world. In particular, they wanted to give voice to work that was new, different, cutting edge.

"A lot of us were members of MWA and ETB (The Encounter on Three Borders, an international crime writers group with members from Cuba, Mexico, the USA and many European countries). We'd meet once a month for dinner and talk about our love of mystery writing," says Raisch.

The conversation, he says, would often turn into a lament about the lack of good markets for mystery short fiction outside the mainstream. "It just seemed to be that most of the markets were only open to teacup and butler mysteries—easy listening and Lawrence Welk stuff—so starting out as an arrogant revolutionary group we wanted to open it up—

play some jazz and rock and roll!" And so *New Mystery* was born.

"We did our first issue for a writer's convention held in Mexico. It contained a lot of hardboiled, Chandler-style stories. There was so much hardboiled material, we risked being pigeon-holed and this was not the way we wanted to go. We wanted to make good on our pledge—to offer the widest variety of work possible." They put out one issue in the first year, two in the second, three in the third; now they are quarterly.

While *New Mystery* continues to publish one or two hardboiled stories each issue, Raisch says he and the other editors try to include all types of mystery from police procedural to malice domestic—even a few cozies. He does not shy away from cutting edge or controversial material, but tries to balance each issue with "softer" works as well. He is striving to include a wider variety of material than was presented in the first issue of the magazine.

As the magazine has grown, Raisch and company have run into some problems with handling the large number of submissions. To deal with the problems, they've had to come up with some formal policies, something all feel is a necessary evil. Raisch is apologetic. "We get so many manuscripts from people who just send out their stuff everywhere, who haven't studied the magazine, and it's hard for a small organization to spend all that time, so we're now stating our policies in our writers' guidelines."

The first submission policy, he says, is that the magazine is not responsible for unsolicited manuscripts. With that said, number two follows that manuscripts will only be accepted through agents or from published writers. Yet, Raisch will take some unsolicited stories for the magazine's debut story, a special feature that highlights the work of new writers. Those interested in submitting a debut story must mark "New Mystery Magazine Debut" or "NMM debut" on the outside envelope. Although Raisch tries to return material, the magazine does not guarantee return of your submission and if you hear nothing within 60 days, he says it should be considered a rejection.

The debut story is a favorite feature for Raisch. "It's very hard to find a new writer for every issue, but we've brought out seven new writers so far and virtually all of them have gone on with their careers. We're very happy about that."

Raisch also looks for a good mix of stories for each issue. "For example, if we're doing a really tough story, we need to balance it with something a little softer. We vary the length, too. So, we might have a story that's really great, but it doesn't fit with the rest of the issue. We'll either hold it or shoot it back."

New Mystery has published some of the top names in the mystery field. "I've been honored to edit stories by John Lutz, Lawrence Block, Andrew Vachss," says Raisch. "I've worked with Andrew Greeley, who is a mystery master and quite a personality. We've published Josh Pachter, one of the best short story writers in the U.S. and, of course, there's William Campbell Gault, Henry Slesar . . . the list goes on and on."

Raisch has close ties to Cuba both professionally and personally (he visits there once a year) and has introduced a number of Cuban writers to American readers. "We've found some very good writers in Havana. Last year we had a story by Justo Vasco, for example," he says. In addition to work from writers in Cuba, *New Mystery* has also published writers from Spain, the Czech Republic, Germany, France, other parts of Europe and Japan. Raisch usually uses translators from the same country as the writer and prefers the two work together whenever possible. Many of the translators he uses are mystery writers themselves.

The magazine also features at least one folk tale or legend each issue. Raisch is particularly proud to be the first to present many of these tales in written form. He gets these stories from a variety of sources and has found academics working in oral history fields to be most helpful. For example, he recently received a collection of plantation tales from the University of Maryland.

"We try to get something ancient. We've had Anansi [pixie] stories from Jamaica, Teutonic folk tales, tribal fragments and tales from the Appalachian Mountains, a place with a long oral tradition. We try to find stories featuring murder and many of these are quite nice; some read like Dashiell Hammett or Agatha Christie."

In addition to the six to ten pieces of fiction he publishes each issue, Raisch also includes several book reviews. "We have had a variety of critics, some who have made big names for themselves in other publications. We have William Goldschein, for example. If he likes you, he really likes you but if he doesn't, he just nails you. I think that can be very helpful for writers sometimes."

Raisch invites many of his fellow mystery writers to review books, which has helped him get a number of different voices into his magazine.

The magazine also includes "The Whole New Mystery Catalog," a section for reviews of movies, CD-ROMs and audio tapes related to mystery.

It's clear *New Mystery* is still evolving. Raisch plans an anthology of the first four years of the magazine. He is also putting together some special issues including a Sherlock Holmes parody issue and one featuring malice domestic stories.

Stories for *New Mystery* are selected by an editorial committee. "We have three graduate students who work part time and they do a lot of reading for us. Most of the initial reading is done rather informally. Yet there are actually only three of us who have the final vote on what to accept if there's a conflict—myself and two other editors."

Raisch says overwriting is a problem in many of the submissions he receives. Some writers try to say too much—so much, he says, that their talent becomes buried. "I often tell people to go for simplicity, cut back on their language.

"In stories I look for competency, grasp, thoughtfulness, style, structure, personality," says Raisch. "I ask 'Is there a story? Do I care about anybody?' In a lot of stuff we get, all the characters are so nasty, I feel why bother to read it? I want to love someone in a story, care about them, empathize."

Address: 175 5th Ave., #2001 The Flat Iron Bldg., New York, NY 10010
Phone: (212)353-1582
Fax: (212)353-3495
How To Contact: Fiction submissions should be sent to Editorial Committee. Make initial contact by sending the complete manuscript. To obtain writing guidelines send a 9×12 SASE with $1.24 postage. Receives 300-400 unsolicited fiction submissions each month. Purchases 10 fiction manuscripts per issue. Occasionally comments on rejected manuscripts. Manuscripts are published 6-12 months after acceptance. Preferred length for fiction manuscripts is 3,000-5,000 words. Submissions on computer diskette should be formatted for WordPerfect 5.1 (IBM). 90% of magazine is mystery/crime fiction. A sample copy is available for $7 with SASE and $1.24 postage. Subscription cost is $27.77 for 4 issues.
Payment: Pays approximately $50-1,000 per story.

NOIR

Established: 1994 • Circulation: 4,000-5,000 • Published: Quarterly •
Number of Pages: 64 • Size: 6½ × 10

Christopher Mills, Editor

CATEGORIES
Private Eye, Suspense, Crime, Hardboiled Detective, Police Procedural,
Espionage

"I like the images that it evoked," says Christopher Mills, explaining
why he chose *Noir* as the title for his magazine. "I liked the classic images
of Humphrey Bogart in his trenchcoat in the fog-enshrouded, neon-lit
streets. It's a romanticized image of what is actually a very non- romantic
form of literature."

It's also, Mills says, a pretty good description of the kind of fiction he
is looking for. "I very much liked the imagery and style of the writers
who have written in what they call the 'noir style.' The stories I want to
publish are in that vein, they're in that tradition." Modern examples,
Mills says, are James Ellroy, Lawrence Block and Max Allan Collins.
"Max Allan Collins is a big favorite of mine. I'm really grateful that he
was involved in the first issue."

Although not strictly a comic book, *Noir* is comic-book-sized and, for
Mills, is the combination of two interests—crime fiction and comic
books. "I'm very much into comic books on a professional level," he
says. "I think the medium has a lot more potential than is currently being
explored. Also, I love crime fiction. I love reading it and I love writing
it. I thought it would be kind of neat to do a magazine, almost in the
tradition of the old pulp magazines, where you had good, solid, exciting
fiction with some really nice, exciting illustrations to it as well. As a

comic book person, I've always liked the juxtaposition of prose and art, and I just think it makes for a more visually interesting magazine." *Noir*, therefore, has a mix of both comics and crime fiction.

Mills started reading crime fiction in junior high. "I had a friend whose father had a very large collection of Gold Medal paperbacks and other crime and espionage-type series. He had a lot of John D. Macdonald, Donald Hamilton, that sort of thing. I started reading those out of his collection and then kept with it."

His interest in comic books comes not just from reading them, but from writing them, as well. Mills has written comic books for small companies over the years, with his most recent project being a science fiction book created by Leonard Nimoy called *Leonard Nimoy's Primortals*.

Mills published what he calls a 'trial issue' of *Noir* in February of 1994, with stories by Ed Gorman and Max Allan Collins. Due to a change of publishers and locales (Mills moved from New York to Florida), he had to suspend publication for over a year. He resumed quarterly publication in April of 1995 with an issue that featured stories by William F. Nolan, Robert J. Randisi and C.J. Henderson. Although the magazine is heavy on professional writers, Mills says "I basically try to mix established professionals with new writers in a given issue."

What Mills seeks for his magazine is the hardboiled private eye story. "I tend to lean toward the more masculine stuff. I like a lot of what's being written now in the female private eye series, but I kind of feel bad that I can't find more written from a male perspective nowadays. Because," he says, laughing, "I'm a guy. I think I relate to that a lot better." He feels that publishers have turned their back on the male private eye in order to pursue novels featuring female sleuths. "There are some very good writers working in the genre of the woman private eye," Mills says, but he feels there needs to be more of a balance between male and female detective fiction.

Cozy-type stories are not *Noir* material. "I'm not really big on little old ladies sitting in small country villages solving thirty crimes a year, or Angela Lansbury traipsing around the world, remaining eternally cheerful even though she stumbles across a dead body every seven days." Stories with horror and fantasy elements aren't what Mills is looking for, either. "I don't care what they deal with, whether it's pornography, drugs or any of the elements that go into today's crime or today's world.

But for my magazine, I really would like it to be a hardboiled, kind of dark tone. That doesn't mean I wouldn't consider publishing something a little more humorous or lighter; even I'm not unrelentingly grim. But the title of the magazine is *Noir*, and the fiction's going to have a little bit of a dark tone."

Two stories that Mills feels particularly exemplify the kind of fiction he is looking for appeared in *Noir*'s premiere issue. The first is a story by Max Allan Collins called "The Love Rack," which evokes what Mills is looking for in the magazine very well. The other is Ed Gorman's "Surrogate," which was subsequently reprinted in a Mickey Spillane anthology called *Murder Is My Business*. "They were very different in style and length. Al Collins's story was very much a fifties crime thing that combined James M. Cain with Mickey Spillane. Ed Gorman's was much more a modern, rural America story which showed that the bleakness and hopelessness that seems to come across in the daily news creeps into these small towns and upper-middle-class environments. I liked both of those stories a great deal."

In addition to the four or five stories in each issue, Mills also runs a book review section and one or two articles. Articles are usually interviews with writers, film reviews, and retrospectives of classic noir films, novels and writers.

Mills says the best way to sell a story to *Noir* is to know the magazine. "If you can't find it, write to me for a sample copy. Look at the magazine, and you'll get a good idea of what I'm looking for from that."

Address: 559 N.E. 46th St. #201, Boca Raton, FL 33431
Phone: (407)368-7497
How To Contact: Fiction submissions should be sent to Christopher Mills, Editor. Make initial contact by sending manuscript. Send a business-sized SASE to obtain writing guidelines. Purchases 3-4 fiction manuscripts per issue. Occasionally comments on rejected manuscripts. Responds to author submissions in 1 month. Manuscripts are published 3-12 months after acceptance. Preferred length for fiction manuscripts is 3,000-5,000 words. Allows simultaneous submissions. 70% of magazine is mystery/crime fiction. A sample copy is available for $4.95.
Payment: Pays approximately 3¢ a word.
Terms: Acquires first North American serial rights. ✧

☼ ☼ ☼ ☼

Cover: Robert Thompson

OVER MY DEAD BODY! THE MYSTERY MAGAZINE

Established: 1993 • Circulation: 1,000 • Published: Quarterly • Number of Pages: 68 • Size: 8½ × 11

Cherie Jung, Editor

CATEGORIES
Private Eye, Cozy, Suspense, Crime, Thrillers, Historical, Hardboiled Detective, Amateur Sleuth, Humorous Mystery, Urban Horror, Dark Mystery, Light Horror, Police Procedural, Malice Domestic, Psychological Suspense, Romantic Suspense, Surrealistic Mystery, Espionage, Courtroom/ Trial

If you pick up a copy of *Over My Dead Body!*, you'll be greeted with an array of short and long fiction, author profiles, interviews with experts in crime, and some commentary. The editor likes to read, and she likes variety. "I'm one of those people who will read anything, including cereal box side panels," says Cherie Jung. She's not kidding. Her reading interests vary from mainstream fiction to Oriental literature to martial arts to science fiction and, of course, mystery.

An avid reader since childhood, Jung acknowledges the drawbacks of her nondiscriminatory approach to reading. "I had the distinction of being the first person—and annoyingly, a female—to read *Run Silent, Run Deep* (the submarine war book by Edward Beach) in my junior high school." Just imagine what her schoolmates thought of the 12 year-old girl dallying in subterranean warfare. Over the years, however, Jung has focused her reading habits; ever since she read Sue Grafton's *C is for Corpse*, mysteries have dominated her reading. She admits devouring four or five of them weekly.

Jung has been writing since the early 1970s, publishing martial arts fiction and a series of columns on women's martial arts in *Black Belt*

Magazine. Such writing led her to editing. "I first got the editing bug when I was publishing my martial arts newsletter," Jung says. "Then my husband and I tried our hand at writing romance novels. I found I just couldn't write the mushy stuff. Couldn't write the sexy parts either. But I just loved to edit his writing. So I think editing is in my blood. Even on rejected manuscripts, I have to resist the temptation to edit as I read." She's been editor of *OMDB!* since its inception in 1993.

Eclecticism, coupled with elasticity in defining what constitutes a mystery, makes *OMDB!* distinctive in the mystery market. Jung says, "We are aiming at the casual mystery reader. We use a really loose definition of the term mystery. Many of our stories would probably be called "cross-over" stories. They often have an element of horror, science fiction, romance, or some other genre mixed with the elements of mystery. We've had mysteries with vampires, with werewolves, with psychics, with aliens, and with ordinary serial killers."

Another distinguishing characteristic of *OMDB!* is Jung's conception of what she's supplying to readers. Her mystery stories don't have to be edifying, just entertaining. *OMDB!* is a magazine, not a textbook. "We publish stories that don't quite fit the normal or more traditional mystery magazine tone. We're not overwhelmingly serious. We also view ourselves as being entertainment oriented. We'd like a reader to be able to pick up a copy of our magazine and find something to pass the time—or to browse—that immediately catches their attention. We don't expect our readers to read us from cover to cover at one sitting."

While Jung publishes mostly short fiction ("My favorites are short short stories of under 2,000 words."), she'll print a longer story. Take, for example, "Deep in the Roaring Fork" by Ty Treadwell, which appeared in the cops mini-theme issue of *OMDB!.* Says Jung, "Ty was told by another small press publisher that the story was too long for them, to give us a try. The story was too long for us, also, but we made space for it because everyone on the staff who read it liked it." If, however, you are interested in publishing long fiction, Jung wants it known that she is currently overstocked on 2,000-6,000 word submissions. But if you think it's good enough, send it.

There's also good news at *OMDB!* for unpublished writers: they want you. "It's wide open for new writers," Jung says, "Most of our writers come from the slush pile. Plus we don't publish reprints. We post requests for new submissions on the Internet in various mystery related areas, but most of our submissions seem to arrive after the writers have noticed our listing in one of the writing source books, such as those published by Writer's Digest."

Regardless of your age, career choice, or writing achievements, *OMDB!* will seriously consider your submission. "We've had stories from a Boeing engineer, from retired police officers, teenagers, and elderly writers just starting a new career. There are many good writers out there just waiting to be discovered. We wish we had room in our magazine to print even more stories."

Although she receives over 500 submissions a month, Jung makes it a point to know and work with writers interested in publishing in *OMDB!*. "We keep track of authors who have submitted manuscripts to us in the past that we either published, or had to return because we'd already accepted something similar. We contact each of those authors within a year of their last submission if they haven't submitted something to us since, just to let them know we want them to continue submitting stories to us. In the past, some of our writers have rewritten stories four or five times to get them 'just right.' We like to work with authors whose stories have potential. If we ask an author to send something back again, we really do mean it."

OMDB! has five people reading manuscripts. "Big name or unpublished writer, everyone is treated equally," says Jung. Each issue contains a mini-theme, and each mini-theme has its own editor. But the mini-theme related stories go to slush pile readers first. Jung thinks having readers besides the mini-theme editor read submissions first lends objectivity to the editorial process. "For instance, when we did the paranormal sleuth mini-theme, the stories with psychics were first read by three readers who did not like paranormal stories. Those stories they read and liked were then passed on to the mini-theme editor. Our slush pile readers look for good stories first, mystery stories second."

However open-minded Jung is regarding submissions, she does have her pet peeves. "Manuscripts drenched in perfume are a turn-off, especially since it brings on asthma attacks for several of our slush pile readers. Taping or stapling the manuscripts inside bomb-proof envelopes is another pet peeve. If we can't get inside the envelope, how are we to read the manuscript?" She also despises twist endings with no story and plots borrowed from TV shows, "of which I've seen many."

As far as gratuitous sex, violence, gore and racism goes, *OMDB!*

"won't automatically reject stories on those subjects. We have some stories that contain strong or offensive language. And the good guys don't always have to win. We've also had manuscripts involving necrophilia—but no pedophilia or cannibalism yet. If it fits the story, we accept it. We're dealing with the darker side of human nature and it often times isn't pretty. We're not X-rated but we're not PG, either."

Like many editors these days, Jung would like to add diversity to her publication. "We could use more humor; it has its place in mystery fiction. Sure, murder isn't funny, usually. But the way others cope with crime can be amusing. I'd also like to see more stories featuring ethnicity—but not just as window-dressing. We've received lots of manuscripts purporting to be ethnic, but in fact, the writer has just thrown in a non-white character or two. Putting a couple of Italian Mafia fugitives on an Indian reservation doesn't make the story ethnic. At least not for us."

A veteran in the writing industry, Jung has advice the mystery writer should heed. "Learn how to apply the basic story elements—plotting, characterization, and dialogue. Learn how to prepare a manuscript properly. And then, tell a good story. There's no substitute for good storytelling, whether it's a natural inclination on the part of the writer or something that has been developed through study and practice. Write what you like to read, not what you think might sell."

Address: P.O. Box 1778, Auburn, WA 98071-1778
Phone: (206)473-4650
How To Contact: Fiction submissions should be sent to Cherie Jung, Fiction Editor. Send complete manuscript. Send a business-sized SASE to obtain writing guidelines. Purchases 10-15 fiction manuscripts per issue. Responds to submissions in 6-12 weeks. Manuscripts are published 6-24 months after acceptance. Preferred length for fiction manuscripts is 250-4,000 words. Allows simultaneous submissions. Submissions on computer diskette should be in WordPerfect 5.1; prefers ASCII. Electronic submissions should be sent to OMDB@aol.com. 50% of magazine is mystery/crime fiction. A sample copy is available for $5. Subscription cost is $12 for 4 issues.
Payment: Pays approximately 1¢ a word fiction; $10-25 an article non-fiction.
Terms: Acquires first North American rights.

Cover: Lissanne Lake

PIRATE WRITINGS

Established: 1992 • Circulation: 7,000 • Published: Quarterly • Number of Pages: 72 • Size: 8 × 10

Edward McFadden, Editor

CATEGORIES
Private Eye, Cozy, Suspense, Crime, Young Adult, Thrillers, Historical, Hardboiled Detective, Amateur Sleuth, Humorous Mystery, Urban Horror, Juvenile, Dark Mystery, Light Horror, Police Procedural, Malice Domestic, Psychological Suspense, Romantic Suspense, Surrealistic Mystery, Espionage, Courtroom/Trial

"The types of mysteries that I've always liked and always enjoyed are the surreal mysteries," says Edward McFadden, founder and editor of *Pirate Writings* magazine. "The mystery work that Poe did was great and surreal, and that's the kind of stuff that I grew up with. It influenced me and what I choose for the magazine." And what McFadden chooses is not your mother's mysteries; he wants cutting-edge fiction.

"I've read a couple of Grisham's books, and that kind of mystery is so common and boring," McFadden says. "You get bored pretty quick. I'm looking for a mystery that kind of breaks some of the classic rules and has a little surrealism. That's not to say I won't buy a straight cop story, because I will, but I'm looking for something a little different."

The difference between *Pirate Writings* and other mystery magazines is evident in the subtitle: *Tales of Fantasy, Mystery & Science Fiction.* McFadden offers a mix of genres in his magazine, with the thought that people want diversity. "If you're in the mood for a mystery tonight, my magazine's got it for you. If you're in the mood for science fiction, I've got it for you. If you're in the mood for fantasy, I've got it for you. If you're in the mood for something you can't put into any of those categories, I've got it for you. So rather than find a real deep niche, like cozy mysteries or mystery in general, I've allowed myself to expand, to grow in copy and in circulation, because I am willing to present a broad range of material." And this, McFadden says, is something that appeals highly to his readers. "They like the fact that they can pick up one magazine and get a pretty complete package. Because the fact of the matter is, very few people read *Asimov's* and *Ellery Queen's* from cover to cover. They maybe read one or two stories. I've got one or two. So for five bucks, they can buy my magazine and read their two stories in each genre, but they only paid five bucks, instead of buying fifteen dollars' worth of magazines and having half the material go unread."

McFadden started *Pirate Writings* in 1992 as just something fun to do. He was looking for a way to combine his undergraduate degree in business with his Master's degree in communications and make the two work together. "I was a starting writer at the time, and I thought it would be fun to put out a little pamphlet or small press magazine where it could help me learn the business and meet some people. I didn't intend for the magazine to become as big as it has when I started." McFadden's first issue had a print run of 200 copies. Now the magazine has a circulation of almost 10,000. "When I started this magazine, my intention was not to wind up with a circulation of 10,000 and be in supermarkets and newsstands. But as I got more into publishing and got to know the business more, I found that the business was for me. It's basically that simple. I love the publishing industry. I think it's a great field. It allows me to utilize my business knowledge and my creative knowledge to one end, and I think that's one of the greatest things about it." But, McFadden cautions, that can be one of its greatest downfalls, too.

"So many guys come up with great ideas, great names, great stories, great layout—everything. But they have absolutely no concept of how to deal with the business side of things, so they get gobbled up. And the reverse is true. You've got these guys who think they know the publishing business, so they can put out a product, but they don't know anything about the creative side, so they put out a bad product. You have to deal with the creative aspect of putting out a product, of dealing with artists, with writers, with the whole layout. But on the other side of the coin, you do have to deal with the business aspects."

Proof of McFadden's business savvy is evident in the rapid growth of *Pirate Writings*. What started out in 1992 as little more than a photocopied pamphlet quickly grew to a saddle-bound digest and is now an 8½ × 11 magazine with a full-color cover and big names like Roger Zelazny, Ian McCleod, J.N. Williamson and Jessica Salmonson.

Despite this growth, McFadden remains very open to new writers. "I'm always looking to give new writers a shot," he says. "I've got two writers in this [Spring 1995] issue that have never been published anywhere. And four more of them, to make six, would be considered small press writers. I push my big-name writers because that's one of the things that sells the magazine, but I publish a lot of new writers, too."

McFadden says that he is specifically looking for more mystery stories. "One of the things we've been trying to do over the past six months is to specifically push the mystery element of the magazine." Because he gets a lot of press in the science fiction arena, McFadden attracts a lot of science fiction and fantasy submissions. "But I have a hard time finding mystery. It's a great place to break into the magazine."

Despite receiving 300 to 400 submissions per month, McFadden says his turnaround time is better than average. He splits his slush pile with his associate editor, Tom Piccirilli, and between the two of them, they read every submission. "Everybody gets read. Every single manuscript that comes in. I'm not going to lie and say we read every manuscript all the way through. If you don't hook me or Tom by the first three pages, you're going to get bounced, because if you're not hooking us, you're not hooking the reader. If after page three we're not into this, I usually scan the rest of the manuscript to see if there's a diamond in the rough in the last six pages that maybe just needs a rewrite." If either editor really loves a story, they show it to the other. If they like it, but they're not "blown away" by it, they'll let it sit for a week or two before reading it again. Everything else is rejected and sent back. "Nobody gets an outright rejection, ever. Never done it and never will." The maximum response time, McFadden says, is six weeks.

While McFadden is very interested in obtaining cutting-edge mysteries, he does not want to see gratuitous sex and foul language. "Too many people these days seem to associate 'cutting- edge' with the word 'f–' and gratuitous sex. They figure if you throw sex in and say 'f–' ten times, it's cutting-edge. That is not what I consider cutting-edge. 'Cutting-edge' to me means something different, something that hasn't been done before. Something that makes you think about something you've never thought about before. Too many people—and I'll be perfectly honest with you;

it's the big names as much as the new writers—they seem to think that when I say I want cutting-edge that I want cursing, I want sex scenes and I want all this crazy stuff going on. That's not what I mean." McFadden says sex is okay, if done tastefully. "If you want to put a sex scene in, read an Ian Flaming novel. James Bond made love to ten women in every book, but it was done with taste, it was done with class, and that's how I would like those types of situations handled in my magazine."

McFadden is also tired of seeing overused plots and cliché characterization. "I'm sick of cats. I'm sick of cops killing themselves. I'm sick of 'husband rapes wife/wife gets revenge.' I get one of each of these a day. These stories usually come from the new writers, the writers who think thay have so many great ideas but when they actually sit down to write, they find that they don't have anything to say. They write a great first paragraph that really pulls you in, but then there's nothing there." Or, McFadden says, they have a good plot and they ruin it with standard, die-cut characters. "I'll be reading a story and I'll be thinking 'You know, they've got some pretty good ideas.' And then they'll throw in that boiler-plate characterization. That just says, well, no, this guy didn't put any thought into his characterization, because this has been done a million times before. The cop that drinks, the cop that kills himself because he can't deal with what he sees every day. This is real life, yes," McFadden says. "However, I'm not looking for real life as much as I am looking for a story that entertains my reader."

Address: 53 Whitman Ave., Islip, NY 11751
Phone: (516)224-1130
Fax: (516)224-1130
How To Contact: Make initial contact by sending cover letter with manuscript. Send a business-sized SASE to obtain writing guidelines. Purchases 50 fiction manuscripts per issue. Comments on rejected manuscripts. Manuscripts are published 1 year after acceptance. Preferred length for fiction manuscripts is 3,000-4,000 words. 33% of magazine is mystery/crime fiction. A sample copy is available for $4.99. Subscription cost is $16.75 for 4 issues.
Payment: Pays approximately 1-5 cents a word.
Terms: Acquires North American serial rights.

Secondary & Foreign
Short Fiction Markets

THE ADVOCATE

Established: 1987 • Circulation: 12,000 • Published: 6 times a year •
Number of Pages: 32 • Size: 10 × 13

J.B. Samuels, Editor

CATEGORIES
Private Eye, Cozy, Suspense, Crime, Young Adult, Thrillers, Historical,
Hardboiled Detective, Amateur Sleuth, Humorous Mystery, Urban Horror,
Juvenile, Dark Mystery, Light Horror, Police Procedural, Psychological
Suspense, Romantic Suspense, Surrealistic Mystery, Espionage, Courtroom/
Trial

"We want more solid and entertaining writing. We also are advocating
new and nonprofessional writers. Just send us your story with an SASE
and we'll consider it."

Address: 301A Rolling Hills Park, Prattsville, NY 12468
Phone: (518)299-3103
How To Contact: Fiction submissions should be sent to Remington
Wright, Editor. Make initial contact by sending manuscript and query
letter with SASE. Send a business-sized SASE to obtain writing guidelines. Receives 40 unsolicited fiction submissions each month. Purchases 6 fiction manuscripts per issue. Occasionally comments on rejected manuscripts. Responds to author submissions in 4-6 weeks.
Manuscripts are published 6-8 months after acceptance. Preferred
length for fiction manuscripts is less than 1,500 words. A sample copy

is available for $3. Subscription cost is $12 for 6 issues.

Payment: Pays approximately 2 contributor's copies.

Terms: Acquires first rights.

BELLETRIST REVIEW

Established: 1992 • Circulation: 500 • Published: Twice a year • Number of Pages: 76 • Size: 8½ × 11

Marlene Dube, Editor

CATEGORIES

Suspense, Thrillers, Humorous Mystery, Light Horror, Malice Domestic, Psychological Suspense

---

"We'd like less cliches and more humor," says Marlene Dube. "We publish mostly psychological suspense pieces, but we are open to other categories of mystery and crime fiction. Just make sure you review at least one sample copy to get an idea of our style." Recently published Daniel Quinn, the author of *Ishmael.*

Address: 17 Farmington Ave., Suite 290, Plainville, CT 06062

How To Contact: Fiction submissions should be sent to Marlene Dube, Editor. Make initial contact by sending manuscript and cover letter. Send a business-sized SASE to obtain writing guidelines. Receives 120 unsolicited fiction submissions each month. Purchases 12 fiction manuscripts per issue. Comments on rejected manuscripts. Responds to author submissions in 6 weeks. Manuscripts are published 6-8 months after acceptance. Preferred length for fiction manuscripts is 2,500-5,000 words. Allows simultaneous submissions. Will print reprints. 10% of magazine is mystery/crime fiction. A sample copy is available for $4.95. Subscription cost is $14.99 for 2 issues.

Payment: Pays in contributor's copy.

Terms: Acquires one-time rights.

BOYS' LIFE

Established: 1911 • Circulation: 1.3 Million • Published: Monthly •
Number of Pages: 75 • Size: 8½×11

Shannon Lowry, Editor

CATEGORIES
Amateur Sleuth, Humorous Mystery, Juvenile

"We'd like to see more mysteries, period, and more suspense in the
mysteries we do see. Study our writer's guidelines and lots of past issues."
Boys' Life recently has published G. Clifton Wisler and Donald J. Sobol.

Address: 1325 West Walnut Hill Lane, P.O. Box 152079, Irving, TX
75015-2079
Phone: (214)580-2366
How To Contact: Fiction submissions should be sent to Shannon Lowry,
Associate Editor. Make initial contact by sending manuscript with
SASE. Send a business-sized SASE to obtain writing guidelines. Pur-
chases 1 fiction manuscript per issue. Responds to author submissions
in 2-8 weeks. Manuscripts are published 4-18 months after accep-
tance. Preferred length for fiction manuscripts is 1,000-1,500 words.
A sample copy is available for $2.50 with 9×12 SASE. Subscription
cost is $15.60 for 12 issues.
Payment: Pays approximately $750 for fiction.
Terms: Acquires first time rights.

BYLINE MAGAZINE

Established: 1981 • Circulation: 3,000 + • Published: Monthly • Number
of Pages: 36 • Size: 8½×11

Kathryn Fanning, Managing Editor

CATEGORIES
Private Eye, Cozy, Suspense, Thrillers, Amateur Sleuth, Police Procedural,
Malice Domestic, Psychological Suspense, Romantic Suspense

Address: P.O. Box 130596, Edmond, OK 73013

Phone: (405)348-5591

Fax: (405)348-5591

How To Contact: Fiction submissions should be sent to Kathryn Fanning, Managing Editor. Make initial contact by sending complete manuscript for short fiction; query otherwise. Send a business-sized SASE to obtain writing guidelines. Receives 200 unsolicited fiction submissions each month. Purchases 1 fiction manuscript per issue. Occasionally comments on rejected manuscripts. Responds to author submissions in 1-2 months. Manuscripts are published 3-6 months after acceptance. Preferred length for fiction manuscripts is 2,000-4,000 words. Allows simultaneous submissions. A sample copy is available for $4. Subscription cost is $20 for 11 issues.

Payment: Pays approximately $100 for short fiction.

Terms: Acquires first North American rights.

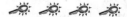

CLUES, A JOURNAL OF DETECTION

Established: 1980 • Circulation: 500 • Published: 2 times a year • Number of Pages: 156 • Size: 5½ × 7

Pat Browne, Editor

CATEGORIES
Hardboiled Detective

"Write about something other than the old standards."

Address: Bowling Green State University, Bowling Green, OH 43403

Phone: (419)372-7861

Fax: (419)372-8095

How To Contact: Make initial contact by sending cover letter. Send a business-sized SASE to obtain writing guidelines. Comments on rejected manuscripts. Responds to author submissions in 3-4 weeks. Manuscripts are published 9-12 months after acceptance. A sample copy is available for $5. Subscription cost is $12.50 for 2 issues.

☀ ☀ ☀ ☀

DAGGER OF THE MIND

Established: 1988 • Circulation: 5,000 • Published: Quarterly • Number of Pages: 80-100 • Size: 8½ × 11

Arthur William Lloyd Breach, Editor

> **CATEGORIES**
> Suspense, Thrillers, Hardboiled Detective, Urban Horror, Dark Mystery, Light Horror, Surrealistic Mystery, Courtroom/Trial

Address: 1317 Hookridge Dr., El Paso, TX 79925
Phone: (915)591-0541
How To Contact: Fiction submissions should be sent to Arthur Breach, Editor. Send a business-sized SASE to obtain writing guidelines. Receives 300-350 unsolicited fiction submissions each month. Purchases 10-20 fiction manuscripts per issue. Comments on rejected manuscripts. Responds to author submissions in 3 months. Manuscripts are published 1 year after acceptance. Allows simultaneous submissions. Submissions on computer diskette should be formatted for WordPerfect. 20% of magazine is mystery/crime fiction. A sample copy is available for $3.50 plus 5 stamps. Subscription cost is $6 for 4 issues.
Payment: Pays approximately 1-1½¢ word.
Terms: Acquires first North American serial rights.

☀ ☀ ☀ ☀

Cover: Steven B. Gould

DEAD OF NIGHT

Established: 1989 • Circulation: 3,200 • Published: Quarterly • Number of Pages: 84 • Size: 8½ × 11

Lin Stein, Editor

CATEGORIES
Suspense, Thrillers, Humorous Mystery, Urban Horror, Dark Mystery, Light Horror, Psychological Suspense, Surrealistic Mystery

"We want mysteries with an element of the supernatural," says Editor Stein. "The mysteries we publish have some mysteriousness to them. There is usually a supernatural/occult/paranormal element to what we publish. Read a sample copy (and if possible, a back issue, as well) to see what we've already done."

Dead of Night recently has published Lois Tilton, Nancy Kilpatrick, Jeanne Kalogridis, Christie Golden, J.N. Williamson, Steve Rasnic Tem, Mort Castle and Gary Braunbeck. "One of our favorite stories was John Maclay's 'Bogart, Mary Astor and the Big Bite of Love.' This was a nostalgic, unique light horror piece that cast Bogie as a vampire."

Address: 916 Shaker Rd, Suite 228, Longmeadow, MA 01106-2416

How To Contact: Fiction submissions should be sent to Lin Stein, Editor. Make initial contact by sending cover letter with manuscript for fiction; query for nonfiction. Send a business-sized SASE to obtain writing guidelines. Receives 100 unsolicited fiction submissions each month. Purchases 8-10 fiction manuscripts per issue. Occasionally comments on rejected manuscripts. Responds to author submissions in 4-6 weeks (2-4 weeks on queries only). Manuscripts are published 6-18 months after acceptance. Preferred length for fiction manuscripts is up to 3,000 words. Will print reprints. 20% of magazine is mystery/crime fiction. A sample copy is available for $4; back issues $2.50. Subscription cost is $15 for 4 issues.

Payment: Pays approximately 3¢ a word for fiction and 2¢ nonfiction.

Terms: Acquires first North American sales rights or reprint rights.

A DIFFERENT BEAT

Established: 1994 • Circulation: 300 • Published: 3 times a year • Number of Pages: 80 • Size: 5½ × 8

Sandra Hutchinson, Editor

CATEGORIES
Humorous Mystery, Urban Horror, Light Horror, Police Procedural,
Surrealistic Mystery

"We'd like more stories set in unusual locales—cops in Faerie, cops on Mars, cops in Hell. Or we'd like stories about cops facing unusual challenges such as werewolves, intergalactic horse thieves, disruptions in the space-time continuum," says Sandra Hutchinson. "Humor also works well for me and I don't see enough of it; I see too much graphic and gory horror."

The cross-genre theme of ordinary law enforcement personnel dealing with unordinary situations makes *A Different Beat* unique in the market. Hutchinson advises writers eager to publish in *A Different Beat* to "portray law enforcement personnel as human beings—neither flawless Galahads nor corrupt villians. Make sure that the speculative element (and there must be one for me to accept a piece) is combined with a good mystery, good characterization and a clear ending."

Devon Monk's "Bar None" is a recently published favorite of Hutchinson's "because of the humor, the use of language, and the unusual cross-genre twist."

Address: 7 Saint Luke's Road, Allston, MA 02134

How To Contact: Fiction submissions should be sent to Sandra Hutchinson, Editor. Make initial contact by sending manuscript with cover letter. Send a business-sized SASE to obtain writing guidelines. Receives 50 unsolicited fiction submissions each month. Purchases 5-10 fiction manuscripts per issue. Occasionally comments on rejected manuscripts. Responds to author submissions in 1 month. Manuscripts are published 4 months after acceptance. Preferred length for fiction manuscripts is under 5,000 words. 90% of magazine is mystery/crime fiction. A sample copy is available for $5. Subscription cost is $12 for 3 issues.

Payment: Pays approximately 1¢ per word.

Terms: Acquires first North American serial rights.

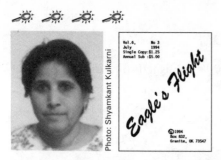

EAGLE'S FLIGHT MAGAZINE

Established: 1989 • Circulation: 200 • Published: Quarterly • Number of Pages: 12 • Size: 8½×7

Shyamkant Kulkarni, Editor

CATEGORIES
Suspense, Crime, Psychological Suspense, Romantic Suspense, Espionage

"We'd like less horror and sex and more intellectual pursuits. We love writing and are devoted to literature. Read previous issues of our magazine and do extensive reading of the type of writing you want to write. Rewrite and rewrite. Then submit." A recent favorite published in *Eagle's Flight* is "To the Picnic" by Agnes Giamona Burkes. "It's realistic and subtle, has very nice form and is heart-warming with good character depiction."

Address: Box 465, Granite, OK 73547-0465
How To Contact: Fiction submissions should be sent to Rekha Kulkarni, Fiction Editor. Make initial contact by sending manuscript. Send a business-sized SASE to obtain writing guidelines. Receives 2-4 unsolicited fiction submissions each month. Purchases 1-2 fiction manuscripts per issue. Responds to author submissions in 6 months. Manuscripts are published 1-3 years after acceptance. Preferred length for fiction manuscripts is 1,000-2,000 words. 25% of magazine is mystery/crime fiction. A sample copy is available for $1.25. Subscription cost is $5 for 4 issues.
Payment: Pays approximately $5-10 per story.
Terms: Acquires first publication rights.

☀ ☀ ☀ ☀

HOUSEWIFE WRITER'S FORUM

Established: 1988 • Circulation: 2,000 • Published: Bimonthly • Number of Pages: 40-48 • Size: 6½ × 10

Emma Bluemel, Editor

CATEGORIES
Suspense, Historical, Humorous Mystery, Psychological Suspense, Romantic Suspense

Address: P.O. Box 780, Lyman, WY 82937

Phone: (307)782-7003

How To Contact: Fiction submissions should be sent to Edward Wahl, Fiction Editor. Make initial contact by calling or writing. Send a business-sized SASE to obtain writing guidelines. Receives 50 unsolicited fiction submissions each month. Purchases 1-2 fiction manuscripts per issue. Responds to author submissions in 3 months. Manuscripts are published 1 year after acceptance. Preferred length for fiction manuscripts is 2,000 maximum words. Allows simultaneous submissions. Will print reprints. A sample copy is available for $4. Subscription cost is $15 for 6 issues.

Payment: Pays approximately 1¢ per word plus contributor's copy.

Terms: Acquires first North American serial rights.

☀ ☀ ☀ ☀

Michael Shores/Debbie Gish
Kracked Mirror Mysteries

KRACKED MIRROR MYSTERIES

Established: 1994 • Circulation: 100 • Published: 3 times a year • Number of Pages: 45-60 • Size: Digest

D.L. Gish, Editor

CATEGORIES
Private Eye, Suspense, Crime, Thrillers, Hardboiled Detective, Amateur Sleuth, Humorous Mystery, Dark Mystery, Police Procedural, Psychological Suspense, Romantic Suspense, Surrealistic Mystery, Espionage, Courtroom/ Trial

"I'd like to have more humorous pieces and stories with believable characters and situations."

Address: 370 E. Woodlawn, Le Center, MN 56057

Phone: (612)357-4884

How To Contact: Fiction submissions should be sent to D.L. Gish, Editor. Make initial contact by sending a query letter. Send a business-sized SASE to obtain writing guidelines. Receives 10-15 unsolicited fiction submissions each month. Purchases 15 fiction manuscripts per issue. Comments on rejected manuscripts. Responds to author submissions in 3-4 weeks. Manuscripts are published within 1 year after acceptance. Preferred length for fiction manuscripts is 2,000 maximum words. Allows simultaneous submissions. Will print reprints. 100% of magazine is mystery/crime fiction. A sample copy is available for $4 plus $1 postage. Subscription cost is $11.50 plus $3 for postage for 3 issues.

Payment: Pays approximately one contributor's copy.

Terms: Acquires first time rights.

☀ ☀ ☀ ☀

Cover: Rinehart Potts

LININGTON LINEUP

Established: 1983 • Circulation: 400 • Published: Bimonthly • Number of Pages: 16 • Size: 8½ × 11

Rinehart Potts, Editor

CATEGORIES
Private Eye, Cozy, Suspense, Crime

Address: 1223 Glen Terrace, Glassboro, NJ 08028-1315
How To Contact: Make initial contact by sending manuscript with summary. No writing guidelines available. Receives 6 unsolicited fiction submissions each month. Occasionally comments on rejected manuscripts. Responds to author submissions in 1 month. Manuscripts are published 6 months after acceptance. Preferred length for fiction manuscripts is 500 words. A sample copy is available for $3. Subscription cost is $12 for 6 issues.
Payment: Pays in contributor's copies.
Terms: Acquires first time rights.

Cover: Sue Feder

MOST LOVING MERE FOLLY

Established: 1988 • Circulation: 300 • Published: Quarterly • Number of Pages: 22 • Size: 8½ × 11

Sue Feder, Editor

CATEGORIES
Suspense, Crime, Historical, Amateur Sleuth, Humorous Mystery, Romantic Suspense

"We want good, strong characters in interesting, well-developed settings. In short, just the sort of thing that makes Ellis Peters so enjoyable. Those wanting to write for us must be of a type to appeal to fans of Ellis Peters. If a writer is unfamiliar with her work, I would recommend he/she stay away from anything except historical mysteries. Although we are nominally a single-author journal, our editorial philosophy of including all material which would be of interest to Ellis Peters/Edith Pargeter fans makes us a rather broad-based, free-wheeling publication. We encourage scholars to lighten up. We've recently published Ellis Peters and Andrew Greeley."

Address: 7815 Daniels Ave., Parkville, MD 21234

Phone: (410)661-2352

How To Contact: Fiction submissions should be sent to Sue Feder, Editor. Make initial contact by sending SASE. No writing guidelines available. Occasionally comments on rejected manuscripts. Responds to author submissions in 1 month. Allows simultaneous submissions. Will print reprints. Submissions on computer diskette should be formatted for ASCII or MS Word/Works or AmiPro. Electronic submissions should be sent to monkshould@aol.com. A sample copy is available for $1. Subscription cost is $15 for 4 issues.

Payment: Pays in contributor's copies.

Terms: Acquires one time rights.

MURDER OF THE MONTH

Established: 1994 • Circulation: 100 + • Published: Monthly • Number of Pages: 16 • Size: 8½ × 11

Rodney Stringfellow, Editor

CATEGORIES
Cozy, Suspense, Humorous Mystery, Dark Mystery

"We're less interested in the mystery than we are in the story. As long as a murder takes place, our requirement has been met. We'd like writers to concentrate on creating unusual stories that are wonderfully written. All our stories are contemporary, take place in or around NYC and during the month the issue is published. In addition to the featured mystery, there is a serial comic and a monthly interview with someone related to an actual murder investigation. If you want to publish, be clever and have your story show a world within New York that few people have seen."

Address: P.O. Box 3888, New York, NY 10185
Phone: (800)229-2110
Fax: (212)388-0312
How To Contact: Fiction submissions should be sent to Rodney Stringfellow, Editor-in-Chief. Make initial contact by writing. Send a business-sized SASE to obtain writing guidelines. Receives 1-2 unsolicited fiction submissons each month. Occasionally comments on rejected manuscripts. Responds to author submissions in 30 days. Manuscripts are published 3 months after acceptance. Preferred length for fiction manuscripts is 3,200 words. Allows simultaneous submissions. 80% of magazine is mystery/crime fiction. A sample copy is free. Subscription cost is $40 for 12 issues.
Payment: Gives a free year's subscription.
Terms: Acquires one time rights.

Cover: Dale L. Power

MURDEROUS INTENT: A MAGAZINE OF MYSTERY & SUSPENSE

Established: 1994 by Madison Publishing Company • Circulation: 4,500 • Published: Quarterly • Number of Pages: 64 • Size: 8½ × 11

Margo Power, Editor

CATEGORIES
Private Eye, Cozy, Suspense, Crime, Thrillers, Hardboiled Detective, Amateur Sleuth, Humorous Mystery, Dark Mystery, Police Procedural, Malice Domestic, Psychological Suspense, Romantic Suspense, Surrealistic Mystery, Espionage, Courtroom/Trial

"We'd like to see more suspense and more humor—something other than husband kills wife or vise versa. Life-like characters and a hint of mystery on the first page are great, but keep suspense high throughout. Tell a good story and mail it to us. Our eclectic mix of articles and fiction interest both writers and readers of mystery. We're stretching the boundaries." *Murderous Intent* has published Ed Gorman, Barbara Paul, Billie Sue Mosiman, Susan Dunlop, MD Lake, Carolyn Hart and Sara Paretsky.

Address: Attn: Margo Power, Madison Publishing Company, P.O. Box 5947, Vancouver, WA 98668-5947
Phone: (360)695-9004
Fax: (360)695-9004
How To Contact: Fiction submissions should be sent to Margo Power, Editor. Make initial contact by sending query for nonfiction and complete manuscript and cover letter for fiction. Send a business-sized SASE to obtain writing guidelines. Receives 50-100 unsolicited fiction submissions each month. Purchases 10-12 fiction manuscripts per issue. Occasionally comments on rejected manuscripts. Responds to author submissions in 2-3 months. Manuscripts are published 4-12 months after acceptance. Preferred length for fiction manuscripts is 200-6,000 words. Allows simultaneous submissions. Will print reprints. Electronic submissions should be sent to madison@teleport.com. 80% of magazine is mystery/crime fiction. Has an annual mystery short story contest. Send SASE for contest guidelines. A sample copy is available for $3.95 + 5 first class stamps. Subscription cost is $15 for 4 issues.
Payment: Pays approximately $10 plus 2 contributor's copies.
Terms: Acquires first North American serial rights.

MYSTERY READERS JOURNAL

Established: 1984 • Circulation: 2,500 • Published: Quarterly • Number of Pages: 80 • Size: 8½ × 7

Janet A. Rudolph, Editor; Leila Laurence, Assistant Editor; Carol Harper, Associate Editor

CATEGORIES
Private Eye, Cozy, Crime, Young Adult, Historical, Hardboiled Detective, Amateur Sleuth, Humorous Mystery, Juvenile, Dark Mystery, Malice Domestic, Espionage, Courtroom/Trial

"We'd like more articles from writers of novels which use the themes of our issues as background: suburban mysteries, San Francisco area mysteries, technology-related mysteries, regional British mysteries. We'd like to know why they chose these as backgrounds for their novel. Our publication is unique because it's thematic in content and we review books both in and out of print. What you write must fit into our issue, and if it fits, then send it."

Address: P.O. Box 8116, Berkeley, CA 94707
Phone: (510)339-2800
Fax: (510)339-8309
How To Contact: Make initial contact by sending cover letter. Send a business-sized SASE to obtain writing guidelines. Occasionally comments on rejected manuscripts. Responds to author submissions in 1 month. Submissions on computer diskette should be formatted for Mac 3.5 disk. A sample copy is available for $7. Subscription cost is $24 for 4 issues.
Payment: Pays one contributor's copy.

MYSTERY TIME MAGAZINE

Established: 1983 • Circulation: 150 • Published: Twice a year • Number of Pages: 44 • Size: 6 × 9

Linda Hutton, Editor

CATEGORIES
Private Eye, Cozy, Suspense, Crime, Amateur Sleuth, Humorous Mystery, Police Procedural, Malice Domestic, Psychological Suspense, Romantic Suspense

"We'd like more humor and more women protagonists over 50. We also welcome new writers/beginning writers and are especially fond of a humorous twist on an old theme. Study a sample copy, then submit a professional-looking story without typos."

Recently published Kristen Neri, Jan Carol Sabin, Guy Belleranti & Sue Marra Byham, and "A Knotty Problem" by Sue Marra Byham, a satire on Miss Jane Marple.

Address: P.O. Box 2907, Decatur, IL 62524

How To Contact: Fiction submissions should be sent to Linda Hutton, Editor. Make initial contact by submitting complete manuscript without cover letter. Send a business-sized SASE to obtain writing guidelines. Receives 25 unsolicited fiction submissions each month. Purchases 15 fiction manuscripts per issue. Occasionally comments on rejected manuscripts. Responds to author submissions in 1 month. Manuscripts are published 3-6 months after acceptance. Preferred length for fiction manuscripts is 1,500 words. Allows simultaneous submissions. Will print reprints. 100% of magazine is mystery/crime fiction. A sample copy is available for $4. Subscription cost is $10 for 2 issues.

Payment: Pays approximately ¼¢ a word.

Terms: Acquires first serial or reprint rights.

NAKED KISS

Established: 1994 • Circulation: 600-700 • Published: Quarterly •
Number of Pages: 48 • Size: 8½×11

Wayne A. Harold, Editor

CATEGORIES
Private Eye, Suspense, Crime, Thrillers, Hardboiled Detective, Urban
Horror, Dark Mystery, Police Procedural, Psychological Suspense

"We'd like less 'shoot-em-up' stories and more with characters having
genuine human emotions. We like strong emotional content. Be sure to
avoid cliches and keep up on the reading. Our magazine handles less
cozy crime fiction than most mystery magazines. The cover and layout
are attractive and easy on the eyes. Ours is a stylish crime fiction magazine with hard-hitting, unconventional stories by top writers, both old
and new." Recently published in *Naked Kiss* are Gary Lovisi, Mike
Black, J.D. Hunt and O'neil DeNoux.

Address: 3160 Brady Lake Rd., Ravenna, OH 44266

How To Contact: Fiction submissions should be sent to Wayne A. Harold,
Editor. Make initial contact by sending manuscript with cover letter
and return postage. Send a business-sized SASE to obtain writing
guidelines. Receives 15 unsolicited fiction submissions each month.
Purchases 6-9 fiction manuscripts per issue. Occasionally comments
on rejected manuscripts. Responds to author submissions in 1-3
months. Manuscripts are published 12-24 months after acceptance.

Preferred length for fiction manuscripts is 2,000-7,000 words. Allows simultaneous submissions. Submissions on computer diskette should be formatted for either Mac or IBM (3.5 disk). Electronic submissions should be sent to NakedKissm@AOl.com. 90% of magazine is mystery/crime fiction. A sample copy is available for $5. Subscription cost is $20 for 4 issues.

Payment: Pays approximately $5-20 per story.

Terms: Acquires first world serial rights.

PHANTASM

Established: 1993 • Circulation: 75 • Published: Quarterly • Number of Pages: 14 • Size: 6 × 9

Betty Mowery, Editor

CATEGORIES

Suspense, Thrillers, Fantasy, Light Horror, Psychological Suspense, Surrealistic Mystery

---

"I want something with a nice, tight writing style and believable plots and characters. Write what you feel comfortable with. Make sure you include an SASE—and no cutesy cover letters."

Address: 1520 7th St., Rock Island, IL 61201

How To Contact: Make initial contact by sending complete manuscript. Send a business-sized SASE to obtain writing guidelines. Receives 12 unsolicited fiction submissions each month. Purchases 16 fiction manuscripts per issue. Occasionally comments on rejected manuscripts. Responds to author submissions in 1 week. Manuscripts are published 2-3 months after acceptance. Preferred length for fiction manuscripts is 500 words. Allows simultaneous submissions. Will print reprints. 90% of magazine is mystery/crime fiction. A sample copy is available for $2. Subscription cost is $10 for 4 issues.

Terms: Acquires first rights.

PLAYBOY MAGAZINE

Established: 1953 • Circulation: 3.7 million • Published: Monthly •
Number of Pages: 162 • Size: 8½ × 11

Alice Turner, Editor

CATEGORIES
Private Eye, Suspense, Crime, Young Adult, Thrillers, Hardboiled
Detective, Amateur Sleuth, Humorous Mystery, Urban Horror, Dark
Mystery, Light Horror, Police Procedural, Malice Domestic, Psychological
Suspense, Romantic Suspense, Espionage

Address: 690 N.Lakeshore Dr., Chicago, IL 60611
Phone: (312)751-8000
How To Contact: Fiction submissions should be sent to Alice Turner,
Fiction Editor. Make initial contact by sending manuscript. Send a
business-sized SASE to obtain writing guidelines. Receives 100 unsolicited fiction submissions each month. Purchases 1 fiction manuscript
per issue. Responds to author submissions in 6-8 weeks. Manuscripts
are published 3-6 months after acceptance. Preferred length for fiction
manuscripts is 7,000 maximum words. Allows simultaneous submissions. Will print reprints. 6% of magazine is mystery/crime fiction. A
sample copy is available for $4.95. Subscription cost is $29.97 for 12
issues.
Terms: Acquires first North American serial rights.

THE POST

Published: 2 times a month • Number of Pages: 32 • Size: 8½ × 11

A.P. Samuels, Editor

CATEGORIES
Suspense, Historical

Address: 1377 K. Street N.W., Suite 856, Washington, DC 20005
Fax: (405)364-4979
How To Contact: Fiction submissions should be sent to A. Samuels, Edi-

tor. Make initial contact by sending manuscript. Send a business-sized SASE to obtain writing guidelines. Receives 50+ unsolicited fiction submissions each month. Purchases 1 fiction manuscript per issue. Responds to author submissions in 2-6 weeks. Preferred length for fiction manuscripts is 8,000-10,000 words.

Payment: Pays approximately 1-3¢ a word.

Terms: Acquires North American serial rights.

RED HERRING MYSTERY MAGAZINE

Established: 1994 • Circulation: 1,500 • Published: Quarterly • Number of Pages: 88 • Size: 7½×10

Polly W. Swafford, Editor

CATEGORIES

Private Eye, Cozy, Suspense, Historical, Amateur Sleuth, Police Procedural, Malice Domestic, Psychological Suspense, Espionage, Courtroom/Trial

"We'd like a larger diversity of voices and tones," says editor Swafford. "Unique plot structures and more character development are also welcome. We publish a diversity of stories, and we're devoted only to short mystery fiction. Send for our guidelines and a sample copy of the magazine. Hone your writing skills, and develop a unique plot and characters. Then send your manuscript."

Recently published in *Red Herring* are Susan Dunlap, Jan Burke, Edie Ramer, J.D. Hunt and Gerry Maddren

Address: P.O. Box 8278, Prairie Village, KS 66208

Phone: (913)642-1503

Fax: (913)642-3128

How To Contact: Make initial contact by submitting complete manuscript with cover letter. Send a business-sized SASE to obtain writing guidelines. Receives 50 unsolicited fiction submissions each month. Purchases 15 fiction manuscripts per issue. Comments on rejected manuscripts. Responds to author submissions in 8-12 weeks. Manuscripts are published 6-12 months after acceptance. Preferred length for fiction manuscripts is 6,000 maximum words. Allows simultaneous submissions. Submissions on computer diskette should be formatted for 3.5" disk; IBM or Mac is fine. 100% of magazine is mystery/crime fiction. A sample copy is available for $4.95. Subscription cost is $15 for 4 issues.

Payment: Pays approximately $5 plus contributor's copy.

Terms: Acquires one time rights.

SHERLOCKIAN TIDBITS

Established: 1988 • Circulation: 220 • Published: Quarterly • Number of Pages: 14 • Size: 8½ × 11

Arnold Korotkin, Editor

CATEGORIES
Historical, Sherlockiana

Only interested in Sherlock Holmes and the Victorian era.

Address: 42 Melrose Place, Montclair, NJ 07042

Phone: (201)783-1463

How To Contact: Send a business-sized SASE to obtain writing guidelines. Comments on rejected manuscripts. Responds to author submissions in 6-8 weeks. Manuscripts are published 1 year after acceptance. Allows simultaneous submissions. Will print reprints. 100% of magazine is mystery/crime fiction. A sample copy is available for $2.

Payment: Pays approximately $75-100.

SHORT STUFF FOR GROWNUPS

Established: 1989 • Circulation: 10,000 • Published: Monthly • Number of Pages: 40 • Size: 8½ × 11

Donna Bowman, Editor

CATEGORIES

Private Eye, Cozy, Suspense, Crime, Historical, Amateur Sleuth, Humorous Mystery, Police Procedural, Malice Domestic, Psychological Suspense, Romantic Suspense, Courtroom/Trial

"We would like to see more humorous submissions. We think weaving a tight story in 1800 words is a real art. I think our writers are outstanding in this ability. If you send to us be sure to include a cover letter with clips or listing credits and a brief autobiographical sketch. We like to include such information when a story is published. We've also published many impressive authors, such as Jane McBride Choate and Dean Ballenger. Yet we're most proud of first-timers who write us later with credits they've gone on to garner. We love giving first chances."

Address: 1015 Roosevelt, Suite G, Loveland, CO 80537

Phone: (303)669-9139

How To Contact: Make initial contact by sending cover letter and complete manuscript. Send a business-sized SASE to obtain writing guidelines. Receives 150 unsolicited fiction submissions each month. Purchases 9-12 fiction manuscripts per issue. Occasionally comments on rejected manuscripts. Responds to author submissions in 3-6 months. Preferred length for fiction manuscripts is 1,800 words. 20% of magazine is mystery/crime fiction. A sample copy is available for $1.50. Subscription cost is $15 for 12 issues.

Payment: Pays approximately $10-50 for pieces over 1,000 words.
Terms: Acquires first North American rights.

SKYLARK

Established: 1971 • Circulation: 700-1,000 • Published: Annually •
Number of Pages: 100 • Size: 8½ × 11

Pamela Hunter, Editor-in-Chief

CATEGORIES
Hardboiled Detective

Address: 2200 169th St., Hammond, IN 46323
Phone: (219)989-2262
How To Contact: Fiction submissions should be sent to Pamela Hunter, Editor-in-Chief. Make initial contact by sending manuscript with SASE and sufficient postage. Send a business-sized SASE to obtain writing guidelines. Receives 30 unsolicited fiction submissions each month. Purchases 10 fiction manuscripts per issue. Occasionally comments on rejected manuscripts. Responds to author submissions in 4 months. Preferred length for fiction manuscripts is under 4,000 words. A sample copy is available for $6. Subscription cost is $6 for 1 issue.
Payment: Pays one contributor's copy.
Terms: Acquires first North American rights.

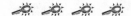

THE SLEUTH

Mary Staub, Editor

CATEGORIES
Private Eye, Cozy, Suspense, Crime, Humorous Mystery

"We'd like less gore, less explicit sex, less stereotyped characters, but more originality."

Address: 1377 K Street NW, Suite 856, Washington, DC 20005
Fax: (405)364-4979
How To Contact: Send a #10 SASE for guidelines. Send complete manuscript. Responds to submissions in 6-8 weeks.
Terms: Acquires first North American serial rights.

Cover: Bothomos

THEMA MAGAZINE

Established: 1988 • Circulation: 300 • Published: 3 times a year • Number of Pages: 200 • Size: 5½ × 8½

Virginia Howard, Editor

CATEGORIES
Private Eye, Cozy, Suspense, Crime, Young Adult, Thrillers, Historical, Hardboiled Detective, Amateur Sleuth, Humorous Mystery, Urban Horror, Dark Mystery, Light Horror, Police Procedural, Malice Domestic, Psychological Suspense, Romantic Suspense, Surrealistic Mystery, Espionage, Courtroom/Trial

Address: P.O. Box 74109, Metairie, LA 70033-4109

Phone: (504)887-1263

How To Contact: Fiction submissions should be sent to Virginia Howard, Editor. Make initial contact by sending a business-sized SASE to obtain writing guidelines. Receives 80 unsolicited fiction submissions each month. Purchases 11 fiction manuscripts per issue. Occasionally comments on rejected manuscripts. Responds to author submissions in 3 months. Manuscripts are published 3 months after acceptance. Preferred length for fiction manuscripts is 6,000 words. Allows simultaneous submissions. Will print reprints. 10% of magazine is mystery/crime fiction. A sample copy is available for $8. Subscription cost is $16 for 3 issues.

Payment: Pays approximately $25, or $10 for short shorts.

TUCUMCARI LITERARY REVIEW

Established: 1988 • Circulation: 150 • Published: Bimonthly • Number of Pages: 42 • Size: 5½ × 8½

Troxey Kemper, Editor

CATEGORIES

Private Eye, Suspense, Crime, Young Adult, Thrillers, Historical, Amateur Sleuth, Humorous Mystery, Juvenile, Dark Mystery, Police Procedural, Psychological Suspense, Espionage, Courtroom/Trial

---

"We'll take whatever comes in the mail if it is good, interesting and less than 1,200 words."

Address: 3108 W. Bellevue Ave., Los Angeles, CA 90026

How To Contact: Fiction submissions should be sent to Troxey Kemper, Editor. Send a business-sized SASE to obtain writing guidelines. Receives 10 unsolicited fiction submissions each month. Purchases 2 fiction manuscripts per issue. Usually comments on rejected manuscripts. Responds to author submissions in 1 week. Manuscripts usually are published 2 months after acceptance. Preferred length for fiction manuscripts is 1,200 words or less. Allows simultaneous submissions. Will print reprints. A sample copy is available for $2. Subscription cost is $12 for 6 issues.

Payment: Pays one contributor's copy.

Terms: Acquires one time rights.

ULTIMATE WRITER MAGAZINE

Established: 1986 • Circulation: 800 • Published: Monthly • Number of Pages: 40-50 • Size: 8½ × 11

Perry Terrell, Editor

CATEGORIES

Private Eye, Cozy, Suspense, Crime, Thrillers, Hardboiled Detective, Amateur Sleuth, Humorous Mystery, Urban Horror, Juvenile, Dark Mystery, Light Horror, Police Procedural, Malice Domestic, Psychological Suspense, Romantic Suspense, Surrealistic Mystery, Espionage, Courtroom/ Trial

"Mysteries challenge the mind to explore possible outcomes. Keep this in mind. Also, comedies are welcome—they take the mind off the gruesome news and day's events."

Address: 4104 Alabama Ave. #8, Kenner, LA 70065

Phone: (504)465-9412

How To Contact: Make initial contact by calling or sending manuscript with SASE. Send a business-sized SASE to obtain writing guidelines. Receives 30-40 unsolicited fiction submissions each month. Occasionally comments on rejected manuscripts. Responds to author submissions in 4-6 months. Manuscripts are published 4-6 months after acceptance. Preferred length for fiction manuscripts is 3,000 maximum words. Allows simultaneous submissions. Will print reprints. Submissions on computer diskette should be formatted for WordPerfect. 50%

of magazine is mystery/crime fiction. A sample copy is available for $3.75. Subscription cost is $27 for 12 issues.

Terms: Acquires one time rights.

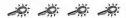

VENERATION QUARTERLY

Established: 1992 • Circulation: 400 • Published: Quarterly • Number of Pages: 50-60 • Size: 8½ × 11

Perry Terrell, Editor

> **CATEGORIES**
> Private Eye, Cozy, Suspense, Crime, Young Adult, Thrillers, Hardboiled Detective, Amateur Sleuth, Humorous Mystery, Urban Horror, Juvenile, Dark Mystery, Light Horror, Police Procedural, Malice Domestic, Psychological Suspense, Romantic Suspense, Surrealistic Mystery, Espionage, Courtroom/Trial

Address: 4104 Alabama Ave. #8, Kenner, LA 70065
Phone: (504)465-9412
How To Contact: Fiction submissions should be sent to Perry Terrell, Editor. Make initial contact by calling or sending manuscript with SASE. Send a business-sized SASE to obtain writing guidelines. Receives 10-15 unsolicited fiction submissions each month. Occasionally comments on rejected manuscripts. Responds to author submissions in 4-6 months. Manuscripts are published 4-6 months after acceptance. Preferred length for fiction manuscripts is 3,000 maximum words. Allows simultaneous submissions. Will print reprints. Submissions on computer diskette should be formatted for WordPerfect. 100% of magazine is mystery/crime fiction. A sample copy is available for $6.50.

Terms: Acquires one time rights.

WHISPER

Established: 1989 • Circulation: 1,000 • Published: 3 times a year • Number of Pages: 24 • Size: 8½ × 11

Anthony Boyd, Editor

CATEGORIES
Suspense, Thrillers, Humorous Mystery, Dark Mystery, Light Horror,
Psychological Suspense, Surrealistic Mystery, Espionage, Courtroom/Trial

Address: P.O. Box 2354, Rohnert Park, CA 94927

How To Contact: Fiction submissions should be sent to Anthony Boyd, Editor. Make initial contact by sending story with SASE. Send a business-sized SASE to obtain writing guidelines. Receives 25 unsolicited fiction submissions each month. Purchases 1 fiction manuscript per issue. Comments on rejected manuscripts. Responds to author submissions in 1 month. Manuscripts are published 9 months after acceptance. Preferred length for fiction manuscripts is 1,200-1,500 words. Will print reprints. Electronic submissions should be sent to whisper@crl.com. A sample copy is available for $2. Subscription cost is $10 for 6 issues.

Payment: Pays 1 or 2 contributor's copies.

Terms: Acquires one time print and electronic rights.

Cover: Troy Taylor

WHITECHAPEL GAZETTE

Established: 1993 • Circulation: 100-150 • Published: 3 times a year •
Number of Pages: 60 • Size: 8½×11

Troy and Alexandra Taylor, Editors

CATEGORIES
Sherlock Holmes

"We're strictly Sherlock Holmes/Sir Arthur Conan Doyle and we do nonfiction pieces on the Victorian Era. We'd like to see more nonfiction

Sherlock Holmes pieces. We are a Sherlock Holmes magazine for everybody. You don't have to be a scholar to enjoy our magazine. We do Basil Rathbone films, too, so we're in this for anyone with an interest in Sherlock Holmes. Stay away from overly scholarly pieces. We don't do footnotes—if you can't say it in the article then we don't want it."

Address: 805 West North St., Decatur, IL 62522
Phone: (217)422-7567
Fax: (217)877-9211
How To Contact: Make initial contact by submitting complete manuscript. Send a business-sized SASE to obtain writing guidelines. Purchases 2 fiction manuscripts per issue. Comments on rejected manuscripts. Responds to author submissions in 2 weeks. Manuscripts are published 3-6 months after acceptance. 25% of magazine is mystery/crime fiction. A sample copy is available for $6.50. Subscription cost is $18 for 3 issues.
Payment: Pays one contributor's copy.
Terms: Acquires one time rights.

WOMAN'S WORLD

Established: 1981 • Circulation: 1.3 million • Published: weekly • Number of Pages: 55 • Size: 8 × 10

Jeanne Muchnick, Fiction Editor

CATEGORIES
Mini Mysteries

Address: 270 Sylvan Ave., Englewood Cliffs, NJ 07632
Phone: (201)569-6699

How To Contact: Make initial contact by sending manuscript with SASE. Send a business-sized SASE to obtain writing guidelines. Receives 100 unsolicited fiction submissions each month. Purchases 1 fiction manuscript per issue. Occasionally comments on rejected manuscripts. Responds to author submissions in 6-8 weeks. Manuscripts are published 10-12 weeks after acceptance. Preferred length for fiction manuscripts is 1,200 words. A sample copy is available for $1.25.
Payment: Pays approximately $500.
Terms: Acquires first North American serial rights.

WRITING WRITERS MAGAZINE

Established: 1992 • Circulation: 1,000 • Published: Monthly • Number of Pages: 36 • Size: Tabloid

Dorothy Cagle, Editor

CATEGORIES
Private Eye, Cozy, Suspense, Crime, Young Adult, Thrillers, Historical, Hardboiled Detective, Amateur Sleuth, Humorous Mystery, Urban Horror, Juvenile, Dark Mystery, Light Horror, Police Procedural, Malice Domestic, Psychological Suspense, Romantic Suspense, Surrealistic Mystery, Espionage, Courtroom/Trial

"We'd like more cloke and dagger stories where the reader has to guess the ending. Try something different."

Address: 786 Birch St., Paradise, CA 95969
How To Contact: Make initial contact by sending cover letter with SASE. Send a business-sized SASE to obtain writing guidelines. Receives 25-30 unsolicited fiction submissions each month. Comments on rejected manuscripts. Responds to author submissions in 1 month. Allows simultaneous submissions. Will print reprints. 50-75% of magazine is mystery/crime fiction. A sample copy is available for $2. Subscription cost is $20.50 for 12 issues.

CANADIAN MAGAZINES

GREEN'S MAGAZINE

Established: 1972 • Circulation: 300 • Published: Quarterly • Number of Pages: 100 • Size: 5⅛ × 8

David Green, Editor

CATEGORIES

Private Eye, Cozy, Suspense, Crime, Young Adult, Thrillers, Historical, Hardboiled Detective, Amateur Sleuth, Humorous Mystery, Urban Horror, Juvenile, Dark Mystery, Light Horror, Police Procedural, Malice Domestic, Psychological Suspense, Romantic Suspense, Surrealistic Mystery, Espionage, Courtroom/Trial

---

"Keep the reader in mind at all times so they will be satisfied to have read the story," says Green. "Justice should still triumph."

Address: P.O. Box 3236, Regina, Saskatchewan, Canada, S4P3H1
Phone: (306)586-3246
How To Contact: Fiction submissions should be sent to David Green, Editor. Make initial contact by writing. Send a business-sized SASE with Int'l reply coupon to obtain writing guidelines. Receives 100 unsolicited fiction submissions each month. Purchases 10 fiction manuscripts per issue. Comments on rejected manuscripts. Responds to author submissions in 8 weeks. Manuscripts are published 6-12 months after acceptance. Preferred length for fiction manuscripts is 2,000-3,000 words. 10% of magazine is mystery/crime fiction. A sample copy is available for $4. Subscription cost is $12 for 4 issues.

Payment: Pays approximately 2 contributor's copies.
Terms: Acquires first North American rights.

THE MYSTERY REVIEW

Established: 1992 • Circulation: 4,000 • Published: Quarterly • Number of Pages: 72 • Size: 8½ × 11

Barbara Davey, Editor

CATEGORIES

Private Eye, Cozy, Suspense, Crime, Young Adult, Thrillers, Historical, Hardboiled Detective, Amateur Sleuth, Humorous Mystery, Juvenile, Dark Mystery, Light Horror, Police Procedural, Malice Domestic, Psychological Suspense, Romantic Suspense, Surrealistic Mystery, Espionage, Courtroom/ Trial

---

Address: P.O. Box 233, Colborne, ON K0K 1S0, Canada,
Phone: (613)475-4440
Fax: (613)475-3400
How To Contact: Fiction submissions should be sent to Barbara Davey, Editor. Make initial contact by submitting a query letter stating your idea. Send a business-sized SASE to obtain writing guidelines. Occasionally comments on rejected manuscripts. Responds to author submissions in 1 month. Manuscripts are published 3-6 months after acceptance. 5% of magazine is mystery/crime fiction. A sample copy is available for $5.95. Subscription cost is $20 for 4 issues.
Payment: Pays a nominal fee.
Terms: Acquires all rights.

WRITER'S BLOCK MAGAZINE

Established: 1994 • Circulation: 25,000 • Published: Quarterly • Number of Pages: 48 • Size: 5¼ × 8

Shaun Donnelly, Editor

CATEGORIES
Private Eye, Suspense, Crime, Thrillers, Historical, Hardboiled Detective, Humorous Mystery, Dark Mystery, Police Procedural, Psychological Suspense, Romantic Suspense, Espionage, Courtroom/Trial

"We'd like more clever plots with surprising twists, as well as well-defined characters and locations. We have a wide mix of genres and an exceptional calibre of writers. Because we pay more than most magazines, we've become a tough market to crack. Send only your best." *Writer's Block* recently has published W.O. Mitchell, Nancy Kilpatrick and Maureen Jennings.

Address: Box 32, 9944 - 33rd Ave., Edmonton, Alberta CANADA, TGN IE8

How To Contact: Fiction submissions should be sent to Shaun Donnelly, Editor. Make initial contact by sending query letter and manuscript. To obtain writing guidelines send Canadian Postage or IRC only. Receives 125 unsolicited fiction submissions each month. Purchases 6 fiction manuscripts per issue. Occasionally comments on rejected manuscripts. Responds to author submissions in 2-6 weeks. Manuscripts are published 1-6 months after acceptance. Preferred length for fiction manuscripts is 2,000-5,000 words. 25% of magazine is mystery/crime fiction. A sample copy is available for $5. Subscription cost is $12 for 4 issues.

Payment: Pays approximately 5¢ a word.

Terms: Acquires first North American serial rights.

UNITED KINGDOM MAGAZINES

A SHOT IN THE DARK

Established: 1994 • Circulation: 1,000 • Published: Quarterly • Number of Pages: 64 • Size: 5¾ × 8¼

Bob Cartwright, Editor

CATEGORIES
Hardboiled Detective

"We would like to carry more fiction but it's a problem of space," says Bob Cartwright. "In our March, 1995 issue, we had a short story that exemplifies the current U.S. Hardboiled sub-genre. We are one of only two magazines specifically related to crime fiction. So give us a try. We're open-minded. We love crime fiction in all its guises. We also respect crime fiction authors and don't do hatchet jobs on their work."

Address: 32 High St. Bonsall, Matlock, Derbyshire, DE4 2AR, UK

Phone: (062)982-2702

How To Contact: Make initial contact by writing. Receives 3-4 unsolicited nonfiction submissions per month. Comments on rejected manuscripts. Responds to author submissions in 2 weeks. Preferred length for nonfiction manuscripts is 500-2,500 words. Will print reprints. Submissions on diskette should be formatted for Quark DTP. 5% of magazine is mystery/crime fiction. Subscription cost is $15 U.S. for 4 issues.

Nonfiction Short Markets

THE ADVOCATE

Established: 1987 • Circulation: 12,000 • Published: 6 times a year • Number of Pages: 32 • Size: 10 × 13

J.B. Samuels, Editor

CATEGORIES
Interviews, Essays, Film Reviews, Poetry, Advice Columns

Address: 301A Rolling Hills Park, Prattsville, NY 12468
Phone: (518)299-3103
How To Contact: Nonfiction should be sent to Cory Reeves, Nonfiction Editor. Make initial contact by sending manuscript and query letter with SASE. Send a business-sized SASE to obtain writing guidelines. Receives 5 unsolicited nonfiction submissions per month. Purchases 1 nonfiction manuscript per issue. Occasionally comments on rejected manuscripts. Responds to author submissions in 4-6 weeks. Manuscripts are published 6-8 months after acceptance. Preferred length for nonfiction manuscripts is less than 1,500 words. A sample copy is available for $3. Subscription cost is $12 for 6 issues.
Payment: Pays 2 contributor's copies.
Terms: Acquires first rights.

Photo: Rosemary Herbert

THE ARMCHAIR DETECTIVE

Established: 1967 • Circulation: 7-10,000 • Published: Quarterly • Number of pages: 126 • Size: 8½x11

Judi Vause, Owner
Kate Stine, Editor-in-Chief

CATEGORIES
Interviews, Essays, Film Reviews, Industry News, New Bookstores, Overseas Reports, Convention Listings, Market Listings

"I don't think you can jump into the mystery field without knowing what you're doing. You can't fake it," says Kate Stine, editor-in-chief of *The Armchair Detective.* "It's very obvious when you're reading a manuscript and the person has just read a couple of magazine articles and has decided he can do a mystery. There has to be a real commitment on the part of the writer. So my first advice to aspiring writers is, don't jump into it without knowing that you're very committed to this field and well-read in it."

Few know this better than she. In addition to running one of the most respected scholarly magazines devoted to the mystery genre, Stine has held editorial jobs at Mysterious Press and Warner Books, and until December of 1994, was editor-in-chief of Otto Penzler Books. Her career history has given her a wealth of information and tips for beginning writers.

"Publishing is an extremely fluid industry," she says, "so it always pays to be courteous. People move from house to house constantly, taking their impressions of a writer's behavior with them. For example, the person answering the phone at a publishing house is usually an editorial assistant. While this is a lowly position in the general scheme of things, it's important to realize that these are apprentice editors. They may not be able to acquire books now—although many assistants are given that opportunity—but they will be able to do it in a year or two." And those assistant editors will most likely move up to become full editors, as Stine did. "When I was an associate editor a few years ago, a writer became very upset with my company's contracts department and subjected me to an abusive name-calling tirade. I wasn't his editor, I had just answered the phone. Two years later, I was assembling a start-up mystery imprint. This same writer—now in need of a publisher—called me, obviously not remembering who I was. Needless to say, I wasn't eager to work with him again."

In addition to being courteous, it also helps for a beginning writer to be published. "Get to know the people at mystery periodicals," Stine advises. "Write them articles, do reviews of books. At *The Armchair Detective*, I'm open to seeing submissions from anyone about critical looks at mystery authors or regional fiction, or an overview of a writer or a certain sub-genre." Although this type of writing doesn't pay much, it gets your name in front of the editors in the field who read these periodicals to keep up on the market. "Editors do look more seriously at writers who have been published," Stine says.

Editors also look more favorably on books with a bit of humor to them. "Humor is always good," Stine says. "It doesn't have to be a joke a page, but I like a nice humorous tone." However, "the first thing that will keep me reading is smoothness of writing style." Character is important, as is setting. "As far as I'm concerned, I'm more drawn to character and setting rather than purely plot elements. You can fix plot elements, but I don't think you can fix the other things like that."

One thing Stine doesn't like is over-the-top violence. "Immediate brutal violence in the first two pages, horrifying violence, tends to turn me off. I think it tends to turn readers in general off. I read Thomas Harris, but if you look at what he's actually writing, he doesn't do that. I think a lot of people have read Thomas Harris and think, 'Well, I can out-gross him.' Well, yes, but they can't out-write him." For beginning writers, Stine feels it's easier to leave the violence out. "I think it takes more technical mastery to handle really violent scenes than it does to leave the violence offstage."

As someone who knows the field, Stine feels there are certain sub-genres to watch and others to avoid. "I think probably the serial killer book is over, unless it's wonderful and then all bets are off. I see more historical mysteries coming out, which has been apparent for the past couple of years. Woman protagonists in mysteries have been going up for some time." Ethnic detective novels are also on the rise. "That's probably something that's going to keep growing in the field. People are very interested in other cultures and they're looking for more of that in their mysteries."

Networking is also important. "Once you're ready to start showing your book around, a really helpful thing to do is to go to writers' conferences and mystery fan conferences. There you can make useful contacts, get to know booksellers, people who do mystery periodicals. You can also probably bump up into an agent or editor. And, more importantly, you can talk to mystery writers who, by and large, are the nicest people in publishing. They're just a wonderful group, and they're very helpful to each other." Over a period of time, Stine says, you'll make some friends among these writers, and they'll read your books and recommend you to an agent or an editor that they know. She suggests Malice Domestic or Left Coast Crime (see convention listings, page 374) as good regional conventions for writers new to the scene. "Bouchercon can be overwhelming if you're new, but a lot of business gets done there," Stine adds. Smaller conventions tend to have a more relaxed feel and you are more likely to have a chance to chat with writers, editors and agents.

Making connections and gaining exposure can be immensely helpful to a new writer in what Stine sees as a shrinking market. Due to overbuying in the eighties, Stine says that publishers have spent the early part of this decade cutting writers, and thus she sees the market getting tighter. It may look grim to a new writer, but Stine says there is hope. "I think a good book *will* get published."

And once your books start getting published, keep a record of them. "When I was editor-in-chief of a start-up mystery imprint, we had to gather basic information on all of our writers," Stine says. "We requested lists of their titles, publication dates, publishers, ISBNs and subsidiary rights sales (e.g. book club, paperback reprint, large print, foreign). An astonishing number of writers could not give us this basic information about their own books. For example, if we wanted to sell the Italian rights to a book, we wouldn't know if any previous books had been sold in Italy, who bought them and for how much money. We might have accepted less money than the same publisher had offered for previous books out of sheer ignorance of the writer's track record." Many writers think that their agents will take care of the record keeping, and they usually do. However, Stine cautions, "the average writer will have several agents and several publishers over the course of his or her career, so it is vital that a writer keep track of these matters personally.

"Writing is not just an art, it's a business," Stine says. "And it definitely benefits a writer to treat it that way."

Address: 129 W. 56th Street, New York, NY 10019
Phone: (212)765- 0902
Fax: (212)265-5478
How To Contact: Nonfiction should be sent to Kate Stine, Editor-in-Chief. Send a business-sized SASE to obtain writing guidelines. Query for guidelines if unfamiliar with the magazine's requirements. Unsolicited essays okay; interviews require a query letter. Receives 10-15 unsolicited nonfiction submissions per month; purchases 5-8 per month. Preferred word length is 3,000-10,000. Responds to author submissions in 1-3 months. Manuscripts are published 3-9 months after acceptance. Allows reprints if article originally appeared in a very small circulation magazine. Send review copies to book review editor at above address. Publishes 50-100 reviews per issue. A sample copy is available for $9. Subscription cost is $31 for 4 issues.
Payment: Pays approximately $12 per printed page, upon publication. Reviewers are paid only in free review books.
Terms: Acquires first North American rights.

BOYS' LIFE

Established: 1911 • Circulation: 1.3 Million • Published: Monthly • Number of Pages: 75 • Size: 8½×11

Mike Goldman, Associate Editor

CATEGORIES
Interviews, Essays, Software Reviews

Address: 1325 West Walnut Hill Lane, P.O. Box 152079, Irving, TX 75015-2079

Phone: (214)580-2366

How To Contact: Nonfiction should be sent to Mike Goldman, Associate Editor. Make initial contact by sending query letter with SASE. Send a business-sized SASE to obtain writing guidelines. Purchases 20 + nonfiction manuscripts per issue. Responds to author submissions in 2-8 weeks. Manuscripts are published 4-18 months after acceptance. Preferred length for nonfiction manuscripts is 450-1,000 words. A sample copy is available for $2.50 with 9 × 12 SASE. Subscription cost is $15.60 for 12 issues.

Payment: Pays approximately $150-1,500 for non-fiction.

Terms: Acquires first time rights.

BYLINE MAGAZINE

Established: 1981 • Circulation: 3,000 + • Published: Monthly • Number of Pages: 36 • Size: 8½ × 11

Kathryn Fanning, Managing Editor

CATEGORIES
Essays, Poetry, Mystery News, Advice Columns, Convention Listings, Market Listings

"We are a writer's magazine, not specifically a mystery magazine," says Marcia Preston, Editor/Publisher.

Address: P.O. Box 130596, Edmond, OK 73013

Phone: (405)348-5591

Fax: (405)348-5591

How To Contact: Nonfiction should be sent to Kathryn Fanning, Managing Editor. Send a business-sized SASE to obtain writing guidelines. Receives 100 unsolicited nonfiction submissions per month. Occasionally comments on rejected manuscripts. Responds to author submissions in 1-2 months. Manuscripts are published 3-6 months after acceptance. Allows simultaneous submissions. A sample copy is available for $4. Subscription cost is $20 for 11 issues.

Payment: Pays approximately $15 for nonfiction fillers to $50 for features on the topic of writing.
Terms: Acquires first North American rights.

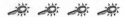

CLUES, A JOURNAL OF DETECTION

Established: 1980 • Circulation: 500 • Published: 2 times a year • Number of Pages: 156 • Size: 5½×7

Pat Browne, Editor

CATEGORIES
Interviews, Essays

Address: Bowling Green State University, Bowling Green, OH 43403
Phone: (419)372-7861
Fax: (419)372-8095
How To Contact: Nonfiction should be sent to Pat Browne, Editor. Make initial contact by sending cover letter. Send a business-sized SASE to obtain writing guidelines. Receives 4-5 unsolicited nonfiction submissions per month. Purchases 20 nonfiction manuscripts per issue. Comments on rejected manuscripts. Responds to author submissions in 3-4 weeks. Manuscripts are published 9-12 months after acceptance. Preferred length for nonfiction manuscripts is 4,500 words. 100% of magazine is mystery/crime nonfiction. A sample copy is available for $5. Subscription cost is $12.50 for 2 issues.

THE CRIMINAL RECORD

Established: 1987 • Circulation: 200 • Published: 6 times a year • Number of Pages: 15 • Size: 5½×8½

Ann M. Williams, Editor

CATEGORIES
Reviews, Essays, Mystery News, Convention Listings, Award Winners

"We look for thoughtful, personal reviews reflecting a variety of viewpoints and tastes. If you're a reviewer, don't give away too much of the plot."

Address: 3131 E. Seventh Ave. Pkwy., Denver, CO 80206
Phone: (303)393-6531
How To Contact: Contributions should be sent to Ann M. Williams, Editor. Publishes 10-15 book reviews per issue. No pay. Preferred length is 300 words or less. Subscription cost is $7 for 6 issues.

DAGGER OF THE MIND

Established: 1988 • Circulation: 5,000 • Published: Quarterly • Number of Pages: 80-100 • Size: 8½ × 11

Arthur William Lloyd Breach, Editor

CATEGORIES
Interviews

Address: 1317 Hookridge Dr., El Paso, TX 79925
Phone: (915)591-0541
How To Contact: Nonfiction should be sent to Aurthur Breach, Editor. Send a business-sized SASE to obtain writing guidelines. Receives 40-50 unsolicited nonfiction submissions per month. Purchases 5-8 nonfiction manuscripts per issue. Comments on rejected manuscripts. Responds to author submissions in 3 months. Manuscripts are published 1 year after acceptance. Allows simultaneous submissions. Submissions on diskette should be formatted for WordPerfect. 25% of magazine is mystery/crime nonfiction. A sample copy is available for $3.50 plus 5 stamps. Subscription cost is $6 for 4 issues.
Payment: Pays approximately 1-1½¢ word.
Terms: Acquires first North American serial rights.

DEAD OF NIGHT

Established: 1989 • Circulation: 3,200 • Published: Quarterly • Number of Pages: 84 • Size: 8½ × 11

Lin Stein, Editor

CATEGORIES
Interviews, Essays, Film Reviews, Poetry, Magazine Reviews

Address: 916 Shaker Rd, Suite 228, Longmeadow, MA 01106-2416
How To Contact: Nonfiction should be sent to Lin Stein, Editor. Make initial contact by sending a query letter for nonfiction. Send a business-sized SASE to obtain writing guidelines. Receives 1-10 unsolicited nonfiction submissions per month. Purchases 3-4 nonfiction manuscripts per issue. Occasionally comments on rejected manuscripts. Responds to author submissions in 4-6 weeks. Manuscripts are published 6-18 months after acceptance. Preferred length for nonfiction manuscripts is up to 2,800 words. Will print reprints. 5% of magazine is mystery/crime nonfiction. A sample copy is available for $4; back issues $2.50. Subscription cost is $15 for 4 issues.
Payment: Pays approximately 2¢ nonfiction.
Terms: Acquires first North American sales rights or reprint rights.

DROOD REVIEW

Established: 1982 • Circulation: 1,600 • Published: Bimonthly • Number of Pages: 20-24 • Size: 8½ × 11

Jim Huang, Editor

CATEGORIES
Interviews, Essays, Mystery News, Software Reviews, Overseas Reports, Convention Listings, Book Reviews

"We are very thoughtful and thorough with our coverage. We work hard to give our readers something to think about. It's not just thumbs up, thumbs down. Our twelve years have given us experience which makes us stand apart. We are very interested in reviewing books from small presses, alternative presses, and first novels."

Address: P.O. Box 50267, Kalamazoo, MI 49005
Phone: (616)349-3006
Fax: (616)383-4403
How To Contact: Nonfiction should be sent to Jim Huang, Editor. Make initial contact by sending a query letter stating your experience. Send a business-sized SASE to obtain writing guidelines. Purchases 25-35 nonfiction manuscripts per issue. Responds to author submissions in 1 month. Manuscripts are published 3 months after acceptance. Preferred length for nonfiction manuscripts is 200-2,000 words. Submissions on diskette should be formatted in ASCII. Electronic submissions should be sent to 73717.663@compuserve.com. 100% of magazine is mystery/crime nonfiction. A sample copy is available for $2.50. Subscription cost is $14 for 6 issues.
Payment: Reviewers get to obtain book reviewed.
Terms: Acquires all rights.

GAUNTLET MAGAZINE

Established: 1990 • Circulation: 10,000 • Published: twice a year • Number of Pages: 176 • Size: 6 × 9

Barry Hoffman, Editor

CATEGORIES
Essays, interviews

"We like hard-hitting, investigative pieces, like our recently published '60 Minutes vs. Scientology' piece."

Address: 309 Powell Rd., Springfield, PA 19064
Phone: (610)328-5476
Fax: (610)328-9929
How To Contact: Make initial contact by sending query letter and SASE. Send a business-sized SASE to obtain writing guidelines. Occasionally comments on rejected manuscripts. Responds to author submissions in 4-8 weeks. Manuscripts are published 6-12 months after acceptance. Allows simultaneous submissions. Will print reprints. A sample copy is available for $9.95 plus $2 postage. Subscription cost is $22 for 2 issues.
Payment: Pays approximately 3¢ a word.
Terms: Acquires first North American rights.

GOTHIC JOURNAL

Established: 1991 • Published: Bimonthly • Number of Pages: 52 • Size: 8½×11

Kristi Lyn Glass, Publisher

CATEGORIES
Interviews, Articles, Author Profiles, Industry Figure Profiles, Market Listings, Letters, Commentary

"Gothic Journal is the only news and review magazine that exclusively covers romantic mysteries, romantic suspense, gothic romance, supernatural romance, and woman-in-jeopardy romance. We have extenseive and unique promotional opportunities for authors. We publish a bimonthly point-of-purchase poster that is distributed free to interested bookstores, including many mystery bookstores; this poster includes review highlights and recommended titles for the period. Our reviews offer at least

50% commentary; the balance is plot description. Read Gothic Journal and understand our readership (readers, writers, and publishers of books in the genre). Understand how we define "gothic" (ask for our 'Genre Definitions' and 'What's in a Category' article reprints). Submit an article that will be of interest to readers, writers, or both—specific to one or more of our genres. We've published comprehensive profiles on many famous authors, including Victoria Holt, Daphne du Maurier, Virginia Coffman, Velda Johnston, Mary Stewart, Dan Ross, Jill Tattersall, Dorothy Daniels, Dorothy Eden, Helen MacInnes, Daoma Winston, Evelyn Anthony, and Anya Seton. Our 'Genre Definitions' piece (Aug/Sept '94) clarifies the market's definitions and use of the multitide of genres and subgenres related to the genres we cover. It explains, for example, the difference between romantic adventure and romantic intrigue."

Address: 19210 Forest Rd. North, Forest Lake, MN 55025-9766
Phone: (612)464-1119
Fax: (612)464-1331
How To Contact: Nonfiction should be sent to Kristi Lyn Glass, Publisher. Make initial contact by sending for guidelines; query first for author profiles. Send a business-sized SASE to obtain writing guidelines. Receives 1-3 unsolicited nonfiction submissions per month. Purchases 1-3 nonfiction manuscripts per issue. Comments on rejected manuscripts. Responds to author submissions in 3-8 weeks. Manuscripts are published 6-18 months after acceptance. Preferred length for nonfiction manuscripts is 250-4,000 words. Will print reprints. Submissions on diskette should be formatted in ASCII for IBM. Electronic submissions should be sent to Internet: kglass@vnet.net. 100% of magazine is nonfiction. A sample copy is available for $4. Subscription cost is $24 for 6 issues.
Payment: Pays $20-30 plus 3 copies for articles; $5-10 per issue for reviews.
Terms: Acquires first rights on articles; on author profiles buys all rights.

HARDBOILED MAGAZINE

Established: 1988 • Circulation: 1,000 • Published: Quarterly • Number of Pages: 100 • Size: 5 × 8

Gary Lovisi, Editor

CATEGORIES
Interviews, Essays, Film Reviews

Address: P.O. Box 209, Brooklyn, NY 11228-0209
How To Contact: Nonfiction should be sent to Gary Lovisi, Editor. Make initial contact by sending query letter. Send a business-sized SASE to obtain writing guidelines. Receives 10 unsolicited nonfiction submissions per month. Purchases 4-5 nonfiction manuscripts per issue. Occasionally comments on rejected manuscripts. Responds to author submissions in 2-4 weeks. Manuscripts are published 6-18 months after acceptance. Preferred length for nonfiction manuscripts is 1,000 words. 30-50% of magazine is mystery/crime nonfiction. A sample copy is available for $6. Subscription cost is $30 for 6 issues.
Payment: Pays approximately $5-50 plus 2 free copies.
Terms: Acquires one time first North American rights.

HOUSEWIFE WRITER'S FORUM

Established: 1988 • Circulation: 2,000 • Published: Bimonthly • Number of Pages: 40-48 • Size: 6½ × 10

Emma Bluemel, Editor

CATEGORIES
Interviews, Essays, Poetry, Mystery News, Advice Columns, Market Listings, Humor, Personal Experience

Address: P.O. Box 780, Lyman, WY 82937
Phone: (307)782-7003
How To Contact: Nonfiction should be sent to Emma Bluemel, Editor. Make initial contact by calling or writing. Send a business-sized SASE

to obtain writing guidelines. Receives 70 unsolicited nonfiction submissions per month. Purchases 10-15 nonfiction manuscripts per issue. Responds to author submissions in 3 months. Manuscripts are published 1 year after acceptance. Preferred length for nonfiction manuscripts is 400-700 words. Allows simultaneous submissions. Will print reprints. A sample copy is available for $4. Subscription cost is $15 for 6 issues.

Payment: Pays approximately 1¢ per word plus contributor's copy.

Terms: Acquires first North American serial rights.

LININGTON LINEUP

Established: 1983 • Circulation: 400 • Published: Bimonthly • Number of Pages: 16 • Size: 8½ × 11

Rinehart Potts, Editor

CATEGORIES
Interviews, Essays, Film Reviews

Address: 1223 Glen Terrace, Glassboro, NJ 08028-1315

How To Contact: Make initial contact by sending manuscript with summary. No writing guidelines available. Receives 6 unsolicited nonfiction submissions per month. Occasionally comments on rejected manuscripts. Responds to author submissions in 1 month. Manuscripts are published 6 months after acceptance. Preferred length for nonfiction manuscripts is 1,000 words. A sample copy is available for $3. Subscription cost is $12 for 6 issues.

Payment: Pays in contributor's copies.

Terms: Acquires first time rights.

MOST LOVING MERE FOLLY

Established: 1988 • Circulation: 300 • Published: Quarterly • Number of Pages: 22 • Size: 8½ × 11

Sue Feder, Editor

CATEGORIES
Interviews, Essays, Film Reviews, Poetry, Overseas Reports, Convention
Listings, Book Previews

Address: 7815 Daniels Ave., Parkville, MD 21234

Phone: (410)661-2352

How To Contact: Nonfiction should be sent to Sue Feder, Editor. Make initial contact by sending SASE. No writing guidelines available. Occasionally comments on rejected manuscripts. Responds to author submissions in 1 month. Allows simultaneous submissions. Will print reprints. Submissions on diskette should be formatted for ASCII or MS Word/Works, or AmiPro. Electronic submissions should be sent to monkshould@aol.com. A sample copy is available for $1. Subscription cost is $15 for 4 issues.

Payment: Pays in contributor's copies.

Terms: Acquires one time rights.

MURDER & MAYHEM

Established: 1993 • Circulation: 1,000 • Published: 6 times a year • Number of Pages: 44 • Size: 8½ × 11

Fiske and Elly-Ann Miles, Editors

CATEGORIES
Essays/Articles, Mystery News, New Bookstores, Overseas Reports,
Convention Listings

"Our most pressing needs are reviews and well-researched articles on mystery topics," say Fiske and Elly-Ann Miles. "Reviewers should avoid plot summary and concentrate on objective analysis and criticism. Include published clips or writing samples with query. We place a premium on skilled writing. We do not publish freelance interviews."

Address: P.O. Box 415024, Kansas City, MO 64141

How To Contact: Nonfiction should be sent to Fiske or Elly-Ann Miles, Editors. Send a business-sized SASE to obtain writing guidelines. Comments on rejected manuscripts. Responds to author submissions in 4 weeks. Manuscripts are published 3-6 months after acceptance. Submissions on diskette should be formatted for MS DOS, WordPerfect or MS Word. 100% of magazine is mystery/crime nonfiction. A sample copy is available for $3.50. Subscription cost is $15 for 6 issues.

Terms: Acquires first North American serial rights.

MURDER CAN BE FUN

Established: 1986 • Circulation: 4,000 • Published: Biannually • Number of Pages: 32 • Size: 5½ × 8½

John Marr, Editor

CATEGORIES
Essays/Articles, True Crime

Address: P.O. Box 640111, San Francisco, CA 94164

Phone: (415)775-8534

How To Contact: Nonfiction should be sent to John Marr, Editor. Make initial contact by sending query with SASE. Send a business-sized SASE to obtain writing guidelines. Receives 5 unsolicited nonfiction submissions per month. Purchases 1 nonfiction manuscript per issue. Responds to author submissions in 4-6 weeks. Manuscripts are published 6 months after acceptance. Preferred length for nonfiction manuscripts is 2,500 words. Will print reprints. 35% of magazine is mystery/crime nonfiction. A sample copy is available for $2. Subscription cost is $5 for 2 issues.

Terms: Acquires all serial rights.

☀ ☀ ☀ ☀

MURDEROUS INTENT: A MAGAZINE OF MYSTERY & SUSPENSE

Established: 1994 • Circulation: 4,500 • Published: Quarterly • Number of Pages: 64 • Size: 8½×11

Margo Power, Editor

CATEGORIES
Interviews, Poetry, Short Fillers

"We have an eclectic mix of nonfiction articles and fiction of interest to both writers and readers of mystery. We're stretching the boundaries."

Address: P.O. Box 5947, Vancouver, WA 98668-5947
Phone: (360)695-9004
Fax: (360)695-9004
How To Contact: Nonfiction should be sent to Margo Power, Editor. Make initial contact by sending query for nonfiction and complete manuscript and cover letter for fiction. Send a business-sized SASE to obtain writing guidelines. Receives 5-6 unsolicited nonfiction submissions per month. Purchases 2-4 nonfiction manuscripts per issue. Occasionally comments on rejected manuscripts. Responds to author submissions in 2-3 months. Manuscripts are published 4-12 months after acceptance. Preferred length for nonfiction manuscripts is 2,000-4,000 words. Allows simultaneous submissions. Will occasionally print reprints. Electronic submissions should be sent to madison@teleport.com. 20% of magazine is mystery/crime nonfiction. A sample copy is available for $3.95 + 5 first class stamps. Subscription cost is $15 for 4 issues.
Payment: Pays approximately $10 plus 2 contributor's copies.
Terms: Acquires first North American serial rights.

☀ ☀ ☀ ☀

MYSTERY FORUM MAGAZINE

Established: 1992 • Circulation: 600+ • Published: 6 times a year • Number of Pages: 48 • Size: 8½×11

Bob Myers, Editor

CATEGORIES
Interviews, Essays, Film Reviews, Mystery News, New Bookstores

Address: 16503 3rd St. North, Independence, MO 64056
Phone: (816)257-0011
How To Contact: Nonfiction should be sent to Bob Myers, Editor. Make initial contact by sending cover letter with short biography and manuscript. Send a business-sized SASE to obtain writing guidelines. Receives 1-2 unsolicited nonfiction submissions per month. Purchases 2 nonfiction manuscripts per issue. Occasionally comments on rejected manuscripts. Responds to author submissions in 60 days. Manuscripts are published 2-6 months after acceptance. Preferred length for nonfiction manuscripts is 2,000-5,000 words. Allows simultaneous submissions. Will print reprints. Submissions on diskette should be formatted for WordPerfect, MS Word or ASCII. 50% of magazine is mystery/crime nonfiction. A sample copy is available for $6. Subscription cost is $18 for 6 issues.
Payment: Pays approximately $30 per story or article.
Terms: Acquires first North American and reprint rights.

MYSTERY READERS JOURNAL

Established: 1984 • Circulation: 2,500 • Published: Quarterly • Number of Pages: 80 • Size: 8½ × 7

Janet A. Rudolph, Editor

CATEGORIES
Interviews, Essays, Mystery News, New Bookstores, Overseas Reports, Convention Listings

"Our publication is unique because it's thematic in content and we review books both in and out of print."

Address: P.O. Box 8116, Berkeley, CA 94707
Phone: (510)339-2800
Fax: (510)339-8309

How To Contact: Nonfiction should be sent to Janet A. Rudolph, Editor. Make initial contact by sending cover letter. Send a business-sized SASE to obtain writing guidelines. Publishes 15-20 nonfiction manuscripts per issue. Occasionally comments on rejected manuscripts. Responds to author submissions in 1 month. Preferred length for nonfiction manuscripts is 1,000-5,000 words. Submissions on diskette should be formatted for Mac 3.5 disk. 100% of magazine is mystery/crime nonfiction. A sample copy is available for $7. Subscription cost is $24 for 4 issues.
Payment: Pays one contributor's copy.

MYSTERY SCENE

Established: 1985 • Circulation: 5,700 • Published: Bimonthly • Number of Pages: 72 • Size: 8½ × 11

Ed and Joe Gorman, Editors

CATEGORIES
Interviews, Essays, Book Reviews, Film Reviews, New Bookstores, Software Reviews, Overseas Reports, Convention Listings, Market Listings

"One of the most competent reviewers is Jon Breen of Ellery Queen Mystery Magazine. Study him for his precision. He's able to give you the story, the theme, the flavor of the book, and his opinion—all very cogently in 50-75 words. We are the news magazine of the mystery field. We reflect the concerns and interests of the professional mystery writer. We've recently featured interviews with Joan Hess, Carolyn Hart, Sue Grafton, Robert Crais, Nicholas Freeling, Lawrence Block, Dean Koontz and Ed McBain."

Address: P.O. Box 669, Cedar Rapids, IA 52406-0669

Fax: (319)363-9895

How To Contact: Nonfiction should be sent to Ed Gorman, Editorial Director. Make initial contact by sending or faxing a query letter. Send a business-sized SASE to obtain writing guidelines. Purchases 10 nonfiction manuscripts per issue. Responds to author queries in 1 week. Allows simultaneous submissions. Will print reprints. Submissions on diskette should be formatted in ASCII on 3.5 disk IBM or MAC. 100% of magazine is mystery/crime nonfiction. A sample copy is available for $1.50. Subscription cost is $35 for 6 issues.

Payment: Pays approximately 1-2¢ a word.

Terms: Acquires first rights.

NAKED KISS

Established: 1994 • Circulation: 600-700 • Published: Quarterly • Number of Pages: 48 • Size: 8½×11

Wayne A. Harold, Editor

CATEGORIES
Interviews, Essays, Film Reviews

Address: 3160 Brady Lake Rd., Ravenna, OH 44266

How To Contact: Nonfiction should be sent to Wayne A. Harold, Editor. Make initial contact by sending manuscript with cover letter and return postage. Send a business-sized SASE to obtain writing guidelines. Receives 2-3 unsolicited nonfiction submissions per month. Purchases 1-2 nonfiction manuscripts per issue. Occasionally comments on rejected manuscripts. Responds to author submissions in 1-3 months. Manuscripts are published 12-24 months after acceptance. Preferred length for nonfiction manuscripts is 1,000-3,000 words. Allows simultaneous submissions. Submissions on diskette should be formatted for either Mac or IBM (3.5 disk). Electronic submissions should be sent to NakedKissm@aol.com. 10% of magazine is mystery/crime nonfiction. A sample copy is available for $5. Subscription cost is $20 for 4 issues.

Payment: Pays approximately $5-30 per article.

Terms: Acquires first world serial rights.

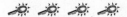

NEW MYSTERY MAGAZINE

Established: 1989 • Circulation: 90,000 • Published: Quarterly • Number of Pages: 96 • Size: 8½ × 11

Charles Raisch, Editor

CATEGORIES
Film Reviews, New Bookstores

Address: 175 5th Ave., #2001 The Flat Iron Bldg., New York, NY 10010
Fax: (212)452-6054
How To Contact: Nonfiction should be sent to Charles Raisch, Editor. Make initial contact by sending complete manuscript. To obtain writing guidelines send a 9 × 12 SASE w/ $1.24 postage. Receives 50 unsolicited nonfiction submissions per month. Purchases 10-20 nonfiction manuscripts per issue. Occasionally comments on rejected manuscripts. Manuscripts are published 6-12 months after acceptance. Preferred length for nonfiction manuscripts is 500-2,000 words. Submissions on diskette should be formatted for WordPerfect 5.1 (IBM). 10% of magazine is mystery/crime nonfiction. A sample copy is available for $7 with SASE. Subscription cost is $27.77 for 4 issues.
Payment: Pays approximately $50-1,000 per story.

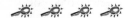

NOIR

Established: 1994 • Circulation: 4,000-5,000 • Published: Quarterly • Number of Pages: 64 • Size: comic book

Christopher Mills, Editor

CATEGORIES
Interviews, Film Reviews, Retrospectives

Address: 559 N.E. 46th St. #201, Boca Raton, FL 33431
Phone: (407)368-7497
How To Contact: Nonfiction should be sent to Christopher Mills, Editor. Make initial contact by sending manuscript. Send a business-sized

SASE to obtain writing guidelines. Purchases 1-2 nonfiction manuscripts per issue. Occasionally comments on rejected manuscripts. Responds to author submissions in 1 month. Manuscripts are published 3-12 months after acceptance. Preferred length for nonfiction manuscripts is less than 2,000 words. Allows simultaneous submissions. 30% of magazine is mystery/crime nonfiction. A sample copy is available for $4.95.

Payment: Pays approximately .03¢ a word.

Terms: Acquires first North American serial rights.

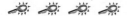

OVER MY DEAD BODY! THE MYSTERY MAGAZINE

Established: 1993 • Circulation: 1,000 • Published: Quarterly • Number of Pages: 68 • Size: 8½ × 11

Cherie Jung, Editor

CATEGORIES
Interviews, Essays, Film Reviews, Mystery News, Profiles

Over My Dead Body recently has published E.W. Count, Joanne Pence, Fred Hunter and Jeffrey Marks.

Address: P.O. Box 1778, Auburn, WA 98071-1778

Phone: (206)473-4650

How To Contact: Nonfiction should be sent to Cherie Jung, Features Editor. Make initial contact by sending complete manuscript or query for nonfiction. Send a business-sized SASE to obtain writing guidelines. Receives 15 unsolicited nonfiction submissions per month. Purchases 5-10 nonfiction manuscripts per issue. Occasionally comments on rejected manuscripts. Responds to author submissions in 6-12 weeks. Manuscripts are published 6-24 months after acceptance. Preferred length for nonfiction manuscripts is 1,500-2,500 words. Allows simultaneous submissions. Submissions on diskette should be formatted for WordPerfect 5.1; prefers ASCII. Electronic submissions should be sent to omdb@aol.com. 50% of magazine is mystery/crime nonfiction. A sample copy is available for $5. Subscription cost is $12 for 4 issues.

Payment: Pays approximately 1¢ a word fiction; $10-25 an article nonfiction.

Terms: Acquires first North American rights.

PLAYBOY MAGAZINE

Established: 1953 • Circulation: 3.7 million • Published: Monthly • Number of Pages: 162 • Size: 8½ × 11

Alice Turner, Editor

CATEGORIES
Interviews, Overseas Reports

Address: 690 N. Lakeshore Dr., Chicago, IL 60611
Phone: (312)751-8000
How To Contact: Nonfiction should be sent to Peter Moore, Senior Articles Editor. Send a business-sized SASE to obtain writing guidelines. Responds in 6-8 weeks. Manuscripts are published 3-6 months after acceptance. Allows simultaneous submissions. Will print reprints. A sample copy is available for $4.95. Subscription cost is $29.97 for 12 issues.

Terms: Acquires first North American serial rights.

REAL CRIME BOOK DIGEST

Established: 1992 • Circulation: 10,000 • Published: Quarterly • Number of Pages: 40 • Size: 8 × 10

Jim Agnew, Editor

CATEGORIES
Interviews, Essays

Address: 1017 W. Wilson Ave., Chicago, IL 60640
Phone: (800)536-8205
Fax: (312)878-9415
How To Contact: Nonfiction should be sent to Jim Agnew, Editor. Send a

business-sized SASE to obtain writing guidelines. Responds to author submissions in 2 weeks. Preferred length for nonfiction manuscripts is 1,000 words. A sample copy is available for $2.95. Subscription cost is $15 for 4 issues.

Terms: Acquires one time rights.

Cover: Richard Valley

SCARLET STREET

Established: 1991 • Circulation: 25,000 • Published: Quarterly • Number of Pages: 100+ • Size: 8×10

Jessie Lilley, Publisher

CATEGORIES
Interviews, Essays/Articles

"We discuss mystery and horror on film, t.v., in books, and in music. We are not a 'true crime' book or fiction magazine. We are an entertainment magazine. *Scarlet Street* is the only one of its kind. Be willing to write for no fee. Also read the magazine before submitting. See what *Scarlet Street* is all about. *Scarlet Street* has recently published Gregory William Mank, Bill Palmer, Tony Earnshaw, Deborah Del Vecchio, Tom Weaver, Ross Care, John Brunas, Michael Brunas, Richard Valley and David Stuart Davies. Check out issue no. 16; Greg Mank's piece on Dwight Frye is super. Greg has a flair for researching lives—just what we like here. We want information we've never seen published anywhere before."

Address: P.O. Box 604, Glen Rock, NJ 07452
Phone: (201)346-9225
Fax: (201)346-9226

How To Contact: Nonfiction should be sent to Richard Valley, Editor-in-Chief. Make initial contact by sending a writing sample. Send a business-sized SASE to obtain writing guidelines. Receives 10 unsolicited nonfiction submissions per month. Purchases 2 nonfiction manuscripts per issue. Occasionally comments on rejected manuscripts. Responds to author submissions in 1-2 months. Manuscripts are published 1-2 years after acceptance. Preferred length for nonfiction manuscripts is 500-3,000 words. Will print reprints. A sample copy is available for $5.95 plus $2 postage. Subscription cost is $20 for 4 issues.

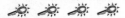

SHERLOCKIAN TIDBITS

Established: 1988 • Circulation: 220 • Published: Quarterly • Number of Pages: 14 • Size: 8½ × 11

Arnold Korotkin, Editor

CATEGORIES
Sherlockiana

Only interested in Sherlock Holmes and the Victorian era.

Address: 42 Melrose Place, Montclair, NJ 07042
Phone: (201)783-1463
How To Contact: Make initial contact by writing. Send a business-sized SASE to obtain writing guidelines. Comments on rejected manuscripts. Responds to author submissions in 6-8 weeks. Manuscripts are published 1 year after acceptance. Allows simultaneous submissions. Will print reprints. A sample copy is available for $2.
Payment: Pays approximately $75-100.

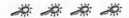

SNAKE RIVER REFLECTIONS

Established: 1990 • Circulation: 200 • Published: 10 times a year • Number of Pages: 10-12 • Size: 5½ × 8½

Bill White, Editor

Address: 1863 Bitterroot Dr., Twin Falls, ID 83301

Phone: (208)734-0746

How To Contact: Nonfiction should be sent to Bill White, Editor. Send a business-sized SASE to obtain writing guidelines. Receives 5-10 unsolicited nonfiction submissions per month. Occasionally comments on rejected manuscripts. Responds to author submissions in 3 weeks. Manuscripts are published 1 month after acceptance. Will print reprints. Electronic submissions should be sent to WJAN@AOL.com. 40% of magazine is mystery/crime nonfiction. Subscription cost is $7.50 for 10 issues.

Payment: Pays one contributor's copy.

Terms: Acquires first rights.

TRUE DETECTIVE

Established: 1924 • Circulation: 100,000 • Published: 7 times a year • Number of Pages: 74 • Size: 8 × 10

Rose Mandelsberg, Editor-in-Chief

Address: 460 W. 34th St., New York, NY 10001

Phone: (212)947-6500

Fax: (212)947-6727

How To Contact: Nonfiction should be sent to Rose Mandelsberg, Editor-in-Chief. Make initial contact by query letter. Send an oversized SASE to obtain writing guidelines. Receives 5 unsolicited nonfiction submissions per month. Purchases 9 nonfiction manuscripts per issue. Comments on rejected manuscripts. Preferred length for nonfiction manuscripts is 5,000 words. 100% of magazine is mystery/crime nonfiction. A sample copy is available for $2.95. Subscription cost is $11.97 for

7 issues.

Payment: Pays approximately $250 for 5,000 words, $500 for 10,000.

Terms: Acquires first North American serial rights.

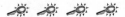

TUCUMCARI LITERARY REVIEW

Established: 1988 • Circulation: 150 • Published: Bimonthly • Number of Pages: 42 • Size: 5½ × 8½

Troxey Kemper, Editor

> **CATEGORIES**
> Essays, Poetry, Nostalgia, Vignettes, Opinion

"We'll take whatever comes in the mail if it is good, interesting and less than 1,200 words."

Address: 3108 W. Bellevue Ave., Los Angeles, CA 90026

How To Contact: Nonfiction should be sent to Troxey Kemper, Editor. Send a business-sized SASE to obtain writing guidelines. Receives 10 unsolicited nonfiction submissions per month. Purchases 2 nonfiction manuscripts per issue. Usually comments on rejected manuscripts. Responds to author submissions in 1 week. Manuscripts usually are published 2 months after acceptance. Preferred length for nonfiction manuscripts is 1,200 words or less. Allows simultaneous submissions. Will print reprints. A sample copy is available for $2. Subscription cost is $12 for 6 issues.

Payment: Pays one contributor's copy.

Terms: Acquires one time rights.

WHITECHAPEL GAZETTE

Established: 1993 • Circulation: 100-150 • Published: 3 times a year • Number of Pages: 60 • Size: 8½ × 11

Troy and Alexandra Taylor, Editors

CATEGORIES
Interviews, Essays, Film Reviews, Overseas Reports, Convention Listings, Sherlock Holmes

"We're strictly Sherlock Holmes/Sir Arthur Conan Doyle and we do nonfiction pieces on the Victorian Era. We'd like to see more nonfiction Sherlock Holmes pieces. We are a magazine for everybody. You don't have to be a scholar to enjoy our magazine. We do Basil Rathbone films, too, so we're in this for anyone with an interest in Sherlock Holmes. Stay away from overly scholarly pieces. We don't do footnotes—if you can't say it in the article then we don't want it."

Address: 805 West North St., Decatur, IL 62522
Phone: (217)422-7567
Fax: (217)877-9211
How To Contact: Make initial contact by submitting complete manuscript. Send a business-sized SASE to obtain writing guidelines. Purchases 3 nonfiction manuscripts per issue. Comments on rejected manuscripts. Responds to author submissions in 2 weeks. Manuscripts are published 3-6 months after acceptance. 75% of magazine is mystery/crime nonfiction. A sample copy is available for $6.50. Subscription cost is $18 for 3 issues.
Payment: Pays in contributor's copy.
Terms: Acquires one time rights.

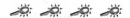

ULTIMATE WRITER MAGAZINE

Established: 1986 • Circulation: 800 • Published: Monthly • Number of Pages: 40-50 • Size: 8½ × 11

Perry Terrell, Editor

CATEGORIES
Essays, Poetry, Advice Columns, Convention Listings, Market Listings

Address: 4104 Alabama Ave. #8, Kenner, LA 70065
Phone: (504)465-9412

How To Contact: Nonfiction should be sent to Perry Terrell, Editor. Make initial contact by calling or sending manuscript with SASE. Send a business-sized SASE to obtain writing guidelines. Occasionally comments on rejected manuscripts. Responds to author submissions in 4-6 months. Manuscripts are published 4-6 months after acceptance. Preferred length for nonfiction manuscripts is 1,500-2,000 words. Allows simultaneous submissions. Will print reprints. Submissions on diskette should be formatted for WordPerfect. A sample copy is available for $3.75. Subscription cost is $27 for 12 issues.
Terms: Acquires one time rights.

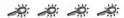

WRITING WRITERS MAGAZINE

Established: 1992 • Circulation: 1,000 • Published: Monthly • Number of Pages: 36 • Size: Tabloid

Dorothy Cagle, Editor

CATEGORIES
Interviews, Essays, Poetry

Address: 786 Birch St., Paradise, CA 95969
How To Contact: Make initial contact by sending cover letter with SASE. Send a business-sized SASE to obtain writing guidelines. Receives 2-3 unsolicited nonfiction submissions per month. Comments on rejected manuscripts. Responds to author submissions in 1 month. Allows simultaneous submissions. Will print reprints. A sample copy is available for $2. Subscription cost is $20.50 for 12 issues.

CANADIAN MAGAZINES

☀ ☀ ☀ ☀

DETECTIVE FILES GROUP

Circulation: 300,000 • Published: Bimonthly • Number of Pages: 68 • Size: 8 × 11

Dominick A. Merle, Editor-in-Chief

CATEGORIES
Real Crime

"We focus on factual accounts of current crimes, told in a Columbo-TV style."

Address: 1350 Sherbrooke St. W., Montreal, Quebec, H3G 2T4
How To Contact: Nonfiction should be sent to Dominick A. Merle, Editor-in-Chief. Make initial contact by sending letter with Int'l Reply Coupons. Receives 25-50 unsolicited nonfiction submissions per month. Purchases 6-8 nonfiction manuscripts per issue. Occasionally comments on rejected manuscripts. Responds to author submissions in 1 month. Manuscripts are published 3-6 months after acceptance. Preferred length for nonfiction manuscripts is 3,500-6,000 words. 100% of magazine is mystery/crime nonfiction. Subscription cost is $17 for 12 issues.
Payment: Pays approximately $250-350 per article.
Terms: Acquires first North American rights.

THE MYSTERY REVIEW

Established: 1992 • Circulation: 4,000 • Published: Quarterly • Number of Pages: 72 • Size: 8½ × 11

Barbara Davey, Editor

CATEGORIES
Interviews, Essays, Film Reviews, Poetry, Mystery News, New Bookstores, Overseas Reports, Convention Listings, Market Listings

"We'd like some word puzzles and more thematic articles of interest to mystery readers. And we'd like articles on true mystery—that is, real-life mysteries that haven't been solved. *Mystery Review* has a very attractive layout and a high quality of writing. We review first time authors and small presses, as well as established authors and major publishers."

Address: P.O. Box 233, Colborne ON K0K 1S0, CANADA
Phone: (613)475-4440
Fax: (613)475-3400
How To Contact: Send a business-sized SASE to obtain writing guidelines. Receives 40 unsolicited nonfiction submissions per quarter. Purchases 12-20 nonfiction manuscripts per issue. Responds to author submissions in 1 month. Manuscripts are published 3-6 months after acceptance. Allows simultaneous submissions. Will print reprints. Submissions on diskette should be formatted in ASCII. Electronic submissions should be sent to 71554.551@compuserve.com. 95% of magazine is mystery/crime nonfiction. A sample copy is available for $5.95. Subscription cost is $20 for 4 issues.
Payment: Pays a nominal fee.
Terms: Acquires all rights.

UNITED KINGDOM MAGAZINES

A SHOT IN THE DARK

Established: 1994 • Circulation: 1,000 • Published: Quarterly • Number of Pages: 64 • Size: 5¾ × 8¼

Bob Cartwright, Editor

CATEGORIES
Interviews, Essays, Mystery News, New Bookstores, Advice Columns, Overseas Reports

---

Address: 32 High St. Bonsall, Matlock, Derbyshire, DE4 2AR, UK
Phone: (062)982-2702
How To Contact: Make initial contact by writing. Receives 5-6 unsolicited nonfiction submissions per month. Comments on rejected manuscripts. Responds to author submissions in 2 weeks. Preferred length for nonfiction manuscripts is 500-2,500 words. Will print reprints. Submissions on diskette should be formatted for Quark DTP. 95% of magazine is mystery/crime nonfiction. Subscription cost is $15 US for 4 issues.

FINDING AN AGENT

How to Find, and Keep, a Top-Notch Mystery Agent

DONALD MAASS

Ask any experienced mystery writer and they will tell you: A good agent can do wonders for your career; a bad agent can really screw it up.

Choosing and working with an agent—the right agent—is clearly important. So where are the courses on this subject? Not in any school that I know about. Most authors learn by trial and error. Once that may have been safe enough, but in the cold, numbers-driven marketplace of the 1990s, early errors can be fatal. I know. My agency gets calls every week from authors whose careers have crashed.

These authors give many reasons for their trouble: low advances, no support, poor covers, orphaned books, etc. The thing is, these problems are routine. Every author faces them, if not sooner, then later. They need not be fatal. All you need is a trusty Sherpa. A good agent. Here's how to find, and keep, yours.

The Search and How It Feels

If you are a new author, the first thing to realize is that you probably feel anxious. Oh, there may be good moments, particularly when you are writing; moments when you feel confident that your work is equal to, or better than, anything out there.

Then there are the bad moments when you remember what you've heard about the odds, slush piles, agents. Maybe you have heard that it is easier to get a contract than to get an agent. Or that without an agent no decent publisher will touch you.

The truth, here, is that you have a choice. Of agents. You may not feel like it, but you do. Understanding that, believing it, is your first challenge. To help you, here are three common feelings that block the empowerment I am talking about. See if any apply to you:

1. *This book is my baby!* Sure it is. You conceived it, grew it, disciplined it. You don't want to let it go. You probably also fear that no one will ever fully appreciate its many qualities.

If this is you, you are sharing a common experience. A lingering emotional attachment to your novel is normal. So is its opposite: finishing it and finding that you hate it. Both are flip sides of the same coin. You've invested a lot in this. It matters.

But you can't sell a baby. You can't even be objective about it. And if you can't be objective about your novel, then how will you be able to evaluate what you hear about it from agents?

2. *What does it matter?* No one's going to want it anyway. You are no fool. You know the score. If you are extremely lucky you might land a decent agent but the odds are against it, right?

If this describes you, you are also having a common experience. Offering your work in the marketplace is risky. The chances of getting hurt—even humiliated—are high. The easiest way to lessen the pain of rejection is to plan for it.

The problem with this defense mechanism is that it leads authors to feel that the process is out of their hands. Why discriminate? Why push? Why feel anything but shock and joy when some randomly-chosen agent finally says "yes." No reason. And so begins many a woeful and tragic publishing tale.

3. *I don't know where to begin.* "Help! There's too much information! All these lists! How do I know which agency would be best?"

There's no panic worse than the panic of beginning a scary task. One way to cope is to put it off. Another is to rush. Witness: Quite often when I respond positively to a query letter, I get back a hurried note: "Disk crashed. I'll send the manuscript next week." Or: "Final revisions in progress. You'll have it in a month."

Final revisions. Probably that means "first draft." Either way, this author rushed. He wrote to me before his novel was ready. Why? He was under-confident, anxious for validation. He could not wait to find out if I would be interested. As a result, the novel that I finally read is going to be less than completely done.

That's a shame, because all that stuff about the odds is correct. The odds are long. To calm these fears and avoid mistakes let's break the agent hunt into its components and find out what really works.

When to Look

First ask, "Do I need to look at all?" That is, as a new author do you really need an agent? Opinions differ. Most professional mystery authors have agents, but it is often said that first timers will not get a noticeably better deal if they are represented.

That is true to a point. With few exceptions advances for first mystery novels are low. An agent may get you a few thousand dollars more up front, yes, but why pay a commission when royalties eventually close the gap anyway? What's the difference?

The difference shows in a couple of ways. First, because many major publishers will not read unagented manuscripts, an agent can open doors. Even more important, a savvy agent who knows individual editors' tastes and publishing houses' relative strengths can be an effective matchmaker, pairing your work with the company best able to make that work a success.

There are also contracts to consider: Advance levels, royalty rates, copyright, options and control of subsidiary rights are all vital issues in which a new author can benefit from an agent's expertise. Take, for instance, the right to publish your novel in German. The unagented author typically cedes control to his publisher, who typically keeps 50% of the proceeds from licensing this right. On a first novel deal, most agents like to retain control. The cost to the author thus drops to 20-25%. More money for you.

How much more? Maybe not much but, hey, money is money. In addition, there's the matter of marketing. One first mystery in a catalog of hundreds of books is not likely to get much help from its publisher. To an agent small subsidiary rights sales matter more.

Okay, let's assume you're convinced. When should you approach agents? Before you start to write? After you've sold a few stories? When you've finished your first novel? When you've got a publisher interested in it; perhaps even an offer on the table?

Working backwards through those options, it should be obvious that approaching agents with an offer in hand is going to produce powerful results. Agents are drawn to commissions like bees to honey. If this is your situation, expect to hear some highly flattering buzz about your writing.

But how deep is that enthusiasm? To find out you will have to listen hard and cut through much self-serving PR. It is wise to begin this scenario with a strong idea of what you want in an agent.

Most authors do not wait so long. Of the 3,000 query letters I receive each year—a relatively modest amount, by the way—most come from writers who have finished a novel. But must you necessarily have completed a manuscript to make contact?

No, but the truth is that it is difficult to the point of impossible to sell a first novel that is not finished. (These days it can even be difficult to move an *established* author from one house to another with only a partial manuscript to show.) Hence, for me there is little point in reading an unfinished manuscript by a first time novelist. Authors with a sales history—particularly a good one—are a different matter.

Short story sales are useful credits to have. Sales to *Ellery Queen's* or *Alfred Hitchcock's* never fail to catch my eye. In and of themselves such credits don't guarantee a brilliant novel. Nor does their absence necessarily mean anything bad. But they do suggest that an author is on the road to being a full time professional. Sell some short stories if you can. It helps.

Last word: The time *not* to contact an agent is before you have written any fiction at all. Unless you are a big name celebrity. (If you are, call. We'll talk.)

Where to Look

This is the easy part. In the pages that follow is an excellent sourcelist of mystery agents. There are excellent general sourcebooks around, too. Check the reference section of your local bookstore.

Still, even in-depth profiles can leave you feeling lost. What happens if your top choices turn you down? What if (happy day!) several agencies want you? On what basis will you choose? Is it possible to know—really *know*—what you are getting into?

To distinguish one agency from another, you must first give yourself permission to gather information. It is true that agents, especially the top ones, are busy folks. They guard their time. Breaking through that barrier can be tough.

Oddly enough, some authors, I find, actually enjoy being seduced by the aura of power and secrecy that surrounds agents. This sort of author does not want to know how agents do their work. They are romantics. They would rather believe in magic.

Still, as an author you are a consumer. And the service you will be buying is quite expensive. You have the right to information, but if you want it you may have to look beyond sourcebooks. One good way to start is to join the *Mystery Writers of America*. This excellent group's national and regional newsletters are helpful. Agents' names, clients and recent sales often turn up in their pages. So do interviews with agents.

To develop a more refined feel for agents' styles and effectiveness, talk to their clients. Here, both MWA events and mystery writers' conventions can be helpful. The bar at the Bouchercon hotel is a great place to hear candid talk about agents. (Be discerning, though: Honest assessments are one thing, gossip is another.) Going online is another option. Network around.

Your goal is to learn not merely who handles who, or which agents are looking for what. You need a sense of agents as people. It is often said that the author-agent relationship is like a marriage. How true! Not only does it involve trust and respect, it also involves getting to know your partner painfully well.

Recognize that you will probably work with your agent for a long time. You owe it to yourself to choose one you like and enjoy; one who lets you feel free. Freedom is the foundation of creative growth.

How to Connect

How to approach an agent? How do you approach anyone? You can do it in person, on the phone, by letter, by fax, by e-mail. Sourcebooks like this one tell you how individual agents prefer to be pitched, but really there are no absolute rules except common sense.

Speaking of common sense, consider how you introduce yourself to someone at a party: Unless you are uncommonly bold, or insensitive, I'll bet you do not march up to total strangers and announce, "Greetings! Here's why you are dying to be my friend . . ."

A pushy manner is off-putting. Amazingly, it is also the most common tone in query letters. I'm not kidding! You'd be astonished how often I receive letters that sound something like this:

Dear Mr. Maass:
    This is your lucky day! I have carefully analyzed the techniques of such bestselling authors such as Stephen King, Jeffrey Archer and John Grisham. As a result I can guarantee you that my terrifying

apocalyptic thriller, GENE POOL-UTION, is a slam-bang page turner that no reader will be able to put down.

In fact, 20 test readers have already confirmed the GENE POOL-UTION was the most frightening reading experience of their lives. Ripped right out of today's headlines, this novel cannot miss. Believe me, you will long remember the day when you rushed to the phone to request my manuscript, etc.

This hard sell disappoints most in that it insists upon making up my mind for me. Test readers? I am sure they genuinely loved his novel, but unless they work in publishing they are unlikely to be able to judge accurately its potential. (And frankly I already have my qualms: DNA-doom thrillers are quite difficult to pull off, Michael Crichton notwithstanding.)

So, if the hard sell is no fun at parties or in query letters, why do authors fall back on it? Insecurity is one big reason, I believe. Another is the advice that authors too often find in writers' magazines; articles that say things like: *You've got to sell yourself! You must show that you understand the market! Get their attention and don't let it go!*

Don't get me wrong: I like authors who know what they have got. Spelling that out for me briefly and knowledgeably is not pushy. It is a plus. But that is far different than the hard sell.

However you approach an agent—in person, by phone, by letter—a relaxed-but-businesslike approach is probably the best. The most effective pitches I get start with an icebreaker: "I notice that you represent Anne Perry, whose mysteries I admire." Or, "My friend Dean Koontz gave me your name." Or even, "I believe that fans of Walter Mosley will enjoy my work, too."

It is easy to overdo comparisons like that last one, but you see my point: There's a real person on the other side of your pitch, and he is not a used-car salesman. He (or she) is a book person. Treat him like a sensitive, intelligent publishing professional and you will be far ahead of the game.

Now, let's get specific. *Should you drop by?* Meetings take time, and besides what is there to talk about until I have read your writing? *Should you phone?* There is not much point unless you have an "in," such as an *in*troduction from a professional to use. *Should you fax?* Faxing is fast. It begs a fast response from someone whose time is already crunched. *Should you write?* You are a writer. Need I say more than that?

More specific still: *Should you send an outline with your query?* If a listing suggests it, yes. If not then it depends on whether you can write an effective synopsis. If so, go for it. If not, stick with a tantalizing capsule description in your letter. *Should you go ahead and send the manuscript?* It takes much longer to read a book than a letter. Do you really want your novel to languish on a slush pile, miles behind the manuscripts that were requested?

Protocol questions: *Is it okay to write/submit to more than one agent at a time?* Yes, but it is also polite to let your prospects know what you are doing. Besides, if they know the heat is on they may get back to you more quickly. *What if an agent demands to have my novel exclusively?* Well, it is up to you. Are you significantly more interested in that agent than in others? What if that agent says, "yes"? Will you really keep looking?

Reading Fees

A brief word about reading fees: Reputable agents generally do not charge them, not even nominal fees to cover handling. In fact, the Cannon of Ethics of the AAR (Association of Authors Representatives) allows reading fees only with extensive advance disclosure to the author, and then only until the end of 1995. Following that, reading fees will be banned altogether to member agents.

Certain non-member agents will continue to charge such fees, I am sure. Should you pay them? I do not recommend doing so for mere consideration, though critiques are sometimes offered for your money. Are these worth it? Ask to see a sample critique ahead of time. Also find out who actually will read your manuscript and how long it will take to get their report.

Even then, there are choices other than literary agents if you want to pay for manuscript analysis. There are plenty of freelance editors and editor/rewriters (known in the trade as "book doctors") from whom to choose. Their services may prove more expensive than agents' critiques, but in the long run those services may also prove more beneficial. For names, look in the industry reference book LMP (Literary Market Place) in the section called Editorial Services. Or contact the Editorial Freelancers Association. Be sure you are paying for quality advice.

What to Ask Agents

I hope you enjoy your agent search. For me it is a fascinating dance. Eventually, though, all authors hope to hear the following: "I've read your novel and I love it. I want to represent you." The usual response is delirious joy. Nothing wrong with that, but do take a moment to ask some important questions.

Most urgent question? Not, *"How much do you charge?"* but, *"What do you think of my novel?"* The answer to that one will tell you volumes about the experience you are about to have.

The first thing you want from the answer is enthusiasm. For agents, handling new mystery writers means taking a loss. Commissions do not usually cover the overhead involved in the first few books. Plus, it is a rough road. It can take years to swing that first sale. Even after that, problems may abound.

What sustains an agent through that? I will tell you: passion. By that I mean an irrational faith in a writer's future or at least the conviction that their writing is worthy, even brilliant. You must have that. Without it you are already sunk.

The second thing you need from the answer is a sense of your prospective agent's editorial vocabulary and approach. *Editorial?* Yes. In all likelihood, your agent is going to serve as your first and most long-standing editor. Surprised? I am, too. I used to think that editors edited and agents sold. That's still true, mostly, but as corporate demands sponge up more and more of editors' time, editorial functions are shifting increasingly to agents. Ask your fellow authors.

So, what is good editorial advice? That depends. If you are a facile, outline-handy, trend-watching sort of author then you probably want an agent to tell you how to tailor your fiction to what's hot, what's selling. If, however, you are the slow, style-conscious, trend-ignoring type then you probably want an agent who nurtures your unique voice.

Above all, you want an agent who understands mystery fiction.

That leads to the second most important question: *How much mystery writing do you handle?* You probably already have some idea, but it is useful to know more. Does this agent do a lot of your type of mystery? Exactly how would he or she describe your work?

And that leads to another crucial question: *What plans do you have for marketing my mystery?* The answer had better be detailed and logical.

Today there are many more strategies to choose from than in years past. For instance, once the best possible hardcover deal was always the top objective; not so anymore. Hard/soft deals with large commercial houses are far smarter for many mysteries. Certain others are best served by original paperback publication. What type is yours? And why? Ask.

Okay, now you may ask *"How much do you charge?"* Fifteen percent on domestic revenues has become standard. A trickier issue is whether expenses are charged on top of that, and if so which? Certainly outside legal, public relations and accounting advice need not be covered by commissions. But policies vary widely on things like copying, messengers, phone charges, overseas postage and such. If charged, must you front some money or will the agent foot it? Do you get advance clearance?

Next vital question: *Are you a member of the AAR (Association of Authors Representatives)?* While membership does not guarantee you will get brilliant representation, it does mean that your prospect has met certain minimum performance standards and has signed a Code of Ethics which addresses the handling of funds, the availability of information, confidentiality, expenses, conflicts of interest, reading fees and other issues important to your writing career.

Keep going: *How many people work at your company? How many are agents? Who will actually handle my work? How are overseas sales and movie/TV sales accomplished? Will you consult with me before closing every deal? Will you ever sign agreements (especially subsidiary rights agreements) on my behalf?*

Still more: *Are you incorporated? When you receive money for me, how quickly will you pay out my share? Will you issue a 1099 tax form at the end of the year? What happens if you die or are incapacitated? How will I receive monies due to me?*

Aren't you glad you are asking these questions now? There's one more biggie; so big that it deserves a section of its own.

The Agency Agreement

I use the simplest and most trusting form of contract between me and my clients: a handshake. I do this because unless there is a high level of mutual respect involved I do not feel that we have a useful working relationship. Also, if my clients are unhappy I feel they should be free to leave at any time.

Not everyone is comfortable with that, however. Most agencies have written agreements between themselves and their clients. Review yours before you sign it. What follows is a discussion of some of the most common provisions you will come across:

Commissions. Naturally commission rates are set out for domestic sales, movie/TV sales, overseas sales, special sales. Expenses to be charged and clearance procedures should also be spelled out.

Works covered. Will your agent handle everything you write, down to essays you dash off for your industry trade journal? Or will only specific work be handled? You may want representation only on a per-project basis. If so, establish that in writing.

Duration. Most agency agreements lock you in for a certain length of time. Two years is typical. After that, the agreement is renewed by mutual consent. A highly important aspect of duration is what happens to unsold rights after termination. Does your agent retain control? If so, for how long? Believe me, when agents and authors split no issue causes more grief than this one. Work out something equitable in advance.

For contracts still in force upon termination (that is, for novels still in print and earning) the agent generally continues to receive funds and his commission, as long as earnings continue. The same holds true for ongoing subsidiary rights income, whether the rights were sold by the agent or by the publisher.

One situation that few agency agreements cover is this one: Your agent submits a project to a publisher, but while it is still under consideration you and your agent split. Now an offer appears but who negotiates the deal and collects the commission, your old or your new agent? That's a tricky one, huh?

Generally ad hoc arrangements are made in these cases. Perhaps the new agent approves the deal, but does not get a commission. Or perhaps the new agent does the deal and splits the commission with the old agent. Whatever the arrangement, be sure you feel comfortable with the way the deal will be handled.

Working with Your Agent

Phew! You made it! Now you and your agent are off and running. What now? How much feedback can you expect? How often should you call?

If you have chosen well, you are probably paired with an agent whose experience, temperament and business style are well suited to your needs. But even author-agent relationships have a honeymoon; after that comes the bumpy breaking-in period.

The important thing here is to accurately identify what you need and communicate it clearly to your agent. That is not always easy. It can be tough to separate, say, a need for reporting on submissions from feelings of anxiety if a novel is not selling. Here you must know yourself. And your agent. Be patient.

One thing that helps, I find, is a career plan. You know that old job interview ploy, "Where do you want to be in five years?" That is a good question for you and your agent to ask. What are your career goals? How will you get there? What specific steps are needed?

A career plan is especially important if you intend to, or already, write more than one type of novel. It is not unusual for mystery authors, in particular, to write more than one series. Is that best done under a pseudonym? Should you stick with your first publisher for both series, or put the new eggs in another basket? Work this stuff out with your agent.

I also find that a career plan gives both me and my clients a way to measure progress. In fact, recently I have begun making up advance *marketing* plans for individual projects. Together with new clients I choose potential publishers. We then follow our progress through the list, adjusting as circumstances change. A sense of participation is healthy.

About calling . . . no one likes to be a pest, but at the same time waiting for news can be depressing. How often should you call? I advise my clients to phone any time they feel a need for information. Some call every few days. A few call twice a year.

As you go forward, you will probably come to rely more and more on your agent for advice and counsel. Some of this is mere "hand-holding" while waiting for offers, contracts, checks. However, some of the comments you hear may change the way you write. Some may even change the entire direction of your career.

Given clear goals, hard work, good communication and a bit of luck the author-agent relationship is usually happy and mutually profitable. Sometimes, though, it does not work out so well. I hate to drop clients. On occasion they leave, and that hurts, too.

Let us examine the first scenario: Being dropped by your agent; or, more usefully, how *not* to be dropped by your agent.

Keeping Your Agent

Oddly enough, I think the key here lies not so much in your relationship with your agent as in your relationship with your writing. Marriages can go stale. So can friendships. So can your engagement with your own fiction, if you do not strive to keep it fresh.

I am talking about growth. Getting better. Taking joy in your strengthening command of mystery technique. The occasional creative plateau will not hold you back, but laziness and/or ego will. There is nothing sadder than an author who thinks that he, or she, knows it all. Such authors do not usually last.

One curse upon creative vigor is anxiety. It can derive from early success, which is daunting to maintain, or from financial pressure, common among authors who have gone full time too soon. Whatever the cause, if the result is writer's block then it can be years before the author's career gets back on track. In such cases I am usually slow to cast a client adrift.

Speaking of creative problems, there is another that often besets mystery writers: weariness with a series. Arthur Conan Doyle got sick of Sherlock Holmes, so why shouldn't you get sick of *your* detective? It will probably happen at some point. When it does you will probably feel pressure to keep everything status quo. And why not? If you have come to this point then the series is undoubtedly successful. So what should you do?

The solutions are as varied as the writers who devise them. Some authors start a second series. Others develop other types of fiction. Still others drink (which I do not suggest). Whatever your solution, stay fresh. If it makes sense, your agent will support your diversification and help you strike a balance between your bread-and-butter mystery writing and your developmental work.

Stay alive, grow, and more likely than not your agent will happily keep you. But what if you do not want to keep your agent? Some thoughts follow.

Moving On

How do you know when it is time to leave your agent? Boy, that is a tough one. Having taken over many authors from other agencies, I can tell you that the level of problems authors experience varies. Some problems are slight, but of long-standing. Others are so sudden and big that it boggles the mind.

One factor that remains constant, though, is this: Leaving your agent sheds light on your own shortcomings as well as your agent's. Smart authors use this opportunity to examine themselves and their writing.

But back to the first question: How do you know? Breakdown of communication is one warning sign. Do your calls go unreturned? Is there no follow-through on routine requests? If so, examine the situation. Are you being unreasonable? Are there differences or disagreements causing bad feelings?

Lack of progress is another worry, but again it is wise to study the situation before making any moves. Say that your advances have hit a plateau: Is this your agent's fault or yours? Maybe your *writing* has hit a plateau. If your sales are not growing either and your publisher is not at fault, well . . . perhaps it is time to take an objective look at your storytelling.

Certainly there are problems for which only your agent is to blame. Blown deals. Lost manuscripts. Misunderstandings with your publisher. That kind of thing is just bad business. Even here, though, I advise caution: Are there mitigating circumstances? Did your agent's spouse recently die? Is he facing surgery?

Once you do decide to move on, try to maintain a businesslike demeanor. You will thank yourself later. Dignity is a precious possession.

And when you hook up with your new agent? Well, you begin a new honeymoon. And soon thereafter, the bumpy part. But if you have taken my advice you will have learned a lot about yourself during the divorce. And that self-knowledge should serve you well as you stride toward new levels of success.

The Ultimate Transaction

I hope that all this talk of agents has left you feeling empowered. There is, however, one relationship that is more important to a mystery writer's career than any other: his relationship with his readers.

When you publish your first novel you invite readers into your imaginary world. If you have painted it well, they will probably return. Think of it as opening a store: Your fans are your repeat customers. They are the foundation under your career. Give them good value, reopen your store on a reliable schedule, and they will eventually make you successful beyond your dreams.

Remember, too, that your fans are unique to you; a discrete subset of all mystery readers, to borrow a phrase from mathematics. They want *your* detective. *Your* setting. *Your* prose. Ultimately, your readers will know your writing better than anyone else.

Think about it: Your query letter gets you, perhaps, one minute of an agent's attention. The cover on your book gets, maybe, a few seconds from a buyer for a bookstore chain. But once that book is sold to a customer, taken home and opened . . . ah! You have hours upon hours in which to lure that reader into your story, then take him on a ride he will never forget.

Given that, where do you think you should put the lion's share of your time and energy? The answer to that one is easy: into your mystery writing. Best of luck!

Agent Listings

ADLER & ROBIN BOOKS, INC.

Established: 1988 • 50 clients

Contact: Lisa Swayne

SPECIALIZES IN
Private Eye, Suspense, Thrillers, Light Horror, Police Procedural

Agency is seeking both new and established writers. Offers a written contract which is binding for 1 year. Author must give 30 days notice to terminate contract. **Recent sales:** *Room To Write* by Bonni Goldberg to Jeremy P. Tarcher, *Kidnet* by Brad and Debra Schepp to HarperCollins. Usually obtains clients upon recommendations from others. Immediately interested in manuscripts that have a strong, clean style and well-paced plot by a writer tackling a subject they know well. "I am not impressed by someone writing a police procedural who has no knowledge of police work. An unusual hook (like food, quirky setting, etc.), a likeable protagonist that readers will want to see again & the potential to develop a book into a series" make a manuscript saleable, agency says. "We promote all of our clients' books for free. This past year, we have placed authors on numerous national television programs, including the Today Show and the Maury Povich Show."

Address: 3409 29th Street, NW, Washington, DC 20008
Phone: (202)363-7410
Fax: (202)686-1804

☀ ☀ ☀ ☀

JAMES ALLEN, LITERARY AGENT

Established: 1974 • Signatory of WGA • 45 clients

Contact: James Allen

SPECIALIZES IN
Amateur Sleuth, Police Procedural

Agency prefers to work with established writers, mostly through referrals. Offers a written contract which is binding for 3 years and automatically renewable. Author must give 30 days notice to terminate contract. **Recent sales:** *Icewater Mansions & Black Water* by Doug Allyn to St. Martin's, *Loving Mollie* by Jeane Renick to HarperCollins. "I reserve the right to pass on extraordinary expenses: international airmail for hardcovers (to market translation rights), copying costs of booklength manuscripts, ordering of additional copies of books from U.S. publishers (again, for marketing foreign rights). I usually pay such bills, then deduct the costs from subsequent earnings received—it's less painful for the author that way. If, having read a newcomer's manuscript, I decline to take the author on as a client, I give a fairly detailed reasoning why. Once on my list, a client gets input, as needed, for ways that a text might be improved for the market. There is no charge for this input, and it varies in degree." Does not offer for-hire criticism service. Usually obtains clients upon recommendations from established clients or editors. Immediately interested in manuscripts that have "truly unusual scenarios. But they're hard to come by. More generally, however, I look for protagonists who have lives outside of their sleuthing. A saleable manuscript must be well-rounded, well-realized, with characters the reader can care about."

Attends the following conferences/conventions: "I attend the Edgars every time I have a nominated client, which means seven times in the last ten years. When it's in the Northeast, I attend Boucheron. I also go to other conferences, especially smaller ones to which I'm invited as a guest speaker."

"Though open to new talent, I'm not actively looking to add new clients to my list, and I prefer to take on only authors with at least one booklength credit behind them. If you'll permit me a horticultural analogy, I prefer to put my energies into helping an already-sprouted sapling to grow into a tree, rather than hoping a still unsprouted seed will break through the ground."

Address: P.O. Box 278, Milford, PA 18337

MARCIA AMSTERDAM AGENCY

Established: 1970 • Signatory of WGA

Contact: Marcia Amsterdam

> **SPECIALIZES IN**
> Private Eye

Agency is seeking both new and established writers. Offers a written contract which is binding for 1 year. **Recent sales:** *Freefall* by Joyce Sweeney to Dell, *Shanghai Star* by William H. Lovejoy to Kensington, *Children of the Dawn* by Patricia Rowe to Warner. Charges author for office expenses, postage, photocopying. Usually obtains clients upon recommendations from others and queries.

Address: 41 W. 82nd St., New York, NY 10024-5613
Phone: (212)873-4945

AUTHOR'S LITERARY AGENCY

Established: 1992 • 15 clients

Contact: Dick Smith

> **SPECIALIZES IN**
> Private Eye, Cozy, Suspense, Crime, Thrillers, Hardboiled Detective, Police Procedural, Espionage, Courtroom/Trial

Agency is seeking both new and established writers. "Query first always, and have a SASE accompany all submissions—otherwise the submission will not be considered." Offers a written contract which is binding for 30 days. Author must give 30 days notice to terminate contract. **Recent sales:** *Fourth and Long: The Kent Woldrep Story* by Kent Woldrep & Susan Malone. Usually obtains clients upon recommendations from others and queries. "Strong characterization and good writing that starts with a strong hook in the first chapter immediately draws me to a manuscript."

Attends the following conferences/conventions: Bouchercon, Golden Triangle, others.

Address: P.O. Box 610582, DFW Airport, TX 75261-0582
Phone: (817)267-1078
Fax: (817)571-4656

BRANDT & BRANDT LITERARY AGENTS, INC.

Established: 1912 • Member: AAR • Signatory of WGA • 150 clients

Contact: Carl Brandt

> **SPECIALIZES IN**
> Private Eye, Cozy, Suspense, Crime, Young Adult, Thrillers, Historical, Hardboiled Detective, Amateur Sleuth, Humorous Mystery, Urban Horror, Juvenile, Dark Mystery, Light Horror, Police Procedural, Malice Domestic, Psychological Suspense, Romantic Suspense, Surrealistic Mystery, Espionage, Courtroom/Trial

Agency prefers to work with established writers, mostly through referrals. Charges author for "such things as manuscript copying." Usually obtains clients upon recommendations from others. "Initially, we are more interested in the writer than the specific book. We look for a long term relationship."

Address: 1501 Broadway, New York, NY 10036
Phone: (212)840-5760
Fax: (212)840-5776

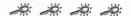

JULIE CASTIGLIA LITERARY AGENCY

Established: 1993 • Member: AAR • 45-50 clients

Contact: Julie Castiglia

> **SPECIALIZES IN**
> Private Eye, Cozy, Suspense, Thrillers, Police Procedural, Psychological
> Suspense, Romantic Suspense, Courtroom/Trial

Agency is seeking both new and established writers, but prefers to work with established writers, mostly through referrals. Offers written contract. Contract has 60 day termination clause. **Recent sales:** *Skywriting* by Margarita Engle to Bantam, *Bridge of No Return* by Mike Dunn to Avon, *Spare Change* by John Pear to St.Martin's. "A deposit is required from unpublished writers to cover marketing fees." Offers criticism service. "We offer criticism only if we decide to represent the project. There is no charge." Usually obtains clients upon recommendations from others, at conferences and conventions and through queries. Advises writers "not to approach an agent until you have attended conferences and workshops and have had the manuscript objectively critiqued (if you are an unpublished writer). If published, you already know all you need to know."

Address: 1155 Camino del Mar, Suite 510, Del Mar, CA 92014
Phone: (619)753-4361
Fax: (619)753-5094

CIRCLE OF CONFUSION LTD.

Established: 1990 • Signatory of WGA • 80 clients

Contact: Rajeev Agarwal

SPECIALIZES IN
Private Eye, Cozy, Suspense, Crime, Young Adult, Thrillers, Historical,
Hardboiled Detective, Amateur Sleuth, Humorous Mystery, Urban Horror,
Juvenile, Dark Mystery, Light Horror, Police Procedural, Malice Domestic,
Psychological Suspense, Romantic Suspense, Surrealistic Mystery,
Espionage, Courtroom/Trial

Agency is seeking both new and established writers. Offers a written
contract which is binding for 1 year. Author must give 60 days notice
to terminate contract.

Address: 666 5th Ave. Suite 303A, New York, NY 10103
Phone: (212)969-0653

DIANE CLEAVER, INC.

Member: AAR

Contact: Diane Cleaver

SPECIALIZES IN
Private Eye, Suspense, Hardboiled Detective, Psychological Suspense,
Courtroom/Trial

Agency is seeking both new and established writers. Usually obtains
clients upon recommendations from others and queries.

Address: 55 5th Ave., New York, NY 10003
Phone: (212)206-5600
Fax: (212)463-8718

FRANCES COLLIN, LITERARY AGENT

Member: AAR • 90 clients

Contact: Frances Collin

> **SPECIALIZES IN**
> Cozy, Suspense, Historical, Urban Horror, Dark Mystery, Light Horror, Romantic Suspense, Surrealistic Mystery, Courtroom/Trial

Agency prefers to work with established writers, mostly through referrals. Charges author for "photocopying manuscripts if necessary and the cost of sending books to foreign agents. Legal bills, copyright registration and renewal cost of books filled by publishers, foreign and film offers also warrant charge." Usually obtains clients upon recommendations from others, and very occasionally from queries.

Address: P.O. Box 33, Wayne, PA 19087

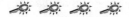

RICHARD CURTIS ASSOCIATES, INC.

Established: 1969 • Member: AAR • Signatory of WGA • 125 clients

Contact: Richard Curtis

> **SPECIALIZES IN**
> Private Eye, Cozy, Suspense, Crime, Young Adult, Thrillers, Historical, Hardboiled Detective, Amateur Sleuth, Humorous Mystery, Urban Horror, Juvenile,Dark Mystery, Light Horror, Police Procedural, Malice Domestic, Psychological Suspense, Romantic Suspense, Surrealistic Mystery, Espionage, Courtroom/Trial

Agency prefers to work with established writers, mostly through referrals. Charges author for additional fees for some office expenses. Usually obtains clients upon recommendations from others, at conferences and through queries. "A salable mystery has three components," says Richard Curtis. "Quality writing, quality story telling, quality characterization."

Address: 171 East 74th St., New York, NY 10021
Phone: (212)772-7363
Fax: (212)772-7393

ANITA DIAMANT LITERARY AGENCY

Established: 1917 • Member: AAR • Signatory of WGA • 125 clients

Contact: Anita Diamant, Robin Rue

> **SPECIALIZES IN**
> Private Eye, Cozy, Suspense, Crime, Thrillers, Hardboiled Detective, Humorous Mystery, Dark Mystery, Police Procedural, Malice Domestic, Psychological Suspense, Romantic Suspense, Espionage, Courtroom/Trial

Agency is seeking both new and established writers. Offers a written contract which is binding for 90 days. Author must give 90 days notice to terminate contract. **Recent sales:** *In the Dark* by Carol Brennan to Putnam, *Jacqueline Kennedy Onassis* by Lester David, *Pearl in the Mist* by VC Andrews to Pocket. Usually obtains clients upon recommendations from others, at conferences, and through queries and unsolicited manuscripts. Immediately interested in manuscripts that have "opening suspense and good characterizations with a fresh, interesting plot."

Attends the following conferences/conventions: Malice Domestic, ABA, RWA conferences.

Address: 310 Madison Ave., New York, NY 10017
Phone: (212)687-1122
Fax: (212)972-1756

DOYEN LITERARY SERVICES INC.

Established: 1988 • 50+ clients

Contact: B.J. Doyen

> **SPECIALIZES IN**
> Cozy, Suspense, Young Adult, Thrillers, Historical, Amateur Sleuth, Humorous Mystery, Romantic Suspense

Agency is seeking both new and established writers. Offers a written contract which is binding for 1 year. Author must give 30 days notice to terminate contract. Usually obtains clients upon recommendations from others, at conferences and through queries. Immediately interested in manuscripts that have "an opening that grabs my interest with polished writing that's suitable for today's marketplace."

Address: 1931 660th St., Newell, IA 50568
Phone: (712)272-3300

THE ETHAN ELLENBERG LITERARY AGENCY

Established: 1984 • 70 clients

> **SPECIALIZES IN**
> Suspense, Thrillers, Police Procedural, Psychological Suspense, Romantic Suspense

Agency is seeking both new and established writers. Offers a written contract which is binding for 1 year. Author must give 60 days notice to terminate contract. Charges author for postage and photocopying. Usually obtains clients upon recommendations from others, at conferences, and through queries, solicitation and unsolicited manuscripts. **Recent sales:** *Forged in Honor* by Leonard Scott to Ballantine, *Eternity Base* by Bob Mayer to Presidio, *Black Wolf* by Tom Wilson to Signet, *The Sentry* by Ross Kasminoff to Crown, *Easy Prey* by Michael Cecilione to Zebra, *A Perfect Match* by Laura Hayden to Harlequin Intrigue, *Danger's Kiss* by Christine Michels to Leisure.

Address: 548 Broadway, #5-E, New York, NY 10012
Phone: (212)431-4554
Fax: (212)941-4652

ANN ELMO AGENCY INC.

Established: 1940 • Member: AAR

Contact: Lettie Lee

Agency is seeking both new and established writers. Usually obtains clients upon recommendations from others.

Address: 60 E. 42 St., New York, NY 10165
Phone: (212)661-2880
Fax: (212)661-2883

THE GARON-BROOKE ASSOC. INC.

Established: 1952 • Member: AAR • Signatory of WGA • 100 clients

Contact: Jay Garon, Nancy Coffee, Jean Free

Offers a written contract which is binding for 3-5 years. Author must give 60 days notice to terminate contract. **Recent sales:** *The Rainmaker* by John Grisham to Doubleday, *Arc Light* by Eric Harry to Simon & Schuster, *Genome* by Ben Mezrich to HarperCollins. Usually obtains clients upon recommendations from others, queries and editorial referrals.

Attends the following conferences/conventions: ABA, Frankfurt Book Fair, New Orleans Writers' Conference.

Note: "We are not taking on category novels or most nonfiction. We want mainstream manuscripts."

Address: 101 West 55th St., Suite 5K, New York, NY 10019

THE GISLASON AGENCY

Established: 1991 • 12 clients

Contact: Barbara J. Gislason, Dara Moskowitz

SPECIALIZES IN
Private Eye, Cozy, Young Adult, Amateur Sleuth, Juvenile, Light Horror,
Romantic Suspense

Agency is seeking both new and established writers. Offers a written contract which is binding for 6 months. Charges author for postage, copying, faxing, long distance calls. Usually obtains clients upon recommendations from others, at conferences and by solicitation. "Clarity of plot, depth of characters, and the charm or strength of prose interest me."

Attends the following conferences/conventions: ABA, Bouchercon, UMBA.

Address: 219 S.E. Main St. Suite 506, Minneapolis, MN 55414
Phone: (612)331-8033
Fax: (612)331-8115

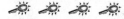

GOLDFARB & GRAYBILL LAW OFFICES

Established: 1965 • Signatory of WGA • 100+ clients

Contact: Nina Graybill

SPECIALIZES IN
Private Eye, Cozy, Suspense, Crime, Thrillers, Historical, Hardboiled
Detective, Amateur Sleuth, Humorous Mystery, Dark Mystery, Light
Horror, Police Procedural, Malice Domestic, Psychological Suspense,
Romantic Suspense, Espionage, Courtroom/Trial

Agency is seeking both new and established writers. Offers written contract. Charges author for "out of pocket expenses: postage, copying, long distance calls, etc." Usually obtains clients upon recommendations from others, at conferences, from queries, by solicitation and unsolicited manuscripts. "What we like are great characters and dialogue, and an interesting, well-executed plot."

Attends the following conferences/conventions: ABA, Frankfurt Book Fair.

Address: 918 16th St. N.W., Suite 400, Washington, DC 20008
Phone: (202)466-3030
Fax: (202)293-3187

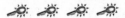

CHARLOTTE GORDON AGENCY

Established: 1985 • 20 clients

Contact: Charlotte Gordon

> **SPECIALIZES IN**
> Cozy, Suspense, Young Adult, Historical, Amateur Sleuth, Humorous Mystery, Juvenile, Police Procedural, Malice Domestic

Agency prefers to work with established writers, mostly through referrals. No fee. Offers written contract. **Recent sales:** *Illegal Motion* by Grif Stockley to Simon & Schuster, *One Mississippi* by Tima Smith to Ballantine. Offers criticism service on an individual basis; it's not a regular service. Usually obtains clients upon recommendations and/or queries. Query with 2 chapters of manuscript and SASE. Immediately interested in manuscripts with good writing and vivid characters.

Address: 235 E. 22nd St., New York, NY 10010
Phone: (212)679-5363

JOHN HAWKINS & ASSOCIATES, INC.

Established: 1893 • Member: AAR • 100+ clients

Contact: Warren Frazier

SPECIALIZES IN
Private Eye, Suspense, Urban Horror, Dark Mystery, Psychological
Suspense, Espionage

Agency is seeking both new and established writers. Charges author for photocopying and marketing fees. Usually obtains clients upon recommendations from others, at conferences, by solicitation and through unsolicited manuscripts.

Address: 71 W. 23rd St., Suite 1600, New York, NY 10010
Phone: (212)807-7040
Fax: (212)807-9555

HULL HOUSE LITERARY AGENCY

Established: 1987 • 35 clients

Contact: David Stewart Hull

SPECIALIZES IN
Suspense, Crime, Amateur Sleuth, Malice Domestic, Psychological Suspense

Agency is seeking both new and established writers. Charges author for photocopying, overseas postage and fax charges, plus Federal Express if necessary. Usually obtains clients upon recommendations from others, and through queries. "I like a good concept with an appealing central character," Hull says. "An ideal manuscript features a strong central character of either sex who is *not* a detective or police person. This character's profession or background does not have to be unusual, but often a regional slant is of particular interest to editors. The manuscript should ideally introduce a series concept which can be carried out in future books. I tell all beginning writers to carefully read all the Edgar nominees for the current year. I think it is particularly valuable to read the books in the 'best first' category."

Address: 240 E. 82nd St., New York, NY 10028
Phone: (212)988-0725
Fax: (212)794-8758

☀ ☀ ☀ ☀

JABBERWOCKY/A LITERARY AGENCY

Established: 1994 • 40 clients

Contact: Joshua Bilmes

> **SPECIALIZES IN**
> Private Eye, Cozy, Suspense, Crime, Young Adult, Thrillers, Historical,
> Hardboiled Detective, Amateur Sleuth, Humorous Mystery, Urban Horror,
> Juvenile, Dark Mystery, Light Horror, Police Procedural, Malice Domestic,
> Psychological Suspense, Romantic Suspense, Surrealistic Mystery,
> Espionage, Courtroom/Trial

Agency is seeking both new and established writers. Authors should query first. Charges author for photocopying, purchase, and international mailing of books and manuscript, plus some long distance calls. Usually obtains clients upon recommendations from others, queries and solicitation. Immediately interested in manuscripts that have "a spark or bounciness in the writing by authors who often write about a character or setting to which they feel a strong connection."

"Saleability," says Bilmes, "is a function of plot, ambiance, characterization, dialogue, innate writing ability and other factors. While a successful book can result from many variations of those skills, there is no successful book which has none of them."

Attends the following conferences/conventions: Malice Domestic.

Address: P.O. Box 4558, Sunnyside, NY 11104-0558
Phone: (718)392-5985
Fax: (718)392-5985

☀ ☀ ☀ ☀

KIDDE, HOYT & PICARD LITERARY AGENCY $\mathcal{P}^d\ 2$

Established: 1980 • Member: AAR • 55 clients

Contacts: Katharine Kidde, Laura Langlie

> **SPECIALIZES IN**
> Private Eye, Suspense, Historical, Amateur Sleuth, Psychological Suspense, Romantic Suspense, Espionage, Courtroom/Trial

Agency is seeking both new and established writers. Charges author for reimbursement for copies, faxes, postage, and long distance calls. Usually obtains clients upon recommendations from others, and through queries. Immediately interested in manuscripts that have "a taut plot, strong style, and an empathetic protagonist."

Address: 335 E. 51st St., New York, NY 10022
Phone: (212)755-9461

☀ ☀ ☀ ☀

⚝PETER LAMPACK AGENCY, INC. ✓

Established: 1977 • 35-40 clients

Contact: Deborah T. Brown

> **SPECIALIZES IN**
> Suspense, Thrillers, Historical, Amateur Sleuth, Psychological Suspense

Agency is seeking both new and established writers. **Recent sales:** A 3 book deal for Judith Kelman to Bantam, *Ties that Bind* by Warren Adler to Donald I. Fine. Charges author for photocopying. "I do give detailed reasons for rejection, and am very editorially inclined when I accept. I only send what I consider a tight manuscript for editors' review." Usually obtains clients upon recommendations from others, at conferences and through queries. Immediately interested in manuscripts that offer "good, tight writing, character development, setting, good narrative drive or suspense line and subtlety of character and clues. Individuality in a key aspect: either the character of the sleuth, the unfolding nature of the crime or the criminal, unusual setting that is intrinsic to the plot, etc. The best quality, though, is seamless plot."

Attends the following conferences/conventions: ABA, Bouchercon.

"We don't have as many mystery writers on board as we'd like, partly because it's such a difficult genre. We've represented Warren Adler's side-line series of Fiona Fitzgerald mysteries and David Osborne's side-line series: Margaret Barlow. Also, Judith Kelman, Karin McQuillan and, our top grossing client, Clive Cussler."

Address: 551 5th Ave., Suite 1613, New York, NY 10176-0187
Phone: (212)687-9106
Fax: (212)687-9109

MICHAEL LARSEN/ELIZABETH POMADA LITERARY AGENTS

Established: 1972 • Member: AAR • 100 clients

Contact: Elizabeth Pomada

> **SPECIALIZES IN**
> Private Eye, Cozy, Suspense, Crime, Thrillers, Historical, Light Horror, Malice Domestic, Psychological Suspense, Romantic Suspense

Agency is seeking both new and established writers. Offers written contract. Author must give 60 days notice to terminate contract. **Recent sales:** *Guerrilla Advertising* by Jay Conrad Levinson to Houghton Miflen, *A Crack in Forever* by Jeannie Brewer to Simon & Schuster, *The Girls with the Grandmother Faces* by Frances Weaver to Hyperion. Charges author for photocopying and foreign mailings. Usually obtains clients upon recommendations from others, at conferences and through queries. Immediately interested in manuscripts that "start on page one with a fast pace."

Attends the following conferences/conventions: Santa Barbara Writer's Conference, Maui Writer's Conference, ASJA and others.

Address: 1029 Jones St., San Francisco, CA 94109
Phone: (415)673-0939

THE LITERARY AGENCY GROUP INTERNATIONAL

Established: 1988 • Signatory of WGA • 100+ clients

Contact: Jessica Wainwright

SPECIALIZES IN
Private Eye, Suspense, Crime, Young Adult, Thrillers, Hardboiled Detective, Amateur Sleuth, Humorous Mystery, Urban Horror, Juvenile, Dark Mystery, Light Horror, Police Procedural, Malice Domestic, Psychological Suspense, Romantic Suspense, Espionage, Courtroom/Trial

Agency is seeking both new and established writers. Offers a written contract which is binding for negotiable length of time. Author must give 30 days notice to terminate contract. Usually obtains clients upon recommendations from others, at conferences and through unsolicited manuscripts. "I want to find characters I fall in love with and can't forget for days after reading, a story I can't put down even if it's time to go to bed, and real people in extraordinary circumstances."

Attends the following conferences/conventions: Bouchercon, World Fantasy Convention, others.

Address: 270 Lafayette St., Suite 1505, New York, NY 10012
Phone: (212)274-1616
Fax: (212)274-9876

NANCY LOVE LITERARY AGENCY

Established: 1984 • 60-65 clients

Contact: Nancy Love

SPECIALIZES IN
Private Eye, Cozy, Suspense, Crime, Thrillers, Amateur Sleuth, Police Procedural, Psychological Suspense, Espionage, Courtroom/Trial

Agency is seeking both new and established writers. Offers written contract. Author must give 60 days notice to terminate contract. **Recent sales:** *Legend of the Dead* by Micah Hackler to Dell, *Thirteen Mountain* by John Reed to St. Martin's, *A Far and Deadly Cry* by Teri Peitso Holbrook to Bantam. Charges author for photocopying, overseas postage. Usually obtains clients upon recommendations from others, through queries, by solicitation and via unsolicited manuscripts. "Freshness of the concept, the quality of writing, and a strong series protagonist all make a manuscript saleable," Love says.

Has attended the following conferences/conventions: Pacific Northwest Writer's Conference, ASJA, Harrietta Austin Writer's Conference.

Address: 250 E. 65th St. 4A, New York, NY 10021
Phone: (212)980-3499
Fax: (212)308-6405

DONALD MAASS LITERARY AGENCY

Established: 1980 • Member: AAR • 75 clients

Contact: Donald Maass, Jennifer Jackson

> **SPECIALIZES IN**
> Private Eye, Cozy, Suspense, Crime, Young Adult, Thrillers, Historical, Amateur Sleuth, Humorous Mystery, Juvenile, Dark Mystery, Police Procedural, Malice Domestic, Psychological Suspense, Romantic Suspense, Surrealistic Mystery, Espionage, Courtroom/Trial

Agency is seeking both new and established writers. **Recent sales:** *As Cain His Brother* by Anne Perry to Fawcett Columbine, *Dead Ahead* by Bridget McKenna to Berkley Prime Crime, *Caught Dead* by Roxanne Longstreet to Kensington Publishing. Charges author for large photocopying jobs, outside legal and tax advice, and other such expenses. All expenses are made by agreement with client. Usually obtains clients upon recommendations from others, at conferences and through queries. "I like a sane, professional approach, prior publishing credits and a great story," Maass says. "A saleable mystery has a great plot, a terrific detective, fascinating milieu and gorgeous prose—not much to ask, is it?" (For more advice from Donald Maass, see "How To Find, and Keep, a Top-Notch Mystery Agent," page 277.) Attends the following conferences/conventions: Bouchercon, Malice Domestic.

Address: 157 W. 57th St., Suite 1003, New York, NY 10019
Phone: (212)757-7755

THE ROBERT MADSEN LITERARY AGENCY $\wp \rangle$ 2

Established: 1992 • 4 clients

Contact: Kim Van Nguyen, Senior Editor

> **SPECIALIZES IN**
> Private Eye, Cozy, Suspense, Crime, Young Adult, Thrillers, Historical, Hardboiled Detective, Amateur Sleuth, Humorous Mystery, Urban Horror, Juvenile, Dark Mystery, Light Horror, Police Procedural, Malice Domestic, Psychological Suspense, Romantic Suspense, Surrealistic Mystery, Espionage, Courtroom/Trial

Agency is seeking both new and established writers. Offers written contract, binding for 3 years; author must give 90 days notice to terminate contract. **Recent sales:** *Diamonds and Gems Buyers' Guide* by Thomas James to Oasis Publishing, *Toward a Free Vietnam* by Thanh Nguyen to Victoria Ngo, Publisher, *Downsizing Your Personal Wealth* by Reginald Lord to Sunset Publications. So far, does not charge fees, "but if we do, it will be a minimal postage fee (third or fourth class postage, amounting to about six dollars per submission, including return postage). Writers are expected to provide clean copies." Usually obtains clients upon recommendations from others and through unsolicited submissions. Immediately interested in manuscripts that have "good writing—plot, setting, characters, tone, atmosphere—it all adds up, and remember, the sum is greater than its parts."

Advice: "Be professional; write well; stay optimistic."

Address: 1331 E. 34th St. #1, Oakland, CA 94602
Phone: (510)223-2090

MANUS & ASSOCIATES LITERARY AGENCY

Established: 1985 • Member: AAR • 60 clients

Contact: Janet Manus, Jillian Manus

SPECIALIZES IN
Cozy, Suspense, Humorous Mystery, Amateur Sleuth

Agency is seeking both new and established writers. Offers a written contract which is binding for 1.3 years. Author must give 45 days notice to terminate contract. 15% of clients are new writers. Usually obtains new clients from recommendation of others, at conferences and conventions, and queries. Attends Bouchercon and Malice Domestic.

THE EVAN MARSHALL AGENCY

Established: 1987 • Member: AAR • 40 clients

Contact: Evan Marshall, Martha Jewett

SPECIALIZES IN
Private Eye, Cozy, Suspense, Crime, Young Adult, Thrillers, Historical, Hardboiled Detective, Amateur Sleuth, Humorous Mystery, Urban Horror, Juvenile, DarkMystery, Light Horror, Police Procedural, Malice Domestic, Psychological Suspense, Romantic Suspense, Surrealistic Mystery, Espionage, Courtroom/Trial

Agency is seeking both new and established writers. Author must give 90 days notice to terminate contract. **Recent sales:** *The Lady Chapel* by Candace M. Robb to St. Martin's, *Death at Face Value* by Joyce Christmas to Fawcett, *Someone to Watch Over* by Trish Macdonald Skillman to Dell. Usually obtains clients upon recommendations from others, at conferences, by query and through solicitation. Immediately interested in manuscripts that have "fresh ideas and technically excellent writing. A good manuscript has a story that is fresh within the current demands of the market; clean, technically accomplished writing with rich characterization. Today's mystery reader wants novels with mystery, not the cardboard-character puzzles of yesterday."

Address: 6 Tristam Place, Pine Brook, NJ 07058-9445
Phone: (201)882-1122
Fax: (201)882-3099

MULTIMEDIA PRODUCT DEVELOPMENT, INC.

Established: 1971 • Member: AAR • 150 clients

Contact: Jane Jordan Browne

> **SPECIALIZES IN**
> Cozy, Suspense, Thrillers, Historical, Amateur Sleuth, Malice Domestic, Psychological Suspense, Romantic Suspense

Agency prefers to work with established writers, mostly through referrals. Offers a written contract which is binding for 2 years. **Recent sales:** *The Eagle Catcher, The Ghost Walker, The Dream Spinner* by Margaret Coel to Berkley, *Fixed in His Folly* by David Walker to St. Martin's, *The Persian Pickle Club* by Sandra Dallas to St. Martin's, and hard cover of *The Eagle Catcher* to University Press of Colorado. Charges author for foreign phone calls, postage, faxing and photocopying. Usually obtains clients upon recommendations from others. Immediately interested in manuscripts that have "excellent writing with a unique story and believable characters. Author should be familiar with the market."

Attends the following conferences/conventions: ABA, RWA, Bouchercon, Dark and Stormy Nights.

Address: 410 S. Michigan Ave., Suite 724, Chicago, IL 60605
Phone: (312)922-3063
Fax: (312)922-1905

DEE MURA ENTERPRISES, INC.

Signatory of WGA

Contact: Dee Mura

> **SPECIALIZES IN**
> Private Eye, Cozy, Suspense, Crime, Young Adult, Thrillers, Historical, Hardboiled Detective, Amateur Sleuth, Humorous Mystery, Urban Horror, Juvenile, Dark Mystery, Light Horror, Police Procedural, Malice Domestic, Psychological Suspense, Romantic Suspense, Surrealistic Mystery, Espionage, Courtroom/Trial

Offers written contract. Author must give 90 days notice to terminate contract. Charges author for office expenses, postage, photocopying. Usually obtains clients upon recommendations from others.

Advice: "The first 25 pages must pull me in. Have an exciting, solid, well-written story. Make the suspense high and the concept original. Have complex characters."

Address: 269 W. Shore Dr., Massapequa, NY 11758; Email: Samurai5-&ix.netcom.com
Phone: (516)795-1616
Fax: (516)795-8797

THE JEAN V. NAGGAR LITERARY AGENCY

Member: AAR • 120 clients

Contact: Jean Naggar

> **SPECIALIZES IN**
> Cozy, Suspense, Thrillers, Historical, Police Procedural

Agency prefers to work with established writers, mostly through referrals. Offers written contract. Author must give 90 days notice to terminate contract. **Recent sales:** *After Dark* by Phillip Margolin to Doubleday/Bantam, *Clouds of Heaven* by Joe De Mers to Dutton/Signet, *Songs in Ordinary Time* by Mary McGarry Morris to Viking/Penguin. Charges author for photocopying, messengers, long distance calls, books, galleys, foreign mailings. Usually obtains clients upon recommendations from others. Immediately interested in manuscripts that have "a unique twist, locale, character, and voice."

Address: 216 E. 75th St., New York, NY 10021
Phone: (212)794-1082

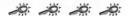

THE NORMA-LEWIS AGENCY

Established: 1980 • 15 clients

Contact: Norma Liebert

SPECIALIZES IN
Private Eye, Cozy, Suspense, Crime, Young Adult, Thrillers, Hardboiled Detective, Amateur Sleuth, Humorous Mystery, Juvenile, Police Procedural, Psychological Suspense, Romantic Suspense, Espionage, Courtroom/Trial

Agency is seeking both new and established writers. Offers written contract. Usually obtains clients upon recommendations from others and through queries.

Advice: "The opening paragraph must motivate me to read on, and my interest must be sustained throughout the book."

Address: 360 W. 53rd St., Suite BA, New York, NY 10019
Phone: (212)664-0807
Fax: (212)664-0462

EDWARD A. NOVAK III LITERARY REPRESENTATION

Established: 1991 • 30 clients

Contact: Edward Novak

SPECIALIZES IN
Suspense, Crime, Psychological Suspense, Espionage, Courtroom/Trial

Agency prefers to work with established writers, mostly through referrals. Offers written contract. Author must give 30 days notice to terminate contract. **Recent sales:** *Rogue's Isles* by Thomas G. Briody to St. Martin's. Charges author for photocopying. Usually obtains clients upon recommendations from others. Charges $50 reading fee for outline and three chapters on unsolicited manuscripts; service includes 500 word critique from agent within four weeks. Interested in stories that offer "good writing, good time and place, and the ability to keep a secret. Good crafting plus a solid background are key to selling a mystery."

Address: 711 N. 2nd St., Suite 1, Harrisburg, PA 17102
Phone: (717)232-8081
Fax: (717)232-7020

OTITIS MEDIA LITERARY AGENCY

Established: 1989 • Signatory of WGA

Contact: Hannibal Harris, Richard Boylan

SPECIALIZES IN
Suspense, Crime, Thrillers, Historical, Light Horror, Espionage

Agency is seeking both new and established writers. Offers a written contract which is binding for 1 year. Author must give 30 days notice to terminate contract. "We prefer writer to supply us with manuscripts, postage if multiple submission or auction is determined." Usually obtains clients upon recommendations from others and queries. Agency looks for writers who present a professional package. "Simple things like spelling, grammar, punctuation, orderly layout of story. Excellent manuscript quality helps—no nine pin or twelve pin dot matrix printers, type dark enough to be readable (hint: install new ribbons and check the toner). Writing quality, overall commanding plot, fast pacing and excellent dialoque" are what make a manuscript saleable, agency says. "Hooks should be planted early and often to drag the reader through the book (or movie)."

Address: 1926 Dupont Ave. South, Minneapolis, MN 55403
Phone: (612)377-4918
Fax: (612)377-3046

SUSAN ANN PROTTER LITERARY AGENT

Established: 1971 • Member: AAR • Signatory of WGA • 35 clients

Contact: Susan Ann Protter

SPECIALIZES IN
Private Eye, Cozy, Thrillers, Amateur Sleuth, Police Procedural, Suspense,
Courtroom/Trial

Agency is seeking both new and established writers. Offers a written contract which is binding for a negotiable length of time (minimum of 18 months.) Author must give 60 days notice to terminate contract. **Recent sales:** *Shutout* by D. Nighbert to St. Martin's, *Beware the Tufted Duck* by L. Adamson to Dutton, and *A Cat on a Winning Street* by L. Adamson to Signet. Charges author for Federal Express, long distance calls, overseas mail, copies, legal fees (if required). Usually obtains clients upon recommendations from others and by queries. Queries must include an SASE. "A writer's ability to involve me immediately—and to sustain such involvement—draws me to a manuscript," Protter says. "A plausible plot, an original sleuth and a well-researched setting will help sell a manuscript."

Address: 110 W. 40th St., Suite 1408, New York, NY 10018
Phone: (212)840-0480

QUICKSILVER BOOKS-LITERARY AGENTS

Established: 1987 • 50+ clients

Contact: Bob Silverstein

SPECIALIZES IN
Suspense, Thrillers

Agency is seeking both new and established writers. Query first with SASE. No reading fee. Charges 15% commission. Offers a written contract which is binding for 1 year. Author must give 2 weeks notice to terminate contract. **Recent sales:** *Deadly Impression* by Dennis Asen to Bantam, *Panther* by Melvin Van Peebles to Thunder's Month Press. Charges author for photocopying and postage charges. Usually obtains clients upon recommendations from others, at conferences, and through queries, solicitation and unsolicited manuscripts. Immediately interested in both book-length adult fiction and nonfiction manuscripts that have narrative intensity, originality of voice and conception, and quality language."

Attends the following conferences/conventions: NWU.

Address: 50 Wilson St., Hartsdale, NY 10530
Phone: (914)946-8748

THE SEYMOUR AGENCY

Established: 1992 • 30 + clients

Contact: Mike and Mary Seymour

SPECIALIZES IN
Suspense, Thrillers, Humorous Mystery, Light Horror, Romantic Suspense

Agency is seeking both new and established writers. Offers a written contract which is binding for 1 year. **Recent sales:** *Fools Paradise* by Tori Phillips to Harlequin, *Beyond Forever* by Lee Ann Dansby to Lion Hearted Publishers, *"Bride"* books by Tamara Leigh to Bantam. Offers criticism service. "There's a $25 fee for the first 50 pages." Agents Mike and Mary Seymour critique the manuscript. Usually obtains clients upon recommendations from others, through queries and by unsolicited manuscript submissions. Immediately interested in manuscripts that have "romantic intrigue of 75,000 words that's fast-paced, with well-developed characters and a believable plot."

Attends the following conferences/conventions: NYS Outdoor Writers and National Outdoor Writers.

"We are published authors/NYS certified teachers who have had success critiquing work and selling it."

Address: 17 Rensselaer Ave., Heuvelton, NY 13654

Phone: (315)344-7223
Fax: (315)344-7223

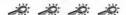

EVELYN SINGER LITERARY AGENCY

Established: 1951 • 25 clients

Contact: Evelyn Singer

SPECIALIZES IN
Suspense

Agency prefers to work with established writers only, mostly through referrals. Must have earned at least $20,000 from prior writing sales to be considered. Offers a written contract which is binding for 3 years. Author must give 3 months notice to terminate contract. **Recent sales:** *Legacy of Vengeance* by John Armistead by Carroll & Graf, *Apple Valley Series* by Nancy Smith to Avon. Charges author for long distance calls, international postage. "We answer all correspondences through mail. Do not phone us. When writing, include SASE, wrapper and postage for manuscript."

Address: P.O. Box 594, White Plains, NY 10602

PATRICIA TEAL LITERARY AGENCY

Established: 1978 • Member: AAR • 50 clients

Contact: Patricia Teal

SPECIALIZES IN
Cozy, Suspense, Amateur Sleuth, Humorous Mystery, Romantic Suspense, Courtroom/Trial

Agency prefers to work with established writers, mostly through referrals. "We want female protagonists in cozy mysteries." Offers a written contract which is binding for 1 year. Author must give 30 days notice to terminate contract. **Recent sales:** *Guilty by Choice* by Patricia D. Benke to Avon, *Fred* Series by Sherry Lewis to Berkley Prime Crime, *Guilt by Silence* by Taylor Smith to Mira (Harlequin). Charges author for xeroxing, postage. Usually obtains clients upon recommendations from others, at coferences and through queries.

Attends the following conferences/conventions: ABA, Romance Writers of America, Bouchercon, California Writers Association, California State University San Diego Writers Conference, various RWA Chapter Conferences.

Advice: "Don't write in any genre you don't enjoy reading."

Address: 2036 Vista Del Rosa, Fullerton, CA 92631
Phone: (714)738-8333
Fax: (714)738-8333

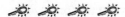

WATKINS-LOOMIS AGENCY

Established: 1908 • 150 clients

Contact: Lily Oei

> **SPECIALIZES IN**
> Private Eye, Suspense, Crime, Young Adult, Historical, Humorous Mystery, Juvenile, Dark Mystery, Psychological Suspense, Romantic Suspense, Surrealistic Mystery

Agency works with both new and established writers. **Recent sales:** Thomas Adcock to Pocket and Walter Mosley to Norton. Charges author for postage, photocopying, phone, faxing. Usually obtains clients upon recommendations from others. "We are interested in how well a story is told, particularly the plausibility of the events."

Address: 133 E. 35th St., New York, NY 10036
Phone: (212)532-0080

SANDRA WATT & ASSOCIATES

Established: 1977 • Signatory of WGA • 35 clients

Contact: Sandra Watt

SPECIALIZES IN
Private Eye, Cozy, Suspense, Crime, Thrillers, Historical, Hardboiled
Detective, Amateur Sleuth, Humorous Mystery, Urban Horror, Juvenile,
Light Horror, Police Procedural, Malice Domestic, Psychological Suspense,
Surrealistic Mystery, Espionage, Courtroom/Trial

Agency is seeking both new and established writers. Offers a written contract which is binding for 1 year. Author must give 30 days notice to terminate contract. **Recent sales:** *Death by Rhubarb series* by Lou Jane Temple to St. Martin's, *Women of Parkwood Lane* to Citadel (movie of the week), *In Cold Love* by Mick Strawser to Citadel (ABC movie of the week). Charges "a $100 marketing fee to a previously unpublished author, for first books only." Usually obtains clients upon recommendations from others, at conferences and through queries. "Style, character and plot must be key elements for a publishable manuscript."

Attends the following conferences/conventions: SDSU and others.

"Most mysteries by unpublished authors I receive are competent but they have no spark of style to distinguish them. Without a distinctive voice, too many mysteries are simply competent and the market is too crowded for the simply competent."

Address: 8033 Sunset Blvd., Suite 4053, Los Angeles, CA 90046
Phone: (213)851-1021

CHERRY WEINER, LITERARY AGENCY

Established: 1977 • 40-50 clients

Contact: Cherry Weiner

Agency prefers to work with established writers, mostly through referrals. Offers written contract. **Recent sales:** *Murder at the Gods Gate* by Lynda Robinson to Walker & Ballantine, *Queen to the Hearts* by Donna Valentino to Harper Paperbacks, *Blood Secrets* Trilogy by Karen Taylor to Zebra. Charges author for special mailings, overseas calls. Offers suggestion service at no charge. Usually obtains clients upon recommendations from others, at conferences and through queries (occasionally). Immediately interested in manuscripts that have "something different—page-turning readability."

Attends the following conferences/conventions: RWA, Western Writers, Mystery Writers, Edgars and others.

Advice:"Write what you *love* to read—not what you think is easiest to get published."

Address: 28 Kipling Way, Manalapan, NJ 07726
Phone: (908)446-2096
Fax: (908)446-2096

WITHERSPOON ASSOCIATES

Established: 1991 • 150+ clients

Agency is seeking both new and established writers. Agency prefers to work with established writers, mostly through referrals. Offers written contract. Author must give 30 days notice to terminate contract. **Recent sales:** *Big Town* by Doug Swanson to HarperCollins, *Fools in the Hill* by Preston Lerner to Pocket Books/Simon & Schuster, *Dream Boat* by Doug Swanson to HarperCollins. Usually obtains clients upon recommendations from others and through solicitation and queries.

Advice: "The novel needs to begin on page one, not page fifty." Attends the following conferences/conventions: ABA, Frankfurt.

Address: 157 W. 57th St., Suite 700, New York, NY 10019
Phone: (212)757-0567
Fax: (212)757-2982

☀ ☀ ☀ ☀

RUTH WRESCHNER, AUTHORS' REPRESENTATIVE

Established: 1982 • 75 clients

Contact: Ruth Wreschner

SPECIALIZES IN
Private Eye, Cozy, Suspense, Crime, Thrillers, Hardboiled Detective, Police Procedural, Psychological Suspense, Romantic Suspense, Courtroom/Trial

Agency is seeking both new and established writers. Agency prefers to work with established writers, mostly through referrals. Offers written contract. Author must give 30 days notice to terminate contract. Charges author for postage and photocopying. Offers criticism service. "I will give a very cursory critique if I am interested in pursuing the book further; if I am not interested in the book, I mostly do not read enough to offer critique. Unfortunately, most manuscripts fall into that range." Usually obtains clients upon recommendations from others, at conferences and through queries. Immediately interested in manuscripts that have "a real page-turning quality, an unusual setting (locale), with strong plot and characterization. Above all, the writing style must shine."

Address: 10 W. 74th St., New York, NY 10023
Phone: (212)877-2605
Fax: (212)595-5843

ANN WRIGHT REPRESENTATIVES

Established: 1961 • Signatory of WGA • 40+ clients

Contact: Dan Wright

SPECIALIZES IN
Private Eye, Suspense, Crime, Thrillers, Hardboiled Detective, Humorous Mystery, Dark Mystery, Police Procedural, Romantic Suspense, Espionage, Courtroom/Trial

Agency is seeking both new and established writers. Offers a written contract which is binding for 2 years. Deducts whatever extra charges at time of sale. Offers criticism service to signed clients only. Usually obtains clients upon recommendations from others and through queries. Immediately interested in manuscripts that immediately involve the reader in the story. Submissions "must have strong motion picture potential."

Address: 165 W. 46th St. #1105, New York, NY 10036
Phone: (212)764-6770
Fax: (212)764-5125

SUSAN ZECKENDORF ASSOCIATES, INC.

Established: 1979

Contact: Susan Zeckendorf

SPECIALIZES IN
Private Eye, Suspense, Crime, Thrillers, Hardboiled Detective, Amateur Sleuth, Urban Horror, Dark Mystery, Police Procedural, Psychological Suspense, RomanticSuspense, Espionage, Courtroom/Trial

Agency is seeking both new and established writers. **Recent sales:** *Cry for Help* by Karen Hanson Shruck to Berkely, *Maybelleen* by Kathleen Wallocking to Henry Holt, Mary Lou Williams biography by Linda Dahl to MacMillan. Charges author for photocopying. Usually obtains clients upon recommendations from others, at conferences, and via queries.

"Characters with nuance and texture appeal to me," Zeckendorf says, "as well as a compelling story line and vivid writing."

Has attended the following conferences/conventions: Writers Connection, Frontiers in Writing, Central Valley Writer's Conference, Golden Triangle, Oklahoma Festival of Books. Member of AAR. No unsolicited material. Send query with SASE.

Address: 171 W. 57th St., New York, NY 10019
Phone: (212)245-2928

More Mystery Agents

The following agents are listed as handling mystery and crime fiction in the *Guide To Literary Agents*, published by Writer's Digest Books. These agents did not respond to our requests for information. Query before submitting full or partial manuscripts.

Acton, Leone, Hanson & Jaffe, Inc., 928 Broadway, Suite #303, New York, NY 10010

Agents Inc. for Medical and Mental Health Professionals, P.O. Box 4956, Fresno, CA 93744-4956

Lee Allan Agency, P.O. Box 18617, Milwaukee, WI 53218-0617

Linda Allen Literary Agency, 1949 Green St., Suite 5, San Francisco, CA 94123

The Axelrod Agency, 54 Church St., Lenox, MA 01240

Malaga Baldi Literary Agency, P.O. Box 591, Radio City Station, New York, NY 10101

Blassingame Spectrum Corp., 111 Eighth Ave., Suite 1501, New York, NY 10011

Reid Boates Literary Agency, P.O. Box 328, 274 Cooks Crossroad, Pittstown, NJ 08867

The Barbara Bova Literary Agency, 3951 Gulfshore Blvd.,PH1-B, Still Maples, FL 33940

The Joan Brandt Agency, 788 Wesley Dr. NW, Atlanta, GA 30305

Marie Brown Associates Inc., 625 Broadway, Room 902, New York, NY 10012

Curtis Brown Ltd., 10 Astor Place, New York, NY 10003-6935

Jane Butler, Art & Literary Agent, P.O. Box 33, Matamoras, PA 18336-1530

Sheree Bykofsky Associates, 211 E. 51st St., Suite 11-D, Box WD,

New York, NY 10022

Cantrell-Colas Inc. Literary Agency, 229 E. 79th St., New York, NY 10021

Maria Carvainis Agency Inc., 235 West End Ave., New York, NY 10023

Francine Ciske Literary Agency, P.O. Box 555, Neenah, WI 54957

Ruth Cohen Inc.,Literary Agency, P.O. Box 7626, Menlo Park, CA 94025

Columbia Literary Associates, Inc., 7902 Nottingham Way, Ellicott City, MD 21043- 6721

Aleta M. Daley/Maximilian Becker, 44 East 82nd St., New York, NY 10028

Elaine Davie Literary Agency, 274 N. Goodman St., Rochester, NY 14607

The Lois de la Haba Agency Inc., 1123 Broadway, Suite 810, New York, NY 10010

Diamond Literary Agency, P.O. Box 117, Arvada, CO 80001

Sandra Dijkstra Literary Agency, 1155 Camino del Mar, #515, Del Mar, CA 92014

Robert Ducas, 350 Hudson St., New York, NY 10014

Dupree/Miller & Associates, 100 Highland Pk. Village, Suite 350, Dallas, TX 75205

Emerald Literary Agency, 1212 N. Angelo Dr., Beverly Hills, CA 90210

Esquire Literary Productions, 1492 Cottontail Lane, La Jolla, CA 92037

Farber Literary Agency Inc., 14 E. 75th St., #2E, New York, NY 10021

Florence Feiler Literary Agency, 1524 Sunset Plaza Dr., St. Louis, MO 63122-5531

Flannery Literary, 34-36 28th St., #5, Long Island City,NY 11106-3516

Fran Literary Agency, 7235 Split Creek, San Antonio, TX 78238-3627

Connie Goddard: Book Development, 203 N. Wabash Ave., Chicago, IL 60601- 2415

Sanford J. Greenburger Associates, 55 Fifth Ave., New York, NY 10003

The **Charlotte Gusay Literary Agency,** 10532 Blythe, Suite 211, Los Angeles, CA 90064

Reece Halsey Agency, 8733 Sunset Blvd., Suites 101, 102, Los Angeles, CA 90069

Gary L. Hegler Literary Agency, P.O. Box 890101, Houston, TX 77289-0101

Herner Rights Agency, P.O. Box 303, Scarsdale, NY 10583

J De S Associates Inc., 9 Shagbark Rd., Wilson Point, South Norwalk, CT 06854

Natasha Kern Literary Agency, P.O. Box 2908, Portland, OR 97208-2908

Harvey Klinger, Inc., 301 W. 53rd St., New York, NY 10019

Barbara S. Kouts, Literary Agent, P.O. Box 558, Bellport, NY 11713

Edite Kroll Literary Agency, 12 Grayhurst Park, Portland, ME 04102

Robert Lantz-Joy Harris Literary Agency Inc., 156 Fifth Ave., Suite 617, New York, NY 10010

Ellen Levine Literary Agency, Inc., 15 E. 26th St., Suite 1801, New York, NY 10010

Ray Lincoln Literary Agency, Elkins Park House, Suite 107-B, 7900 Old York Rd., Elkins Park, PA 19117

Wendy Lipkind Agency, 165 E. 66th St., New York, NY 10021

Lyceum Creative Properties, Inc., P.O. Box 12370, San Antonio, TX 78212

Margret McBride Literary Agency, 7744 Fay Ave., Suite 201, La Jolla, CA 92037

Gina Maccoby Literary Agency, 1123 Broadway, Suite 1009, New York, NY 10010

Helen McGrath, 1406 Idaho Ct., Concord, CA 94521

March Tenth, Inc., 4 Myrtle St., Haworth, NJ 07641

The Denise Marcil Literary Agency, 685 West End Ave., New York, NY 10025

Barbara Markowitz Literary Agency, 117 N. Mansfield Ave., Los Angeles, CA 90036

Howard Morhaim Literary Agency, 175 Fifth Ave., Suite 709, New York, NY 10010- 7703

Fifi Oscard Agency Inc., 24 W. 40th St., New York, NY 10018

The Otte Company, 9 Goden St., Belmont, MA 02178-3002

The Richard Parks Agency, 138 E. 16th St., 5th Floor, New York,

NY 10003

Rodney Pelter, 129 E. 61st St., New York, NY 10021

L. Perkins Associates, 5800 Arlington Ave., Riverdale, NY 10471

Alison J. Picard Literary Agent, P.O. Box 2000, Cotuit, MA 02635-2000

Julie Popkin, 15340 Albright St. #204, Pacific Palisades, CA 90272

Roberta Pryor, Inc., 24 W. 55th St., New York, NY 10019

Helen Rees Literary Agency, 308 Commonwealth Ave., Boston, MA 02116

Renaissance: A Literary/Talent Agency, 152 N. La Peer Dr., Los Angeles, CA 90048- 3011

Rock Literary Agency, P.O. Box 625, Newport, RI 02840

Rose Agency, 2033 Ontario Circle, Ft. Wayne, IN 46802-6737

Pesha Rubinstein Literary Agency, 37 Overlook Terrace, #1D, New York, NY 10033- 2216

Russell-Simenauer Literary Agency, P.O. Box 43267, Upper Montclair, NJ 07043- 2501

Blanche Schlessinger Agency, 433 Old Gulph Rd., Penn Valley, PA 19072

Harold Schmidt Literary Agency, 343 W. 12th St., #1B, New York, NY 10014

Susan Schulman, A Literary Agency, 454 W. 44th St., New York, NY 10036-5205

Lynn Seligman, Literary Agent, 400 Highland Ave., Upper Montclair, NJ 07043

Bobbe Siegel Literary Agency, 41 W. 83rd St, New York, NY 10024-5246

Philip G. Spitzer Literary Agency, 50 Talmage Farm Lane, East Hampton, NY 11937

Lyle Steele & Co. Ltd., 511 E. 73rd St., Suite 6, New York, NY 10021

Stepping Stone, 59 W. 71st St., New York, NY 10023

Gloria Stern Literary Agency, 2929 Buffalo Speedway, Houston, TX 77098-1707

H.N. Swanson Inc., 8523 Sunset Blvd., Los Angeles, CA 90069

Mary Jack Wald Associates, 111 E. 14th St., New York, NY 10003

Wallace Literary Agency, Inc., 177 E. 70 St., New York, NY 10021

John A. Ware Literary Agency, 392 Central Park West, New York, NY 10025-5801

The **Weingel-Fidel Agency**, 310 E. 46th St., #21E , New York, NY 10017

Westchester Literary Agency, 4278 D'Este Court, Suite 203, Lake Worth, FL 33467

Wieser & Wieser, Inc., 118 E. 25th St., 7th Floor, New York, NY 10010-2915

EDITORS AT WORK

☀ ☀ ☀ ☀ ☀

Anatomy of a Sale: "Me and Mr. Harry" to *Ellery Queen's Mystery Magazine*

J A N E T   H U T C H I N G S
Editor-in-Chief, Ellery Queen's Mystery Magazine

Some editors provide specific guidelines for authors, while others reply to that perennial author's question *What are you looking for?* with the frustrating editorial truism, *Good stories.* I belong to the latter group. I won't provide a do or don't list of topics because I believe that almost any subject can be made fresh and interesting by a writer who has learned to create believable characters.

Characterization is central to our genre because unlike science fiction, which has been described as a genre of ideas, mystery fiction is always concerned in some way with justice and morality, and, consequently, with the motives, intentions, and values of its characters.

The story you are about to read provides a particularly strong example of convincing characterization. It made its way into my "must read" pile with its first couple of paragraphs by immediately creating a question about its central character and her situation. Although the author had not previously published any crime fiction, it was clear from those opening paragraphs that she understood the key to creating suspense—involving the reader in the inner lives of the characters. Since discussing the specific mechanisms that move Batya Swift Yasgur's elegantly constructed piece may spoil its initial impact on you, I'd like you to read the story first, and then we'll take a look at how she achieved such good effects.

Me and Mr. Harry
BATYA SWIFT YASGUR

And isn't it just like my parents to mess it all up for me, just when it was so nice?

So I'm sitting here, in that stuffy green room just outside the principal's office, waiting for that fat, blousy lady, the social worker, to talk to me again. Mrs. Morris. Her voice is thick and powdery and sweet like the makeup she smears on her face; her hair is all puffed and twisted and piled on top of her head. When she smiles, her mouth is like a big cave you can fall into.

"You can tell me everything, dear." She leans over her desk and I shrink back into my chair. It's a big armchair, cozy, like a nest, and I'm a little bird snuggling into it. I won't talk. She can't make me.

She's getting rattled. I can tell.

"Wouldn't you like to talk about it?"

Like hell I would. I make my eyes into little slits, flare my nostrils—just a tiny bit—and tighten my lips. The Satanic look, my mother calls it. Gets them every time.

Now Mrs. Morris is even more rattled.

"I'm only here to help you." Her voice shakes some.

Right, lady. And I'm a flying ant. I'll keep my mouth shut, thanks.

She fidgets with her pen, breathes onto her glasses, and writes something down in a manilla folder. I curl myself up into a ball and sink back farther into the chair.

I want Mr. Harry. That's all.

Mommy comes home early every night now. She never used to. Used to work all the time, and I'd let myself in with the key. Made myself cereal and milk and the TV kept me company till she came home. Then it was why didn't I do my homework, and why didn't I make my bed, and why didn't I sweep. Oh, and why didn't I set the table, didn't I know what a long day she had, and how hard she and Daddy work. Then dinner and bath and bed, maybe two minutes of hello from Daddy before he got on the phone. And I used to lie there wondering whether my math teacher would yell at me again for getting the wrong answer, or my science teacher would laugh at me for my "stupid" mistakes.

Until Mr. Harry. Homework times went by so fast with him. I never even thought of TV when I was over at his house. He always had the yummiest cookies and we'd have a great time eating and watching the birds at his feeder. Or that time we shoveled his walk, and we made that giant snowman with a carrot nose and a funny hat, and then he made me hot chocolate.

I hate it when Mommy tries to help me with my homework. "Let's make this a nice family time!" she chirps brightly. "Then how about some pizza?"

I just want things the way they used to be. I want Mr. Harry back.

I'm smoking again. I lift the cigarettes from Daddy's jacket pocket. Mr. Harry got me to stop. Told me all this stuff about cancer, showed me how a cigarette burned a black hole through his handkerchief, and said the same thing would happen to my lungs. "Who cares," I said, puffing away. That's when he hugged me the first time. I swear, he had tears in his eyes. "I care," he told me. And he did.

Why did they have to go and put him in jail?

They won't even let me call him. Or write. Nothing.

Oops! I'm out of cigarettes. Better go get one before Daddy gets out of the shower.

The court is a great big brick building with so many corridors and hallways it's like one of those mazes we built in science class for the poor rats. It's not going to be a trial like on TV, they told me. I'm going to see the judge in his room.

I'm pretty nervous about meeting a judge. I expect someone with a black robe, a big wig, and a hammer, who's going to bang and yell "Order!" all the time. But no, he's a little guy with yellow wispy hair, like an old doll's, when I'd washed it too many times. He keeps making grumpy, harrumphy noises in his throat and wiping his nose with a red handkerchief. There are no armchairs.

"When did you first start going to Harry Wrightson's place?"

Another throat noise, another sniffle. I sit up straighter. I don't have to tell this guy anything, even if he is a judge.

I make my slitted-eye face. I can stare him down.

"Answer the question," my mother says, giving my shoulder a squeeze.

I go on staring.

"Yes, yes." The judge clears his throat. "This is hard for you, I know."

No you don't.

He tries again. "When did he touch you the first time?"

I can't hear those words and keep looking at him. I look at the floor. That day, after I failed my science test, when I cried and Mr. Harry held me, warm and tight and cuddly. Stroked my hair and whispered, "Science isn't what counts. Love is. And you're an expert at that." Oh, and I had to ask him what an "expert" is. And he *didn't* tell me to "go look it up."

The judge is asking another question, but I'm not listening anymore. The school is running this program called "Bad Touch/Good Touch." Mrs. Morris keeps looking at me while they're play-acting these stupid skits on stage, but I make believe I don't see. Mr. Harry's touching—that wasn't bad. Sure, it felt kind of funny at first. But it was—what was his word—*special*. Because I'm special. He said so.

More dumb doctors. One asks lots of questions, you know, some kind of a test. A little like school, but also different. Boxes to fill in, shapes to complete, splatters of ink on some cards, and he wants to know what they look like to me. My mouth is zipped shut. He keeps shaking his head and writing stuff down in this folder. "No little girl has ever behaved like this in here," he says as I'm leaving.

Good. I really am special after all.

They think that 'cause I don't talk, I also can't hear. They're saying more and more in front of me.

I keep hearing them talking about me. Whispers, of course. Lots about a "residence." I *did* look that one up, and it means "home." I don't get it. I already have a home. Correction: I have a house. Only at Mr. Harry's did I ever really feel home.

I'm back in the cozy armchair in Mrs. Morris's office. Mommy and Daddy are there too. Mommy keeps crying and wiping her eyes with this gross wet tissue that has big holes and is falling apart. Daddy keeps tapping her on the arm and saying, "Now, Bertha."

"Honey." Mommy sounds quivery like the wings on the humming-bird outside Mr. Harry's window as he used to hover (now *there's* a nice vocabulary word for you, a free gift from Mr. Harry and me) over his feeder.

I won't even turn to look at her. I let the chair cuddle me.

"Talk to Mrs. Morris!" How many times since it happened have I heard Daddy say that in his "punishment" voice. But nothing can make me talk. Not when they yell. Not when they hit. Not when they cry.

"Don't you want to make sure he doesn't do this to another little girl?"

I almost laugh. What we had, Mr. Harry and me, was just between the two of us. He wouldn't do this with anyone else, 'cause no one is special like me.

Looks like I'm going to be shipped off to this place they call the "residence." Seems like it's some kind of orphanage. I don't get it. My parents are alive. I thought orphan homes are for kids whose parents are dead. Of course, for all I care, they could be. Mr. Harry is gone and that's what matters.

Mommy's eyes are teary all the time, but Daddy does a lot of barking. "Please, honey, won't you even talk to us?" Mommy begs. "You're ruining your life, young lady, I hope you know that!" is all I hear from Daddy.

Who cares.

I hear them talking on the phone. I don't know who they're talking to, but I've picked up on the upstairs extension. They don't know I'm listening, of course. Just like they don't know about the time Daddy yelled at Mommy about the bank and the morgidge (is that how you spell it?) in their bedroom, and I was hiding in my spot in the linen closet outside their door. Or that night when I heard all those strange bumps and thumps and groany noises. Or the time Mommy cried when she thought she was going to have another baby. "I can hardly handle one. How am I ever going to manage with two!" I've got eavesdropping down to a science (probably the only science I'll ever be good at).

"What do you mean, they're going to release him?" Daddy's angriest voice.

"Just what I said." The man I don't know is talking.

"But that's outrageous!" Mommy is crying, as usual.

"Your daughter won't talk, so there isn't enough evidence."

"What she said that time, that wasn't enough? That's how we found out about it in the first place!"

"No."

"What about the other little girl? Doesn't her testimony count for something?"

My hand, holding the phone receiver, turns to ice. I'm afraid I'm going to throw up.

And when I hear myself screaming, Mommy and Daddy drop the

phone and are running up the stairs. My voice sounds rusty, like a broken machine that's been lying around too long.

"*What other little girl?*"

Characterization and Suspense in "Me and Mr. Harry"

The mystery/crime field is very broad and the suspense story is only one of its legitimate offspring. Yet many of the principles at work in a good suspense story apply to the genre's other forms too. Rather than try to identify all the elements that go into making "Me and Mr. Harry" a good story, I want to focus on the author's techniques for characterization. From her example you will probably be able to gather some ideas that will help you with whatever type of mystery fiction you write.

One of the first principles of good characterization is to establish a point of view early on and maintain it. This is especially important in writing a short story, where you generally are not following a character through an extended period of life, and where you have very few words in which to create a picture of the character for the reader. Batya Swift Yasgur wastes not a single sentence. She immediately establishes four important points relevant to her story's point of view:

1. the story will be related by a child;
2. there is an immediate source of conflict between the child and his or her parents;
3. the child's attitude towards the parents is hostile;
4. the child has a sarcastic turn of mind.

Telling a story from a child's viewpoint isn't easy, especially when the narrative is in the first person, since all the information readers must have to grasp what is going on—including the setting of the scene—has to be conveyed in terms a child would understand. The author of this piece does a remarkable job of filtering the facts needed by the reader through her young protagonist's consciousness. New writers are usually advised to avoid difficult viewpoints such as this, but in the end, your choice must be dictated by the needs of your story.

The use of a child as narrator may have helped Batya Yasgur to avoid one of the common pitfalls of authors who write about social issues such as child abuse. At the beginning of this essay I said we have no stated restrictions on subject matter at *EQMM*, no list of taboos; there are, however, subjects I approach with a strong expectation of not liking what I'm about to read. Child abuse heads that list, for the simple reason that so few writers seem able to treat the subject without explicit moralizing. When authors give in to the temptation to play the moralist—or sociologist or psychologist—it is often at the cost of truth in characterization, since they may then also be tempted to make the victim of the abuse as sympathetic and good as possible. By telling her story in the first person, from the child's point of view, Ms. Yasgur is able to peel away the gloss that often surrounds children portrayed as victims. In "Me and Mr. Harry," the opportunity to superimpose adult judgments about what has occurred is limited since the child, who is telling the story, doesn't yet have quite the same concepts as the adults as to what is right and wrong. Mystery fiction exists against a background of moral judgments. They are what we measure the heinousness of a crime in terms of, and understand characters' motives in relation to, but such judgments should be part of the unnoticed backdrop to the story and not made to intrude upon the reader's consciousness. By choosing a viewpoint that does not force upon the reader the conventional adult appraisal of actions, Ms. Yasgur has heightened, not lessened, the moral impact of her story.

Seeing what point of view will work best for a given story is one thing; maintaining and developing it consistently to the last page is another. Many writers lose their focus somewhere in the middle pages. Batya Yasgur does not, and some of the techniques she employs (consciously or otherwise) may be helpful to you. The effectiveness of Ms. Yasgur's portrayal of the protagonist of "Me and Mr. Harry" derives partly from reiteration of the attitudes she equips her character with in the story's opening lines. For instance, all the adults in the story but Mr. Harry are depicted as in some way sloppy and repellent: The social worker is a fat, blousy lady whose "voice is thick and powdery and sweet like the makeup she smears on her face"; Mommy wipes her eyes with "this gross wet tissue that has big holes and is falling apart"; the judge "keeps making grumpy, harrumphy noises in his throat and wiping his nose with a red handkerchief"; and Daddy smokes cigarettes, which Mr. Harry tells her burn black holes through the lungs. The narrator's descriptions in all these cases sound again the note of the opening lines. She is derisive, she sees the adults—not only her parents, it turns out, but other adults in positions of authority over her—as necessarily opposed to her and physically unappealing. The repetition of this type of description functions as a kind of *leitmotif*. We see it and recognize that we're inside this character and no one else.

Believable characters have attitudes we can recognize and predict; they can't be changing willy nilly. And yet a degree of complexity and areas of conflict and inconsistency are required if the character is to claim our interest. First person narratives afford ample opportunity for an author to digress on the conflicted thoughts of the central character/narrator. In fact, one of the reasons the first person is often chosen for private-eye stories is that such digressions have become a convention of the form. Generally speaking, however, thoughts do not work as well as feelings and visceral reactions in bringing out the conflicts that motivate a character. Notice how easily Batya Yasgur leads us to the heart of her child narrator's predicament with these two lines: "I shrink back into my chair. It's a big armchair, cozy, like a nest, and I'm a little bird snuggling into it." Right away we know that this is a little girl who for all her snideness about the adults in her life desires the comfort and protection that only adults and a home can provide. And from that we immediately get a picture of what her home life is like without ever needing access to her thoughts. To characterize by conveying a visceral experience of the character, as the author does in this case, is more economical than giving the reader her thoughts, and when you're writing a short story, economy is of great importance.

The author of this piece is skilled at making the elements of her story work in a variety of ways at once. She has compressed a very complex set of relationships into five short pages, and she could not have done so had she needed to tell us all we come to understand. She relies instead on feelings and associations. The phlegmy, makeup-besmeared, cigarette-puffing adults make me think of the Europeans in Jonathan Swift's *Gulliver's Travels* whose skins are so fine when viewed by others of their size but appear to have pores like grotesque craters when observed from the standpoint of the Lilliputians. Such associations, which will be different for different readers, are irrelevant except insofar as they help us to make connections between what the author specifically tells us, and what she wants us to pick up on for ourselves—in this case the powerlessness of the child in relation to the gargantuan adults who people her world. For a story to spark such associations, it must allow us to feel and react as its characters do; it must affect us on a visceral as well as a cognitive level.

So far we've talked about the ways in which a good writer will flesh-out and build aspects of character. But it is equally important in the mystery story to know what information about a character to withhold. The surprise and horror in Batya Swift Yasgur's story does not come from the discovery of what happened to the child (we know that almost from the beginning), but from our grasping what the child felt about it. The suspense in this story is tied to a revelation about the character, and it is therefore very important, if suspense is to be maintained, that this aspect of her psychological makeup be revealed at the right time. To a greater or lesser extent, the idea of holding back some crucial piece of the psychological puzzle applies to most mystery stories. Even in the classical detective story the question of whodunit is usually linked to the question of what makes certain characters tick. Learning when to allow the reader to make these discoveries about a character is just as important as learning how to place clues and uncover evidence. And if you can allow readers to figure out for themselves what drives your characters, the impact of the discovery will be greater.

In Batya Yasgur's story it's obvious from the beginning that a child has been abused—a social worker has been called in, a man is in jail, a judge is initiating proceedings—but we're halfway through the narrative before any mention is made of Mr. Harry's touching the victim. By with-holding discussion of the crime, the author creates a question in the reader's mind as to just how serious the abuse was and how it has affected the child. Now remember that the child is telling the story, so if it takes her this long to get to what Mr. Harry's accused of doing, and she mentions it in such an offhand way, then we can probably conclude that she doesn't think it's very important—at least not as long as it's linked to her being *special*. But isn't that a striking attitude? In answering the question in the reader's mind about what happened, Ms. Yasgur immediately creates a more interesting question about the child's inner life, a question she's not going to answer for us until the very last line.

The suspense that skillful characterization can generate often turns on the complexity of a character's personality. In all of us there are currents moving the psyche of which we are not entirely aware. A believable characterization will reflect this complexity. The child in "Me and Mr. Harry" is a good example. She may not feel that there is anything very significant about Mr. Harry's touching her, but of course there is. It simply lies coiled at a deeper level of her psyche, ready to spring when she discovers that she is not, after all, special. We don't realize how profoundly the sexual relationship has affected her until the last line of the story when she discovers the facts of which everyone else has been aware. Thus there is a perfect merging in the end of those aspects of the story that have to do with facts and circumstances and those that have to do with the inner life of the protagonist. The story's real punch, however, comes from the psychological revelation, and that's why the story is such a good example of how the development of character functions in creating suspense.

Summary

When a story comes across my desk at *EQMM*, I try to keep an open mind: I'm reluctant to say what it is I'm looking for, or to state my personal preferences, because a good writer will almost always be able to surprise me into liking what I thought I wouldn't. Batya Swift Yasgur proved the point with her very first work of fiction, "Me and Mr. Harry." From her opening paragraphs she convinced me that she had a fresh voice, unhindered by preconceptions about her subject matter, and would deliver truthful characterizations.

Her story illustrates three principles of characterization that you will find at work in most successful mystery/suspense stories. She

1. established a recognizable point of view for her protagonist and maintained it throughout the story;
2. relied more on the gut reactions of her character than on her thoughts to convey what makes her tick; and
3. created a question about the character that carried through the story to create and maintain suspense.

By mastering these important elements of storytelling, Batya Yasgur not only sold "Me and Mr. Harry" to *EQMM*, she won (for "Me and Mr. Harry") the 1995 Robert L. Fish Award for best short story by a new author.

Anatomy of a Sale: *The Innocents* to Walker & Company

M I C H A E L   S E I D M A N
Mystery Editor, Walker & Company

A hundred times a week I open an envelope or package that contains the promise of a manuscript I must acquire for my list. I publish 20 novels and one anthology a year.

Each of those submissions—query letter, partial or complete manuscript—is sent in good faith by an author or an agent. As often as not I'm told why I will want to publish the book: It is, of course, wonderfully well written; it is bound to be a bestseller because there are nine million golfers, each of whom will identify with *The Deadly Caddy*; it is exactly like such other successful and popular novels as—well, you fill in the blank, there; it won second place in a contest; everyone in the author's critique group loved it, as did most of the author's immediate family; and, certainly, it meets my guidelines.

Of the 20 novels on my list, at least ten, and as many as 15, may be second or third or later books in an on-going series: option books. Two or three may be novels by established authors who have, for one reason or another, chosen to publish with Walker.

Of the 5,200 submissions received each year, 90 percent are first novels, many written by people who've heard that mysteries are hot, so that is what they should be writing. That their knowledge of the genre is minimal—based on reading three novels and one how-to book before they sat down to write their own—doesn't seem to be of concern to anyone but me.

Because Walker is a small, independent house, the 20 novels on my list each year are an integral part of a business plan as well as representative of a publishing philosophy: They are not chosen, edited, and published because there's a slot to fill. Because of the needs and nature of category fiction, some books will be "traditional": a whodunit easily identified by a potential reader as a book they will want to spend some hours with and, it is hoped, will make them want to spend more time with that author later, either by going to the backlist, or waiting anxiously for the next novel.

At the same time, I'm always looking for a book that is somehow special and different, a story that is going to appeal to those who won't be rounded up with the rest of the usual suspects, a book that is going to "break out" and be embraced by all readers, regardless of their usual reading interests.

There is another requirement: balance. While I suppose it is possible to put together a list that appeals to only one segment of a broad market—readers of cozies, for instance—it is an infinitely boring way to spend one's day. There are, of course, some things I don't like or have found that I cannot publish successfully; that is why, for instance, a 150,000 word novel about a psychic detective proving that the Ghost of Christmas Past is the murderer will be rejected without comment.

And then there are the things I particularly like; at the top of that list is a writer with an understanding of the purposes of fiction and the ability to use that understanding in a compelling way. As an editor and a reader (the two should be inseparable), my interests and the things I'm looking for are the same. I want an author who writes with clarity, but without simplification, who uses all the power of the English language, who understands that people cause events and thus creates story people that fulfill the dictum presented by Heraclitus: A man's character is his fate. I'm looking for situations I haven't encountered before or, failing that, an innovative—rather than trite—reinvention of the wheel. Finally, I don't want to know how the book is going to end; I want to be surprised by a series of events that follow a question implicit in the beginning of the story.

My rejection rate is necessarily high. Most of the time, I know within three pages whether I even want to keep reading; the majority of manuscripts offer absolutely no reason to go on. I know, immediately, that if I don't care enough, I won't be able to get anyone else in the company to care. When I do decide to acquire something, however, I know that the novel is one that I can get behind and support wholeheartedly, and that I will be able to get the support of the entire marketing department to back the publication. That's a minimum desire; every once in a while, I lean back, smile, and yell "Eureka!"

The Innocents, a first novel by Richard Barre, was submitted through his agent Philip Spitzer after a conversation during which I outlined what it was I wanted for my Spring, 1995 list.

The cover letter did not tell me that the novel was set in Southern California, that it featured a male private investigator; it did not categorize the book in any way. Phil simply said that it was a crime novel. That allowed me to approach my reading without any expectations or biases; I simply expected a well-told tale. (It is entirely possible that I would not have read as quickly or with as much interest if I'd known it was a P.I. novel; I already had two on the list and a third would have weighted the scales too heavily. Remember, a list requires balance.)

The story begins with a flashback, set in 1967. Nine paragraphs, with a foreshadowed threat at the end: "He would never do it again." We know the thoughts are those of a child, and we believe that those six words are both a frightened child's promise and a clear statement of fact.

The scene shifts to California, 1990. "Dawn was bringing shape to the greasewood by the time they unearthed the skeleton and sifted for clues. Montoya, part of the initial wave of law. . ." Was this the body of the boy in the opening? Odds were it was. Simple, so far.

As the scene evolves, details are revealed, slowly and in place. Montoya, feeling the cold of the desert winter, wonders if the child liked to swim . . . "certainly his did." Montoya is a father. "Jesus, what next, he thought, rubbing his eyes. In fourteen years he'd seen children die . . . " We get a bit of background and then this: "This one was different, though, put in the ground with intent; chilling beyond the sadness of it. Montoya recalled his first glimpse of the skull, multicolored quartz chips embedded in the small eye sockets." The pacing of the sentence, as well as the intent of it, grabbed me immediately.

The point of view shifts to that of a reporter, calling in to her boss. She's heard about the discovery of the skeleton on her scanner and decided to go to the scene. The last line of the chapter is frightening and to the point, and by the time I got there, I knew this was a manuscript I was going to read to the end.

In the next chapter, we meet Wil Hardesty; he is the (private) detective, the setting is Southern California. There is no other similarity, however, to Raymond Chandler's or Ross Macdonald's Southern California novels; Barre and Hardesty are their own men.

The story that evolves in *The Innocents* is not about who buried the child in the desert (we are introduced to the killer quickly) but about why and about how Hardesty is going to obtain justice for the victims. En route to the end, Barre takes us through twists and turns, philosophical as well as novelistic, keeping reader interest high. The pacing never flags, nor does Barre resort to the old ploy of bringing in a man with a gun when the action slows.

Then, for good measure, about a third of the way through, Barre creates a murder scene that a lesser writer would have used as the opening hook. It is one of the most powerful scenes of its kind that I've ever read, turns the story in yet another direction, and makes it impossible to put the book down until the reader has gotten to the last words on the last page.

Additionally, in the course of telling the story, Barre puts Hardesty through the various stages of a Campbellian hero's journey; the hell the detective fights through—a hell his character would not allow him to avoid—tempers him in such a way that the Hardesty who emerges is a very different man than the one who began the investigation. You know these are events Hardesty will not forget, that the things he does in his next outing will be colored by the experience.

You also know there will be a next outing; that Richard Barre—even before his first novel has been exposed to the world—will be a continuing presence on the Walker list. I can guarantee it: After all, when I finished reading the manuscript I went to my boss, placed the pages on his desk and said, "George, you gotta read this one. It's the book I've been looking for."

Why? Because it was written by a man who engages all the senses of the reader, and who understands murder and death and loss: The killings in *The Innocents* are important, but they are not simply plot points, the excuse for the novel. All too often, I find mystery writers have no understanding at all of what violent crime represents to the victims—the living victims—of the event. You can't have a murder mystery without a corpse, so the body is there. But the passions are lacking. I'm not saying that you have to kill someone in order to write about murder, but you have to feel the emotions or comprehend the lack of them. Barre does.

That all important in-house support began as soon as George Gibson, Walker's publisher, read the manuscript: Our negotiation with Philip

Spitzer was for two books.

Richard Barre and *The Innocents* are the reason I'm willing to open a hundred submissions a week and are a good indication to those looking to sell a crime novel (at least to me) of what it takes.

The Innocents
RICHARD BARRE

Mexico, 1967

The man's hand was hurting his—he wanted to pull away, to run. He said he was sorry about the medal. Why couldn't they understand?

Papa must know that Gilberto had put him up to it. Gilberto was jealous. Gilberto fooled him and now look what happened. First the beating from Papa and now the man taking him away. Sad faces, his brother not looking at him, Mama crying.

Yesterday had been so happy. He wanted to go back to the bright time with the shouts and the blindfold and the clay rooster he'd whacked with the long stick. Even getting up at dawn had been exciting—before the church bells, before anyone. All winter they'd coughed in the chill wind off the mountains. But it was warmer now, and night rain had washed the sky leaving pinks and golds.

Finally he couldn't stand it so he woke them, all but Mama, who stayed behind. How could they have been so slow—hanging back to tease him, laughing as he tried to hurry them along. In church, with Papa watching, he'd been good the whole time. Even the old priest went to sleep, but not him. Next year he would join his brothers at the rail, receive the wafer, feel the shiny disk touch his throat before it moved on. Then he would close his eyes and taste the Bodyblood. Made him want to make a face, but he'd be brave.

Mass was endless, his toes jumping beans—and then it was over. Skipping home in the sunshine, ahead of Papa and the rest. The door opening suddenly. Mama there and the flowers and the piñata and the singing: Happy Birthday to him! As they sucked on little sugar cones, Papa gave it to him, the most beautiful thing he'd ever seen, silver with his name on it and everything. It was only later, when he and Gilberto were alone examining the medal that Gilberto dared him. "Pretend it's first communion. Go on, don't be a baby." He was no baby. He showed Gilberto.

Papa's willow switch had stung like fire through his thin pants. Never had he seen his father so angry. At least he knew Gilberto hurt just as much.

But that was yesterday. Now the man's hand was tightening on his, pulling him toward the door. Papa met his eyes and looked down, then Gilberto. Was the man going to take Gilberto away because of the medal, too? Mama was crying again, Papa holding her now.

He didn't like the man, didn't want to go. Would God know where to find him? Couldn't they give him another chance?

He would never do it again.

California, 1990

Dawn was bringing shape to the greasewood by the time they unearthed the skeleton and sifted for clues. Montoya, part of the initial wave of law, watched as first light touched Saddleback Butte and the Tehachapis. It had been a long night, wind off the Angeles Crest dogging them for most of it, rising again with the sun.

Soon they'd kill the generator-powered kleigs.

Montoya slugged down the last of the coffee, raised the fur collar of his jacket as a gust stung him. Still snow up there, obviously; months before the warm desert evenings, the kids laughing in the backyard pool.

He wondered if the kid they'd found liked to swim. All kids liked to swim, certainly his did. Jesus, what next, he thought, rubbing his eyes. In fourteen years he'd seen children die in smash-ups, a baby electrocuted, a family of five wiped out in a fire. This one was different, though, put in the ground with intent; chilling beyond the sadness of it. Montoya recalled his first glimpse of the skull, multicolored quartz chips embedded in the small eye sockets.

He scratched his scalp under the LA County Sheriff's cap. From the looks, this one was about his daughter's age. Hard not to think it.

The coroner and crime scene people were nearly finished, the grave site photographed, evidence bagged. Montoya, who'd supervised until the homicide team from downtown arrived, tossed the thermos in the 4WD then crunched over coarse gravel defining the flash flood channel.

"Can't tell much yet from the bones." *Parks* the name tag read; Montoya remembered her from a Palmdale rape-murder she and her partner drew a couple of years ago. Her breath showed in the morning cold.

"We maybe got lucky, though." She held up a clear plastic bag, something small and round inside.

Montoya took the bag, felt the St. Christopher medal. It was a cheap-plated one with some of the silver around the figure holding the staff and the lamb stripped away. He turned the bag over. The engraving was worn but deep enough to read:

Vaya con Dios, Benito. Papa, 1967.

Montoya puzzled a moment; something clicked. "What about a chain? One turn up?"

She exhaled, "Not so far. Kind of expect one, wouldn't you, Sergeant. Certainly it would have lasted as long as the medal."

"Detective Parks," a voice called. "Over here."

One of the Lancaster deputies was hunched over something several feet from the area they'd combed. "More bones," he said. "Spotted 'em as it got lighter. Look there."

They looked. Barely visible outside the circle of artificial light, beside the exposed roots of a mesquite bush, white finger bones poked up from gray gravel. Like the others they were small, perfect. A child's hand.

There was a moan of wind, a crackle from one of the radios.

Parks spoke first. "Merry Christmas," she said.

"Son of a bitch," Montoya added.

━━ ◆ ━━

"Slow it down, Patty, how many?"

The news director was trying to open his eyes and find his glasses at the same time. From the floor where he'd knocked the alarm, the hour glowed early, too early for somebody who worked as late as he did.

"What's the source?" he mumbled. She was calling mobile; he could hear truck sounds and a car radio in the background. McGann wasn't the best field jockey on his news team, but she was young and ambitious and covered a lot of ground. Things he liked.

"Scanner, Chief, heard it coming home from a date. At first it was a single kid's remains out near Saddleback Butte—some man and his son shooting at cans found 'em. I got curious, made coffee and sat with it. After a while they came on again and upped it to three. Figured I'd get rolling."

The news director grunted, sat up, fumbled on bifocals; he'd crossed the line now, more awake than asleep. "Okay. How quick can you get there?"

"I'm on the Golden State near Burbank," she said, "Traffic's a bitch. An hour if I step on it."

"Step on it, then. Any idea about the three?"

"Not yet."

The news director heard a horn and a muffled curse, half-smiled, reached for his cigarettes. He'd spent twelve years in the field, knew the pressure the kid was under. Delays were slow death.

"Too early to tell, I guess," she said. "Scanner's been pretty sketchy. I just hope I got the jump."

"Stay with it, you'll be fine. You got a shooter yet?"

"Lombardi's a mile or so back." Gears shifted. "Here we go," she said. "Might scoop this one yet, Chief."

"Just get there in one piece, okay?"

"Rodge."

He was about to hang up and put the department on alert when he heard Patty McGann swear again, only this time it was full of wonder. A little prickle went up the news director's spine. He'd heard a CBS correspondent swear much the same way passing a shot-up rifle company near Hue, 1968. It had been him.

McGann came back, but her voice sounded far away.

"Scanner just updated. They've got five so far." There was a pause. "My God, they're still counting."

T W O

Pumping for speed, Hardesty dropped down the waveface, hit bottom then angled up for a move off the lip. After reentry and a cutback, he'd close it out with five on the nose—maybe ten—show 'em how it's done. Nirvana coming up.

Then the wind. All day it had stoked the breakers, turning wavetops into needle spray that reached windshields driving past the Rincon. All day it had been his friend.

He was coming off the top when it hit, a maverick burst of gusting energy. Unbalanced and overcompensating, he staggered then flipped headfirst into the green wall, the weight of it rolling over him like a highballing freight. He came up breathless, tasting salt. The longboard, like a dog on a leash, tugged on the cord strapped to his ankle.

Gringo flashed by him on the next swell, "Too old for this shit, Wil."

Hardesty grinned. He and his board were relics to these kids and their racy tri-fin thrusters. They knew him, though, got a bang out of his wipeouts. What the hell, so did he.

Even with the wind the day was perfect: lapis sky, clouds long gone, Channel Islands clear enough to see the canyons etched like claw marks in the hills. And two miles south, the roof of his La Conchita house. Lisa'd have the Viennese brewing by now, burnt bitter stuff—words that madehim wonder if it wasn't the way the marriage was heading.

Hardesty ducked under an incoming. The late December swells were the best he'd surfed in years: ten foot bluebirds, the pulse of far-off storms, a blast to the younger guys like Gringo. But for Wil Hardesty, the waves ebbed and flowed in his veins, part of him.

He'd started at the Wedge, bodysurfing at fourteen, and nearly drowned, The exhilaration, though, stuck around long after the water had left his lungs. In a month he was riding breakers under the Newport Beach pier—shooting the shit afterwards with the foggy morning crowd, sharing lukewarm coffee and sugary Winchells with sand on the glaze. Life then was surf odyssey and outlaw-freedom mystique, San Onofre to Malibu to even-then Rincon, Mickey-this and Corky-that, slow dances to tremolo guitar bands, Coppertone on warm skin. Fun to kick around now when he bumped into other surfing graybeards.

Back then he'd even done some money gigs before walking away. Ultimately, it had come down to him and the water.

Thinking how much Devin would have loved it today, he headed in.

Anatomy of a Sale: *Felony Murder* to St. Martin's Press/Thomas Dunne Books

RUTH CAVIN
Senior Editor/Associate Publisher, St. Martin's Press

A summer Sunday morning finds me in my office prepared to spend the day dealing with some 35 to 40 manuscripts that are waiting on my shelf. I pick one up. It's obviously a "no" from its tired page one. The second requires little more. Four chapters into number three, it's clear that it's the same old same old. And then I pick up Joe Klempner's *Felony Murder,* and that's the end of my plans for clearing off my submissions shelves that day; I can't stop until I've finished the last page—and it's not a short book.

St. Martin's Press publishes a whopping percentage of the several hundred hardcover mystery novels that appear annually in the United States. Inevitably, then, my colleagues and I are the recipients of hundreds or more manuscripts each year. I myself receive an average of about six or seven submissions a week—some from agents, and some just, in the publishing world's inelegant but also rather dashing phrase, "over the transom." (Which is much better than "slush pile," anyhow.)

The big question then becomes, how do I choose which of all these submissions to publish and which to send back. A few (although not so many as you might expect) are just plain bad. For the most part, however, the main objection is that they are just like 90% of the other manuscripts that come in: acceptable as to plot, getting by on characterization, etc., but on the whole, very predictable and almost as though they'd been written by the same person. So the manuscript I say "yes" to has to have something special if I'm going to add it to my list of 45 or so mysteries a year.

And that's why *Felony Murder,* a first novel by Joseph T. Klempner, will be published by the time you are reading these lines. The kind of suspense and excitement generated by the book would alone almost be enough to clinch a place on my list. Almost. There are books on the bestseller list that have little to recommend them except page-turning high-voltage suspense. But I ask that the ones I do publish meet all the other standards of a good novel as well. I have to believe the characters and care about them, for good or ill. I have to feel a strong sense of where the story takes place. The action must be logical, the prose must be clean and "accurate" (I'll explain my special meaning of that later) and—this is very important and at the same time very hard to define— the author must have an individual voice that makes his or her book stand out from the rest.

Let's see how Joseph Klempner's book has done this:

At the beginning we are introduced to a character who is one of the urban homeless. But unlike so many homeless people who turn up in fiction these days (as, sadly, they turn up in life), Joey Spadafino is not just another part of the atmosphere, like the sheet of newspaper that blows across a wet sidewalk, or a tree whose leaves have shaken off in the fall winds. The author makes clear right away that this is a person whose humanity he, Klempner, is very aware of.

Then we leave Joey and find ourselves in a New York restaurant where a bunch of high-level cops have been eating and drinking. The Police Commissioner is having some physical problems, problems that could be trivial, but that the author knows how to make us feel are important. Leaving us with that rather ominous impression, Klempner takes us back to Joey, just when his and the commissioner's paths cross: Joey, seeing the man reeling and taking him to be not ill, but drunk, decides to rob him. Not too unexpected; we know all about unsafe city streets—and yet, we've been shown enough of Joey's condition to understand why he's going to do this. This is something that I find a very good sign— that the book will have characters who are neither all good nor all bad, but human beings with their own strengths and weaknesses.

And now we learn there's someone who from her window sees the commissioner lying on the snowy sidewalk, and Joey bending over him. She's Janet, a single mother, up at this hour to feed her infant daughter. She is not only an attractive personality, but a good citizen; she sees something going down and phones the police about it. But just what *has* she seen? Has Joey knocked down the commissioner and then robbed him, or has the commissioner fallen, and Joey gone through his pockets afterward? What Janet saw and didn't see becomes an even more complex issue than it may seem right now.

Joey tries to run away, but is quickly nabbed by the cops responding to Janet's call.

The first chapter prepares us for the rest of the story. It has action, both physical and emotional. (Contrary to what some inexperienced authors think, "action" is not only George punches Harold in the nose; it's the twists and turns that people make in responding to outside forces and inner tugs.) It has fine atmosphere; we are with the characters in Greenwich Village on a snowy night. Already we're aware that things may not be as they seem; that this is not just a cut-and-dried mugging. And although it has not yet brought in the principal character—Dean Abernathy, the young lawyer assigned to defend Joey Spadafino—he'll soon be confronted with the case and his unpromising client.

In chapter two, Dean meets his client and explains to him—and to us—just what "felony murder" is, and a basis is laid for their growing relationship. Later on, we get to know more about Dean himself, and what his life is like; the author has had the savvy to do this with significant details—the kind that give us a good picture of the man and how he lives.

As an editor, I am happy about the writing; it is accurate. Writing is accurate when the words and phrases themselves say what the author wants them to say, rather than, as too often is true, some just-missing approximation of it. The dialogue not only reads like real people talking, it is differentiated; one person's way of saying something is not exactly like the way another would. (Obviously, within limits; neither Judy O'Grady nor the Colonel's lady could ring much of a variation on "It's raining.") We get more about the dead police commissioner and his background from the newspaper story on the case. And we learn more about his physical condition—that he recently had a "minor" heart attack, and that he had been feeling "under the weather" for several days.

Chapter two sets the stage naturally for some important plot elements without dragging them in by the heels. The suspense mounts and mounts, the complications are fresh and fascinating, the characters become real people with whom the reader is very involved, and nothing is predictable. And there is plenty of physical action as well. But as I came near the end of the manuscript, I found that the last part of the story wasn't working very well.

It's obvious that no matter how good the rest of the work is, the plot of a mystery has to be right. *But*—unlike two-dimensional characterization or bad writing, *plots can almost always be fixed,* (assuming the basic premise isn't as flawed as the proposal I once got for a book about neckties that strangled their wearers on their own initiative). After I bought *Felony Murder,* the author and I worked on that final section, and he fixed it.

An editor has a private life and private preferences, but it's necessary for us to separate personal preferences from more general ones. There may be a particular kind of subgenre that I don't choose to read for pleasure, but if a manuscript in that subgenre comes to me, and it's well-done, and I know that there are many readers out there who will enjoy it, I'll take it on. Publishing is a business, and the editor's job is to select works that will live up to the standards of story-telling excellence and will entice people to buy them.

I should point out that I didn't buy *Felony Murder* because "legal thrillers are in." They have been very popular, what with Scott Turow and all, but it's foolish to buy something because it's in; I don't do that. By the time your book is published there may be a completely other "in." Anyhow, there are much more important considerations. The most important is that it's a good book. When it comes right down to it, that's what I look for. Happily, that's often what I find, and what I found in *Felony Murder.*

Felony Murder

JOSEPH T. KLEMPNER

ONE

Joey Spadafino is cold. Cold and wet. He huddles in the doorway and shifts his weight from one foot to the other, trying to wriggle his toes inside his shoes to keep them from becoming numb. His breath sends the snowflakes scattering from in front of his face, as they pick up the lights of Bleecker Street.

It's not the coldest night he has spent on the street, but it's already the worst. Unlike rain, which Joey has found comes pretty much straight down and allows you to get out of by taking refuge in a doorway, snow blows sideways. In fact, it now seems to Joey, the snow sometimes blows *up,* like it's coming from underneath him. And it's not a dry snow that you can shake off you. It's these big, wet flakes that seem to be made out of melting ice, that make your clothing wet as soon as they land on you, and soak the soles of your shoes.

Joey has no watch, but he knows it's well after midnight. He slept for an hour or so earlier, but he's afraid to fall asleep again. He's heard stories of people on the street freezing to death in their sleep cause they got cold and wet and stopped moving, and got found dead the next morning. So he keeps moving his feet, keeps wriggling his toes, concentrates on making it through the night.

Joey thinks about lighting another cigarette. He scored two dollars from a lady walking a dog early in the evening, when the snow was just starting. She'd asked him didn't he have a place to go to get out of the snow, and he'd said no, he was afraid of the shelters, which was true, and she'd reached into her purse and had taken out two dollars which she'd handed him. He'd thought about snatching the purse and taking off with it, but he hadn't done it, hadn't had the nerve. He had thanked her instead. It was a big dog she was walking, anyway.

He'd taken the two dollars and bought a pack of cigarettes. He'd figured the cigarettes would get him through the night better than a slice of pizza would of. They'd last longer, they'd occupy him. But by now he's smoked half the pack, and his mouth tastes like a goddam ashtray, and his stomach's empty, and he wishes he had the slice of pizza.

The meeting had broken up at 0230. If you could call it a meeting. The P.C., his two deputies, Pacelli and Childress, and Haber, who headed up Internal Affairs. They had sat in the corner table at Chandler's, gradually substituting good whiskey for mediocre food, and talking about the old days. It had been Pacelli's idea that they meet, the First Dep saying they needed to talk about restructuring the patrol force in the wake of another round of anticipated budget cuts. But talk had soon turned to the days when a cop could be a cop instead of a public relations expert, and how respect for the uniform was a thing of the past, and how overconcern for minorities was destroying morale. The last was a somewhat delicate topic, since the P.C. himself was black, and the meeting had broken up shortly thereafter, to a glass-draining toast to the days when dinosaurs patrolled the streets.

The brass had split up outside, shaking hands and slapping backs under the streetlamps in the gusting snow. Santana, the P.C.'s chauffeur, had the motor running in the Department auto, and it was warm inside, too warm.

"Turn the heat down, willya?" the P.C. said, sitting down next to his driver. He refused to ride in the back.

"Yessir," said Santana, reaching forward and fumbling with a dial on the dashboard. But if he did anything about it, it didn't seem to help. The P.C. reached to loosen his tie, but it was already undone. He felt like he might vomit. Had he drunk that much? Was he getting the flu, like so many of his men? He tried to crack his window open, but the automatic control seemed to respond to his commands too quickly. Unable to stop it from opening just a bit, he settled for leaving it half open, with snowflakes blowing into the car and over him.

"Home, Sir?"

"Yes, home," the P.C. said.

Santana drove carefully through midtown, down to the Village, toward the Bleecker Street townhouse. He slowed for the red lights before taking them, skidding slightly each time he accelerated again. The snow seemed trapped in the beam of the headlights. They were about to take the turn into Bleecker when the P.C. said, "Pull it over. I'll get out here and walk the block. I can use the air."

"You sure, sir?"

"Yes, I'm sure."

Santana pulled to the curb. The P.C. thanked him for the ride and stepped out into the snow, slamming the door behind him. Santana waited and watched the P.C. turn up his collar and begin the walk up Bleecker Street. Then he pulled away from the curb and continued down Seventh Avenue.

At the moment he first notices the man whose death will so profoundly affect his own life, Joey Spadafino is playing a game with himself, trying to keep warm. He's trying to think of the hottest place he's ever been. Not just like Rockaway Beach in August, when the sand gets so hot in the afternoon it can burn the soles of your feet, but places like that elevator in the Polo Grounds Projects Joey had got stuck in between floors for an hour and a half, or the place behind the big boiler in P.S. 6 where he and Chico used to get high.

When he sees the man walking toward the doorway where he's huddled, Joey's first thought is that the guy's drunk. A black man, taller than Joey and heavier. But old, must be sixty. Well dressed, an expensive-looking overcoat. And totally wasted. Walking with his head down, weaving back and forth. Every several steps he seems to sort of misjudge the height of the pavement, so his foot strikes it before he thinks it's going to, and each time he's got to correct himself and find his rhythm all over again.

Joey looks up and down the block. Empty. The falling snow acts like an early warning system. The flakes light up from the headlights of a car pulling into the block, even before the headlights themselves come into view. Nothing.

In seconds the man's going to pass by him. If he wants to, Joey can take this guy off easy. He holds his breath, feels his pulse pound in his chest. He raises himself up slightly on the balls of his feet, becomes taller, more menacing. The guy's fifteen feet away, ten feet, five. . . .

Janet Killian had just put her baby daughter down in her crib following what was supposed to have been her two o'clock feeding, although it was actually more like two thirty. While she envied those mothers whose babies slept through the night from the time they came home from the hospital, the truth was she kind of liked nursing Nicole in the quiet darkness of the early morning. It was perhaps their closest time together. Janet Killian was a single mother, a working single mother, and quiet time with her daughter was a precious commodity, even if it was a commodity that came at the price of sleeping through the night.

She pulled the blanket over the baby's shoulders, felt the warmth of the tiny back, already rising and falling in the regular breathing of sleep. She walked to the window to see if it was still snowing.

Drawing the curtain back, Janet watched the flakes blowing by, catching the street light. The sidewalk had turned white, although the snow had a slushy look to it, rather than the powdery appearance of her Midwestern memories. Then, across the street, something commanded her attention. A man, kneeling, bent over something in the snow. She squinted to see better, cupped her hands around her face to shield off any light from within the apartment. The something, she realized, was another person, another man, lying on his side on the sidewalk. And the first man was now going through the fallen man's pockets.

"Hey," Janet said, but in keeping her voice quiet so as not to wake her baby, it came out as little more than a whisper against the window glass. She reached for the phone, heard the dial tone, hesitated, then forced herself to dial 911. She continued to watch the man going through the other man's pockets, now taking something, now holding it up to the light.

"Emergency Operator 23," a woman's voice was saying. "May I help you?"

"Yes," said Janet. "I'm watching a crime," was all she could think of.

"What sort of crime, Ma'am?"

"A robbery, I guess, a mugging."

"Where is this occurring, Ma'am?"

"Right across the street," said Janet. "Across from 77 Bleecker Street."

"What are the cross streets, Ma'am?"

"What?" Janet did not understand. The first man had stood up now. It looked like he was standing on the fallen man, or straddled him.

"77 Bleecker Street, Ma'am," the woman's voice was saying. "What street is that between."

"Oh," said Janet. "Sixth and Seventh."

"Sixth and Seventh," the woman repeated. "Ma'am, I'm going to ask you to hold a moment. What's your phone number, in case we get disconnected?"

But Janet was now staring into the face of the standing man, who was looking directly up at her. She lowered the phone to her side, hearing, "Ma'am? Ma'am? Ma'am," continuing to come from it. She could see that he was a white man, and young. She could see him look away from her window, to what must be another window. Now he stepped back from the fallen man, looked down at him and backed away further.

"Ma'am? Ma'am?" the voice was still coming from the phone at her side. The young man started walking toward the corner, slowly at first, then faster. . . .

"Hey, get away from him!" Joey is suddenly aware of a man's voice somewhere above him, aware of lights coming from windows in the building behind him. And across the street a woman in a window is staring at him.

"Shit," Joey says. He looks at the wad of bills held together in a money clip, thinks of dropping the money, pockets it instead. Fighting the impulse to run, he starts walking toward Seventh Avenue, muttering, "Shit, shit, shit, shit," over and over.

When he seems to be getting no closer to the corner, he breaks into a jog, concentrating on not losing his footing on the snow. At the corner, he turns uptown, dropping back into a fast walk. But there are cars, and the oncoming headlights light up the front of his body. He turns around, begins walking downtown, hears the first siren off in the distance. Tries to concentrate on what he's got here, tries to think. Fingers the wad of bills in his pocket, feels the money clip, slips it off and palms it in his pocket.

The siren's getting louder. Joey cocks his head, trying to locate it. Thinks at first it's coming from his right, then from downtown, from in front of him. He considers turning around again, but is afraid to.

At the corner, he walks close by a wire trash can, and drops the money clip in. An alley appears on his right, and he turns into it. But a noise from the blackness startles him, and he's back on Seventh with the siren getting louder, breaking into a jog again, a run. . . .

T W O

A glance in his calendar book reminded Dean Abernathy that today was the day he was supposed to call the Assigned Counsel Office to see if they had any assigned cases they wanted him to handle. They had called him Friday and left a message on his answering machine. The cases didn't pay much, since the hourly rates he had to bill for at the end of each case were so low, but private criminal cases were hard to come by in these times. Besides, it was better to be busy than to sit around.

Still, it was only nine o'clock, and there might not be anyone in the Assigned Counsel Office yet. So Dean assembled the files he would need in court that morning, and reviewed each one before putting them in his briefcase. Run of the mill stuff. A "buy and bust" drug sale to an undercover cop, where they had caught the defendant five minutes later with "stash" (more drugs packaged identically to those sold) and "cash" (the pre-recorded money the undercover cop had used to buy the drugs). A D.W.I. for whom Dean would try to get a reduced plea, from Intoxicated to Impaired, so he could at least get a provisional license to drive to and from his job. A guy who had thrown a plate at his girlfriend because she had rejected the dinner he had cooked her and instead fed it to their dog. Dean snapped the briefcase shut and put on his scarf and coat. It had snowed last night, and the walk to court would be a cold one.

On a chance, he dialed the number of the Assigned Counsel Office. It rang three times. He would give it four.

"Assigned Counsel," said a woman's voice.

"Hi, this is Dean Abernathy. Someone called me late Friday about taking a couple of cases, and I'm returning the call."

"What panel are you on?"

"Felony," Dean answered.

"Let me see," she said. Then, "No, nothing at the moment. They must have found somebody to take those."

"No problem," Dean said.

"You're not on the Homicide Panel, are you?"

"Yes, I am." The Homicide Panel was made up of the most experienced criminal defense lawyers who took court-appointed cases. It paid no more than the other panels, but membership on it carried a bit of prestige, a rare commodity indeed in the Criminal Court Building.

"Well, Judge Mogel just called from AR-1. He's going to need someone this morning on the Wilson murder. Are you interested?"

"Wilson murder?" Dean was embarrassed to say he didn't know who Wilson was or what the Wilson murder was.

"Didn't you listen to the news this morning?"

"I guess not." The truth was, Dean confined his morning listening to the weather and the traffic. Later, in court, he'd read the *Times* folded behind the lid of his open briefcase.

"Police Commissioner Wilson was murdered last night. Died during a mugging."

"Wow," said Dean, slowly and stupidly.

"Do you want it?"

Reflexively, "Yeah, sure."

"Okay," she said. "I don't have a docket number yet, but the defendant's name is Joseph Spadafino, S-P-A-D-A-F-I-N-O. He's 28, and he's being arraigned this morning in AR-1."

"Very good," said Dean, having no idea yet if it was very good or not, still digesting the fact that the Police Commissioner had been killed. "Thanks." He hung up the phone, took a blank manilla file folder from a box, and wrote the name "JOSEPH SPADAFINO" on it. He added it to the files in his briefcase and headed for court.

One Hundred Centre Street, the Criminal Court Building. If our prisons are terrible places because we want them to be, thought Dean Abernathy as he entered the revolving door, then our courthouses are designed to be almost as bad, a sort of preview of coming attractions. Poorly lit, filthy, noisy, overcrowded, smoke-infested, too cold in the winter, too hot in the summer. It was as if they were kept that way intentionally, to prepare the defendants and their families alike for what the next step, prison, would be like, to soften the shock of what lay in store.

He flashed his attorney I.D. at the court officer, who permitted Dean to bypass the line at the metal detector. He wound his way through defendants, police officers, jurors, court personnel and others to the rear of the first floor lobby, to the felony arraignment part known as AR-1. He pushed his way through the double doors and saw that Judge Mogel was already on the bench, waiting for cases to be called.

Murray Mogel's chronic poor health made him look older than his sixty-six years. To most, he was a cynical, sarcastic man who had little patience for prosecutor or defense lawyer. To Dean, who had known Mogel since the days they were both Legal Aid lawyers, Mogel was indeed both cynical and sarcastic. But his cynicism was even-handed: he disbelieved police officers with the same disdain that he disbelieved defendants, with the result, as most defense attorneys knew, that he was a good judge to waive a jury in front of and take one's chances with. Not that that mattered today, when Mogel, as the arraignment judge, would simply be setting bail and an adjourned date on defendants making their very first appearance in court since their arrests. And in Dean's case, in the case of the People versus Joseph Spadafino, there would be no bail, since there seldom was in murder cases.

"Come up, Mr. Abernathy." Judge Mogel had spotted Dean and, characteristically, did not wait for Dean to have to ask to approach the bench. Dean unhooked the chain that separated the audience portion of the courtroom from the well, where the participants stood, and walked up to the bench, behind which Judge Mogel sat.

"Good morning, Judge."

"Hello, Dean." Judge Mogel extended his hand, and Dean shook it. It was thin, and cold from the circulatory problems that came with a bad heart. "I hear you've been assigned to the Wilson case."

Dean nodded, not missing the nuance that the case, in which the deceased was a well-known public figure and the defendant an anonymous ex-convict, had taken on the name of the victim.

"Well, the papers aren't ready yet, but your client's inside." Judge Mogel waved vaguely in the direction of the door to the holding pen which contained prisoners waiting for their arraignments. "Talk to him and let me know if you have any objection to the TV cameras. They've made a request for a pool camera." This time Judge Mogel waved toward the far side of the courtroom.

Dean turned and saw a dozen or so people huddled in groups of three and four. They were unmistakably press: technicians with head sets and wires and rolls of duct tape; well-dressed men and women who fussed with their hair or neckties. Dean now recalled seeing an "Eyewitness News" van parked on the sidewalk outside, its antenna telescoped to full height. This was the show today.

"Whose handling it for the D.A.'s Office?" he asked.

"Walter Bingham. Good man," Judge Mogel added. "Know him?"

"Yeah, he's okay." Walter Bingham was one of the senior trial assistants in the New York County District Attorney's Office. He was pleasant enough, easy to talk to, and a good seat-of-the-pants lawyer whose good looks and imposing height didn't hurt him, and who had a nice way with a jury. If Dean had any reservation about Bingham, it concerned his somewhat narrow view of what information a prosecutor was required to share with the defense. More than once, Dean recalled, Bingham had been slow to turn over some document or reveal some small bit of evidence that contradicted his theory of proof.

Dean stepped back from the bench, left the well area, and walked to the front row of seats, reserved for lawyers and police officers. He folded his coat, put it on one of the empty seats. There was no such thing as a coat rack here. He placed his inexpensive briefcase on top of his coat, leaving it unlatched. That way, if someone reached over from the second row to try to steal his coat, the briefcase would fall to the floor, spilling its contents and serving as an alarm. This was the Criminal Court, after all: there were criminals around.

Dean took out his Department of Corrections pass, reentered the well, and headed to the holding pen. He was stopped in his tracks by Mike Pearl, the veteran courthouse reporter from the *Post*.

"I hear you're representing Spadafino," said Pearl.

"I guess so," Dean said.

"Anything you can tell me about him? You know, criminal record, family, personal stuff. Anything."

"Mike, I haven't even met the guy yet. You know as much as I do."

"I hear he's got a prior robbery."

"You see," Dean said, "you know *more* than I do."

Dean found Joseph Spadafino sitting alone in the farthest pen, the one usually reserved for prisoners the Corrections Officers kept segregated from the main bullpen of adult males. At various times of the day or night it was used for females, youths, "homos" (Correction's stubbornly archaic term for gays and transvestites), and "obsos" (mentally disturbed prisoners who needed special observation). And celebrities, high profile prisoners whose notoriety required extra precautions. Joseph Spadafino was a celebrity.

"Mr. Spadafino?"

"Yeah."

"My name is Dean Abernathy, and I'm the lawyer who's going to be representing you. Hang onto this." Dean handed him a business card. The prisoner studied it, then read from it.

"Ab-er-ath. . . ."

"Abernathy. Call me Dean, that's easier. What do they call you?"

"Joey."

"Okay, Joey, nice to meet you." Dean extended his hand, and they shook. Dean figured shaking hands with inmates cost him four colds a year. In the age of AIDS, Hepatitis B and drug-resistant strains of TB, it was a practice most of his colleagues had abandoned. But Dean would be damned if he was going to start off an interview by creating more distance between himself and his client. There was enough to begin with.

He looked at Joey Spadafino. Small, several inches shorter than

Dean's own five-eleven. Skinny, no more that a hundred and thirty-five pounds. Handsome once, probably, but it looked like his features had sort of given way somewhere along the line. A nose that had been broken more than once. Curly brown hair that looked dull and dirty. A fair share of scars, scabs, cuts and bruises, some old, some fresh. Bloodshot eyes peering out from dark sockets, suggesting he had been awake for a good forty-eight hours. And a faint but decidedly putrid smell that seemed to come in alternating waves of unwashed body odor, stale cigarette smoke, and something else Dean could not quite identify.

Nice overall impression, thought Dean.

"Excuse me Counsellor," came a voice from behind Dean, who turned to see a uniformed Court Officer at the door. "The papers have come up. This is your copy." He handed Dean a folded set of papers. Dean thanked him, and he left.

"Okay, this is good," Dean said to Joey, "we can go over these and see what they're saying.

"This yellow cover means you're being charged with a felony. You know what that is, a crime that you could get state time for, more than a year. This," Dean said, turning to the first page of the stapled packet, "is the complaint. The important part of it says," his eyes scanning over the legalese and focusing on the charges and factual allegations, "that, according to Detective Zysmanski of the Manhattan South Homicide Division, this morning, at approximately 0240—that's two forty A.M.—in front of 76 Bleecker Street, you committed the crimes of Murder in the Second Degree, Robbery in the Second Degree and Robbery in the Third Degree, under the following circumstances: Zysmanski is informed by persons whose names and addresses are known to the District Attorney that, by means of physical force or threat, you removed personal property and United States currency from Edward Wilson, and that during the commission of the crime or the immediate flight therefrom, Edward Wilson, who was not a perpetrator, died. And it says," Dean added "that you made statements."

"I didn't kill anybody, Mr. Aba—"

"Dean. And I know that. At least I know they're not even saying that you did. What they're saying is that you were robbing him, and he happened to die of a heart attack while you were robbing him."

"That's different," Joey said.

"Well, it is and it isn't," Dean said, smiling in what he hoped was a kind way, even if the lesson was about to be a cruel one. "But first, this business about the statements. What did you tell them?"

"I told them what happened, that I took his money, yeah, but I didn't hurt him or nuthin. I mean he was drunk, real drunk. He just kinda fell down. So I took his money. But I didn' *kill* him, I didn' *murder* him!"

"Who'd you tell this to?"

"Jesus, everybody who asked me. Lissen, I ain't got nuthin to hide here. I took the fuckin money. But I didn' *kill* nobody, they know that." Joey held his hands out, palms upward.

"Who's everybody, Joey? Who did you tell? Uniform guys? Detectives?"

"Detectives, yeah. Lots of 'em."

"Did they give you your rights?"

"No. Yeah. I dunno. Later, yeah."

Dean suppressed a smile at the multiple-choice answer, asked instead, "Later, did a tall guy from the D.A.'s Office show up?"

"Yeah. Guy with a mustache." That would be Bingham.

"Did they videotape it?"

"Yeah."

"Okay," Dean took a deep breath. "You want the bad news or the bad news?"

"All's I got is bad news." Joey looked down at his shoes. Dean's eyes followed. The laces had been removed as a precaution.

"I'm afraid so. First, of course, the guy was the Police Commissioner. Second is the felony murder rule. We'll be talking about that a lot, but basically what it says is that if I'm committing a certain felony, and the victim dies during it for any reason—heart attack, accident, runs into a car, shoots himself trying to defend himself, gets shot by a cop, *whatever*—I'm guilty of murder."

"That's not fair."

"Life isn't always fair," Dean said, without wondering if the rule was fair or not. "It's the rule." Then, "We're going to be going in front of the judge in a few minutes. All that's going to happen is he's going to remand you—there won't be any bail set—and give us a date next week. They'll be presenting the case to the grand jury, which is going to indict you. The next time we come to court it'll be upstairs, in Supreme Court, where we'll plead not guilty. In the meantime, I'll be investigating the case, trying to find out as much as I can. If you like, I can have you brought over before next week, so we can sit down to-gether and talk more. Would you like that?"

Joey nodded mechanically.

"Okay. In the meantime, there's a couple of things I want you to do. Number one, most important, *keep your mouth shut!* You've done enough talking already. This is a big case. There's a lot of guys in here would like nothing better than to hear you say something about the case, then drop a dime on you to help themselves. So *nothing*. Under-stand?"

Another nod.

"Next, can you read and write?" It was a precaution Dean had adopted after an embarrassed defendant had reluctantly admitted being illiterate only after Dean had pressed him repeatedly to write down his account of his arrest. The illiteracy had in turn undermined the credibil-ity of the arresting officer, who had claimed that the defendant had read a confession written out by the officer before signing his name to it. But Dean had almost missed it.

"Yeah," said Joey.

"Well, get a hold of some paper and a pencil, and in the next day or two, write down everything that happened. That day before the incident, the incident itself, the arrest, everything that happened at the precinct, everything until you met me. Can you do that?"

"Yeah."

"I want as much detail as possible. It's just for us, for the next time we meet, before you start forgetting things. Don't lose it. Don't show it to anybody but me. Okay?"

"Yeah." Joey probably had not been very good with homework as-signments in school, Dean decided. He would not hold his breath. But it was worth a try. Sometimes little details remembered shortly after an arrest became pivotal months later at trial.

"Next thing," said Dean, "the television people are out there. They've asked the judge for permission to have a camera in the court-room. He has to let them. The best I can do is to strike a deal so that nothing prejudicial gets said in front of the cameras, like your record. Okay?"

A nod.

"Do you have any people?" Dean asked. "Anybody out there you want me to try to get in touch with for you?"

"Yeah. No, not really." Multiple choice again. "I got a mother and a sister somewhere. But I been on the street. I've sorta lost contact, you know what I mean." It was not a question.

"On the street, like homeless?"

"Yeah."

"How bad is your sheet?" Dean turned in the packet of papers to the computer printout of the defendant's criminal record. It was several pages long.

"Not that bad," said Joey. Dean had once asked a fortyish prostitute the same question and got the same answer. Her printout had showed a hundred and twenty-two arrests in the past five years.

"Been upstate?"

"One time," Joey nodded. "Two-to-four for a sale."

It was Dean's turn to nod. A sale meant drugs. Two-to-four years was a sentence reserved for second felony offenders. So Joey Spadafino had at least two prior felony convictions behind him, no family to speak of, no home. He had admitted on videotape robbing the victim and, thanks to the felony murder rule, had thereby admitted murdering him. And the victim just happened to be the very popular Police Commissioner of the City of New York. Not bad for starters.

Back in the courtroom it had become standing room only. Police brass, beefed-up court security, more press, and the just plain curious, come to see who had mugged the Police Commissioner and caused his death. Dean spotted Walter Bingham, the Assistant District Attorney who had taken the videotaped statement from Joey and who would be prosecuting him. As Dean neared him he saw Bingham had not shaved.

"Hello, Walter," Dean said. "Looks like you spent the night at the precinct."

"Yeah, thanks to your client. How've you been, Dean?"

"Okay."

"Mr. Abernathy, Mr. Bingham, please step up," Judge Mogel was calling from the bench. As they approached, the courtroom hushed as spectators strained to hear what would be said.

"I've got this application from NBC, joined in by the other networks and a bunch of local stations" said Judge Mogel, quietly enough to frustrate all but the lip-readers in the audience. "If it were up to me I'd tell them to go to hell, but the Court of Appeals says that absent good cause they're allowed to televise this. I don't want a circus, so I've already told them they'll be allowed one pool camera, and they'll all have to work off that. Any objection, Dean?"

"No objection, Judge, if we can have a couple of ground rules."

"Such as?"

"Such as, number one, no mention of the defendant's record. I'm not asking for bail."

"That's fair. What else?"

"No mention of any statements. I intend to oppose any coverage of a *Huntley* hearing, if we ever get that far." A *Huntley* hearing was an inquiry into, among other things, whether the police had warned a suspect of his constitutional rights before questioning him.

"Judge," protested Bingham, "I've got to serve statement notice. I'm required to do it on the record."

"Fine, you'll do it," said Mogel. "You'll say, 'The People serve notice pursuant to CPL 170.10.' Nothing else. As to what the statements were, you'll provide them to Mr. Abernathy in writing, within the fifteen-day statutory period. Anything else?"

"No," Dean said.

"No," said Bingham.

"All right, it'll take them a while to set up their camera. Come back in twenty minutes."

Dean spent the twenty minutes prying information out of Walter Bingham and dodging reporters. He didn't like trying his cases in the media, even on the rare occasion when he had a case in which the media was interested. Besides, today he really had nothing to say to them that could help his client.

From Bingham he learned that Joey Spadafino had admitted the robbery to several detectives during the hours following his arrest, but had hedged by the time Bingham took the "Q and A," the videotaped question and answer session. Dean asked Bingham when he could get a copy of the video.

"Are you going to have him testify before the grand jury?" Bingham wanted to know first.

"No," said Dean, "I think he's helped you enough already."

"Next week," was Bingham's answer. What it meant was that he was playing it close to the vest. He was required to give the defense a copy of the video, but he would wait until the grand jury had heard the evidence and voted its indictment before turning it over. That way, in case the defendant chose the somewhat unusual step of testifying before the grand jury, he would have to do so without first seeing—or having his lawyer see—what he had said during the Q and A. Dean had mixed feelings about the rule. On the one hand, it did serve to prevent a defendant from tailoring his testimony to what he had said earlier. But it sure felt like walking through a mine field without it.

The arraignment was a non-happening, insofar as it brought no drama, no surprises and no substantive developments in the case whatsoever. None of that prevented the media from treating it like a major news event. Commissioner Wilson had been a popular figure, a black man who had come out of the squalor of Brooklyn's Bedford-Stuyvesant section. Born Deshawn African Wilson to a single mother, orphaned at six, raised by a nearly blind grandmother who had somehow managed to keep him and his three sisters fed, clothed and in school, he had entered the Police Academy at eighteen with the borrowed birth certificate of an older cousin, Edward Lee Wilson. Though he had confessed the ruse after making Sergeant at the age of twenty-eight, it had cost him his first and middle names, and he was stuck for life with the less mellifluous Edward Lee. Twice seriously wounded in the line of duty, Wilson had earned a string of decorations exceeded only by the legendary Mario Biaggi. Unlike Biaggi, however, he had simultaneously retained a reputation as a scrupulously honest cop and a commander of absolute moral integrity. As he rose through the ranks to Captain, Deputy Inspector and eventually Chief of Patrol, that reputation had brought him national recognition. Three years ago the Mayor had named him Commissioner, bypassing several whites and other blacks who outranked him in both title and years on the Department.

As Commissioner, Edward Wilson had been innovative and popular. A champion of the uniformed force that had spawned him, he put more men back on the street where he felt they belonged. He streamlined paperwork, brought the Department into the computer age and hired civilian employees to perform many of the clerical tasks that police officers had traditionally spent so much time doing so poorly. He was a fierce advocate of minorities within the ranks, and he defined minorities as women, blacks, Latinos, Asians, gays, and any other group of one or more who chose to wear beards, mustaches, sideburns, ponytails, earrings, garlic cloves or anything else that their hearts desired. But as tolerant as he was of what he termed these "superficial distinctions," he gave no quarter in two areas: corruption and brutality. Under him, the New York City Police Department had regained its stature as a worldwide model, and Edward Wilson had himself become a familiar face on national magazine covers and Sunday morning panel discussions. There had even been talk of a run for the Governor's mansion, should Mario Cuomo ever decide to hang up his spikes. That thought, if indeed Wilson entertained it, had apparently been put on hold a year ago, when a heart attack that sidelined him for six weeks had raised concerns about his long-term health.

Watching himself on the ten o'clock news that evening, Dean Abernathy was secretly pleased at his sudden fame. He had said virtually nothing at the arraignment itself. The camera had focused on Joey Spadafino being led in front of the bench, on Judge Mogel's ordering him held without bail pending action by the grand jury, and on Walter Bingham's announcement that the presentation would begin that very afternoon; back to Spadafino, looking small and lost as he stood bracketed between Dean and a large Uniformed Court Officer. Then Dean on the courthouse steps, staring directly and sincerely into the camera and stating that, while he could not yet comment on the facts, the public could be sure that "there's more than meets the eye here." Whatever that meant, Dean laughed to himself, clicking the channel selector back to the Knicks-Pistons game in time to see Patrick Ewing miss a free throw. The score appeared, superimposed over Ewing's face, dripping sweat as he concentrated on his second free throw.

DETROIT 68

NEW YORK 60

"Shit," said Dean, clicking off the set. He got up, walked to the kitchen, and opened the refrigerator. A visual inventory revealed a pitcher containing either apple juice or iced tea, he could not remember which. Something scary in a Chinese food container. Six clementines: Dean generally succumbed to the will of the Korean grocer, who in this case had marked them six for ninety-nine cents, but made it a point of maintaining the illusion of free will by rejecting the penny change. A bruised tomato. Two carrots that would either require a peeler—which Dean had temporarily misplaced—or taste like earth.

Dean closed the refrigerator door and tried the freezer. Much better. A box that promised pizza made on French bread. A package of tender, tiny peas. Several plastic containers of mysterious leftovers. A number of foil-wrapped objects of different shapes and sizes, none suggesting food. He settled on the French bread pizza.

Rejecting the microwave his brother Alan had bought him after watching Dean go through a pack of matches trying to light his oven without sacrificing body parts, Dean deftly lit the flame on the second try. He had learned to hold the match with something other than his fingers: a pair of pliers worked best, though tonight he could not locate one, and settled for an old roach clip left over from his marijuana days.

Dean lived alone, partly by choice, partly by virtue of the fact that Brigit Terjesen, his one-time roommate and sometimes bedmate, had six months earlier left him a note one evening in place of herself and her worldly belongings. He still had the note.

Dear Dean:

I cannot compeat for your attention with your work any longer. I know you are "on trial," as you call it. But when you get home at midnight, as you have every night this week, and then ignore me it is too much. I have kneads too.

I wish you a good life.

Brigit

It was just as well, thought Dean. Who wants a girlfriend with kneads, anyway? Dean walked back into the living room, settled into the overstuffed chair that had over the years taken on the shape of his own body, and clicked the game back on in time to see Joe Dumars hit from three-point range.

DETROIT 77
NEW YORK 62

He clicked the game off again and picked up his copy of the *Times*, which he had not had a chance to read during the day.

SECTION VII

RESOURCES

Organizations, Conventions and Awards

ROBERT J. RANDISI

While the actual act of writing is a solitary business, even seasoned pros find it beneficial to discuss the *craft* of writing. Luckily there are writers' organizations in existence, as well as conventions and workshops taking place across the country throughout the year. Most writers would have you believe that they enjoy the solitary nature of their work, but once you've attended a convention you'll see that they are social creatures, as well.

Organizations are generally for both beginning as well as professional writers. They consist of a governing body (president, vice-president, secretary and treasurer) located in the founding city. Chapters are then set up in various cities. Most offer monthly meetings; all publish newsletters with information about the craft and business of writing. Some of them present awards each year—such as The Private Eye Writers of America's Shamus Award and the Mystery Writers of America's Edgar Award. They all offer an opportunity to talk with other writers, which is probably their most important contribution to writing.

In a *workshop* writers are usually asked to bring a short story, novel or section of a novel—a work in progress—to be read aloud and discussed by the class. The program runs a day or two, and is conducted by a published writer. To discover workshops in your area check the book section of your local newspaper, contact the public library or call the writing department of the nearest university. Workshops specifically dealing with mystery writing are discussed later on in this article.

Conventions are attended by unpublished writers (we prefer not to use the phrase "would be"), beginning writers, veteran writers, publishers, editors, agents, booksellers and fans who are all gathering for the sole purpose of discussing writing and books. There are panel discussions, social gatherings and banquets.

Now let's look at each in greater depth and help you decide which is best for you.

Organizations

Mystery writers' organizations are important to established writers and aspiring writers alike. For years the only organization in existence was the Mystery Writers of America, but within the last decade others have cropped up offering more specialized memberships and a wider variety of options. In many cases these organizations have members in common, but they all have something unique to offer.

The American Crime Writer's League (ACWL)

This organization was founded in 1987, to offer mystery writers an alternative to the Mystery Writers of America.

The first president was Charlotte MacLeod and the vice-president was Les Roberts. The house publication is called the BULLETin. Unlike other writers' organizations the ACWL restricts its memberships to published writers, which was the intended major reason for its formation. It does not give an award. One thing it does for members is include a list of member's agents—both names and addresses—in its directory. It was hoped that the ACWL would be less political than other organizations, both in and out of the mystery field.

It is sometimes difficult to discover a contact address for the organization, as it has no permanent base of operation. Your best bet would be to watch the mystery publications. As of this writing, the President of the ACWL is Joan Hess.

Contact address: 3168 Katherine Ave., Fayetteville, AR 72703.

Crime Writer's Association (CWA)

The CWA was founded in 1953. Its main purpose is to support and promote the crime novel in Great Britain. One of the founding members and first chairperson was John Creasey. They present a Gold Dagger Award to the best novel, and a Silver Dagger Award to the runnerup. They also have a Diamond Dagger Award, sponsored by Cartier, which is presented to a writer for his or her career contribution. It is the counterpart to the MWA Grand Master Award. (When Cartier was approached about this, the idea of being associated with the award appealed to them.

However, the actual award—a diamond studded quill pen stuck in a book—is not given to the winner. It is shown to them, and then kept in a vault at Cartier's. The author is then given a pin to wear that resembles the award.)

Since 1973 the CWA has also given a John Creasey award for the best first crime novel. (They prefer to refer to the genre as "crime" writing rather than "mystery" writing.) In an interesting bit of innovation they also offer an award for best "comic" mystery novel.

Unlike the ACWL, the CWA offers memberships to writers of fiction and nonfiction alike, and also has associate memberships available to publishers, editors, agents, reviewers, and other professions connected to the crime novel.

Contact address: The Secretary, Crime Writers Association, P.O. Box 172, Tring, Herts, Great Britain HP23 5LP.

Crime Writers of Canada (CWC)

Memberships in CWC are open to writers of fiction or nonfiction, critics and historians, publishers, editors, agents and booksellers. It was founded in 1982. They publish a quarterly newsletter and present an annual award called The Arthur Ellis Award for best novel, best first novel, best short story, best true crime book and best critical or reference work. The name "Arthur Ellis" is the traditional pseudonym of Canada's official hangman. They also present a "Derrick Murdoch" Award for Life Achievement. Their aim, as with other organizations, is to support crime fiction and crime writers in Canada.

Contact address: Director, Crime Writers of Canada, 225 Carlton St., Ontario, Canada M5A 2L2.

International Association of Crime Writers (IACW)

This association was founded internationally in 1986. A North American chapter was established in 1987. There are 15 chapters, each comprised of more than one country. Each chapter presents a Dashiell Hammett Award for outstanding work in a particular language. Considered by many early on to be more a political organization than anything else, the IACW now strives to bring equality and worldwide translation to mystery writers and their work. There is an annual conference in Gignon, Spain called *Semana Negra,* and other meetings called, at one time or another Three Borders or Four Borders in Florida and Cuba.

Contact address: Executive Secretary, JAF Box 1500, New York, NY 10116, (212)757-3915.

The Mystery Writers of America (MWA)
Established in 1945, MWA's membership is currently in the thousands, with nine chapters. Their purpose is to promote, protect and support mystery writers in the United States. Their motto is "Crime Does Not Pay—Enough!"

Each regional chapter holds monthly meetings, with the organization as a whole meeting during "Edgar" Week in New York, when the annual Edgar Allan Poe Awards are presented. There is a national monthly newsletter called *The Third Degree,* and each regional chapter has its own newsletter. Memberships are open to active and associate members, including agents, publishers, editors, booksellers, critics, and aspiring writers. Memberships are not limited to the written word, but include audio and visual works as well. There are also affiliate memberships for fans.

Contact address: Executive Secretary, Mystery Writers of America, 17 E. 47th St., New York, NY 10017.

The Private Eye Writers of America (PWA)
Founded in 1981, the aim of PWA was to elevate the private eye story from a sub-genre of the mystery to a genre all its own. Its further aim is to continue to foster support and respect for the P.I. genre. The first president was Bill Pronzini, the first vice president Robert J. Randisi. Randisi also created the SHAMUS Award that same year. In 1982, PWA presented awards for best novel, best first novel and best paperback original. They also presented a Life Achievement Award called "The Eye." The first recipient was Ross Macdonald, posthumously. Other winners have been Mickey Spillane, Richard Prather, Michael Collins, Bill Pronzini, Marcia Muller and Stephen J. Cannell. The following year they added a SHAMUS for best short story. The awards are voted on by committee. Early on the organization experimented with having the membership vote, but went to committees.

Contact address: Martha Derickson, Membership Chair, 407 W. Third St., Moorestown, NJ 08057.

Sisters in Crime (SinC)

Founded in 1986 the aim of SinC was basically to combat discrimination against women in the mystery field. The membership presently stands at over 2,000, with memberships open to men as well as women, as long as the men are committed to the good of the organization and its goals. Like the ACWL, SinC has no established award. They offer their members invaluable assistance in networking and publicity. Indeed, this is the strong point of the organization and it is well worth joining for this reason.

Contact address: Executive Secretary, Sisters in Crime, P.O. Box 442124, Lawrence, KS, 66044-8933.

Conventions

There was a time, they tell us, when there was only one convention. It was called Bouchercon, and for 20 years it remained the only game in town, until regional conventions began to pop up with regularity. While Bouchercon's attendance figures have swelled from hundreds in those early days to thousands now, the regional cons continue to be small, cozy gatherings of several hundred, where during the course of the weekend you can virtually touch or talk to everyone on your "want" list.

Conventions all have some things in common. They all feature panel discussions on both mystery writing and the mystery field in general. They all feature "multiple track" programming, usually two, but sometimes as many as three and four, panels going on at one time. The larger conventions—such as Bouchercon, with its 1,200 to 1,500 attendance—can support four-track programming while the smaller cons—with 200 to 400 attendees—cannot.

Most of the cons give writers' organizations an opportunity to meet, scheduling breakfasts and luncheons. They also afford opportunities for publishers to sponsor get-togethers ranging from a cocktail hour to a full blown party.

For the things that are individual to each con, let's cover all these conventions chronologically:

Left Coast Crime

Every February since 1991 there has been a convention called *Left Coast Crime,* so called because it's usually held in a city that is on the "left" coast. In 1991 and 1992 it was held in San Francisco; in '93 and '94,

Anaheim. In 1995 Left Coast Crime was held in Scottsdale, Arizona. In '96 the site will be Denver, Colorado. There is talk of this convention traveling up into Alaska.

The next convention is hosted by whoever wins the "bid" at the current convention. Bids are put in by groups that wish to put on the next convention. Sometimes bids are taken two and three years in advance. Attendance is usually in the two or three hundreds. There are panels, meet-the-author interviews, author autographing sessions and a banquet, at which the guest of honor speaks. There are no awards. Left Coast Crime was the first mystery convention to feature a mass signing, with all the authors appearing in one room to sign books. It has worked well, and continues to be a popular gathering at the convention.

By all accounts each Left Coast Crime convention has been a success. Watch for ads in magazines such as *Mystery Scene* and *The Armchair Detective*.

Sleuth Fest

In March *Sleuth Fest* is held in Fort Lauderdale, Florida, sponsored by the southern Florida chapter of The Mystery Writers of America. It is actually a combination convention and workshop, as three such shops are held. The workshops are held on Friday, the convention on Saturday and Sunday. There is also a short story contest. The featured speaker at the Saturday night banquet in 1995 was Stuart Kaminsky.

Contact address: Sleuth Fest, 4570 127th Trail North, West Palm Beach, FL 33411.

ABA

While not a convention by definition, every June finds all of the publishing world gathered at *ABA*—The American Booksellers Association "show." Starting in 1995 this show is permanently based in Chicago. Many best selling mystery authors like Robert B. Parker, Sue Grafton, Mary Higgins Clark, Patricia Cornwell and others are often featured at publishers' booths, or at signings. Mystery writers Sandra West Prowell, Gar Anthony Haywood, Michael Collins, Wendy Hornsby, Melodie Johnson Howe, John Lescroart and Stephen White were seen in attendance in 1995.

ABA is ostensibly held for members of the publishing community, but for a fee anyone can enter and attend.

Watch *Publishers Weekly* for announcements about ABA.

Malice Domestic

Held in May is *Malice Domestic,* a gathering of writers and fans of the traditional or "cozy" mystery novel. It is always held in Baltimore. Panel discussions, a high tea, a hat contest and a banquet have been held in the past. They also present the Agatha Award, for the best in the traditional field. This is an extremely intimate convention definitely not for fans of P.I., police procedural or crime writing. Although Peter Lovesy, Aaron Elkins and several other male writers have been known to attend, it is primarily attended by female writers. Fans of Nancy Pickard, Margaret Maron and Sharon McCrumb need apply.

Contact address: Malice Domestic, P.O. Box 31137, Bethesda, MD 20824-1137.

Buffcon

A new convention, *Buffcon,* was also held in May of 1995, in Buffalo, New York, with plans to continue every year. Panels, signings and readings were held. There were two tracks of programming, one specifically for how-to topics. The guest of honor was Lawrence Block.

Contact address: BUFFCON, Medaille College, Agassiz Circle, Buffalo, NY 14214.

Eyecon

Eyecon, the first Private Eye Writers of America convention, was held in Milwaukee, Wisconsin, in June of 1995. The guest of honor was Sue Grafton, Toastmaster was Les Roberts. PWA's president and vice-president—'95 office holders unknown at this time—and founder Robert J. Randisi were also present, as well as a host of private eye writers. At this time it is unknown whether there will be a second and subsequent *Eyecons.* Since the 1995 Bouchercon was in Nottingham, England, The Private Eye Writers of America decided to try their own convention.

There was a luncheon at which the winner of the Private Eye Writers of America/St. Martin's Press First P.I. Novel Contest Award was presented, as well as **The Eye,** the PWA Life Achievement Award.

The PWA Shamus Awards—traditionally presented at Bouchercon—were handed out at a Saturday night banquet.

Eyecon also hosted the first PWA Writer's Conference, an all day symposium conducted by members of the Private Eye Writers of America, including Jeremiah Healy, Les Roberts, John Lutz, and others.

Watch mystery publications such as *The Armchair Detective, Mystery Scene* and *The Mystery News* for announcements about the next Eyecon.

Bouchercon

Bouchercon is traditionally held the first weekend of October. There have been some variations, but this is the norm.

The father—or grandfather—of all cons, Bouchercon has been in existence for 25 years. In the past few years special interest groups such as Sisters in Crime and The Private Eye Writers of America have been meeting on the Thursday or Friday morning of the convention. Panel discussions begin Friday morning around 9:30 or 10 and continue through Sunday afternoon. Some of the recent conventions have had as much as four track scheduling, with the fourth track sometimes being a movie. This creates quite a variety of choices for attendees.

Gat Heat, a mystery talk show, has become a staple at most of the conventions. The name was taken from the title of a Richard S. Prather "Shell Scott" novel of the same name. "Gat" is slang for a gun, and "Heat" is obvious. It is hosted by Bob Randisi, who kicks things off with a monologue à la Dave Letterman or Jay Leno, and then goes on to welcome guests who are usually writers. Gat Heat has appeared as early as Friday and as late as Sunday. It does not occupy a regular time slot. Look for it on the program.

Anything can happen at a Bouchercon. There have been mystery talk shows and pies in the faces of panelists. Also, you never know when Max Collins and his band, Crusin', will show up to perform, sometimes with other writers—Doug Allyn (Omaha in 1993)—sitting in.

At the Saturday night banquet the guest of honor speaks, and the Anthony Awards—voted on by the attendees of Bouchercon—are presented. Bouchercon and Malice Domestic are the only conventions to feature their own fan awards.

Bouchercon '95 was in Nottingham, England; '96 will be in St. Paul/Minneapolis and '97, San Francisco.

Magna Cum Murder

First held in 1994, in October over Halloween weekend, *Magna Cum Murder,* is a mystery con held in Muncie, Indiana, near the campus of

David Letterman's alma mater, Ball State University. Gat Heat opened the first convention, and the 200 plus attendees went on from there to have a good weekend. They have already reserved the convention center—a converted post office building—and the Roberts Hotel for 1995 and 1996. The Roberts is a wonderful old hotel that was undergoing some outside renovation during the convention. As a con site it is a refreshing change from the usual "chain" hotels, and should continue to be a major draw for the con.

In '94 the "Mistress of the Revels" was Nancy Pickard. In '95 the "Master of the Revels" was Parnell Hall.

Contact address: Kathryn Kennison, Ball State University, Muncie, IN 47306-0380.

Mid-Atlantic Mystery Book Fair

The Mid-Atlantic Mystery Book Fair has been held the past four years in Philadelphia toward the end of November. Attendance is held at somewhere around 400. This is the only convention that does not have a banquet night. In the past Mid-Atlantic has been a very intimate gathering of authors and fans, giving attendees the opportunity to see or talk to almost everyone. The venue is small, which also adds to the feeling of intimacy.

Contact address: Deen Kogan, % Detecto Mysterioso Books at Society Hill Playhouse, 507 S. 8th St., Philadelphia, PA 19147.

Mid-Atlantic is the third convention held within 30 days of each other, which means some people have to make a choice as to which to attend. Not everyone has the time or the money to attend every one. Because some of the cons are regional, though, it does make sense to choose according to your location. Authors who live on the West Coast are more likely to attend a Left Coast Crime than a Mid-Atlantic, while those on the East Coast would choose to go to Philadelphia. There were only three New York authors at the very first Left Coast Crime in 1991, but subsequent cons have boasted many more. However, the attendance of authors is still greatly determined by their location. Keep this is mind when planning your next convention or workshop.

Workshops

There are general writing workshops offering mystery classes, but here are workshops strictly for mystery writing; basically there are four:

Sleuth Fest

Sleuth Fest, held in Fort Lauderdale, Florida, in March combines convention and workshop formats, by holding a workshop on Friday, and then the convention on Saturday and Sunday. In 1994 they held short story, mystery and screenplay shops.

For information write: Sleuth Fest, 4570 127th Trail North, West Palm Beach, FL 33411.

Buffcon

While not strictly a workshop, *Buffcon* does hold how-to panel discussions as part of the convention schedule.

For information write: Buffcon, Medaille College, Agassiz Circle, Buffalo, NY 14214.

Of Dark And Stormy Nights

Of Dark and Stormy Nights is a workshop conducted in May by the Chicago chapter of the Mystery Writers of America. The locale has changed from year to year, which makes it necessary to track the workshop through the usual mystery publications. It is a one day seminar conducted by published authors covering various categories, such as characterization, and short story writing. Students will be asked to send a work in progress that can be evaluated by the instructor beforehand, and then discussed in depth at the workshop.

For more information write: 2969 S. Bonfield, Chicago, IL 60608.

Eyecon

The first Private Eye Writers of America Writers Workshop was held at *Eyecon* in Milwaukee, in June '95. The Sunday after the convention was the designated day. Workshops on various areas of P.I. writing were held, conducted by top P.I. writers in the field such as Jeremiah Healy, John Lutz and Les Roberts, among others. At this time it is unknown if there will be another one in '96. The aim is to hold one annually, with the money going toward PWA's expenses (newsletters, postage, Shamus Awards, and such).

For more information write: Workshop Director, % PWA, 4239A Barcelos Dr., St. Louis, MO 63129.

Awards

Awards in any field are given varying degrees of importance. The Academy Award can certainly give a boost to the career of the recipient, as can an Emmy or a Tony. There is some speculation, however, as to whether literary awards can give a shot in the arm to the winner's career. Whether it can or cannot, it is certainly nice to be honored by your peers.

Here are some of the awards in the mystery field.

The Agatha

The Agatha Christie Award is presented annually at the Malice Domestic Convention. It honors the best works in the cozy genre. Past winners are Nancy Pickard and Margaret Maron. It is voted on by the attending membership. Like the "Anthony" it is not strictly a professional award, but what might be termed a "convention" award.

The Anthony

While not a professional award the Anthony has nevertheless become a viable award. It is named for Anthony Boucher and presented annually at the Bouchercon mystery convention. It is voted on by the attending members of the convention, so that the votes come from fans and writers alike. Categories vary from convention to convention, but best novel, best first novel and best short story are usually on the ballot. Past winners are Bob Crais, Linda Barnes and Marcia Muller.

The John Creasey Award

Presented by the Crime Writers Association of Great Britain to the year's best first novel.

The Edgar

The Edgar Allan Poe award is presented by the Mystery Writers of America to the best novel, best first novel, best paperback original novel, best short story, best juvenile novel, and best critical/biographical work. They also present awards to movies and television. The award is given at the annual Edgar Awards Banquet, held in New York City in the spring. It is voted on by committees made up of members.

The Arthur Ellis Award
This award is presented by the Crime Writers of Canada in various categories, including best novel, best first novel and best short story, among others. It is named for "Arthur Ellis" the pseudonym for Canada's official hangman. They also present a "Derrick Murdoch" Award for Life Achievement.

The Eye
This is the Private Eye Writers of America Life Achievement Award. Past recipients have been Ross Macdonald, Michael Collins, Richard S. Prather and Mickey Spillane. The winner is selected by the officers of PWA.

The Golden Dagger
This award is presented by the Crime Writers Association of Great Britain in various categories, including best novel. A Silver Dagger is awarded to the runner-up novel.

The Grand Master Award
This is presented by the Mystery Writers of America to a writer for a body of work during a career. The winners are selected by the board of directors. Recent recipients have been Donald E. Westlake and Lawrence Block.

The Hammett Award
This award is presented by the International Association of Crime Writers and named, obviously, for Dashiell Hammett. Each of its 15 chapters presents one for works in a particular language.

Online Resources

D O N   P R U E S

While it will be quite some time before dust jackets become a thing of the past, writers cannot run from the latest in communication technology. In fact, most of you probably already have an account with at least one online service. If you don't, you should; otherwise, you'll continue denying yourself an extraordinary world of information, knowledge, networking and pleasure.

Writers use the online medium for many reasons: to correspond, to conduct research, to participate in critique groups, to interact with established authors, to get acquainted with other mystery aficionados, to purchase books, to express opinions, and just to have fun. There are other enticing benefits. You can take electronic writing courses. You can receive prompt feedback on your manuscripts. You can even talk simultaneously with several writers from various cities, like a call-in radio talk show (except you're typing). What's more, you can easily email numerous copies of your manuscripts to unlimited numbers of people—no wasting time and money on copies or postage. And you can go online 24 hours a day, every day.

There are, however, some drawbacks once you go online. It takes a few hours to acquaint yourself with your particular service and understand how it works. Sometimes you won't know where or how to begin, because there are just too many resources out there. Getting online support can also be difficult, especially if 2 million other users are encountering the same problems at the same time. But such occurrences are rare.

Money is another concern. Most online services have a flat monthly fee (about $10) which is billed to your credit card. With this fee you're usually granted 5 or so hours of online time, depending on the service. Once you've depleted these given hours, you are then charged an hourly rate, usually $3-5 dollars per hour. Still dirt cheap compared to the cost of telephone calls.

Assuming you want to take the online plunge, there's still one question that must be answered: Which online service is best for you? Sure, you can ask your friends who have an online account if they're happy with their service, but will that same service be the most suitable for you? Unfortunately, the only objective way to ascertain which service suits your fancy is to try them all. If, however, you don't have time to spend testing each service, here's a sampling of what the major online services offer for mystery writers and readers.

America Online

One of the nation's largest commercial online services, AOL is a networking hub for America's mystery writers. In the Writers Club (KEYWORD: WRITERS), there is a public bulletin board (BB) specifically for mystery writers in which message folders exist for writers, agents, editors, readers, and for such organizations as the American Crime Writers League, the Mystery Writers of America, and Sisters in Crime. Within the Writers Club is the "Mystery Writers" folder, where famous authors hobnob with unpublished scribes and others interested in the field, including police officers, private detectives, and forensic scientists. You can also participate in live chats for mystery writers or take one of several eight week interactive online courses in mystery writing and related subjects.

Also of interest to mystery aficionados is St. Martin's Press's "Dead Letter," a newsletter devoted to its new mystery line that includes reviews of upcoming titles and interviews with St. Martin's authors. And there's Critics' Choice (KEYWORD: CRITIC), an online entertainment magazine featuring mystery reviews, author interviews, live conferences, weekly Top Ten lists, and a monthly listing of new book previews called Hot Off the Press. In the Critics' Choice area you'll also find an online book club and numerous mystery discussion folders. Just click on the "You're the Critic" icon and find the appropriate groups and folders. Other services from the *New York Times Book Review* (KEYWORD: @TIMES) to *American Bookseller* magazine (KEYWORD: AMERBK) can be found on AOL.

If you have any questions, contact: LaryCrews@aol.com ("Mystery Writers" folder creator and *Mystery Scene* columnist), Darylr4596@aol. com (Mystery Chat moderator), or ThopeB@aol.com (sysop for writers). To receive AOL software, call (800) 827-6364.

Compuserve

While AOL uses keywords, CompuServe—another commercial online giant—uses the "go" command to take you from one area to another. There are many features and forums for writers on CompuServe. Geared exclusively for writers, the Writer's Forum (GO WRITERS) is the place to discuss all aspects of writing. For both writers and readers, however, are the Literary Forum (GO LITFORUM) and the Author's Forum (GO TWAUTHORS). Time Warner Electronic Publishing sponsors the Author's Forum, where you'll find information about publishing news, conferences, new publications, tours, signings and contests. You can also download book excerpts, audio excerpts from books on tape, author photos, games, and covers of legendary novels and magazines. Writers can upload chapters of their books into libraries and invite critiques (you must go to the Mystery message section to do this).

You will also find online bookstores by Time Warner (GO TWEPB) and Random House (GO RANDOM). And there's Books on Tape (GO BOT) which offers over 3,000 full length books for rent. Unlike the above bookstores, this area is not controlled by any particular publisher. Other areas of interest are the Book Collectors Forum (GO COLLECT) and the Crime Forum (GO TWCRIME), where you can download video footage of court trials and discuss true crime books, murder and terrorism, or anything related to crime. And you might be interested in Modus Operandi, an online mystery game.

Contact Kate Grilley (71764.3206@compuserve.com) if you have any questions. To receive CompuServe software, call (800) 848-8990.

Delphi

Still text-based, Delphi doesn't offer the graphic appeal of other popular services, but it does have an active writer's area. In the Groups and Clubs area (found in the main menu) there is the "Writer's Group," which contains a conference room, a forum for swapping manuscripts, and a database for downloading files. If you find writing an altogether too-lonesome affair, check out "Collaborative Novels," where one person starts a novel and others add to it. See it evolve chapter by chapter. There's also a special interest area in the main menu called "Custom Forums." Here you'll find "Murder Online," a mystery forum devoted to mystery novel discussions, and the "Writer's Workshop" which is really a give-and-take critique folder. "Book and Candle Pub" (described as a bar) and the "Electronic Book Club" are casual places to discuss all types of books.

To browse, sample and order books, software and other merchandize, or to find reviews, author tour dates, and other bookish affairs, go to the HarperCollins Online Bookstore, found in the "Shopping" menu in the main menu.

Contact Michael Rose (MROSE@delphi.com) if you have any questions. To receive Delphi software, call (800) 695-4005.

eWorld

Although initially limited to Mac users, eWorld now can be accessed by any Windows computer. (You still need a modem, of course). If you want to partake in writers-only activities on eWorld, there's one good place to go: *Writer's Digest* magazine. From Town Square (the main menu) click on "Arts and Leisure" and then "Performing and Literary Arts." Here you'll find *Writer's Digest*. A short cut for Apple users is to hit the open Apple and G keys at the same time and then type "writers."

There are seven forums for writers in the *Writer's Digest* area. Click on the "Reading for Writers" icon to obtain articles to help improve your writing and marketing skills from current, past, and future issues of the magazine. In "The Writing Life" forum you can share ideas and opinions about the writing lifestyle. The "Critique & Commentary" forum allows you to post opinions about your fellow writers and their work. If you've sold an article or two already (mostly nonfiction), you might want to click on the "Writers for Hire" icon and then post your resume and samples of what you've already published. Magazine editors wander in here on occasion looking for good writing and ideas. Perhaps most helpful for unpublished fiction writers is "Author to Author," a chat room featuring critique groups, conferences with mystery authors and specialists in the field, and bulletin boards. There's also the "Writer's Digest Bookstore," where you can order magazines, books, and other resources to help you write better, and the "Writer's Calendar" which informs you of on-and off-line events you might want to know about.

If you have any questions, contact Writersdig@eworld.com (*Writer's Digest* magazine). To receive eWorld software, call (800) 775-4556.

GEnie

GEnie seems to be the service of choice for Sisters in Crime members. GEnie is divided into Round Tables, each devoted to one special interest and made up of bulletin boards, file libraries, and a conference area. You want the Writer's Round Table; and the mystery category is CAT 10. Here you can discuss all aspects of mystery, from plotting a novel to real crime. Also in CAT 10 are two police officers and an assistant D.A. who answer questions about procedure. Other topics include cozy, conventions, Edgar winners, mystery writers' pseudonyms, etc. *Mystery Scene* magazine maintains a topic in CAT 10 as well. There's a CAT 11 mystery category operated by the Sisters in Crime, open only to members.

In addition, GEnie has a Reader's Round Table for those interested in books but hesitant to enter an area earmarked for writers. Each month the Reader's RT sponsors a "Featured Writer of the Month." Mystery authors are regular and popular guests.

If you have any questions, contact bpaul@genie.geis.com. To receive GEnie software, call (800)638-9636.

Prodigy

Prodigy has a large number of writing areas, all under the Books & Writing Bulletin Board umbrella (JUMP: BOOKS & WRITING). The boards cover fiction, nonfiction, romance, mystery, and other genres. You want "Topic-Mystery Novels." Within this topic, various subjects cover authors, signings, general mystery discussion, a mystery book club, and a Sherlock Holmes area. You'll also want to check out the "Writing Technique/Fiction" forum, in which there's a special mystery area addressing everything from style to finding agents to how many words are in an average mystery novel. Noted book critic and *Playboy* columnist Digby Diehl is the Board Leader.

Many such bulletin boards are loaded with published writers, including best-selling mystery authors, who offer suggestions. Novelist Harry Arnston posts a free course called Novels 101 four times a year. The course is a 53-part primer on the writing business. Also on Prodigy is a Collector's BB (JUMP: COLLECTORS) which discusses books from a collector's point of view.

If you have any questions, contact Harry Arnston (DSMGO3A@Prodigy.com) or Digby Diehl (AFMC80A@Prodigy.com). To receive Prodigy software, call (800) 822-6922.

The Internet

The Internet has gained popularity all over the world. Unlike the other online services, the Net isn't owned or controlled by any independent company. The Department of Defense created the Net in the 60s to link government agencies with universities. It has since grown as a medium for scholastic research and exchange, as well as a vast resource for obtaining information on just about anything. But, because no one really regulates or directs its operations, the Net is like a vast jungle of information. If you don't know which path to take, you'll easily get lost, perhaps never finding your destination.

DorothyL Digest is the main mystery forum on the Internet. Named after Dorothy L. Sayers, it's not a gathering place as such, but it's a list server or newsletter. You can post a theme or request information regarding mystery and DorothyL will send you something (usually everyday) regarding your particular interest. This is a very active area, wrought with mystery aficionados from all over the globe. For information on DorothyL and instructions on how to become a subscriber, send email to: dkovacs@kentvm.bitnet or to krobinso@kentvm.kent.edu. In addition to DorothyL, you can find the Mystery mailing list, a resource for posting user reviews of mysteries (no discussions). Send submission for the list to mystery@lunch.engr.sgi.com. And there's MysteryL, which had much hype but as of late is little more than review postings. To contact MysteryL, email: mystery@lunch.asdsgi.com. Finally, there's Gaslight, a discussion list that includes mysteries from the late 19th and early 20th centuries. Stephen Davies is the Gaslight moderator (sdavies@ mtroyal.a b.ca).

Two Usenet news groups are geared toward the mystery writer. First, the Miscellaneous Writing (misc.writing) Usenet has mystery folders for you to discuss and exchange information about mystery writing, including your own work. And there's the Mystery Usenet group (rec.arts.mystery), with individual folders devoted to one author. If you're interested in critique groups, contact Rheal Nadeau at fiction-request@psuvm.p su.edu. She'll direct you to the appropriate place. Plus one World Wide Web (WWW) site is devoted solely to mystery writing. It's really a search engine which will help you find anything on the Web related to mystery. Contact http://lycos.cs.cmu.edu.

Finally, there are four quite useful WWW resources on the Internet. The United Kingdom Police & Forensics Web includes a help/advice area where questions can be posted relative to police and forensics. It also allows for subscription options to POLICE—L listserv (open to all interested in forensics). Links to other sites include World Directory of Criminology Institutes, CIA, FBI, Metro-Dade Police Department Crime Lab and others. This email address is: http://www.innotts.co.uk/mick2me/ukpolice.html. And there's the Cop Net page, which provides access to city, county, college, state, and federal law enforcement agencies in the U.S., including the ATF, U.S. Customs Service, DEA, FBI, FEMA, IRS and other government agencies. Email: http://copnet.uwyo.edu/flintw.

Perhaps the definitive Web sites for mystery writers are http://www.db.dk/dbaa/jbs/homepage.htm and http://www.db.dk/dbaa/jbs/tsguide.-htm. The first site provides link-access to other mystery-related listservs. The second site offers a list of mystery publications, 43 screens long, from all over the world. Both sites are maintained by Jan B. Steffensen (jbs@db.dk).

If you have any questions regarding the Internet, contact J. Alec West (alecwest@teleport.com).

In addition to the aforementioned services are the AT&T, MCI, BIX, and Microsoft Network online services, none of which provided any information for this book.

OTHER ELECTRONIC RESOURCES

While not commercial online services, here are a few mystery-related electronic resources we thought worth noting.

HMS PRESS is an electronic publisher in the UK. It considers publishing all mystery categories. Editor Wayne Ray says, "HMS Press no longer publishes paperbound books. We only publish books on disk, but we are accepting any well written manuscript in any genre on any subject. No hard copy submissions accepted. Payment in kind plus royalties. "Accepts unsolicited manuscripts. Receives 5-10 unsolicited manuscripts each month. Submit full manuscript. Send email queries to Wayne.Ray@onlinesys.com. Allows simultaneous submissions. Submissions on computer diskette should be formatted for WordPerfect 5.1. 100% of accepted manuscripts are submitted through agents. Responds to queries in 4 weeks. Reports on manuscripts in 2 months. Occasionally comments on rejected manuscripts. Send SASE for writer's guidelines. Authors are paid in royalties of 10% minimum and receive $75 from book club. Purchases First North American computer rights. Send queries and manuscripts to Wayne Ray at P.O. 340 Stub, London Ontario N6A4W1 or call (519) 433-8994.

OVER MY DEAD BODY! THE MYSTERY BULLETIN BOARD is a computer based bulletin board (BBS) for mystery readers, writers and fans. The service provides news, reviews and information regarding mystery organizations and events for callers. Most callers do not belong to any mystery organizations, nor do they subscribe to other mystery publications. Information on the BBS is processed quickly, so they keep close track of mystery events. If you have just sold a novel, produced a play, written a screenplay or whatever, let them know and they'll pass the information on to other callers. You need a computer, a modem and a communications package such as BitCom, ProComm, SmartCom, etc. to hook up to the BBS. The phone number is (206) 473-4522. For more information, call Cherie Jung at (206) 473-4650.

SERENDIPITY SYSTEMS is a multimedia publisher. Editor John Galuszka says, "We do not publish genre fiction. However, we will consider publishing mystery novels if the work includes hypertext, multimedia aspects, programmed text or other advanced computer features." Serendipity publishes an average of 1-2 first novels per year and accepts unsolicited manuscripts. Receives 15-20 unsolicited manuscripts each month. Submit full manuscript. Send email queries to J.Galuszka@genie.geis. com. Submissions on computer diskette should be formatted for IBM. Responds to queries in 2 weeks. Reports on manuscripts in 2 weeks. Send SASE for writer's guidelines. Authors are paid in royalties of 33% of net price. Purchases electronic rights only. Manuscript is published an average of 1-4 months after acceptance. 10 free copies of book go to author. Contact John Galuska at P.O. Box 140, San Simeon, CA 93452.

Reference Books, Periodicals and Other Resources

There are many excellent reference materials available to mystery writers. Most can be found at your local library, but a few of the following might be hard to find outside of actually writing the publisher. As of press time, all were in print and available to the public.

THE ARMCHAIR DETECTIVE BOOK OF LISTS

The Armchair Detective Book of Lists published its revised second edition in 1995, and it is stuffed with useful facts and interesting tidbits for mystery writers and fans. Edited by Kate Stine, the book lists all the winners of all the major mystery awards, going back to each award's first presentation (which, for the Edgar, was 1946). It doesn't stop there, however. TAD's *Book of Lists* also includes critics' choices for best mysteries of all time, the top ten mystery movies and TV shows, fan clubs and newsletters, mystery booksellers' favorites and much more. Available at your local bookstore, *The Armchair Detective Book of Lists* is $12.95 U.S., $17.50 Canada.

DEADLY SERIOUS: REFERENCES FOR WRITERS OF DETECTIVE MYSTERY & CRIME FICTION

Deadly Serious is a great reference source for mystery writers. Established in 1993, *Deadly Serious* has a circulation of over 400 subscribers. "We offer references on a broad range of topics but the topics are always interpreted to include other references. A topic like art crime will include references to help with vocabulary (art speak), materials and techniques, history, the art world, museum politics, art registries, etc." Also has information on new bookstores, industry news, convention listings and market listings. 100% of magazine is mystery/crime nonfiction. A sample copy is available for $4. Subscription cost is $36 for 10 issues. Contact: Sharon Villines, Editor & Publisher. Address: P.O. Box 1045, New York, NY 10276-1045. Phone: (212)473-5723.

GILA QUEEN'S GUIDE TO MARKETS

Gila Queen's is a monthly reference source which includes complete guidelines for fiction markets. Every issue covers the markets in detail: address changes, dead markets, conferences, contests, moving editors, anthologies, and publishing news in general. They also publish articles on writing topics, and review software and books of interest to writers. Single copies are $5 per year, and subscriptions are $28 per year for the U.S., $32 for Canada, and $45 for overseas. The *Yearly Index of Markets* is available for $3 plus SASE. *Dead Market Listings* are available for $4. Write P.O. Box 97, Newton, NJ 07860-0097 for information.

THE HOWDUNIT SERIES

Published by Writer's Digest Books, the Howdunit Series is a line of reference books for mystery writers, explaining the details of various aspects of police work and criminology in laymen's terms. Current titles are:

Armed & Dangerous: A writer's guide to weapons
Cause of Death: A writer's guide to death, murder and forensic medicine
Deadly Doses: A writer's guide to poisons
Malicious Intent: A writer's guide to how murderers, robbers, rapists and other criminals think
Modus Operandi: A writer's guide to how criminals work
Police Procedural: A writer's guide to the police and how they work
Private Eyes: A writer's guide to private investigators

Priced at $16.99 each, these books can be found at your local bookstore or ordered from Writer's Digest Books at 1-800-289-0963.

LAW & ORDER

Law & Order is a monthly magazine for professional law enforcement personnel. Established in 1953, the magazine has a circulation of 30,000. Editor Bruce Cameron publishes nonfiction pieces that deal directly with law enforcement, such as essays, management techniques, and anything else for the law professional. Subscriptions are $20 for 12 issues. Contact Bruce Cameron at 1000 Skokie Blvd., Wilmette, IL 60091 or (708) 256-8555.

MURDER MOST COZY

Murder Most Cozy is a new bi-monthly newsletter for fans of cozy mysteries. The editor promises interviews with American and British authors, an on-going cozy checklist, information on the latest cozies and more. For a sample copy, send $2 to: *Murder Most Cozy*, P.O. Box 561153, Orlando, FL 32856. For information, call Jan Dean at (407)481-9481.

MYSTERY FORUM

Mystery Forum is a nationally syndicated television talk show which interviews mystery and suspense authors. Interview segments run four to eight minutes, allowing the author to comment on background, locale and main characters. Publishing news, book and film reviews are all geared to mystery fans. Guests may need to travel to Kansas City, Missouri for taping. For further information, contact *Mystery Forum*, 16503 3rd St. North, Independence, MO 64056.

P. I. MAGAZINE

P.I. Magazine publishes true crime only. 80-85% of its readers are professional private investigators. Editor Bob Mackowiak wants personality profiles or articles on techniques, equipment or the like. All true crime stories must include a real P.I. Has a circulation of 3,500. Pays $50 per article. Says Mackowiak, "The easiest way to get into *P.I. Magazine* is to contact a real P.I. and write about one of his or her most interesting cases—that's our constant need." Send complete manuscript with cover letter to 755 Bronx, Toledo, OH 43609 or call (419) 382-0967.

SCAVENGER'S NEWSLETTER

Scavenger's Newsletter was established in 1984 by Janet Fox to spotlight small magazine markets for science fiction, fantasy, horror and mystery. It is chock-full of markets and, even at 28 pages, it looks like Fox is running out of room. The core of the newsletter is the "Scroungings" section, which contains up to 40 market listings, most of which include personal notes from the editors in addition to information on how to submit, payment and needs. Fox separates listings from the United Kingdom in "UK Update," and includes shorter listings, notes on various publications, and brief comments on markets by writers in "Slim Pickins."

Fox also includes a number of articles on issues in the small press, which are written by contributors: a " Flea Market" area listing magazine copies and subscriptions for sale; "The Dip List," listings of publications that will review writers' work; and "The Skeptic Tank," which includes magazine reviews by contributor Jim Lee. "Junk Mail" is a lively letters-to-the-editor page, and, with Fox's policy of allowing rebuttal, it's home to a number of ongoing "discussions."

A single copy is available for $2. Subscriptions are $7 for one-half year, $14 for one year in the U.S. Canadian subscriptions are available for $8.50 for one-half year, $17 for one year (in U.S. funds). Overseas subscriptions are $11.50 for one-half year, $23 for one year (also in U.S. funds). Contact Janet Fox at 519 Ellingwood, Osage City, KS 66523, or call (913)528-3538.

THOMAS INVESTIGATIVE PUBLICATIONS

Thomas Investigative Publications publishes how-to manuals for private investigators. Contact Ralph Thomas at Box 142226, Austin, TX 78714 or call (512) 928-8190.

THE WRITER'S COMPLETE CRIME REFERENCE BOOK

The Writer's Complete Crime Reference Book, by Martin Roth, is a complete guide to the procedures of the law—and the lawless. It includes general, yet accurate, information about every aspect of crime, including the fundamentals of investigations; the policies and procedures of law enforcement agencies; escape methods; rules of evidence; jargon used by criminals and the police; plus much more. Priced at $19.99, this book can be found at your local bookstore or ordered from Writer's Digest Books at 1-800-289-0963.

WRITER'S DIGEST MAGAZINE

Writer's Digest is filled with instructional articles for writers, editors and self-publishers. They list markets for fiction, including many slanted toward mystery and crime fiction. "We inspire the writer to write, instruct him or her on how to improve that work, and direct it toward appropriate markets." *Writer's Digest* can be found in just about every bookstore and newsstand, or single copies can be ordered for $3.25 (includes postage and handling). Subscriptions are $27 per year in the U.S. To subscribe, write Box 2123, Harlan, IA 51593. For other information, write to Tom Clark, Editor, 1507 Dana Ave., Cincinnati, OH 45207.

THE 7-STEP FORMULA TO WRITING SUCCESS

STEP 1 Start with the right idea. Find out where to locate sources of story ideas that never run dry. Uncover the essential ingredients for a compelling "who-done-it," and how to test the success of an idea before you write.

STEP 2 Set the stage. Learn how to use the five essential ingredients of story backgrounds. Discover how the pros research unfamiliar places and people, and how they effectively weave together setting and story.

STEP 3 Create unforgettable characters. Find out what makes readers love, hate, and even fear the people in your stories—and how to invent heroes and villains who will keep readers eagerly turning pages.

STEP 4 Thicken the plot. Guide your story from irresistible start to climactic end. Begin with a solution and move back to the crime, or start with a clue and work it into a plot. Plus, find out dozens more tips the experts use to make their stories move.

STEP 5 Write scenes that excite and thrill, twist and build. Tease your readers with clues. Puzzle them with red herrings. Titillate them with romance and sex. Remember...it's all in the art of building scenes that keeps the heat on from beginning to end.

STEP 6 Finish with an ending that keeps them wanting more. (As Mickey Spillane says, "Your first page sells the story and your last page sells the next one.") Learn how to edit and polish so readers will clamor for anything else you write.

STEP 7 Sell your story. Find out how to prepare your manuscript in a professional manner, locate the perfect publisher for your particular style, and protect your rights when you get a letter of acceptance.

Mail this card today for FREE information!

NO POSTAGE
NECESSARY
IF MAILED
IN THE
UNITED STATES

BUSINESS REPLY MAIL
FIRST CLASS MAIL   PERMIT NO. 17   CINCINNATI, OH

POSTAGE WILL BE PAID BY ADDRESSEE

Writer's Digest School
1507 DANA AVENUE
CINCINNATI OH 45207-9965

Bookstore Listings

Here you'll find a selection of booksellers from across the United States, in Canada and even a few in Great Britain that either specialize or have an extensive stock in mystery. We've attempted to make this list as complete as possible.

Mystery bookstores can help you further your writing career in a few ways. First, these stores are more likely to carry a wider selection of mystery magazines, both fiction and non-fiction, and books that might be harder to find elsewhere. Mystery bookstores are also excellent places to meet other writers, both professional and beginning. Some sponsor writing groups or at least are aware of local writers' meetings, and many have published authors in for readings and book signings.

Also listed here are mail-order booksellers. These booksellers will send books anywhere in the world, and can be a great help if there are no mystery bookstores in your area. They often have a wide selection of classic and rare titles, as well as non-fiction books and back issues of mystery magazines.

AMERICAN BOOKSTORES

ALABAMA

WAYNE MULLINS BOOKS
Address: 2337 Marshell Rd., Wetumpka, AL 36092
Phone: (205) 567-4102
Owner/Contact Person: Wayne Mullins
Established: 1991
Profile: Buys and sells used books. Trades books. 90 percent of stock is old or rare books. Write for a catalog. Prefers catalog sales; shelf-viewing by appointment only.

ARIZONA

FOOTPRINTS OF A GIGANTIC HOUND
Address: 123 South Eastbourne, Tucson, AZ 85716
Phone: (602) 326-8533
Owner/Contact Person: Elaine Livermore
Established: 1986
Profile: Conducts author signings.

JANUS BOOKS, LTD.
Address: P.O. Box 40787, Tucson, AZ 85717
Phone: (602) 881-8192
Owner/Contact Person: Michael S. Greenbaum
Established: 1979
Profile: Buys and sells used books. Trades books. 90 percent of stock is old or rare books. Sells memorabilia. Write for a catalog. Specializes in first editions of detective, mystery and suspense fiction; carries related bibliography, criticism and reference. Also carries Sherlockiana.

THE POISONED PEN
Address: 7100 E. Main St., Scottsdale, AZ 85251
Phone: (602) 947-2974
Established: 1989
Profile: Buys and sells used books. 20 percent of stock is old or rare books. Sells memorabilia. Carries 10 mystery related magazines. Conducts author signings and readings. Write for a catalog. Specializes in historical mysteries, Southwestern and regional mysteries and British mysteries. Has a readers' advisory service, a bookshopping service, a mystery-of-the-month mail-order club, an impressive newsletter and a monthly discussion group.

CALIFORNIA

ANDY'S BOOKS

Address: P.O. Box 2686, Cypress, CA 90630
Phone: (714) 527-6935
Owner/Contact Person: Janis Langwiser
Established: 1992
Profile: Buys and sells used books. Trades books. 10 percent of stock is old or rare books. Write for a catalog. Specializes in detective, mystery, horror. Offers a free search service.

BLOODY DAGGER BOOKS

Address: 3817 Shasta St., #D, San Diego, CA 92109
Phone: (619) 581-9134
Owner/Contact Person: Nick Pappas
Established: 1992
Profile: Buys and sells used books. 100 percent of stock is old or rare books. Sells memorabilia. Write for a catalog. This is a mail-order only business specializing in mystery, crime and detective fiction. Publishes a price guide titled *Bloody Dagger Reference; A Price Guide to Mystery—Crime—Detective Fiction.*

BOOK CARNIVAL

Address: 348 S. Tustin, Orange, CA 92666
Phone: (714) 538-3210
Owner/Contact Persons: Ed and Pat Thomas
Established: 1981
Profile: Buys and sells used books. Trades books. 70 percent of stock is old or rare books. Sells memorabilia. Carries 2 mystery related magazines. Conducts author signings. Carries signed first editions.

BOOKS WEST

Address: P.O. Box 417760, Sacramento, CA 95841
Phone: (916) 331-4746

Owner/Contact Persons: Gary Hollcroft & Judy Hurley

Established: 1991

Profile: Buys and sells used books. 25 percent of stock is old or rare books. Write for a catalog. Mail order only. Offers affordably priced paperback, vintage paperback and hardcover mysteries, police procedurals, horror, gothic. Most books are readers copies. Carries some first editions.

LAST SEEN READING

Address: P.O. Box 1423, Palo Alto, CA 94302

Phone: (415) 321-3348

Owner/Contact Persons: Bonnie & David Pollard

Established: 1983

Profile: Buys and sells used books. Trades books. 90 percent of stock is old or rare books. Sells memorabilia. Carries 3 mystery related magazines. Write for a catalog. Specializes in out of print mysteries and juvenile series fiction.

M.C. NEWBURN BOOKS

Address: 950 San Pablo Ave., Albany, CA 94706

Phone: (510) 524-1370

Owner/Contact Person: Maurice C. Newburn

Established: 1989

Profile: Buys and sells used books. Conducts author signings and readings. Has excellent children's and general fiction departments.

MITCHELL BOOKS

Address: 1395 E. Washington Blvd., Pasadena, CA 91104

Phone: (818) 798-4438

Owner/Contact Person: John Mitchell

Established: 1980

Profile: Buys and sells used books. 70 percent of stock is old or rare books. Sells memorabilia. Carries 1 mystery related magazine. Write for a catalog. Specializes in mystery. Houses over 40,000 hardcovers.

MYSTERIOUS BOOKSHOP WEST

Address: 8763 Beverly Blvd., West Hollywood, CA 90048
Phone: (310) 659-2959
Manager: Sheldon MaCarthur
Established: 1989
Profile: Buys and sells used books. Trades books. 70 percent of stock is old or rare books. Sells memorabilia. Carries 6 mystery related magazines. Conducts author signings and readings. Write for a catalog. Specializes in mystery, crime, espionage, true crime, first editions, vintage paperbacks, criticism, new and used books. "We are the source for mystery and crime fiction; the West Coast version of one of the first mystery bookstores in the U.S.—The Mysterious Bookshop in New York City." Owned by Otto Penzler.

RAVEN BOOKS

Address: P.O. Box 939, Artesia, CA 90702
Phone: (310) 924-7285
Owner/Contact Person: Robert Samoian
Established: 1976
Profile: Buys and sells used books. 50 percent of stock is old or rare books. Write for a catalog. Mail order only. Issues 4 to 6 catalogs annually, usually 8 pages long.

SAN FRANCISCO MYSTERY BOOKSTORE

Address: 746 Diamond St., San Francisco, CA 94114
Phone: (415) 282-7444
Owner/Contact Person: Bruce Taylor
Established: 1976
Profile: Buys and sells used books. Trades books. 50 percent of stock is old or rare books. Sells memorabilia. Carries 12 mystery related magazines. Conducts author signings. "We *don't* have a store cat."

SECRET STAIRCASE BOOKSHOP

Address: 2223 Broadway, Redwood City, CA 94063

Phone: (415) 366-1222
Owner/Contact Person: Diane Blakely
Established: 1992
Profile: Buys and sells used books. Conducts author signings and readings. Specializes in children's books. Publishes monthly newsletter; offers special request mail orders.

SHERLOCK IN L.A.

Address: 1741 Via Allena, Oceanside, CA 92056
Phone: (619) 630-2013
Owner/Contact Persons: Vincent & Flavia Brosnan
Established: 1981
Profile: Buys and sells used books. Trades books. 95 percent of stock is old or rare books. Sells memorabilia. Send $2.50 for a catalog. Specializes in Sherlockiana, Doyle, and Victoriana. Accepts want lists and services Sherlockians world wide. Visits by appointment only.

TALL STORIES

Address: 2141 Mission Street, Suite 301, San Francisco, CA 94110
Phone: (415) 255-1915
Owner/Contact Person: Donna Rankin
Established: 1991
Profile: Buys and sells used books. 100 percent of stock is old or rare books. Conducts author signings. Focuses on anitquarian books and used modern titles. "We are a co-op with 17 dealers covering many subjects."

LEN UNGER'S RARE BOOKS

Address: 631 N. Wilcox Ave. Ste. 3B, Los Angeles, CA 90004
Phone: (213) 962-7929
Established: 1980
Profile: Buys and sells used books. 50 percent of stock is old or rare books. Write for a catalog. Specializes in "books of merit."

COLORADO

THE BOOK SLEUTH, INC.
Address: 2501 W. Colorado, Suite 105, Colorado Springs, CO 80904
Phone: (719) 632-2727
Owner/Contact Person: Mrs. Helen Randal
Established: 1984
Profile: Buys and sells used books. Trades books. 1 percent of stock is old or rare books. Conducts author signings.

THE RUE MORGUE
Address: 946 Pearl St., Boulder, CO 80302
Phone: (303) 443-8346
Owner/Contact Persons: Tom and Enid Schantz
Established: 1970
Profile: Buys and sells used books. 50 percent of stock is old or rare books. Carries 4 mystery related magazines. Conducts author signings and readings. Write for a catalog. Carries numerous signed books and offers a national mail order service for all mystery books published. Publishes "The Purloined Letter," a monthly newsletter with annotated, critical listings of all new mysteries.

CONNECTICUT

DUNN & POWELL BOOKS
Address: P.O. Box 2544, Meriden, CT 06450
Phone: (207) 288-4665
Owner/Contact Person: Steve Powell
Established: 1991
Profile: Buys and sells used books. Trades books. 95 percent of stock is old or rare books. Sells memorabilia. Write for a catalog. Houses a very large stock of quantity editions (20-25 titles) with emphasis on pre-1960 titles. Catalogs over 10,000 books annually.

GEORGIA

SCIENCE FICTION AND MYSTERY BOOKSHOP

Address: 2000-F Cheshire Bridge Rd. N.E., Atlanta, GA 30324
Phone: (404) 634-3226
Owner/Contact Persons: Mark Stevens & William Amis
Established: 1983
Profile: Carries 7 mystery related magazines. Conducts author signings. Houses "maybe the largest true crime section anywhere."

ILLINOIS

BEASLEY BOOKS

Address: 1533 W. Oakdale, 2nd Floor, Chicago, IL 60657
Phone: (312) 472-4528
Owner/Contact Persons: Beth and Paul Garon
Established: 1979
Profile: Buys and sells used books. 100 percent of stock is old or rare books. Write for a catalog. Inventory can be viewed by appointment only.

CENTURIES & SLEUTHS BOOKSTORE

Address: 743 Garfield, Oak Park, IL 60304
Phone: (708) 848-7243
Owner/Contact Person: August Paul Aleksy, Jr.
Established: 1990
Profile: Carries 3 mystery related magazines. Conducts author signings and readings. Specializes in history and mystery with strong Sherlockian/Victorian flavor. Regular mystery and history discussion groups. Also publishes a newsletter.

THE MYSTERY NOOK

Address: Illinois Antique Center, 308 S.W. Commercial, Peoria, IL 61614

Phone: (309) 685-3840
Owner/Contact Persons: Kathy Miller and Joyce Welsch
Established: 1991
Profile: Buys and sells used books. 40 percent of stock is old or rare books. Write for a catalog. Carries mystery, crime fiction, and children's mysteries. Has a second location at The Antique Mall of Chenoa, R24, Chenoa, IL.

FRANK S. POLLACK, BOOKSELLER
Address: 1214 Green Bay Rd., Highland Park, IL 60035
Phone: (708) 433-2213
Owner/Contact Person: Frank S. Pollack
Established: 1987
Profile: Buys and sells used books. Trades books. 75 percent of stock is old or rare books. Write for a catalog. Specializes in the best of collectible and rare first editions in mystery, detective and modern literature. Lots of hard to find books. Carries only books in first edition and in great condition. Features new books and makes recommendation to collectors.

UNCLE BUCK'S MYSTERIES
Address: 390 Oak Hill Dr., Belleville, IL 62223
Phone: (618) 397-3568
Owner/Contact Person: Roger Wuller
Established: 1986
Profile: Buys and sells used books. 50 percent of stock is old or rare books. Write for a catalog.

INDIANA

THE CORNER SHOP
Address: 116 E. Water St., Portland, IN 47371
Phone: (219) 726-4090
Owner/Contact Person: Miss E.M. Cheeseman
Established: 1982

Profile: Buys and sells used books. 98 percent of stock is old or rare books. Specializes in mystery and adventure books. Offers a search service and special orders of in print titles.

MURDER AND MAYHEM

Address: 6411 Carrollton Avenue, Indianapolis, IN 46220
Phone: (317) 254-8273
Owner/Contact Person: Jane Syrk
Established: 1991
Profile: Buys and sells used books. 1 percent of stock is old or rare books. Sells memorabilia. Carries 10 mystery related magazines. Conducts author signings and readings. Write for a catalog.

TIMOTHY P. SLONGO BOOKS

Address: 714 E. Yoke St., Indianapolis, IN 46203
Phone: (317) 783-3497
Owner/Contact Person: Timothy P. Slongo
Established: 1991
Profile: Buys and sells used books. 95 percent of stock is old or rare books. Write for a catalog. Specializes in genre fiction. Carries advance review and uncorrected proof copies.

KANSAS

RAVEN BOOKSTORE

Address: 6 E. 7th St., Lawrence, KS 66044
Phone: (913) 749-3300
Owner/Contact Persons: Pat Kehde and Mary Lou Wright
Established: 1987
Profile: Buys and sells used books. Conducts author signings and readings.

MAINE

DUNN & POWELL BOOKS

Address: 1 The Hideaway, Bar Harbor, ME 04609
Phone: (207) 288-4665
Owner/Contact Person: Steve Powell
Established: 1991
Profile: Buys and sells used books. Trades books. 95 percent of stock is old or rare books. Sells memorabilia. Write for a catalog. Houses a very large stock of quantity editions (20-25 titles) with emphasis on pre-1960 titles. Catalogs over 10,000 books annually.

MARYLAND

MYSTERY BOOKSHOP

Address: 7700 Old Georgetown Rd., Bethesda, MD 20814
Phone: (301) 657-2665
Owner/Contact Persons: Jean and Ron McMillen
Established: 1989
Profile: Buys and sells used books. 1 percent of stock is old or rare books. Sells memorabilia. Carries 10 mystery related magazines. Conducts author signings and readings. Write for a catalog. Specializes in mystery, detective fiction, and reference books. Offers quality customer service.

MYSTERY LOVES COMPANY

Address: 1730 Fleet St., Baltimore, MD 21231
Phone: (410) 276-6708
Owner/Contact Persons: C. Paige Rose and Katherine Harig
Established: 1991
Profile: Buys and sells used books. Trades books. 20 percent of stock is old or rare books. Carries 8 mystery related magazines. Conducts author signings and readings. Write for a catalog. Specializes in mystery and signed first editions. Has a bookstore dog named Toby and is located in an historic area founded in the 1700's.

QUILL & BRUSH

Address: P.O. Box 5365, Rockville, MD 20848
Phone: (301) 460-3700
Owner/Contact Persons: Allen and Patricia Ahearn
Profile: Buys and sells used books. 90 percent of stock is old or rare books. Carries 100 mystery related magazines. Conducts author signings. Write for a catalog. Carries first edition 19th and 20th century literature.

SECOND STORY BOOKS

Address: 12160 Park Lawn Dr., Rockville, MD 20852
Phone: (301) 770-0477
Owner/Contact Person: Nelson Freck
Established: 1992
Profile: Buys and sells used books. Trades books. 100 percent of stock is old or rare books. Write for a catalog.

MASSACHUSETTS

KATE'S MYSTERY BOOKS (MURDER UNDER COVER, INC.)

Address: 2211 Massachusetts Ave., Cambridge, MA 02140
Phone: (617) 491-2660
Owner/Contact Person: Kate Mattes
Established: 1983
Profile: Buys and sells used books. Trades books. 40 percent of stock is old or rare books. Sells memorabilia. Carries 12 mystery related magazines. Conducts author signings and readings. Write for a catalog. Contains several special sections—autographed, women, historical, gay & lesbian, New England, traditional, British, etc. Publishes a newsletter: $6 annual fee. Will send a sample containing news about events, reviews by customers and listings of new books.

SPENSER'S MYSTERY BOOKSHOP

Address: 314 Newbury Street, Boston, MA 02115

Phone: (617) 262-0880
Owner/Contact Person: Andy Thurnaver
Established: 1983
Profile: Buys and sells used books. Trades books. 60 percent of stock is old or rare books. Carries 6 mystery related magazines. Affiliated with Time & Again Books, 364 Main St., N. Andover, MA 01845.

MICHIGAN

DEADLY PASSIONS BOOKSHOP
Address: 157 S. Kalamazoo Mall, Kalamazoo, MI 49007
Phone: (616) 383-4402
Owner/Contact Persons: Jim Huang & Jennie G. Jacobson
Established: 1992
Profile: Buys and sells used books. Trades books. 5 percent of stock is old or rare books. Carries 6 mystery related magazines. Conducts author signings and readings. Write for a catalog. Offers a frequent buyer's discount program; has monthly discussion groups for both mystery and science fiction lovers.

ELSE FINE BOOKS
Address: P.O. Box 43, Dearborn, MI 48126
Phone: (313) 924-1529
Owner/Contact Persons: Louise Oberschmidt & Allen M. Hemlock
Established: 1982
Profile: Buys and sells used books. 99 percent of stock is old or rare books. Write for a catalog. Carries collectors' books and specializes in first editions in mystery, detective, thriller. Antiquarian Booksellers Association of America (ABAA) member.

MINNESOTA

FOOTSTOOL DETECTIVE BOOKS
Address: 3148 Holmes Ave. S., Minneapolis, MN 55408
Phone: (612) 825-8941

Owner/Contact Person: Norman Riger
Established: 1984
Profile: Buys and sells used books. Trades books. 2 percent of stock is old or rare books. Sells memorabilia. Send $1 for a catalog. Carries 5,000 paperbacks—mystery, thriller, gothic, spy, horror, suspense. Liquidates book sales and stores and collections at cheap prices. Offers uniform pricing: $1.50 paperbacks, $3 hardcovers. Has a separate warehouse at 2115 Como Ave. SE, Minneapolis, MN 55414. Mostly mail order; in house sales by appointment only.

GREEN LION BOOKS
Address: 2402 University Ave. W., Suite 409, St. Paul, MN 55114
Phone: (612) 644-9070
Owner/Contact Person: L. Goodman
Established: 1979
Profile: Buys and sells used books. Trades books. 95 percent of stock is old or rare books. Sells memorabilia. Write for a catalog. Carries numerous paperbacks from the 40's and 50's, especially paperback originals for such authors as J.D. MacDonald, Jim Thompson, etc. Stocks "hard-to-find" books—titles or editions generally not found at other used bookshops. Receives mail orders; visits are by appointment only.

ONCE UPON A CRIME
Address: 604 W. 26th St., Minneapolis, MN 55405
Phone: (612) 870-3785
Owner/Contact Person: Steve Stilwell
Established: 1987
Profile: Buys and sells used books. Trades books. 15 percent of stock is old or rare books. Carries 8 mystery related magazines. Conducts author signings and readings. Write for a catalog. Prides itself on being a small store with a large stock and very knowledgeable staffers. "Author Jeremiah Healy calls the store's newsletter, *The Blotter*, 'one of the best, if not the best, newsletter in the country.'"

UNCLE EDGAR'S MYSTERY BOOKSTORE
Address: 2864 Chicago Ave. S., Minneapolis, MN 55407
Phone: (612) 824-9984
Owner/Contact Person: Don Blyly
Established: 1980
Profile: Buys and sells used books. Trades books. 50 percent of stock is old or rare books. Carries 4 mystery related magazines. Conducts author signings and readings. Write for a catalog. Publishes a science fiction and mystery newsletter. Shares building with Uncle Hugo's SF Bookstore.

MISSOURI

BIG SLEEP BOOKS
Address: 239 N. Euclid, St. Louis, MO 63108
Phone: (314) 361-6100
Owner/Contact Persons: Chris King and Helen Simpson
Established: 1988
Profile: Buys and sells used books. Trades books. 15 percent of stock is old or rare books. Conducts author signings and readings. Focuses on mystery, espionage and adventure novels.

NEW HAMPSHIRE

MYSTERY LOVERS INK
Address: 8 Stiles Rd., Salem, NH 03079
Phone: (603) 898-8060
Owner/Contact Person: Joanne L. Romano
Established: 1985
Profile: Carries 3 mystery related magazines. Conducts author signings and readings. Write for a catalog. Publishes a monthly newsletter. Catalog costs $2.

NEW JERSEY

MCCOY'S RARE BOOKS

Address: 121 Choctaw Ridge Rd., Branchburg, NJ 08876
Phone: (908) 722-7064
Owner/Contact Persons: Jamie and Patti McCoy
Established: 1988
Profile: Buys and sells used books. Trades books. 90 percent of stock is old or rare books. Sells memorabilia. Write for a catalog.

PATTERSON SMITH

Address: 23 Prospect Terrace, Montclair, NJ 07042
Phone: (201) 744-3291
Owner/Contact Person: Patterson Smith
Established: 1955
Profile: Buys and sells used books. 100 percent of stock is old or rare books. Sells memorabilia. Write for a catalog. Sells true crime only.

NEW MEXICO

SKULLDUGGERY HOUSE BOOKS

Address: P.O. Box 1851, Alamogordo, NM 88311
Phone: (505) 434-6641
Owner/Contact Persons: Jim and Sharon Smith
Established: 1991
Profile: Buys and sells used books. 20 percent of stock is old or rare books. Write for a catalog. Specializes in mystery writers from the 30s and 40s. Carries a large number of young adult mysteries.

NEW YORK

BLACK AND WHITE BOOKS

Address: 111 Hicks Street, #11F, Brooklyn, NY 11201
Phone: (718) 855-2598

Owner/Contact Person: Rushton H. Potts
Established: 1987
Profile: Buys and sells used books. 90 percent of stock is old or rare books. Write for a catalog. Focuses on mystery/detective fiction and science fiction & fantasy. Carries related reference material.

CERTO BOOKS
Address: P.O. Box 322, Circleville, NY 10919
Phone: (914) 361-1190
Owner/Contact Person: Nick Certo
Established: 1987
Profile: Buys and sells used books. Trades books. 90 percent of stock is old or rare books. Write for a catalog. Specializes in mail orders and out-of-prints. Stocks pulp magazines, early fanzines and first editions, mostly hardcover; pre-1960 vintage paperbacks.

METROPOLIS MYSTERY BOOKSHOP & TEA ROOM
Address: 31 Union Square West PH#2, New York, NY 10003
Owner: Small group of mystery writers
Established: 1991
Profile: Buys and sells used books. Trades books. 20 percent of stock is old or rare books. Sells memorabilia. Carries 20 mystery related magazines. Conducts author signings and readings. Houses an extensive variety of titles. Send $5 and a 9 × 12 SASE for catalog. Customers are invited for teas by invitation only. Send postcard with phone number to schedule an appointment.

THE MYSTERIOUS BOOKSHOP
Address: 129 West 56th St., New York, NY 10019
Phone: (212) 765-0900
Owner/Contact Person: Otto Penzler
Established: 1980
Profile: Buys and sells used books. 50 percent of stock is old or rare books. Sells memorabilia. Conducts author signings. Write for a catalog. Carries many signed new titiles, has access to finding out-of-print

and first editions for clients. Stocks reference and biography books related to mystery, and has an extensive Sherlock Holmes section.

MYSTERY BOOKSTORE (OCEANSIDE BOOKS)

Address: 173 A. Woodfield Road, W. Hempstead, NY 11552
Phone: (516) 565-4710
Owner/Contact Person: Adrienne Williams
Established: 1973
Profile: Buys and sells used books. 20 percent of stock is old or rare books. Sells memorabilia. Write for a catalog. "Our main focus is 'vintage' mystery & detective [fiction] when we can obtain it. Our stock includes out-of-print up to date—first with dust jacket in very good condition (and we mean very good). Our reputation has been built on customer service, building collections in the best possible condition. We also carry out-of-print paperbacks (used). We leave the new to the chains." Publishes an extensive catalog and specializes in reference and bibliographic material on mystery authors.

PARTNERS & CRIME

Address: 44 Greenwich Avenue, New York, NY 10011
Phone: (212) 243-0440
Owner/Contact Persons: John Douglas and partners
Established: 1994
Profile: Buys and sells used books. 15 percent of stock is old or rare books. Conducts author signings and readings. Write for a catalog. Carries many out-of-print books. "We have a rental library in addition to our regular retail shop, a meeting room avaiable for rental, classes for new writers and reading groups. Our meeting room is panelled with an oak floor and a faux fireplace with tricks."

SCIENCE FICTION, MYSTERIES & MORE!

Address: 140 Chambers Street, New York, NY 10007
Phone: (212) 385-8798
Owner/Contact Person: Alan Zimmerman
Established: 1992

Profile: Buys and sells used books. Trades books. 25 percent of stock is old or rare books. Sells memorabilia. Carries 8 mystery related magazines. Conducts author signings and readings. "Our focus is science fiction and mysteries. We try to be a community center for the fans of both genres. We have monthly readings, parties for new books and discussion groups on fact and fiction. We have a workshop on writing taught by an editor from Simon & Schuster (John Ordover) and a workshop on the Tarot taught by Alexandra Honigsberg. Our Star Trek costume parties have been on TV."

TIM'S BOOKS
Address: 31 Hewlett Road, Red Hook, NY 12571
Phone: (914) 758-2555
Owner/Contact Person: Tim Murphy
Established: 1994
Profile: Buys and sells used books. 100 percent of stock is old or rare books. Write for a catalog. Company is mail-order only, specializing in vintage/collectable paperbacks and digests.

NORTH DAKOTA

PANDORA'S BOOKS LTD.
Address: Box 54, Neche, ND 58265
Phone: (204) 324-8548
Owner/Contact Person: Grant Thiessen
Established: 1973
Profile: Buys and sells used books. Trades books. 100 percent of stock is old or rare books. Carries 90 mystery related magazines.Write for a catalog. Specializes in mystery and science fiction. Mail orders only, and out-of-prints only. Operation is 100% computerized, so your order can be instantly confirmed. Over 200,00 titles available.

OHIO

THE BOOK HARBOR
Address: 32 W. College Ave., Westerville, OH 43081
Phone: (614) 895-3788
Owner/Contact Persons: George and Fredrica Spurgeon
Established: 1988
Profile: Buys and sells used books. 60 percent of stock is old or rare books. Sells memorabilia. Will search for paperback mystery. Also carries handmade silver and gemstone jewelry.

GRAVE MATTERS BOOKSTORE
Address: Box 32192, Cincinnati, OH 45232
Phone: (513) 242-7527
Owner/Contact Persons: Alice Ann Carpenter and John Leininger
Established: 1986
Profile: Buys and sells used books. 50 percent of stock is old or rare books. Carries 15 mystery related magazines. Write for a catalog. Houses a large collection of mystery reference, Sherlockiana and older crime fiction; also carries new books.

HAHN'S HOUSE OF MYSTERY
Address: 8414 Arundel Ct., Cincinnati, OH 45231
Phone: (513) 521-8046
Owner/Contact Person: Robert C. Hahn
Established: 1992
Profile: Buys and sells used books. Trades books. Write for a catalog. Carries modern first editions, proofs, advance reading copies, and signed books in collectible condition. Visits made via appointment only.

MURDER IS SERVED
Address: 5273 Bittersweet Dr., Dayton, OH 45424
Phone: (513) 438-0211

Owner/Contact Person: John W. Bierman
Established: 1993
Profile: Buys and sells used books. 100 percent of stock is old or rare books. Write for a catalog. Carries collectible and reading copy mysteries in first, XL and BC editions. Prefers mail orders, but with advance notice visitors are welcome.

MYSTERIES FROM THE YARD
Address: 253 B Xenia Ave., Yellow Springs, OH 45387
Phone: (513) 767-2111
Owner/Contact Person: Mary Frost-Pierson
Established: 1979
Profile: Buys and sells used books. Trades books. 20 percent of stock is old or rare books. Sells memorabilia. Carries 1 mystery related magazine. Conducts author signings. Specializes in children's mysteries and puzzle books, media mystery, and Sherlockiana.

STRANGE BIRDS BOOKS
Address: P.O. Box 12639, Norwood, OH 45212
Phone: (513) 631-3336
Owner/Contact Person: Ken Hughes
Established: 1992
Profile: Buys and sells used books. Trades books. 10 percent of stock is old or rare books. Write for a catalog. Carries good used mystery paperbacks and hardcovers. Catalog includes reviews and tidbits of information about selected authors.

ROY WILLIS, BOOKSELLER
Address: 195 Thurman Ave., Columbus, OH 43206
Phone: (614) 443-4004
Owner/Contact Person: Roy Willis
Established: 1972
Profile: Buys and sells used books. 90 percent of stock is old or rare books.

OREGON

MURDER BY THE BOOK

Address: 3210 SE Hawthorne Blvd., Portland, OR 97214

Phone: (503) 232-9995

Owner/Contact Persons: Carolyn Lane and Jill Hinckley

Established: 1983

Profile: Buys and sells used books. Trades books. 10 percent of stock is old or rare books. Carries 5 mystery related magazines. Conducts author signings and readings. Write for a catalog. Carolyn and Jill are proud of their customer service record. Rents hardcovers and audio tapes; has mysteries for kids and good reference material for mystery writers.

PENNSYLVANIA

BUCKINGHAM BOOKS

Address: 8058 Stone Bridge Road, Greencastle, PA 17225

Phone: (717) 597-5657

Owner/Contact Persons: Len and Nancy Buckingham

Established: 1988

Profile: Buys and sells used books. 65 percent of stock is old or rare books. Sells memorabilia. Write for a catalog. Sells through catalog only.

CLOAK & DAGGER BOOKS

Address: 227 Lurgan Ave., Shippensburg, PA 17257

Phone: (717) 532-8213

Owner/Contact Person: Robert Wynne

Established: 1988

Profile: Buys and sells used books. Trades books. 75 percent of stock is old or rare books. Write for a catalog.

CLOAK AND DAGGER BOOKS

Address: 219 East Main Street, Mechanicsburg, PA 17055
Phone: (717) 795-7470
Owner/Contact Person: Debbie Beamer
Established: 1990
Profile: Buys and sells used books. 25 percent of stock is old or rare books. Sells memorabilia.

GRAVESEND BOOKS

Address: Box 235, Pocono Pines, PA 18350
Phone: (717) 646-3317
Owner/Contact Person: Enola Stewart
Established: 1971
Profile: Buys and sells used books. 90 percent of stock is old or rare books. Sells memorabilia. Carries 20 mystery related magazines. Write for a catalog. Specializes in detective fiction. Unlike many stores that come and go, Gravesend has been around 24 years.

MYSTERY LOVERS BOOKSHOP & CAFE

Address: 514 Allegheny River Blvd., Oakmont, PA 15139
Phone: (412) 828-4877
Owner/Contact Persons: Mary Alice Gorman and Richard Goldman
Established: 1990
Profile: Sells memorabilia. Carries 4 mystery related magazines. Conducts author signings and readings. Write for a catalog. Houses extensive children's section with multimedia titles. Full cafe in store. Provides catered events for school groups, book clubs and others. Publishes a very impressive newsletter which customers can subscribe to for $5 per year. "Masters of Mystery" program offers discounts based on the number of purchases made. Orders can also be made online by sending request to 71652,2654@Compuserve.com.

WHODUNIT?

Address: 1931 Chestnut St., Philadelphia, PA 19103

Phone: (800) 567-1478
Owner/Contact Person: Art Bourgean
Established: 1977
Profile: Buys and sells used books. Trades books. 75% of bookstore is old or rare books. Sells memorabilia. Carries 2 mystery related magazines. Write or call for a catalog.

RHODE ISLAND

MURDER BY THE BOOK
Address: 1281 N. Main St., Providence, RI 02940
Phone: (401) 331-9140
Owner/Contact Person: Kevin Barbero
Established: 1978
Profile: Buys and sells used books. Trades books. 90 percent of stock is old or rare books. Write for a catalog. Specializes in mystery detective fiction and critical works.

TEXAS

BOOK TREE
Address: 702 University Village, Richardson, TX 75081
Phone: (214) 437-4337
Owner/Contact Persons: Terry Phillips and Barry Phillips
Established: 1987
Profile: Buys and sells used books. Trades books. 2-3 percent of stock is old or rare books. Carries 7 mystery related magazines. Conducts author signings. Write for a catalog. Sisters In Crime "Deadly Allies" meets every 2nd Sunday at the store. Also carries new comics and rents audio books.

MORDIDA BOOKS
Address: P.O. Box 79322, Houston, TX 77279
Phone: (713) 467-4280
Owner/Contact Person: Richard D. Wilson

Established: 1987
Profile: Buys and sells used books. Trades books. 100 percent of stock is old or rare books. Write for a catalog. Carries first editions of mystery and detective novels. Prefers mail order; shelf-viewing by appointment only.

MURDER BY THE BOOK
Address: 2342 Bissonnet, Houston, TX 77005
Phone: (713) 524-8597
Owner/Contact Person: Martha Farrington
Established: 1980
Profile: Buys and sells used books. 5 percent of stock is old or rare books. Sells memorabilia. Carries 5 mystery related magazines. Conducts author signings and readings. Write for a catalog. Focuses on "simply the best in mystery fiction." One store manager, Dean James, is a widely published reviewer and the co-author of *By A Woman's Hand: A Guide to Mystery Fiction by Women*(Berkley Books, 1994).

MYSTERIES & MORE
Address: 11139 N. IH 35 #176, Austin, TX 78753
Phone: (512) 837-6768
Owner/Contact Persons: Elmer and Jan Grape
Established: 1990
Profile: Buys and sells used books. Trades books. 60 percent of stock is old or rare books. Carries 3 mystery related magazines. Conducts author signings and readings. Write for a catalog. Sells mostly mysteries. Carries large collection of modern first editions.

WASHINGTON

CARDINAL BOOKS
Address: 4010 NE 136th St., Vancouver, WA 98686
Phone: (206)576-9070
Owner/Contact Person: Larry and Linda Johnson
Profile: Buys and sells used books. Trades books. 50% of stock is old or

rare books. Sells memorabilia. Write or call for catalog.

KILLING TIME MYSTERY BOOKS

Address: 2821 NE 55th St., Seattle, WA 98105
Phone: (206) 525-2266
Owner/Contact Persons: Susan M. Nevins and Miriam Uhlig
Established: 1992
Profile: Buys and sells used books. Trades books. 5 percent of stock is old or rare books. Carries 3 mystery related magazines. Conducts author signings and readings. Publishes a newsletter (just write for a copy) and offers a preorder discount program on hardcovers; also gives frequent buyer discounts.

SEATTLE MYSTERY BOOKSHOP

Address: 117 Cherry Street, Seattle, WA 98104
Phone: (206) 587-5737
Owner/Contact Person: Bill Farley
Established: 1990
Profile: Buys and sells used books. Trades books. 40 percent of stock is old or rare books. Carries 6 mystery related magazines. Conducts author signings. Has a broad selection of in-print and out-of-print mysteries for readers and collectors. Specializes in Northwest authors. Takes mail and phone orders. Carries signed copies. Publishes a news-letter. Offers searches.

WISCONSIN

BOOKED FOR MURDER, LTD.

Address: 2701 University Avenue, Madison, WI 53705
Phone: (608) 238-2701
Owner/Contact Person: Mary Helen Becker
Established: 1988
Profile: Buys and sells used books. 1 percent of stock is old or rare books. Carries 6 mystery related magazines. Conducts author signings and readings. Write for a catalog. Bookstore personnel have an "expert

knowledge of mysteries" and strive to create a cozy atmosphere.

MYSTERY ONE BOOKSHOP

Address: 2109 N. Prospect Ave., Milwaukee, WI 53202
Phone: (414) 347-4077
Owner/Contact Person: Richard Katz
Established: 1993
Profile: Buys and sells used books. Trades books. 20 percent of stock is old or rare books. Sells memorabilia. Carries 1 mystery related magazine. Conducts author signings and readings. Specializes in American crime fiction. Publishes a newsletter—just write or call to receive a copy.

P.I.E.S.

Address: P.O. Box 341218, Milwaukee, WI 53234
Owner/Contact Person: Gary Warren Niebuhr
Established: 1990
Profile: Buys and sells used books. Trades books. 90 percent of stock is old or rare books. Sells memorabilia. Mail order catalog specializing in P.I. novels. Carries books for both the reader and the collector.

WEST'S BOOKING AGENCY

Address: P.O. Box 406, Elm Grove, WI 53122
Phone: (800) 754-8677
Owner/Contact Person: Richard West
Established: 1975
Profile: Buys and sells used books. 95 percent of stock is old or rare books. Sells memorabilia. Carries 100 mystery related magazines. Specializes in private eye fiction and paperback originals. Houses a large stock of mystery and crime fiction.

CANADA

ANN'S BOOKS AND MOSTLY MYSTERIES

Address: 225 Carlton St., Toronto, Ontario M5A 2L2 Canada
Phone: (416) 962-7947
Owner/Contact Person: David Srene-Melvin
Profile: Buys and sells used books. 100 percent of stock is old or rare books. Write for a catalog. Sells self-published books.

HENRI LABELLE

Address: 1162 Lesage St., P.O. Box 561, Prevost, Quebec J0R 1T0 Canada
Phone: (514) 224-2813
Owner/Contact Person: Henri Labelle
Established: 1987
Profile: Buys and sells used books. 85 percent of stock is old or rare books. Sells memorabilia. Carries many mystery related magazines. Write for a catalog. Mail order only. Also deals in non-sports trading cards and comic books from the 1950-60's, and T.V./movie memorabilia.

THE MYSTERY MERCHANT BOOKSTORE

Address: 1952 West 4th Ave., Vancouver, British Columbia V6J 1M5 Canada
Phone: (604) 739-4311
Owner/Contact Persons: Noah Stewart, Manager/Sandra Leef, Manager
Established: 1992
Profile: Buys and sells used books. 100 percent of stock is old or rare books. Carries 4 mystery related magazines. Conducts author signings and readings. Write for a catalog. The oldest, largest and most beautiful mystery bookstore west of Toronto. Well-organized stock, highly computerized data retrieval and storage and an extremely well-read staff. Over 8,000 new and 3,000 used titles in stock. Want lists are maintained on computer. Staff has developed a computer database called Noah's Archives which tracks mysteries by author, title, subject,

character names, location, etc. (i.e. can create a list of all mysteries set in Portugal and featuring female private eyes, or can find the title of the third book in a particular series). Database currently has over 6,500 books listed, each with up to seven different tags, and is added to daily. It may become commercially available on CD-ROM in the future.

PRIME CRIME BOOKS

Address: 891 Bank St., Ottawa, Ontario K1S 3W4 Canada
Phone: (613) 238-2583
Owner/Contact Person: James Reicker
Profile: Buys and sells used books. Trades books. 5 percent of stock is old or rare books. Conducts author signings and readings. Specializes in detective and mystery fiction.

SLEUTH OF BAKER STREET

Address: 1595 Bayview Ave., Toronto, Ontario M4G 3B5 Canada
Phone: (416) 483-3111
Owner/Contact Person: J.D. Singh
Established: 1979
Profile: Buys and sells used books. 25 percent of stock is old or rare books. Conducts author signings and readings. Write for a catalog. Knowledgeable staff and owners, search service offered and mail order. "Best selection of crime/detective fiction in North America. Or so our customers tell us."

GREAT BRITIAN

A1 CRIME FICTION

Address: Westridge House, 3 Horsecastles Lane, Sherborne, Dorset DT9 6DW England
Phone: (093) 581-4989
Owner/Contact Person: D.C. Ireland
Established: 1966
Profile: Buys and sells used books. Trades books. 95 percent of stock is

old or rare books. Write for a catalog. 25,000 books in stock. Store's focus is entirely crime, detective and spy fiction.

BLACK HILL BOOKS

Address: The Wain House, Black Hill, Clunton, Craven Arms, Shropshire SY7 0JD England
Phone: 0588-640551
Owner/Contact Persons: Guy N. Smith and Jean M. Smith
Established: 1972
Profile: Buys and sells used books. Trades books. 100 percent of stock is old or rare books. Carries 150 mystery related magazines. Write for a catalog. Crime Fiction hardcover catalog, Vintage paperbacks catalog and Guy N. Smith catalog each published 4 times per year. "We have a special Guy N. Smith bookroom: signed books, manuscripts, T-shirts, ephemera, fan club, etc."

ERGO BOOKS

Address: 46 Lisburne Rd., London NW3 2NR England
Phone: (071) 482-4431
Owner/Contact Person: Elliot Greenfield
Established: 1976
Profile: Buys and sells used books. Trades books. 98 percent of stock is old or rare books. Sells memorabilia. Carries many mystery related magazines. Write for a catalog. "Ephemera (especially Sherlockiana) is big with us." Greenfield also says, "I see people by appointment at any time. I've made appointments for 2 a.m.! I operate from home where 2 book rooms contain a great deal."

MING BOOKS UK

Address: 110 Gloucester Ave., London NW1 8JA England
Phone: 0171-483-2681
Owner/Contact Persons: Robin and Marion Richmond
Established: 1982
Profile: Buys and sells used books. Trades books. 95 percent of stock is old or rare books. Carries many mystery related magazines. Write for

a catalog. Ming focuses on obtaining the "best UK 1st editions" and out of print titles. Offers free search service.

MURDER ONE

Address: 71-73 Charing Cross Road, London, WC2H 0AA England
Phone: (071) 734-3483
Owner/Contact Person: Maxim Jakubowski
Established: 1989
Profile: 10 percent of stock is old or rare books. Carries 12 mystery related magazines. Conducts author signings. Write for a catalog. "Largest mystery bookshop in the world!"

ZARDOZ BOOKS

Address: 20 Whitecroft, Dilton Marsh, Westbury, Wiltshire BA134DJ England
Phone: (0373) 865371
Owner/Contact Person: M. Flanagan
Profile: Buys and sells used books. Trades books. 95 percent of stock is old or rare books. Sells memorabilia. Carries 10 mystery related magazines. Send $1 US for a catalog. Mail order only, specializing in paperback first printings.

IRELAND

MAINLY MURDER BOOKSTORE

Address: 2a Paul St., Cork Ireland
Phone: (021) 272413
Owner/Contact Person: Patricia Barry
Profile: Buys and sells used books. 10 percent of stock is old or rare books. Write for a catalog. "Only bookshop in Ireland specializing in crime and detection."

Must Reading

We asked editors, agents and bookstore owners what novels they would recommend to a beginning mystery writer—the "A" list of crime fiction. While they chose a number of different titles, a few of the same authors kept popping up. Here are the top ten, according to our survey.

1. Raymond Chandler
2. Dashiell Hammett
3. Agatha Christie
4. Sir Arthur Conan Doyle
5. Sue Grafton -
6. Dorothy L. Sayers
7. James Lee Burke
8. Rex Stout
9. Tony Hillerman
10. Ross Macdonald

About the Contributors

Contributors to the Instructional Articles

Jack M. Bickham

Jack Bickham is the author of more than 75 published novels, including the popular Brad Smith series for Forge/Tor Books. He has also written extensively about the craft of fiction, both in *Writer's Digest* magazine and in several books published by Writer's Digest Books.

Ruth Cavin

Ruth Cavin was born and raised in Pittsburgh, and is a graduate of what was then Carnegie Tech, with a Bachelor of Science degree in General Studies. After 50 years or more in other climes, she is still a Pirates fan (some people never learn). She is the author of several published books, none of them adult fiction, and has started a number of mystery writers on their way, from Aaron Elkins to Laurie R. King. She has all these plaques on her wall: The Ellery Queen Award from Mystery Writers of America (given to outstanding people in the mystery-publishing field); the Lifetime Achievement Award from the Midwest Mystery and Suspense Convention; and the Mid- Atlantic Mystery and Book Fair Award.

Robin Gee

Robin Gee is a senior editor at Writer's Digest Books and editor of *Novel & Short Story Writer's Market*, the annual directory of information and opportunities for fiction writers. She is also a freelance writer, editor and film reviewer for Critics' Choice, an online entertainment magazine which publishes in America Online, Delphi and eWorld. In addition to writing the marketing articles for this edition, Robin also interviewed Joe Blades at Ballantine, Cathleen Jordan at *Alfred Hitchcock Mystery*

Magazine, Gary Lovisi at *Hardboiled* magazine, Charles Raisch at *New Mystery* magazine, and Natalee Rosenstein at Berkley Books.

Jan Grape

In addition to owning and operating the *Mysteries & More* bookstore in Austin, Texas, with her husband Elmer, Jan Grape writes mystery fiction and has been a contributing editor to *Mystery Scene* magazine for the past seven years. She also writes a regular column for *Mystery Scene* called "What's New in Publishing," and has been the editor of the Private Eye Writers of America's "Refelections in a Private Eye" newsletter for the last four years. Jan has also served as Regional President of the Southwest Chapter of the Mystery Writers of America, and as Treasurer of the Heart of Texas Chapter of Sisters in Crime.

Janet Hutchings

Janet Hutchings is the editor-in-chief of *Ellery Queen's Mystery Magazine*, and is only the third person to hold that position since the magazine's beginning in 1941. Since being chosen for the job in 1991 by previous editor Eleanor Sullivan, Janet has published many fine stories by the biggest names in the mystery field, and has launched the careers of some of today's hot new writers.

Donald Maass

Donald Maass is an independent New York literary agent who represents 80 authors of mystery, suspense, science fiction, fantasy, horror and other types of commercial fiction. He is also the author of 14 psuedonymous novels published by Avon, Bantam, Pocket, Silhouette and Troll Associates. His column "The Bottom Line" on publishing topics appears in *Mystery Scene* and other writers' magazines. He is a member of the Association of Authors Representatives, Science Fiction Writers of America and Mystery Writers of America.

Don Prues

Don Prues is the Sourcebook Series production editor at Writer's Digest Books. For this edition he wrote the *Online Resources* section and interviewed Eamon Dolan at HarperCollins, Cherie Jung at *Over My Dead Body!* and Bob Myers at *Mystery Forum*. He has contributed to the poetry journal *Sagetrieb*, and he is a magazine columnist for Critics' Choice, an online entertainment magazine which is published on America Online, Delphi and eWorld.

Robert Randisi

You may meet Robert J. Randisi someday; he's everywhere in the mystery field. Bob was co-founder of the Private Eye Writers of America (with Bill Pronzini), and attends several mystery conventions each year. He can usually be found at Eyecon and Magna Cum Murder hosting "Gat Heat," a mystery talk show in the style of David Letterman's *The Late Show*. Bob also writes the popular Miles Jacoby mystery series and edits anthologies of mysteries by Private Eye Writers of America members. He recently co-edited *Deadly Allies II: A PWA-Sisters in Crime Collaborative Anthology*, with Susan Dunlap.

Michael Seidman

A 30-year publishing veteran, Michael Seidman is the mystery editor at Walker & Company. A *Writer's Digest* magazine correspondent, he is the author of two books for writers, *From Printout to Published: A Guide to the Publishing Process*, and *Living the Dream: An Outline for a Life in Fiction*. He is presently at work on two new books, one a question and answer volume based on his syndicated column, "Ask Michael," and the other a collection of essays tentatively titled *Writing Outside the Lines: Commerce, Art and Category Fiction*.

Sharon Gwyn Short

Sharon Gwyn Short is the author of the Patricia Delaney mystery series, which features a computer-whiz private investigator and is set in Cincinnati, Ohio. The first two books in the series are *Angel's Bidding* and *Past Pretense*. The next book in the series, *The Death We Share*, was due out in December, 1995.

Contributors to the Market Profiles

Chantelle Bentley
Chantelle Bentley is the production editor for *Poet's Market* and *Novel & Short Story Writer's Market*. She lives in Batavia, Ohio, with her husband and daughter. Chantelle interviewed Keith Kahla at St. Martin's Press for this edition.

Dorothy Maxwell Goepel
Dorothy Maxwell Goepel works as a freelance writer for ad agencies, hospitals and businesses, and serves as a Public Affairs Specialist in the U.S. Air Force Reserve. Her articles have appeared in magazines and newspapers including *Marketing News, Mature Living, Kentucky Living Magazine* and *Capper's*. Two of her short stories were finalists in the 1993 and 1994 *Writer's Digest* magazine's Writing Competitions. She resides in Cincinnati. Dorothy interviewed Kate Miciak of Bantam Crimeline for this edition.

Heather K. Hardy
Heather K. Hardy is a graduate of the College of Charleston with a degree in English. She lives in Cincinnati, Ohio, and works for Paragon Advertising Inc. Heather interviewed Sarah Gallick at Kensington Publishing for this edition.

Jack Heffron
Jack Heffron is an editor at Writer's Digest Books. He has published fiction and nonfiction in a number of magazines including the *Black Warrior Review, North American Review, TriQuarterly Review,* and the *Utne Reader*. Jack interviewed Michael Seidman at Walker & Company for this edition.

Jeffrey Marks
Jeffrey Marks is a freelance writer whose work has appeared in a number of magazines including *Mystery Scene* and *The Armchair Detective*. His biography of mystery writer Craig Rice has appeared in a French anthology of Rice's works. Jeff was also the winner of the 1994 Malice Domestic Grant for his novel, *The Scent of Murder*. Jeff interviewed Joseph Pittman at Dutton/Signet for this edition.

Kelly O'Donnell
Kelly O'Donnell, a freelance writer living in Cincinnati, is a former reporter for Thomson Newspapers, *The African Expedition Gazette* and Press Community Newspapers. She began her association with Writer's Digest Books on the premiere edition of the *Science Fiction Writer's Marketplace and Sourcebook*. Kelly interviewed Jason Jacob Poston at Donald I. Fine Publishing for this edition.

H. Robert Perry
H. Robert Perry is a Cincinnati writer whose short fiction has appeared in *Tomorrow Speculative Fiction, Gaslight, The Stake, Tense Moments* and *Mean Lizard* magazines. Rob interviewed Barbara Grier at The Naiad Press for this edition.

Robert Schofield
Robert Schofield is a freelance writer whose fiction and nonfiction have been published in *Figment: Tales from the Imagination, Sorcerer's Apprentice, Compute!'s Gazette*, and *Ahoy* magazines. He is employed by Proctor & Gamble as a systems analyst. Rob interviewed Camille Cline at Forge/Tor for this edition.

David G. Tompkins
David G. Tompkins is a former editor for Betterway Books. He recently edited the *Science Fiction Writer's Marketplace and Sourcebook* for Writer's Digest Books. David interviewed Elisa Wares at Random House for this edition.

Glossary of Mystery Terms

In the following glossary we've included general publishing terms as well as specific mystery terms. The mystery terms are set in boldface type.

Advance—Payment by a publisher to an author prior to the publication of a book, to be deducted from the author's future royalties.

All rights—The rights contracted to a publisher permitting a manuscript's use anywhere and in any form, including movie and book-club sales, without additional payment to the writer.

Amateur sleuth—The character in a mystery (usually the protagonist) who does the detection but who is not a professional private investigator or police detective. The amateur sleuth has another career or is independently wealthy and becomes involved in the murder by circumstance, chance or interest.

Auction—Publishers sometimes bid against each other for the acquisition of a manuscript that has excellent sales prospects.

Bickering team or cohort mystery—Usually a mystery series in which there are two detectives working together. This may be a married couple or friends, or the two may start out with nothing in common. Although the detection of the crime is still the primary focus, the relationship between the pair is developed throughout the series.

Book producer/packager—An organization that develops a book for a publisher based upon the publisher's idea, or that plans all elements of a book—from its initial concept to writing and marketing strategies—and then sells the package to a book publisher and/or movie producer.

Caper—A crime story, usually told from the viewpoint of the perpetrator. The tone is often lighthearted or even comical, and the crime is a theft rather than a murder. Favorite caper targets: art or jewelry.

Cliffhanger—Fictional event in which the reader is left in suspense at the end of a chapter or episode, so that interest in the story's outcome will be sustained.

Contributor's copy—Copy of a magazine or published book sent to an author whose work is included.

Copyright—The legal right to exclusive publication, sale or distribution of a literary work.

Courtroom/Trial—A mystery in which the focal point is the courtroom itself. Relies heavily on verbal rhetoric and persuasive legal arguments from both the prosecution and the defense.

Cover letter—A brief letter sent with a complete manuscript submitted to an editor.

Cozy or English cozy—A murder mystery set in a small English or New England town and featuring an amateur sleuth who is often a genteel old lady or gentleman. The setting is refined and the violence subdued.

Crime—A story which details the account of how a crime was committed, including information from police detectives, autopsy findings, coroner's inquest reports, and newspaper clippings. All this helps author and reader find out what happened. Such a story usually has much action, emotion and suspense.

Dark mystery—Similar to noir, with hardboiled detectives and bleak settings, but also with mild horror elements mixed in.

Electronic rights—A nebulous term, the definition of which varies from publisher to publisher. Generally, 'electronic' rights refers to the right to publish a work on CD-ROM, computer diskette and online sources.

Espionage—Involves spying to gather information about the plans and activities of a foreign government or a competing company.

First North American serial rights—The right to publish material in a periodical before it appears in book form, for the first time, in the United States or Canada.

Galleys—The first typeset version of a book that has not yet been divided into pages.

Gothic mystery—A mystery with a decidedly dark, brooding tone, often set at an old estate. A gothic contains elements of romantic suspense and sometimes even supernatural overtones.

Hard-boiled detective—A detective character type popularized in the 1940s and 1950s, now a mainstay in mystery fiction. The hard-boiled detective is usually male, streetwise and hardened by life.

Heist—A mystery involving a theft, which is more serious than the caper. The focus is on solving the crime, but emphasis is placed on the planning and execution of the theft as well.

Historical—A story rooted in some past historical setting, as in a mystery involving the death of Queen Elizabeth's butler.

House—A press or publishing company. (Publishing house).

Imprint—Name applied to a publisher's specific line (e.g. Owl, an imprint of Henry Holt).

Juvenile mystery—A mystery novel geared toward children ages 9-12. Often the protagonist and/or narrator manifests characteristics (jealousy of a sibling, parental resentment, etc.) with which kids in this age group can identify.

Light horror—A story involving horror elements, but with less intensity and gore than traditional horror.

Locked room puzzle—A classic mystery format in which a murder takes place within a room locked from the inside, with no visible way the murderer could have entered or exited.

Maguffin—A sort of red herring, or a story element that distracts the reader from the real solution.

Malice domestic—A mystery featuring a murder among family members, such as the murder of a spouse or parent.

Mass market paperback—Softcover book on a popular subject, usually measuring around 4×7 inches, directed to a general audience, and sold in drugstores and groceries as well as in bookstores.

Ms(s)—Abbreviation for manuscript(s).

Noir—A style of mystery involving hard-boiled detectives and bleak settings.

Novella (also novelette)—A short novel or long story, approximately 7,000-15,000 words.

One-time rights—Permission to publish a story in periodical or book form one time only.

Outline—A summary of a book's contents, often in the form of chapter headings with a few sentences under each one describing the action of the story; sometimes part of a book proposal.

Over the transom—Slang for the path of an unsolicited manuscript into the slush pile.

Page rate—A fixed rate paid to an author per published page of fiction.

P.I.—Private investigator, also known as a private eye, a gumshoe, and other slang terms.

Playing fair with the reader—Planting clues in such a way that the reader encounters everything needed to solve the crime, though the reader can (and should) be distracted from those clues.

Police procedural—A mystery featuring a police detective or officer who uses standard professional police practices to solve the crime.

Private eye—A professional independent investigator. Many mystery series feature private eyes.

Proofs—A typeset version of a manuscript used for correcting errors and making changes, often a photocopy of the galleys.

Proposal—An offer to write a specific work, usually consisting of an outline of the work and one or two completed chapters.

Psychological suspense—A story which focuses not so much on physical action but on the workings of the mind, usually told from the perpetrator's perspective.

Query—A letter written to an editor to elicit interest in a story the writer wants to submit.

Red herring—False clues written into a mystery story with the intention of throwing the reader off track. The term comes from the practice of dragging a smoked red herring through the woods to disrupt a fox hunt by throwing the hounds off the fox scent.

Reporting time—The number of weeks or months it takes an editor to report to an author about a query or manuscript.

Reprint rights—Permission to print an already published work after one-time rights have been sold to another magazine or book publisher.

Romantic suspense—A mystery or suspense story with strong elements of romance, usually between the detective and the victim or the detective and the suspect.

Royalties—A percentage of the retail price paid to an author for each copy of the book that is sold.

SASE—Self-addressed stamped envelope.

Second serial rights—Permission for the reprinting of a work in another periodical after its first publication in book or magazine form.

Serial rights—The rights given by an author to a publisher to print a piece in one or more periodicals.

Serialized novel—A book-length work of fiction published in sequential issues of a periodical.

Series—Novels that feature a common detective—Agatha Christie's many novels starring Miss Marple, for instance. The novel series is more common in mystery fiction than in any other kind of fiction, with the possible exception of the Western.

Shamus—Sleuth or private eye.

Simultaneous submission—The practice of sending copies of the same manuscript to several editors or publishers at the same time. Some people refuse to consider such submissions.

Slush pile—A stack of unsolicited manuscripts in the editorial offices of a publisher.

Subsidiary—An incorporated branch of a company or conglomerate (e.g. Alfred Knopf, Inc., a subsidiary of Random House, Inc.).

Subsidiary rights—All rights, other than book publishing rights included in a book contract, such as paperback, book-club and movie rights.

Surrealistic mystery—A novel with a strange, dreamlike atmosphere, often involving unnatural juxtapositions of time and place with no clear-cut plot.

Suspense story—Although in recent years mystery and suspense have been used interchangeably, a suspense story is one in which the main action (crime or murder) has not yet taken place and the culprit may be known or at least suspected. The emphasis is on the tension built by the anticipation of the outcome, such as stopping a murderer from striking again. A mystery, on the other hand, starts with a murder and emphasizes the solving of the crime.

Synopsis—A brief summary of a story, novel or play. As part of a book proposal, it is a comprehensive summary condensed in a page or page and a half.

Tearsheet—Page from a magazine containing a published story or article.

Thriller—Story intended to arouse feelings of excitement and suspense, typically centers around illegal activities, espionage, sex and violence. Usually a detective story in which the forces of good are pitted against the forces of evil in a kill-or-be-killed situation.

Trade paperback—A soft bound volume, usually measuring 5×8 inches, published and designed for the general public, available mainly in bookstores.

True crime—Nonfiction about actual murders and serial killings, often told with "new journalism" fiction techniques made famous by Truman Capote's *In Cold Blood*.

Unsolicited manuscript—A story or novel manuscript that an editor did not specifically ask to see.

Urban horror—A horror story set in a city or modern suburb, usually involving a crime or murder committed by a supernatural being or element.

Watson—A detective's assistant or friend who narrates the story, named after Dr. Watson of the Sherlock Holmes novels.

Whodunit—Another name for the classic mystery in which the focus is on finding out the identity of the murderer.

Work-for-hire—Work that another party commissions you to do, generally for a flat fee. The creator does not own the copyright and therefore cannot sell any rights.

World or World English rights—The rights contracted to a publisher permitting a manuscript's sale anywhere in the world, including the right to license it to other publishing companies in other countries. World English rights limit the publisher to use of the manuscript in the English language only, not translation into other language.

Young adult—The general classification of books written for readers ages 12 to 18.

EDITOR INDEX

A

Agnew, Jim 266
Amara, Philip D. 134

B

Barksdale, Cal 115
Beguin, Rebecca 142
Benison, Diane 139
Bent, Tim 115
Blades, Joe 62
Bluemel, Emma 218, 256
Boojamra, Lee 147
Bowman, Donna 231
Boyd, Anthony 236
Breach, Arthur William Lloyd 214, 251
Browne, Pat 213. 250

C

Cagle, Dorothy 239, 272
Cartwright, Bob 243, 275
Cline, Camille 84
Colgan, Tom 117
Couch, Chris 134

D

Daniel, Glenda 125
Davey, Barbara 241, 274
Day, Peter 164
Dicks, Barbara 130
Dolan, Eamon 91
Donnelly, Shaun 241
Dryden, Emma 140
Dube, Marlene 211
Duncan, Karen 115

E

Engelke, Doris 161

F

Fanning, Kathryn 212, 249
Feder, Susan 220, 257
Ferron, Carrie 117
Fletcher, Susan J. 167
Freed, Sara Ann 98

G

Gallick, Sarah 95
Gilbert, Carol 141

Gilbert, L.D. 125
Gill, Stephen 159
Gish, D.L. 218
Glass, Kristi, Lyn 254
Goldman, Mike 248
Gordon, R.W. 144
Gorman, Ed 262
Gorman, Joe 262
Goss, Leonard G. 124
Green, David 240
Grier, Barbara 101
Gruch, Mr. 161

H

Hammer, David 130
Harold, Wayne A. 226, 263
Harryman, Joan 123
Hawkridge, Janis 149
Hoffman, Barry 253
Howard, Virginia 233
Huang, Jim 252
Hunter, Pamela 232
Hutchings, Janet 183
Hutchinson, Sandra 215
Hutchison, James 158
Hutton, Linda 225

J

Johnson, Oliver 164
Jordan, Cathleen 180
Jung, Cherie 202, 265
Jurjevics, Juris 150

K

Kager, Kelly 151
Kahla, Keith 107
Kannenstine, Louis 88
Kemper, Troxey 234, 270
Kern, Judy 129
Klein, Mr. 161
Korotkin, Arnold 230, 268
Kulkarni, Shyamkant 217

L

Lanman, Jonathan J. 116
Lilley, Jessie 267
Lombard, Erica 135
Lombard, MaryAnn 119

Lovisi, Gary 131, 187, 255
Lowry, Shannon 212

M

McCarthy, E.J. 145
McCawley, Tony 127
McFadden, Edward 206
Mandelsberg, Rose 269
Markland, Marcia 117
Marr, John 259
Merle, Dominick A. 273
Miciak, Kate 66
Miles, Fiske and Elly-Ann 258
Miller, Anita 114
Mills, Christopher 199, 264
Montgomery, Gwen 117
Morgan, Charles 148
Mowery, Betty 227
Muchnick, Jeanne 238
Munoz, Mr. 163
Myers, Bob 191, 260

O

O'Brien, Dorrie 155
Ormsby, Mrs. 168
O'Shaughnessy, Marianne 146

P

Paton, Jean 157
Pittman, Joseph 76
Poston, Jason Jacob 79
Potts, Rinehart 219, 257
Power, Margo 222, 260

R

Raisch, Charles 195, 264
Ralbovsky, Marianne 141
Rejt, Maria 169
Rich, Jamie S. 128
Roberts, Susan L. 121
Rosenstein, Natalee 72
Rudolph, Janet A. 224, 261
Rutherford, Donna 138

S

Samsa, George 123
Samuels, A.P. 228
Samuels, J.B. 210, 244
Schrier, Jane 118
Seaver, Jeanette 115
Seaver, Richard 115
Seidman, Michael 110
Shepard, Judith 143
Silgardo, Melanie 170
Simon, Gerd 160, 162
Smittenaar, H.G. 133
Starr, Nancy 137
Staub, Mary 233
Stein, Lin 214, 252
Stine, Kate 245
Stocker, Midge 152
Stringfellow, Rodney 221
Swafford, Polly W. 229
Szanta, David 115

T

Taylor, Alexandra 237, 270
Taylor, Troy 237, 270
Terrell, Perry 235, 236, 271
Turner, Alice 228, 266

V

Von Beust, Joachim 160

W

Walter, Elizabeth 166
Wares, Elisa 104
Weinberger, Jane 154
White, Bill 268
Williams, Ann M. 250
Williams, Maria 127

Z

Zagury, Caroyln 153
Zagury, David 153
Zylberstein, Mr. 159

Amateur Sleuth: Academy Chicago 114; Accord Communications 115; Atheneum Books for Young Readers 116; Avalon Books 117; Avon Flare Books 117; Baker Book House Company 118; Ballantine Books 62; Bantam Books 66; Berkley Publishing Group 72; Bethel Publishing 120; bePuzzled 119; Cedar Bay Press 121; Crime Club, The 166; Crossway Books 124; Dancing Jester Press 125; Dare To Dream Books 127; Doubleday 129; Eichborn Verlag 161; Fawcett 130; Fine, Donald I. Inc. 79; Forge 84; Foul Play Press 88; HarperCollins Publishers 91; Headline Book Publishing PLC 167; Henry Holt & Company 132; KBV (Klein & Blechinger Verlag) GMBH 162; Kensington Publishing Corp. 95; Little, Brown and Company, Inc. 136; Lucky Books 138; Macmillan Crime Case 169; Madwoman Press, Inc. 139; Mega-Books 141; Mysterious Press 98; Naiad Press Inc., The 101; New Readers Press 141; New Victoria Publishers, Inc. 142; Random House 104; Red Crane Books 146; Rising Tide Press 147; St. Martin's Press 107; Severn House Publishers, Ltd. 170; Simon & Pierre Publishing Co. Ltd. 157; Singer Media Corp. 149; Soho Press Inc. 150; Spinsters Ink 151; 10/18 (an imprint of UGE) 159; Third Side Press 152; Vesta Publications, Ltd. 159; Victor Gollancz, Ltd. 166; Virago Press, Ltd. 170; Vista Publishing, Inc. 153; Walker & Company 110; Windswept House Publishers 154; Write Way Publishing 155

Courtroom/Trial: Academy Chicago 114; Avalon Books 117; Avon Flare Books 117; Ballantine Books 62; Bantam Books 66; Berkley Publishing Group 72; Bethel Publishing 120; Crossway Books 124; Dancing Jester Press 125; Doubleday 129; Fawcett 130; Fine, Donald I. Inc. 79; Forge 84; HarperCollins Publishers 91; Henry Holt & Company 132; Little, Brown and Company, Inc. 136; Longmeadow Press 137; Lucky Books 138; Madwoman Press, Inc. 139; Mega-Books 141; Naiad Press Inc., The 101; New Readers Press 141; Random House 104; Red Crane Books 146; Rising Tide Press 147; St. Martin's Press 107; Singer Media Corp. 149; Soho Press Inc. 150; Third Side Press 152; Vesta Publications, Ltd. 159; Vista Publishing, Inc. 153; Write Way Publishing 155

Cozy: Academy Chicago 114; Accord Communications 115; Avalon Books 117; Avon Flare Books 117; Baker Book House Company 118; Ballantine Books 62; Bantam Books 66; Berkley Publishing Group 72; Bethel Publishing 120; bePuzzled 119; Cedar Bay Press 121; Constable & Co., Ltd. 165; Crime Club, The 166; Crossway Books 124; Doubleday 129; Fawcett 130; Fine, Donald I. Inc. 79; Forge 84; Foul Play Press 88; Headline Book Publishing PLC 167; Henry Holt & Company 132; Kensington Publishing Corp. 95; Lucky Books 138; Macmillan Crime Case 169; Madwoman Press, Inc. 139; Mega-Books 141; Mysterious Press 98; Naiad Press Inc., The 101; New Readers Press 141; Random House 104; Red Crane Books 146; Rising Tide Press 147; St. Martin's Press 107; Simon & Pierre Publishing Co. Ltd. 157; Spinsters Ink 151; Vesta Publications, Ltd. 159; Victor Gollancz, Ltd. 166; Walker & Company 110; Windswept House Publishers 154; Write Way Publishing 155

Crime: Academy Chicago 114; Arcade Publishing 115; Avalon Books 117; Avon Flare Books 117; Bantam Books 66; Berkley Publishing Group 72; Bethel Publishing 120; bePuzzled 119; Cedar Bay Press 121; Comicart Publishing Company 123; Creative Arts Book Company 123; Crossway Books 124; Dancing Jester Press 125; Dark Horse Comics 128; Doubleday 129; Fawcett 130; Forge 84; Foul Play Press 88;

Gryphon Publications 131; Henry Holt & Company 132; Intercontinental Publishing 133; KBV (Klein & Blechinger Verlag) GMBH 162; Little, Brown and Company, Inc. 136; Lucky Books 138; Madwoman Press, Inc. 139; Mega-Books 141; Naiad Press Inc., The 101; New Readers Press 141; New Victoria Publishers, Inc. 142; Permanent Press 143; Random House 104; Red Crane Books 146; Rising Tide Press 147; St. Martin's Press 107; Scribner Crime Novels 149; Simon & Pierre Publishing Co. Ltd. 157; Singer Media Corp. 149; Turnstone Press 158; Vesta Publications, Ltd. 159; Walker & Company 110; Write Way Publishing 155

Dark Mystery: Academy Chicago 114; Avon Flare Books 117; Ballantine Books 62; Cedar Bay Press 121; Creative Arts Book Company 123; Crossway Books 124; Dark Horse Comics 128; Doubleday 129; Forge 84; Foul Play Press 88; HarperCollins Publishers 91; Henry Holt & Company 132; Kitchen Sink Press 134; Little, Brown and Company, Inc. 136; Lucky Books 138; Margaret K. McElderry Books 140; Mega-Books 141; Naiad Press Inc., The 101; New Readers Press 141; Random House 104; Red Crane Books 146; Rising Tide Press 147; Singer Media Corp. 149; Third Side Press 152; Vesta Publications, Ltd. 159; Walker & Company 110; Write Way Publishing 155

Espionage: Academy Chicago 114; Arcade Publishing 115; Avon Flare Books 117; Ballantine Books 62; Bantam Books 66; Cedar Bay Press 121; Comicart Publishing Company 123; Crossway Books 124; Dancing Jester Press 125; Doubleday 129; Forge 84; Henry Holt & Company 132; Little, Brown and Company, Inc. 136; Longmeadow Press 137; Lucky Books 138; Mega-Books 141; Naiad Press Inc., The 101; New Readers Press 141; Random House 104; Red Crane Books 146; Rising Tide Press 147; St. Martin's Press 107; Singer Media Corp. 149; Soho Press Inc. 150; Third Side Press 152; Vesta Publications, Ltd. 159; Vista Publishing, Inc. 153; Write Way Publishing 155

Hard-boiled Detective: Academy Chicago 114; Allison & Busby Crime 164; Avalon Books 117; Avon Flare Books 117; Ballantine Books 62; Bantam Books 66; Berkley Publishing Group 72; Bethel Publishing 120; bePuzzled 119; Cedar Bay Press 121; Century Books 164; Constable & Co., Ltd. 165; Creative Arts Book Company 123; Crossway Books 124; Dancing Jester Press 125; Dare To Dream Books 127; Dark Horse Comics 128; Doubleday 129; Foul Play Press 88; Gryphon Publications 131; Henry Holt & Company 132; Hodder & Stoughton, Ltd. 168; KBV (Klein & Blechinger Verlag) GMBH 162; Little, Brown and Company, Inc. 136; Lucky Books 138; Macmillan Crime Case 169; Madwoman Press, Inc. 139; Mega-Books 141; Mysterious Press 98; Naiad Press Inc., The 101; New Readers Press 141; Presidio Press 145; Random House 104; Red Crane Books 146; Rising Tide Press 147; St. Martin's Press 107; Severn House Publishers, Ltd. 170; Singer Media Corp. 149; Soho Press Inc. 150; Vesta Publications, Ltd. 159; Victor Gollancz, Ltd. 166; Vista Publishing, Inc. 153; Walker & Company 110; Write Way Publishing 155

Historical: Academy Chicago 114; Avon Flare Books 117; Ballantine Books 62; Bantam Books 66; Berkley Publishing Group 72; Bethel Publishing 120; Century Books 164; Comicart Publishing Company 123; Crossway Books 124; Dancing Jester Press 125; Doubleday 129; Eichborn Verlag 161; Fawcett 130; Forge 84; HarperCollins Publishers 91; Henry Holt & Company 132; Kitchen Sink Press 134; Little, Brown and Company, Inc. 136; Lucky Books 138; Margaret K. McElderry Books 140; Mega-Books 141; New Readers Press 141; New Victoria Publishers, Inc. 142; Random House 104; Red Crane Books 146; Rising Tide Press 147; St. Martin's Press 107; Simon & Pierre Publishing Co. Ltd. 157; Soho Press Inc. 150; 10/18 (an imprint of UGE) 159; Third Side Press 152; Vesta Publications, Ltd. 159;

Vista Publishing, Inc. 153; Walker & Company 110; Write Way Publishing 155

Humorous Mystery: Academy Chicago 114; Accord Communications 115; Avon Flare Books 117; Ballantine Books 62; Bantam Books 66; Berkley Publishing Group 72; Bethel Publishing 120; bePuzzled 119; Cedar Bay Press 121; Crossway Books 124; Dancing Jester Press 125; Dare To Dream Books 127; Doubleday 129; Eichborn Verlag 161; Fawcett 130; Foul Play Press 88; HarperCollins Publishers 91; Henry Holt & Company 132; Kitchen Sink Press 134; Little, Brown and Company, Inc. 136; Lucky Books 138; Madwoman Press, Inc. 139; Margaret K. McElderry Books 140; Mega-Books 141; Naiad Press Inc., The 101; New Readers Press 141; New Victoria Publishers, Inc. 142; Random House 104; Red Crane Books 146; Rising Tide Press 147; St. Martin's Press 107; Simon & Pierre Publishing Co. Ltd. 157; Soho Press Inc. 150; Third Side Press 152; Turnstone Press 158; Vesta Publications, Ltd. 159; Vista Publishing, Inc. 153; Walker & Company 110; Write Way Publishing 155

Juvenile: Academy Chicago 114; Atheneum Books for Young Readers 116; Avon Flare Books 117; Bantam Books 66; Bethel Publishing 120; bePuzzled 119; Cedar Bay Press 121; Crossway Books 124; Dancing Jester Press 125; Dark Horse Comics 128; Dutton/Signet 76; Henry Holt & Company 132; Little, Brown and Company, Inc. Children's Division 135; Lucky Books 138; Margaret K. McElderry Books 140; Mega-Books 141; New Readers Press 141; Random House 104; Red Crane Books 146; Royal Fireworks Press 148; St. Martin's Press 107; Victor Gollancz, Ltd. 166; Windswept House Publishers 154

Light Horror: Academy Chicago 114; Avon Flare Books 117; Ballantine Books 62; Bantam Books 66; Cedar Bay Press 121; Crossway Books 124; Dark Horse Comics 128; Doubleday 129; Forge 84; Longmeadow Press 137; Lucky Books 138; Mega-Books 141; Naiad Press Inc., The 101; New Readers Press 141; Random House 104; Red Crane Books 146; Rising Tide Press 147; St. Martin's Press 107; Singer Media Corp. 149; Third Side Press 152; Vesta Publications, Ltd. 159; Write Way Publishing 155

Malice Domestic: Academy Chicago 114; Accord Communications 115; Allison & Busby Crime 164; Avalon Books 117; Avon Flare Books 117; Baker Book House Company 118; Ballantine Books 62; Bantam Books 66; Berkley Publishing Group 72; Bethel Publishing 120; bePuzzled 119; Constable & Co., Ltd. 165; Crime Club, The 166; Crossway Books 124; Dancing Jester Press 125; Doubleday 129; Fine, Donald I. Inc. 79; Forge 84; Headline Book Publishing PLC 167; Henry Holt & Company 132; Hodder & Stoughton, Ltd. 168; Little, Brown and Company, Inc. 136; Longmeadow Press 137; Lucky Books 138; Macmillan Crime Case 169; Mega-Books 141; Mysterious Press 98; New Readers Press 141; Random House 104; Red Crane Books 146; Rising Tide Press 147; St. Martin's Press 107; Severn House Publishers, Ltd. 170; Soho Press Inc. 150; Third Side Press 152; Vesta Publications, Ltd. 159; Walker & Company 110; Write Way Publishing 155

Police Procedural: Academy Chicago 114; Allison & Busby Crime 164; Arcade Publishing 115; Avalon Books 117; Avon Flare Books 117; Ballantine Books 62; Bantam Books 66; Berkley Publishing Group 72; Bethel Publishing 120; Century Books 164; Constable & Co., Ltd. 165; Crime Club, The 166; Crossway Books 124; Dancing Jester Press 125; Doubleday 129; Fawcett 130; Fine, Donald I. Inc. 79; Forge 84; Foul Play Press 88; Gryphon Publications 131; Headline Book Publishing PLC 167; Henry Holt & Company 132; Hodder & Stoughton, Ltd. 168; Intercontinental Publishing 133; Little, Brown and Company, Inc. 136; Longmeadow Press 137; Lucky Books 138; Macmillan Crime Case 169; Madwoman Press, Inc. 139;

Mega-Books 141; Mysterious Press 98; Naiad Press Inc., The 101; New Readers Press 141; Presidio Press 145; Random House 104; Red Crane Books 146; Rising Tide Press 147; St. Martin's Press 107; Severn House Publishers, Ltd. 170; Singer Media Corp. 149; Soho Press Inc. 150; Spinsters Ink 151; 10/18 (an imprint of UGE) 159; Third Side Press 152; Vesta Publications, Ltd. 159; Victor Gollancz, Ltd. 166; Vista Publishing, Inc. 153; Walker & Company 110; Write Way Publishing 155

Private Eye: Academy Chicago 114; Allison & Busby Crime 164; Arcade Publishing 115; Avalon Books 117; Avon Flare Books 117; Ballantine Books 62; Bantam Books 66; Berkley Publishing Group 72; Bethel Publishing 120; Buest Verlag 160; bePuzzled 119; Cedar Bay Press 121; Century Books 164; Comicart Publishing Company 123; Constable & Co., Ltd. 165; Crime Club, The 166; Crossway Books 124; Dancing Jester Press 125; Dare To Dream Books 127; Doubleday 129; Eichborn Verlag 161; Fine, Donald I. Inc. 79; Forge 84; Foul Play Press 88; Gasogene Press Ltd. 130; Gryphon Publications 131; HarperCollins Publishers 91; Headline Book Publishing PLC 167; Henry Holt & Company 132; Hodder & Stoughton, Ltd. 168; KBV (Klein & Blechinger Verlag) GMBH 162; Little, Brown and Company, Inc. 136; Longmeadow Press 137; Lucky Books 138; Macmillan Crime Case 169; Madwoman Press, Inc. 139; Mega-Books 141; Munoz Moya Editores SA 163; Mysterious Press 98; Naiad Press Inc., The 101; New Readers Press 141; New Victoria Publishers, Inc. 142; Players Press Inc. 144; Presidio Press 145; Random House 104; Red Crane Books 146; Rising Tide Press 147; St. Martin's Press 107; Severn House Publishers, Ltd. 170; Singer Media Corp. 149; Soho Press Inc. 150; Spinsters Ink 151; Third Side Press 152; Turnstone Press 158; Verlagsburo Simon & Magiera 162; Vesta Publications, Ltd. 159; Victor Gollancz, Ltd. 166; Virago Press, Ltd. 170; Vista Publishing, Inc. 153; Walker & Company 110; Write Way Publishing 155

Psychological Suspense: Academy Chicago 114; Arcade Publishing 115; Avalon Books 117; Avon Flare Books 117; Ballantine Books 62; Bantam Books 66; Berkley Publishing Group 72; Cedar Bay Press 121; Crossway Books 124; Dancing Jester Press 125; Dark Horse Comics 128; Doubleday 129; Eichborn Verlag 161; Forge 84; Foul Play Press 88; Gryphon Publications 131; Henry Holt & Company 132; Kitchen Sink Press 134; Little, Brown and Company, Inc. 136; Longmeadow Press 137; Lucky Books 138; Macmillan Crime Case 169; Margaret K. McElderry Books 140; Mega-Books 141; Naiad Press Inc., The 101; New Readers Press 141; Random House 104; Red Crane Books 146; Rising Tide Press 147; St. Martin's Press 107; Singer Media Corp. 149; Third Side Press 152; Vesta Publications, Ltd. 159; Vista Publishing, Inc. 153; Walker & Company 110; Write Way Publishing 155

Romantic Suspense: Academy Chicago 114; Avalon Books 117; Avon Flare Books 117; Ballantine Books 62; Bantam Books 66; Bethel Publishing 120; Cedar Bay Press 121; Crossway Books 124; Doubleday 129; Fine, Donald I. Inc. 79; Forge 84; HarperCollins Publishers 91; Henry Holt & Company 132; Kensington Publishing Corp. 95; Little, Brown and Company, Inc. 136; Lucky Books 138; Madwoman Press, Inc. 139; Mega-Books 141; Naiad Press Inc., The 101; New Readers Press 141; New Victoria Publishers, Inc. 142; Random House 104; Red Crane Books 146; Rising Tide Press 147; Severn House Publishers, Ltd. 170; Singer Media Corp. 149; Third Side Press 152; Vesta Publications, Ltd. 159; Victor Gollancz, Ltd. 166; Vista Publishing, Inc. 153; Windswept House Publishers 154; Write Way Publishing 155

Surrealistic Mystery: Academy Chicago 114; Avon Flare Books 117; Ballantine Books 62; Bantam Books 66; Cedar Bay Press 121; Crossway Books 124; Doubleday

129; Forge 84; Henry Holt & Company 132; Kitchen Sink Press 134; Little, Brown and Company, Inc. 136; Lucky Books 138; Mega-Books 141; New Readers Press 141; Random House 104; Red Crane Books 146; Rising Tide Press 147; Third Side Press 152; Vesta Publications, Ltd. 159; Walker & Company 110; Write Way Publishing 155

Suspense: Academy Chicago 114; Arcade Publishing 115; Avalon Books 117; Avon Flare Books 117; Ballantine Books 62; Bantam Books 66; Berkley Publishing Group 72; Bethel Publishing 120; bePuzzled 119; Cedar Bay Press 121; Creative Arts Book Company 123; Crossway Books 124; Dancing Jester Press 125; Dare To Dream Books 127; Dark Horse Comics 128; Doubleday 129; Eichborn Verlag 161; Forge 84; Foul Play Press 88; Gryphon Publications 131; HarperCollins Publishers 91; Henry Holt & Company 132; Intercontinental Publishing 133; KBV (Klein & Blechinger Verlag) GMBH 162; Little, Brown and Company, Inc. 136; Longmeadow Press 137; Lucky Books 138; Madwoman Press, Inc. 139; Margaret K. McElderry Books 140; Mega-Books 141; Munoz Moya Editores SA 163; Naiad Press Inc., The 101; New Readers Press 141; Permanent Press 143; Random House 104; Red Crane Books 146; Rising Tide Press 147; St. Martin's Press 107; Scribner Crime Novels 149; Singer Media Corp. 149; Soho Press Inc. 150; Third Side Press 152; Vesta Publications, Ltd. 159; Vista Publishing, Inc. 153; Walker & Company 110; Write Way Publishing 155

Thrillers: Academy Chicago 114; Arcade Publishing 115; Avalon Books 117; Avon Flare Books 117; Ballantine Books 62; Bantam Books 66; Berkley Publishing Group 72; Bethel Publishing 120; Buest Verlag 160; Cedar Bay Press 121; Crossway Books 124; Dancing Jester Press 125; Dare To Dream Books 127; Dark Horse Comics 128; Doubleday 129; Fawcett 130; Forge 84; HarperCollins Publishers 91; Henry Holt & Company 132; Intercontinental Publishing 133; Little, Brown and Company, Inc. 136; Longmeadow Press 137; Lucky Books 138; Madwoman Press, Inc. 139; Mega-Books 141; Naiad Press Inc., The 101; New Readers Press 141; Presidio Press 145; Random House 104; Red Crane Books 146; Rising Tide Press 147; St. Martin's Press 107; Singer Media Corp. 149; Soho Press Inc. 150; Verlagsburo Simon & Magiera 162; Vesta Publications, Ltd. 159; Virago Press, Ltd. 170; Vista Publishing, Inc. 153; Write Way Publishing 155

Urban Horror: Academy Chicago 114; Avon Flare Books 117; Ballantine Books 62; Bantam Books 66; Crossway Books 124; Dark Horse Comics 128; Doubleday 129; Eichborn Verlag 161; Forge 84; Gryphon Publications 131; Kitchen Sink Press 134; Longmeadow Press 137; Lucky Books 138; Mega-Books 141; New Readers Press 141; Random House 104; Red Crane Books 146; Rising Tide Press 147; Singer Media Corp. 149; Vesta Publications, Ltd. 159; Write Way Publishing 155

Young Adult: Academy Chicago 114; Atheneum Books for Young Readers 116; Avon Flare Books 117; Berkley Publishing Group 72; Bethel Publishing 120; Cedar Bay Press 121; Comicart Publishing Company 123; Crossway Books 124; Dancing Jester Press 125; Dutton/Signet 76; Fawcett 130; Henry Holt & Company 132; Kensington Publishing Corp. 95; Little, Brown and Company, Inc. Children's Division 135; Lucky Books 138; Margaret K. McElderry Books 140; Mega-Books 141; New Readers Press 141; Random House 104; Red Crane Books 146; Royal Fireworks Press 148; Singer Media Corp. 149; Vesta Publications, Ltd. 159; Victor Gollancz, Ltd. 166; Windswept House Publishers 154

Advice Column/Articles: Advocate, The 244; Byline Magazine 249; Housewife Writer's Forum 256; Shot in the Dark, A 275; Snake River Reflections 268; Ultimate Writer Magazine 271

Amateur Sleuth: Advocate, The 210; Alfred Hitchcock Mystery Magazine 180; Boys' Life 212; Byline Magazine 212; Ellery Queen's Mystery Magazine 183; Green's Magazine 240; Kracked Mirror 218; Most Loving Mere Folly 220; Murderous Intent: A Magazine of Mystery & Suspense 222; Mystery Forum Magazine 191; Mystery Readers Journal 224; Mystery Review, The 241; Mystery Time Magazine 225; New Mystery Magazine 195; Noir 199; Over My Dead Body! The Mystery Magazine 202; Pirate Writings 206; Playboy Magazine 228; Red Herring Mystery Magazine 229; Short Stuff Magazine 231; Thema Magazine 233; Tucumcari Literary Review 234; Ultimate Writer Magazine 235; Veneration Quarterly 236; Writing Writers Magazine 239

Convention Listings: Armchair Detective, The 245; Byline Magazine 249; Criminal Record, The 250; Drood Review 252; Most Loving Mere Folly 257; Murder & Mayhem 258; Mystery Readers Journal 261; Mystery Review, The 274; Mystery Scene 262; Snake River Reflections 268; Ultimate Writer Magazine 271; Whitechapel Gazette 270

Courtroom/trial: Advocate, The 210; Alfred Hitchcock Mystery Magazine 180; Dagger of the Mind 214; Ellery Queen's Mystery Magazine 183; Green's Magazine 240; Hardboiled Magazine 187; Kracked Mirror 218; Murderous Intent: A Magazine of Mystery & Suspense 222; Mystery Forum Magazine 191; Mystery Readers Journal 224; Mystery Review, The 241; Noir 199; Over My Dead Body! The Mystery Magazine 202; Pirate Writings 206; Red Herring Mystery Magazine 229; Short Stuff Magazine 231; Thema Magazine 233; Tucumcari Literary Review 234; Ultimate Writer Magazine 235; Veneration Quarterly 236; Whisper 236; Writer's Block Magazine 242; Writing Writers Magazine 239

Cozy: Advocate, The 210; Alfred Hitchcock Mystery Magazine 180; Byline Magazine 212; Ellery Queen's Mystery Magazine 183; Green's Magazine 240; Linington Lineup 219; Murder of the Month 221; Murderous Intent: A Magazine of Mystery & Suspense 222; Mystery Forum Magazine 191; Mystery Readers Journal 224; Mystery Review, The 241; Mystery Time Magazine 225; New Mystery Magazine 195; Over My Dead Body! The Mystery Magazine 202; Pirate Writings 206; Red Herring Mystery Magazine 229; Short Stuff Magazine 231; Sleuth, The 233; Thema Magazine 233; Ultimate Writer Magazine 235; Veneration Quarterly 236; Writing Writers Magazine 239

Crime: Advocate, The 210; Eagle's Flight Magazine 217; Ellery Queen's Mystery Magazine 183; Green's Magazine 240; Hardboiled Magazine 187; Kracked Mirror 218; Linington Lineup 219; Most Loving Mere Folly 220; Murderous Intent: A Magazine of Mystery & Suspense 222; Mystery Forum Magazine 191; Mystery Readers Journal 224; Mystery Review, The 241; Mystery Time Magazine 225; Naked Kiss 226; New Mystery Magazine 195; Noir 199; Over My Dead Body! The Mystery Magazine 202; Pirate Writings 206; Playboy Magazine 228; Short Stuff Magazine 231; Sleuth, The 233; Thema Magazine 233; Tucumcari Literary Review 234; Ultimate Writer Magazine 235; Veneration Quarterly 236; Writer's Block

Magazine 242; Writing Writers Magazine 239

Dark Mystery: Advocate, The 210; Dagger of the Mind 214; Dead of Night 214; Ellery Queen's Mystery Magazine 183; Green's Magazine 240; Hardboiled Magazine 187; Kracked Mirror 218; Murder of the Month 221; Murderous Intent: A Magazine of Mystery & Suspense 222; Mystery Forum Magazine 191; Mystery Readers Journal 224; Mystery Review, The 241; Naked Kiss 226; Over My Dead Body! The Mystery Magazine 202; Pirate Writings 206; Playboy Magazine 228; Thema Magazine 233; Tucumcari Literary Review 234; Ultimate Writer Magazine 235; Veneration Quarterly 236; Whisper 236; Writer's Block Magazine 242; Writing Writers Magazine 239

Espionage: Advocate, The 210; Alfred Hitchcock Mystery Magazine 180; Eagle's Flight Magazine 217; Ellery Queen's Mystery Magazine 183; Green's Magazine 240; Hardboiled Magazine 187; Kracked Mirror 218; Murderous Intent: A Magazine of Mystery & Suspense 222; Mystery Forum Magazine 191; Mystery Readers Journal 224; Mystery Review, The 241; New Mystery Magazine 195; Noir 199; Over My Dead Body! The Mystery Magazine 202; Pirate Writings 206; Playboy Magazine 228; Red Herring Mystery Magazine 229; Thema Magazine 233; Tucumcari Literary Review 234; Ultimate Writer Magazine 235; Veneration Quarterly 236; Whisper 236; Writer's Block Magazine 242; Writing Writers Magazine 239

Essays: Advocate, The 244; Armchair Detective, The 245; Boys' Life 248; Byline Magazine 249; Clues, A Journal of Detection 250; Criminal Record, The 250; Dead of Night 252; Drood Review 252; Gauntlet Magazine 253; Gothic Journal 254; Hardboiled Magazine 256; Housewife Writer's Forum 256; Linington Lineup 257; Most Loving Mere Folly 257; Murder & Mayhem 258; Murder Can Be Fun 259; Mystery Forum Magazine 260; Mystery Readers Journal 261; Mystery Review, The 274; Mystery Scene 262; Naked Kiss 263; Over My Dead Body! The Mystery Magazine 265; Real Crime Book Digest 266; Scarlet Street 267; Sherlockian Tidbits 268; Shot in the Dark, A 275; Snake River Reflections 268; Ultimate Writer Magazine 271; Whitechapel Gazette 270; Writing Writers Magazine 272

Film Reviews: Advocate, The 244; Armchair Detective, The 245; Dead of Night 252; Hardboiled Magazine 256; Linington Lineup 257; Most Loving Mere Folly 257; Mystery Forum Magazine 260; Mystery Review, The 274; Mystery Scene 262; Naked Kiss 263; New Mystery Magazine 264; Noir 264; Over My Dead Body! The Mystery Magazine 265; Whitechapel Gazette 270

Hard-boiled Detective: Advocate, The 210; Alfred Hitchcock Mystery Magazine 180; Clues, A Journal of Detection 213; Dagger of the Mind 214; Ellery Queen's Mystery Magazine 183; Green's Magazine 240; Hardboiled Magazine 187; Kracked Mirror 218; Murderous Intent: A Magazine of Mystery & Suspense 222; Mystery Forum Magazine 191; Mystery Readers Journal 224; Mystery Review, The 241; Naked Kiss 226; New Mystery Magazine 195; Noir 199; Over My Dead Body! The Mystery Magazine 202; Pirate Writings 206; Playboy Magazine 228; Shot in the Dark, A 243; Skylark 232; Thema Magazine 233; Ultimate Writer Magazine 235; Veneration Quarterly 236; Writer's Block Magazine 242; Writing Writers Magazine 239

Historical: Advocate, The 210; Alfred Hitchcock Mystery Magazine 180; Ellery Queen's Mystery Magazine 183; Green's Magazine 240; Housewife Writer's Forum 218; Most Loving Mere Folly 220; Mystery Forum Magazine 191; Mystery Readers Journal 224; Mystery Review, The 241; Noir 199; Pirate Writings 206; Post, The 228; Red Herring Mystery Magazine 229; Sherlockian Tidbits 230; Short Stuff Magazine 231; Thema Magazine 233; Tucumcari Literary Review 234; Veneration

Quarterly 236; Woman's World 238; Writer's Block Magazine 242; Writing Writers Magazine 239

Humorous Mystery: Advocate, The 210; Alfred Hitchcock Mystery Magazine 180; Belletrist Review 211; Boys' Life 212; Dead of Night 214; Different Beat, A 215; Ellery Queen's Mystery Magazine 183; Green's Magazine 240; Housewife Writer's Forum 218; Kracked Mirror 218; Most Loving Mere Folly 220; Murder of the Month 221; Murderous Intent: A Magazine of Mystery & Suspense 222; Mystery Forum Magazine 191; Mystery Readers Journal 224; Mystery Review, The 241; Mystery Time Magazine 225; New Mystery Magazine 195; Noir 199; Over My Dead Body! The Mystery Magazine 202; Pirate Writings 206; Playboy Magazine 228; Short Stuff Magazine 231; Sleuth, The 233; Thema Magazine 233; Tucumcari Literary Review 234; Ultimate Writer Magazine 235; Veneration Quarterly 236; Whisper 236; Writer's Block Magazine 242; Writing Writers Magazine 239

Industry News: Armchair Detective, The 245; Byline Magazine 249; Criminal Record, The 250; Detective Files Group 273; Drood Review 252; Housewife Writer's Forum 256; Murder & Mayhem 258; Mystery Forum Magazine 260; Mystery Readers Journal 261; Mystery Review, The 274; Over My Dead Body! The Mystery Magazine 265; Shot in the Dark, A 275; Snake River Reflections 268; True Detective 269

Interviews: Advocate, The 244; Armchair Detective, The 245; Boys' Life 248; Clues, A Journal of Detection 250; Dagger of the Mind 251; Dead of Night 252; Drood Review 252; Gauntlet Magazine 253; Gothic Journal 254; Hardboiled Magazine 256; Housewife Writer's Forum 256; Linington Lineup 257; Most Loving Mere Folly 257; Murderous Intent: A Magazine of Mystery & Suspense 260; Mystery Forum Magazine 260; Mystery Readers Journal 261; Mystery Review, The 274; Mystery Scene 262; Naked Kiss 263; Noir 264; Over My Dead Body! The Mystery Magazine 265; Playboy 266; Real Crime Book Digest 266; Scarlet Street 267; Shot in the Dark, A 275; Tucumcari Literary Review 270; Whitechapel Gazette 270; Writing Writers Magazine 272

Juvenile: Advocate, The 210; Boys' Life 212; Ellery Queen's Mystery Magazine 183; Green's Magazine 240; Mystery Forum Magazine 191; Mystery Readers Journal 224; Mystery Review, The 241; Noir 199; Over My Dead Body! The Mystery Magazine 202; Pirate Writings 206; Tucumcari Literary Review 234; Ultimate Writer Magazine 235; Veneration Quarterly 236; Writing Writers Magazine 239

Light Horror: Advocate, The 210; Belletrist Review 211; Dagger of the Mind 214; Dead of Night 214; Different Beat, A 215; Ellery Queen's Mystery Magazine 183; Green's Magazine 240; Mystery Forum Magazine 191; Mystery Review, The 241; Over My Dead Body! The Mystery Magazine 202; Phantasm 227; Pirate Writings 206; Playboy Magazine 228; Thema Magazine 233; Ultimate Writer Magazine 235; Veneration Quarterly 236; Whisper 236; Writer's Block Magazine 242; Writing Writers Magazine 239

Malice Domestic: Advocate, The 210; Belletrist Review 211; Byline Magazine 212; Different Beat, A 215; Ellery Queen's Mystery Magazine 183; Green's Magazine 240; Murderous Intent: A Magazine of Mystery & Suspense 222; Mystery Forum Magazine 191; Mystery Readers Journal 224; Mystery Review, The 241; Mystery Time Magazine 225; New Mystery Magazine 195; Noir 199; Over My Dead Body! The Mystery Magazine 202; Pirate Writings 206; Playboy Magazine 228; Red Herring Mystery Magazine 229; Short Stuff Magazine 231; Thema Magazine 233; Ultimate Writer Magazine 235; Veneration Quarterly 236; Writing Writers Magazine 239

Market Listings: Armchair Detective, The 245; Byline Magazine 249; Gothic Journal 254; Housewife Writer's Forum 256; Mystery Review, The 274; Mystery Scene 262; Ultimate Writer Magazine 271

New Bookstores: Murder & Mayhem 258; Mystery Forum Magazine 260; Mystery Readers Journal 261; Mystery Review, The 274; Mystery Scene 262; New Mystery Magazine 264; Shot in the Dark, A 275

Overseas Reports: Armchair Detective, The 245; Drood Review 252; Most Loving Mere Folly 257; Murder & Mayhem 258; Mystery Readers Journal 261; Mystery Review, The 274; Mystery Scene 262; Playboy 266; Shot in the Dark, A 275; Whitechapel Gazette 270

Poetry: Advocate, The 244; Byline Magazine 249; Dead of Night 252; Most Loving Mere Folly 257; Murderous Intent: A Magazine of Mystery & Suspense 260; Mystery Review, The 274; Snake River Reflections 268; Tucumcari Literary Review 270; Ultimate Writer Magazine 271; Writing Writers Magazine 272

Police Procedural: Advocate, The 210; Alfred Hitchcock Mystery Magazine 180; Byline Magazine 212; Ellery Queen's Mystery Magazine 183; Green's Magazine 240; Hardboiled Magazine 187; Kracked Mirror 218; Murderous Intent: A Magazine of Mystery & Suspense 222; Mystery Forum Magazine 191; Mystery Readers Journal 224; Mystery Review, The 241; Mystery Time Magazine 225; Naked Kiss 226; New Mystery Magazine 195; Noir 199; Over My Dead Body! The Mystery Magazine 202; Pirate Writings 206; Playboy Magazine 228; Red Herring Mystery Magazine 229; Short Stuff Magazine 231; Thema Magazine 233; Tucumcari Literary Review 234; Ultimate Writer Magazine 235; Veneration Quarterly 236; Writer's Block Magazine 242; Writing Writers Magazine 239

Private Eye: Advocate, The 210; Alfred Hitchcock Mystery Magazine 180; Byline Magazine 212; Ellery Queen's Mystery Magazine 183; Green's Magazine 240; Hardboiled Magazine 187; Kracked Mirror 218; Linington Lineup 219; Murderous Intent: A Magazine of Mystery & Suspense 222; Mystery Forum Magazine 191; Mystery Readers Journal 224; Mystery Review, The 241; Mystery Time Magazine 225; Naked Kiss 226; New Mystery Magazine 195; Noir 199; Over My Dead Body! The Mystery Magazine 202; Pirate Writings 206; Playboy Magazine 228; Red Herring Mystery Magazine 229; Short Stuff Magazine 231; Sleuth, The 233; Thema Magazine 233; Tucumcari Literary Review 234; Ultimate Writer Magazine 235; Veneration Quarterly 236; Whitechapel Gazette 237; Writer's Block Magazine 242; Writing Writers Magazine 239

Psychological Suspense: Advocate, The 210; Belletrist Review 211; Byline Magazine 212; Dead of Night 214; Eagle's Flight Magazine 217; Ellery Queen's Mystery Magazine 183; Green's Magazine 240; Hardboiled Magazine 187; Housewife Writer's Forum 218; Kracked Mirror 218; Murderous Intent: A Magazine of Mystery & Suspense 222; Mystery Forum Magazine 191; Mystery Review, The 241; Mystery Time Magazine 225; Naked Kiss 226; New Mystery Magazine 195; Noir 199; Over My Dead Body! The Mystery Magazine 202; Phantasm 227; Pirate Writings 206; Playboy Magazine 228; Red Herring Mystery Magazine 229; Short Stuff Magazine 231; Thema Magazine 233; Tucumcari Literary Review 234; Veneration Quarterly 236; Whisper 236; Writer's Block Magazine 242; Writing Writers Magazine 239

Romantic Suspense: Advocate, The 210; Byline Magazine 212; Eagle's Flight Magazine 217; Ellery Queen's Mystery Magazine 183; Green's Magazine 240; Housewife Writer's Forum 218; Kracked Mirror 218; Most Loving Mere Folly

220; Murderous Intent: A Magazine of Mystery & Suspense 222; Mystery Forum Magazine 191; Mystery Review, The 241; Mystery Time Magazine 225; New Mystery Magazine 195; Noir 199; Over My Dead Body! The Mystery Magazine 202; Pirate Writings 206; Playboy Magazine 228; Short Stuff Magazine 231; Thema Magazine 233; Ultimate Writer Magazine 235; Veneration Quarterly 236; Writer's Block Magazine 242; Writing Writers Magazine 239

Software Reviews: Boys' Life 248; Drood Review 252; Mystery Scene 262

Surrealistic Mystery: Advocate, The 210; Dagger of the Mind 214; Dead of Night 214; Different Beat, A 215; Green's Magazine 240; Hardboiled Magazine 187; Kracked Mirror 218; Murderous Intent: A Magazine of Mystery & Suspense 222; Mystery Forum Magazine 191; Mystery Review, The 241; New Mystery Magazine 195; Over My Dead Body! The Mystery Magazine 202; Phantasm 227; Pirate Writings 206; Sleuth, The 233; Thema Magazine 233; Ultimate Writer Magazine 235; Veneration Quarterly 236; Whisper 236; Writing Writers Magazine 239

Suspense: Advocate, The 210; Alfred Hitchcock Mystery Magazine 180; Belletrist Review 211; Byline Magazine 212; Dagger of the Mind 214; Dead of Night 214; Eagle's Flight Magazine 217; Ellery Queen's Mystery Magazine 183; Green's Magazine 240; Hardboiled Magazine 187; Housewife Writer's Forum 218; Kracked Mirror 218; Linington Lineup 219; Most Loving Mere Folly 220; Murder of the Month 221; Murderous Intent: A Magazine of Mystery & Suspense 222; Mystery Forum Magazine 191; Mystery Review, The 241; Mystery Time Magazine 225; Naked Kiss 226; New Mystery Magazine 195; Noir 199; Over My Dead Body! The Mystery Magazine 202; Phantasm 227; Pirate Writings 206; Playboy Magazine 228; Post, The 228; Red Herring Mystery Magazine 229; Short Stuff Magazine 231; Sleuth, The 233; Thema Magazine 233; Tucumcari Literary Review 234; Ultimate Writer Magazine 235; Veneration Quarterly 236; Whisper 236; Writer's Block Magazine 242; Writing Writers Magazine 239

Thrillers: Advocate, The 210; Belletrist Review 211; Byline Magazine 212; Dagger of the Mind 214; Dead of Night 214; Ellery Queen's Mystery Magazine 183; Green's Magazine 240; Hardboiled Magazine 187; Kracked Mirror 218; Murderous Intent: A Magazine of Mystery & Suspense 222; Mystery Forum Magazine 191; Mystery Review, The 241; Naked Kiss 226; New Mystery Magazine 195; Noir 199; Over My Dead Body! The Mystery Magazine 202; Phantasm 227; Pirate Writings 206; Playboy Magazine 228; Thema Magazine 233; Tucumcari Literary Review 234; Ultimate Writer Magazine 235; Veneration Quarterly 236; Whisper 236; Writer's Block Magazine 242; Writing Writers Magazine 239

Urban Horror: Advocate, The 210; Dagger of the Mind 214; Dead of Night 214; Different Beat, A 215; Ellery Queen's Mystery Magazine 183; Green's Magazine 240; Hardboiled Magazine 187; Mystery Forum Magazine 191; Mystery Review, The 241; Naked Kiss 226; Over My Dead Body! The Mystery Magazine 202; Pirate Writings 206; Playboy Magazine 228; Thema Magazine 233; Tucumcari Literary Review 234; Ultimate Writer Magazine 235; Veneration Quarterly 236; Writing Writers Magazine 239

Young Adult: Advocate, The 210; Green's Magazine 240; Mystery Forum Magazine 191; Mystery Readers Journal 224; Mystery Review, The 241; Noir 199; Over My Dead Body! The Mystery Magazine 202; Pirate Writings 206; Playboy Magazine 228; Thema Magazine 233; Tucumcari Literary Review 234; Veneration Quarterly 236; Writing Writers Magazine 239;

Amateur Sleuth: Charlotte Gordon Agency 302; Cherry Weiner, Literary Agency 319; Circle of Confusion Ltd. 295; Dee Mura Enterprises, Inc. 311; Donald Maass Literary Agency 308; Doyen Literary Services Inc. 298; Evan Marshall Agency 310; Gislason Agency 301; Goldfarb & Graybill Law Offices 301; Hull House Literary Agency 303; Jabberwocky/A Literary Agency 304; James Allen, Literary Agent 292; Kidde, Hoyt & Picard Literary Agency 305; Literary Agency Group International 307; Manus & Associates Literary Agency 309; Multimedia Product Development, Inc. 311; Nancy Love Literary Agency 307; Norma-Lewis Agency 313; Patricia Teal Literary Agency 317; Peter Lampack Agency, Inc. 305; Richard Curtis Associates, Inc. 297; Robert Madsen Literary Agency 309; Sandra Watt & Associates 318; Susan Ann Protter Literary Agent 315; Susan Zeckendorf Associates, Inc. 322; Witherspoon Associates 320

Courtroom/trial: Anita Diamant Literary Agency 298; Ann Wright Representatives 322; Author's Literary Agency 293; Cherry Weiner, Literary Agency 319; Circle of Confusion Ltd. 295; Dee Mura Enterprises, Inc. 311; Diane Cleaver, Inc. 296; Donald Maass Literary Agency 308; Edward A. Novak III Literary Representation 313; Evan Marshall Agency 310; Frances Collin, Literary Agent 296; Garon-Brooke Assoc. Inc. 300; Goldfarb & Graybill Law Offices 301; Jabberwocky/A Literary Agency 304; Julie Castiglia Literary Agency 295; Kidde, Hoyt & Picard Literary Agency 305; Literary Agency Group International 307; Nancy Love Literary Agency 307; Norma-Lewis Agency 313; Patricia Teal Literary Agency 317; Richard Curtis Associates, Inc. 297; Robert Madsen Literary Agency 309; Ruth Wreschner, Authors Representative 321; Sandra Watt & Associates 318; Susan Ann Protter Literary Agent 315; Susan Zeckendorf Associates, Inc. 322; Witherspoon Associates 320

Cozy: Anita Diamant Literary Agency 298; Author's Literary Agency 293; Charlotte Gordon Agency 302; Cherry Weiner, Literary Agency 319; Circle of Confusion Ltd. 295; Dee Mura Enterprises, Inc. 311; Donald Maass Literary Agency 308; Doyen Literary Services Inc. 298; Evan Marshall Agency 310; Frances Collin, Literary Agent 296; Gislason Agency 301; Goldfarb & Graybill Law Offices 301; Jabberwocky/A Literary Agency 304; Jean V. Naggar Literary Agency 312; Julie Castiglia Literary Agency 295; Manus & Associates Literary Agency 309; Michael Larsen/Elizabeth Pomada Literary Agents 306; Multimedia Product Development, Inc. 311; Nancy Love Literary Agency 307; Norma-Lewis Agency 313; Patricia Teal Literary Agency 317; Richard Curtis Associates, Inc. 297; Robert Madsen Literary Agency 309; Ruth Wreschner, Authors Representative 321; Sandra Watt & Associates 318; Susan Ann Protter Literary Agent 315; Witherspoon Associates 320

Crime: Anita Diamant Literary Agency 298; Ann Wright Representatives 322; Author's Literary Agency 293; Cherry Weiner, Literary Agency 319; Circle of Confusion Ltd. 295; Dee Mura Enterprises, Inc. 311; Donald Maass Literary Agency 308; Edward A. Novak III Literary Representation 313; Evan Marshall Agency 310; Goldfarb & Graybill Law Offices 301; Hull House Literary Agency 303; Jabberwocky/A Literary Agency 304; Literary Agency Group International 307; Michael Larsen/Elizabeth Pomada Literary Agents 306; Nancy Love Literary Agency 307; Norma-Lewis Agency 313; Otitis Media Literary Agency 314; Richard Curtis Associates, Inc. 297; Robert Madsen Literary Agency 309; Ruth Wreschner, Authors Representative 321; Sandra Watt & Associates 318; Susan Zeckendorf Associates,

Inc. 322; Watkins-Loomis Agency 318; Witherspoon Associates 320

Dark Mystery: Anita Diamant Literary Agency 298; Ann Wright Representatives 322; Cherry Weiner, Literary Agency 319; Circle of Confusion Ltd. 295; Dee Mura Enterprises, Inc. 311; Donald Maass Literary Agency 308; Evan Marshall Agency 310; Frances Collin, Literary Agent 296; Goldfarb & Graybill Law Offices 301; Jabberwocky/A Literary Agency 304; John Hawkins & Associates, Inc. 302; Literary Agency Group International 307; Richard Curtis Associates, Inc. 297; Robert Madsen Literary Agency 309; Susan Zeckendorf Associates, Inc. 322; Watkins-Loomis Agency 318; Witherspoon Associates 320

Espionage: Anita Diamant Literary Agency 298; Ann Wright Representatives 322; Author's Literary Agency 293; Cherry Weiner, Literary Agency 319; Circle of Confusion Ltd. 295; Dee Mura Enterprises, Inc. 311; Donald Maass Literary Agency 308; Edward A. Novak III Literary Representation 313; Evan Marshall Agency 310; Garon-Brooke Assoc. Inc. 300; Goldfarb & Graybill Law Offices 301; Jabberwocky/A Literary Agency 304; John Hawkins & Associates, Inc. 302; Kidde, Hoyt & Picard Literary Agency 305; Literary Agency Group International 307; Nancy Love Literary Agency 307; Norma-Lewis Agency 313; Otitis Media Literary Agency 314; Richard Curtis Associates, Inc. 297; Robert Madsen Literary Agency 309; Sandra Watt & Associates 318; Susan Zeckendorf Associates, Inc. 322; Witherspoon Associates 320

Hard-boiled Detective: Anita Diamant Literary Agency 298; Ann Wright Representatives 322; Author's Literary Agency 293; Cherry Weiner, Literary Agency 319; Circle of Confusion Ltd. 295; Dee Mura Enterprises, Inc. 311; Diane Cleaver, Inc. 296; Evan Marshall Agency 310; Goldfarb & Graybill Law Offices 301; Jabberwocky/A Literary Agency 304; Literary Agency Group International 307; Norma-Lewis Agency 313; Richard Curtis Associates, Inc. 297; Robert Madsen Literary Agency 309; Ruth Wreschner, Authors Represenative 321; Sandra Watt & Associates 318; Susan Zeckendorf Associates, Inc. 322; Witherspoon Associates 320

Historical: Charlotte Gordon Agency 302; Cherry Weiner, Literary Agency 319; Circle of Confusion Ltd. 295; Dee Mura Enterprises, Inc. 311; Donald Maass Literary Agency 308; Doyen Literary Services Inc. 298; Evan Marshall Agency 310; Frances Collin, Literary Agent 296; Garon-Brooke Assoc. Inc. 300; Goldfarb & Graybill Law Offices 301; Jabberwocky/A Literary Agency 304; Jean V. Naggar Literary Agency 312; Kidde, Hoyt & Picard Literary Agency 305; Michael Larsen/Elizabeth Pomada Literary Agents 306; Multimedia Product Development, Inc. 311; Otitis Media Literary Agency 314; Peter Lampack Agency, Inc. 305; Richard Curtis Associates, Inc. 297; Robert Madsen Literary Agency 309; Sandra Watt & Associates 318; Watkins-Loomis Agency 318; Witherspoon Associates 320

Humorous Mystery: Anita Diamant Literary Agency 298; Ann Wright Representatives 322; Charlotte Gordon Agency 302; Cherry Weiner, Literary Agency 319; Circle of Confusion Ltd. 295; Dee Mura Enterprises, Inc. 311; Donald Maass Literary Agency 308; Doyen Literary Services Inc. 298; Evan Marshall Agency 310; Goldfarb & Graybill Law Offices 301; Jabberwocky/A Literary Agency 304; Literary Agency Group International 307; Manus & Associates Literary Agency 309; Norma-Lewis Agency 313; Patricia Teal Literary Agency 317; Richard Curtis Associates, Inc. 297; Robert Madsen Literary Agency 309; Sandra Watt & Associates 318; Seymour Agency 316; Watkins-Loomis Agency 318; Witherspoon Associates 320

Juvenile: Charlotte Gordon Agency 302; Cherry Weiner, Literary Agency 319; Circle of Confusion Ltd. 295; Dee Mura Enterprises, Inc. 311; Donald Maass Literary Agency 308; Evan Marshall Agency 310; Gislason Agency 301; Jabberwocky/A Literary Agency 304; Literary Agency Group International 307; Norma-Lewis

Agency 313; Richard Curtis Associates, Inc. 297; Robert Madsen Literary Agency 309; Sandra Watt & Associates 318; Watkins-Loomis Agency 318; Witherspoon Associates 320

Light Horror: Adler & Robin Books, Inc. 291; Cherry Weiner, Literary Agency 319; Circle of Confusion Ltd. 295; Dee Mura Enterprises, Inc. 311; Evan Marshall Agency 310; Frances Collin, Literary Agent 296; Gislason Agency 301; Goldfarb & Graybill Law Offices 301; Jabberwocky/A Literary Agency 304; Literary Agency Group International 307; Michael Larsen/Elizabeth Pomada Literary Agents 306; Otitis Media Literary Agency 314; Richard Curtis Associates, Inc. 297; Robert Madsen Literary Agency 309; Sandra Watt & Associates 318; Seymour Agency 316; Witherspoon Associates 320

Malice Domestic: Anita Diamant Literary Agency 298; Charlotte Gordon Agency 302; Cherry Weiner, Literary Agency 319; Circle of Confusion Ltd. 295; Dee Mura Enterprises, Inc. 311; Donald Maass Literary Agency 308; Evan Marshall Agency 310; Goldfarb & Graybill Law Offices 301; Hull House Literary Agency 303; Jabberwocky/A Literary Agency 304; Literary Agency Group International 307; Michael Larsen/Elizabeth Pomada Literary Agents 306; Multimedia Product Development, Inc. 311; Richard Curtis Associates, Inc. 297; Robert Madsen Literary Agency 309; Sandra Watt & Associates 318; Witherspoon Associates 320

Police Procedural: Adler & Robin Books, Inc. 291; Anita Diamant Literary Agency 298; Ann Wright Representatives 322; Author's Literary Agency 293; Charlotte Gordon Agency 302; Cherry Weiner, Literary Agency 319; Circle of Confusion Ltd. 295; Dee Mura Enterprises, Inc. 311; Donald Maass Literary Agency 308; Ethan Ellenberg Literary Agency 299; Evan Marshall Agency 310; Goldfarb & Graybill Law Offices 301; Jabberwocky/A Literary Agency 304; James Allen, Literary Agent 292; Jean V. Naggar Literary Agency 312; Julie Castiglia Literary Agency 295; Literary Agency Group International 307; Nancy Love Literary Agency 307; Norma-Lewis Agency 313; Richard Curtis Associates, Inc. 297; Robert Madsen Literary Agency 309; Ruth Wreschner, Authors Represenative 321; Sandra Watt & Associates 318; Susan Ann Protter Literary Agent 315; Susan Zeckendorf Associates, Inc. 322; Witherspoon Associates 320

Private Eye: Adler & Robin Books, Inc. 291; Anita Diamant Literary Agency 298; Ann Elmo Agency Inc. 299; Ann Wright Representatives 322; Author's Literary Agency 293; Brandt & Brandt Literary Agents, Inc. 294; Cherry Weiner, Literary Agency 319; Circle of Confusion Ltd. 295; Dee Mura Enterprises, Inc. 311; Diane Cleaver, Inc. 296; Donald Maass Literary Agency 308; Evan Marshall Agency 310; Gislason Agency 301; Goldfarb & Graybill Law Offices 301; Jabberwocky/A Literary Agency 304; John Hawkins & Associates, Inc. 302; Julie Castiglia Literary Agency 295; Kidde, Hoyt & Picard Literary Agency 305; Literary Agency Group International 307; Marcia Amsterdam Agency 293; Michael Larsen/Elizabeth Pomada Literary Agents 306; Nancy Love Literary Agency 307; Norma-Lewis Agency 313; Richard Curtis Associates, Inc. 297; Robert Madsen Literary Agency 309; Ruth Wreschner, Authors Represenative 321; Sandra Watt & Associates 318; Susan Ann Protter Literary Agent 315; Susan Zeckendorf Associates, Inc. 322; Watkins-Loomis Agency 318; Witherspoon Associates 320

Psychological Suspense: Anita Diamant Literary Agency 298; Cherry Weiner, Literary Agency 319; Circle of Confusion Ltd. 295; Dee Mura Enterprises, Inc. 311; Diane Cleaver, Inc. 296; Donald Maass Literary Agency 308; Edward A. Novak III Literary Representation 313; Ethan Ellenberg Literary Agency 299; Evan Marshall Agency 310; Garon-Brooke Assoc. Inc. 300; Goldfarb & Graybill Law Offices

301; Hull House Literary Agency 303; Jabberwocky/A Literary Agency 304; John Hawkins & Associates, Inc. 302; Julie Castiglia Literary Agency 295; Kidde, Hoyt & Picard Literary Agency 305; Literary Agency Group International 307; Michael Larsen/Elizabeth Pomada Literary Agents 306; Multimedia Product Development, Inc. 311; Nancy Love Literary Agency 307; Norma-Lewis Agency 313; Peter Lampack Agency, Inc. 305; Richard Curtis Associates, Inc. 297; Robert Madsen Literary Agency 309; Ruth Wreschner, Authors Representative 321; Sandra Watt & Associates 318; Susan Zeckendorf Associates, Inc. 322; Watkins-Loomis Agency 318; Witherspoon Associates 320

Romantic Suspense: Anita Diamant Literary Agency 298; Ann Wright Representatives 322; Charlotte Gordon Agency 302; Circle of Confusion Ltd. 295; Dee Mura Enterprises, Inc. 311; Donald Maass Literary Agency 308; Doyen Literary Services Inc. 298; Ethan Ellenberg Literary Agency 299; Evan Marshall Agency 310; Frances Collin, Literary Agent 296; Garon-Brooke Assoc. Inc. 300; Gislason Agency 301; Goldfarb & Graybill Law Offices 301; Jabberwocky/A Literary Agency 304; Julie Castiglia Literary Agency 295; Kidde, Hoyt & Picard Literary Agency 305; Literary Agency Group International 307; Michael Larsen/Elizabeth Pomada Literary Agents 306; Multimedia Product Development, Inc. 311; Norma-Lewis Agency 313; Patricia Teal Literary Agency 317; Richard Curtis Associates, Inc. 297; Robert Madsen Literary Agency 309; Ruth Wreschner, Authors Represenative 321; Susan Zeckendorf Associates, Inc. 322; Seymour Agency 316; Watkins-Loomis Agency 318

Surrealistic Mystery: Cherry Weiner, Literary Agency 319; Circle of Confusion Ltd. 295; Dee Mura Enterprises, Inc. 311; Donald Maass Literary Agency 308; Evan Marshall Agency 310; Frances Collin, Literary Agent 296; Jabberwocky/A Literary Agency 304; Richard Curtis Associates, Inc. 297; Robert Madsen Literary Agency 309; Sandra Watt & Associates 318; Watkins-Loomis Agency 318; Witherspoon Associates 320

Suspense: Adler & Robin Books, Inc. 291; Anita Diamant Literary Agency 298; Ann Wright Representatives 322; Author's Literary Agency 293; Charlotte Gordon Agency 302; Cherry Weiner, Literary Agency 319; Circle of Confusion Ltd. 295; Dee Mura Enterprises, Inc. 311; Diane Cleaver, Inc. 296; Donald Maass Literary Agency 308; Doyen Literary Services Inc. 298; Edward A. Novak III Literary Representation 313; Ethan Ellenberg Literary Agency 299; Evelyn Singer Literary Agency 317; Evan Marshall Agency 310; Frances Collin, Literary Agent 296; Goldfarb & Graybill Law Offices 301; Hull House Literary Agency 303; Jabberwocky/A Literary Agency 304; Jean V. Naggar Literary Agency 312; John Hawkins & Associates, Inc. 302; Julie Castiglia Literary Agency 295; Kidde, Hoyt & Picard Literary Agency 305; Literary Agency Group International 307; Manus & Associates Literary Agency 309; Michael Larsen/Elizabeth Pomada Literary Agents 306; Multimedia Product Development, Inc. 311; Nancy Love Literary Agency 307; Norma-Lewis Agency 313; Otitis Media Literary Agency 314; Patricia Teal Literary Agency 317; Peter Lampack Agency, Inc. 305; Quicksilver Books-Literary Agents 315; Richard Curtis Associates, Inc. 297; Robert Madsen Literary Agency 309; Ruth Wreschner, Authors Represenative 321; Sandra Watt & Associates 318; Seymour Agency 316; Susan Zeckendorf Associates, Inc. 322; Watkins-Loomis Agency 318; Witherspoon Associates 320

Thrillers: Adler & Robin Books, Inc. 291; Anita Diamant Literary Agency 298; Ann Wright Representatives 322; Author's Literary Agency 293; Cherry Weiner, Literary Agency 319; Circle of Confusion Ltd. 295; Dee Mura Enterprises, Inc. 311; Donald Maass Literary Agency 308; Doyen Literary Services Inc. 298; Ethan Ellenberg Literary Agency 299; Evan Marshall Agency 310; Garon-Brooke Assoc.

Inc. 300; Goldfarb & Graybill Law Offices 301; Jabberwocky/A Literary Agency 304; Jean V. Naggar Literary Agency 312; Julie Castiglia Literary Agency 295; Literary Agency Group International 307; Michael Larsen/Elizabeth Pomada Literary Agents 306; Multimedia Product Development, Inc. 311; Nancy Love Literary Agency 307; Norma-Lewis Agency 313; Otitis Media Literary Agency 314; Peter Lampack Agency, Inc. 305; Quicksilver Books-Literary Agents 315; Richard Curtis Associates, Inc. 297; Robert Madsen Literary Agency 309; Ruth Wreschner, Authors Represenative 321; Sandra Watt & Associates 318; Seymour Agency 316; Susan Ann Protter Literary Agent 315; Susan Zeckendorf Associates, Inc. 322; Witherspoon Associates 320

Urban Horror: Cherry Weiner, Literary Agency 319; Circle of Confusion Ltd. 295; Dee Mura Enterprises, Inc. 311; Evan Marshall Agency 310; Frances Collin, Literary Agent 296; Jabberwocky/A Literary Agency 304; John Hawkins & Associates, Inc. 302; Literary Agency Group International 307; Richard Curtis Associates, Inc. 297; Robert Madsen Literary Agency 309; Sandra Watt & Associates 318; Susan Zeckendorf Associates, Inc. 322; Witherspoon Associates 320

Young Adult: Charlotte Gordon Agency 302; Cherry Weiner, Literary Agency 319; Circle of Confusion Ltd. 295; Dee Mura Enterprises, Inc. 311; Donald Maass Literary Agency 308; Doyen Literary Services Inc. 298; Evan Marshall Agency 310; Gislason Agency 301; Jabberwocky/A Literary Agency 304; Literary Agency Group International 307; Norma-Lewis Agency 313; Richard Curtis Associates, Inc. 297; Robert Madsen Literary Agency 309; Watkins-Loomis Agency 318; Witherspoon Associates 320

GENERAL INDEX

ABA 375
Academy Chicago 114
Accord Communications 115
Adler & Robin Books, Inc. 291
Advocate, The 210,244
Agatha, The 380
Alfred Hitchcock Mystery Magazine 180
Allison & Busby Crime 164
America Online 383
American Crime Writer's League 371
Andy's Books 397
Anita Diamant Literary Agency 298
Ann Elmo Agency, Inc. 299
Ann Wright Representatives 322
Ann's Books and Mostly Mysteries 422
A1 Crime Fiction 423
Anthony, The 380
Arcade Publishing 115
Armchair Detective Book of Lists, The 390
Armchair Detective, The 245
Arthur Ellis Award 381
Atheneum Books for Young Readers 116
Author's Literary Agency 293
Avalon Books 117
Avon Flare Books 117

Baker Book House Company 118
Ballantine Books 62
Bantam Books 66
Beasley Books 402
Belletrist Review 211
Berkley Publishing Group 72
Bethel Publishing 120
Big Sleep Books 409
Black and White Books 410
Black Hill Books 424
Bloody Dagger Books 397
Book Carnival 397
Book Harbor, The 414
Book Sleuth, Inc., The 401
Book Tree 418
Booked For Murder, Ltd. 420
Books West 397
Bouchercon 377
Boys' Life 212, 248

Brandt & Brandt Literary Agents, Inc. 294
Buckingham Books 416
Buest Verlag 160
Buffcon 376, 379
Byline Magazine 212, 249
bePuzzled 119

Cardinal Books 419
Cedar Bay Press 121
Centuries & Sleuths Bookstore 402
Century Books 164
Certo Books 411
Charlotte Gordon Agency 302
Cherry Weiner, Literary Agency 319
Circle of Confusion Ltd. 295
Cloak & Dagger Books 416
Cloak and Dagger Books 417
Clues, A Journal of Detection 213, 250
Comicart Publishing Company 123
CompuServe 384
Constable & Co., Ltd. 165
Corner Shop, The 403
Creative Arts Book Company 123
Crime Club, The 166
Crime Writer's Association 371
Crime Writers of Canada 372
Criminal Record, The 250
Crossway Books 124

Dagger of the Mind 214, 251
Dancing Jester Press 125
Dare To Dream Books 127
Dark Horse Comics 128
Dead of Night 214, 252
Deadly Passions Bookshop 407
Deadly Serious 390
Dee Mura Enterprises, Inc. 311
Delphi 384
Detective Files Group 273
Diane Cleaver, Inc. 296
Different Beat, A 215
Donald Maass Literary Agency 308
Doubleday 129
Doyen Literary Services Inc. 298
Drood Review 252
Dunn & Powell Books 401, 405
Dutton/Signet 76

Eagle's Flight Magazine 217
Edgar, The 380
Edward A. Novak III Literary Representation 313
Eichborn Verlag 161
Ellery Queen's Mystery Magazine 183
Else Fine Books 407
Ergo Books 424
Ethan Ellenberg Literary Agency 299
Evan Marshall Agency 310
Evelyn Singer Literary Agency 317
Eye, The 381
Eyecon 376, 379
eWorld 384

Fawcett 130
Fine, Donald I. Inc. 79
Footprints of a Gigantic Hound 396
Footstool Detective Books 407
Forge 84
Foul Play Press 88
Frances Collin, Literary Agent 296
Frank S. Pollack, Bookseller 403

Garon-Brooke Assoc. Inc. 300
Gasogene Press Ltd. 130
Gauntlet Magazine 253
GEnie 385
Gila Queen's Guide to Markets 391
Gislason Agency 301
Golden Dagger, The 381
Goldfarb & Graybill Law Offices 301
Gothic Journal 254
Grand Master Award, The 381
Grave Matters Bookstore 414
Gravesend Books 417
Green Lion Books 408
Green's Magazine 240
Gryphon Publications 131

Hahn's House of Mystery 414
Hammett Award, The 381
Hardboiled Magazine 187, 256
HarperCollins Publishers 91
Headline Book Publishing PLC 167
Henri Labelle 422
Henry Holt & Company 132
Hodder & Stoughton, Ltd. 168
Housewife Writer's Forum 218, 256
Howdunit Series, The 391
Hull House Literary Agency 303

Intercontinental Publishing 133

International Association of Crime Writers 372
Internet, The 386

Jabberwocky/A Literary Agency 304
James Allen, Literary Agent 292
Janus Books, Ltd. 396
Jean V. Naggar Literary Agency 312
John Creasey Award 380
John Hawkins & Associates, Inc. 302
Julie Castiglia Literary Agency 295

Kate's Mystery Books (Murder Under Cover, Inc.) 406
KBV (Klein & Blechinger Verlag) GMBH 162
Kensington Publishing Corp. 95
Kidde, Hoyt & Picard Literary Agency 305
Killing Time Mystery Books 420
Kitchen Sink Press 134
Kracked Mirror 218

Last Seen Reading 398
Law & Order 391
Left Coast Crime 374
Len Unger's Rare Books 400
Linington Lineup 219, 257
Literary Agency Group International 307
Little, Brown and Company, Inc. 136
Little, Brown and Company, Inc. Children's Division 135
Longmeadow Press 137
Lucky Books 138

McCoy's Rare Books 410
Macmillan Crime Case 169
Madwoman Press, Inc. 139
Magna Cum Murder 377
Mainly Murder Bookstore 425
Malice Domestic 376
Manus & Associates Literary Agency 309
Marcia Amsterdam Agency 293
Margaret K. McElderry Books 140
M.C. Newburn Books 398
Mega-Books 141
Metropolis Mystery Bookshop & Tea Room 411
Michael Larsen/Elizabeth Pomada Literary Agents 306
Mid-Atlantic Mystery Book Fair 378

Ming Books UK 424
Mitchell Books 398
Mordida Books 418
Most Loving Mere Folly 220, 257
Multimedia Product Development, Inc. 311
Munoz Moya Editores SA 163
Murder & Mayhem 258
Murder and Mayhem 404
Murder By The Book 416, 418, 419
Murder Can Be Fun 259
Murder Is Served 414
Murder Most Cozy 392
Murder One 425
Murder of the Month 221
Murderous Intent: A Magazine of Mystery & Suspense 222, 260
Mysteries & More 419
Mysteries From The Yard 415
Mysterious Bookshop, The 411
Mysterious Bookshop West 399
Mysterious Press 98
Mystery Bookshop 405
Mystery Bookstore (Oceanside Books) 412
Mystery Forum 392
Mystery Forum Magazine 191, 260
Mystery Lovers Bookshop & Cafe 417
Mystery Lovers Ink 409
Mystery Loves Company 405
Mystery Merchant Bookstore, The 422
Mystery Nook, The 402
Mystery One Bookshop 421
Mystery Readers Journal 224, 261
Mystery Review, The 241, 274
Mystery Scene 262
Mystery Time Magazine 225
Mystery Writers of America 373

Naiad Press Inc., The 101
Naked Kiss 226, 263
Nancy Love Literary Agency 307
New Mystery Magazine 195, 264
New Readers Press 141
New Victoria Publishers, Inc. 142
Noir 199, 264
Norma-Lewis Agency 313

Of Dark and Stormy Nights 379
Once Upon A Crime 408
Otitis Media Literary Agency 314
Over My Dead Body! The Mystery Magazine 202, 265

P.I. Magazine 392
P.I.E.S. 421
Pandora's Books Ltd. 413
Partners & Crime 412
Patricia Teal Literary Agency 317
Patterson Smith 410
Permanent Press 143
Peter Lampack Agency, Inc. 305
Phantasm 227
Pirate Writings 206
Playboy 266
Playboy Magazine 228
Players Press Inc. 144
Poisoned Pen, The 396
Post, The 228
Presidio Press 145
Prime Crime Books 423
Private Eye Writers of America 373
Prodigy 385

Quicksilver Books-Literary Agents 315
Quill & Brush 406

Random House 104
Raven Books 399
Raven Bookstore 404
Real Crime Book Digest 266
Red Crane Books 146
Red Herring Mystery Magazine 229
Richard Curtis Associates, Inc. 297
Rising Tide Press 147
Robert Madsen Literary Agency 309
Roy Willis, Bookseller 415
Royal Fireworks Press 148
Rue Morgue, The 401
Ruth Wreschner, Authors Represenative 321

St. Martin's Press 107
San Francisco Mystery Bookstore 399
Sandra Watt & Associates 318
Scarlet Street 267
Scavenger's Newsletter 392
Science Fiction and Mystery Bookshop 402
Science Fiction, Mysteries & More! 412
Scribner Crime Novels 149
Seattle Mystery Bookshop 420
Second Story Books 406
Secret Staircase Bookshop 399
Severn House Publishers, Ltd. 170
Seymour Agency 316
Sherlock in L.A. 400

Sherlockian Tidbits 230, 268
Short Stuff Magazine 231
Shot in the Dark, A 243, 275
Simon & Pierre Publishing Co. Ltd. 157
Singer Media Corp. 149
Sisters in Crime 374
Skullduggery House Books 410
Skylark 232
Sleuth Fest 375, 379
Sleuth of Baker Street 423
Sleuth, The 233
Snake River Reflections 268
Soho Press Inc. 150
Spenser's Mystery Bookshop 406
Spinsters Ink 151
Strange Birds Books 415
Susan Ann Protter Literary Agent 315
Susan Zeckendorf Associates, Inc. 322

Tall Stories 400
10/18 159
Thema Magazine 233
Third Side Press 152
Thomas Investigative Publications 393
Timothy P. Slongo Books 404
Tim's Books 413
Tor Books (see Forge 84)
True Detective 269
Tucumcari Literary Review 234, 270
Turnstone Press 158

UGE (see 10/18 159)
Ultimate Writer Magazine 235, 271
Uncle Buck's Mysteries 403
Uncle Edgar's Mystery Bookstore 409

Veneration Quarterly 236
Verlagsburo Simon & Magiera 162
Vesta Publications, Ltd. 159
Victor Gollancz, Ltd. 166
Virago Press, Ltd. 170
Vista Publishing, Inc. 153

Walker & Company 110
Watkins-Loomis Agency 318
Wayne Mullins Books 395
West's Booking Agency 421
Whisper 236
Whitechapel Gazette 237, 270
Whodunit 417
Windswept House Publishers 154
Witherspoon Associates 320
Woman's World 238
Write Way Publishing 155
Writer's Block Magazine 242
Writer's Complete Crime Reference
    Book, The 393
Writer's Digest Magazine 393
Writing Writers Magazine 239, 272

Zardoz Books 425

More Great Books for Writers!

Writer's Market—Let this completely revised and updated edition help you realize your writing dreams. This edition contains information on 4,000 writing opportunities. You'll find all the facts vital to the success of your writing career, including an up-to-date listing of buyers of books, articles and stories, listings of contests and awards, plus articles and interviews with top professionals. *#10432/$27.99/1008 pages*

Writing Mysteries—Sue Grafton weaves the experience of today's top mystery authors into a mystery writing "how-to." You'll learn how to create great mystery, including making stories more taut, more immediate, and more fraught with tension. *#10286/$18.99/208 pages*

Writing the Modern Mystery—If you're guilty of plot, character, and construction murder, let this guide show you how to write tightly crafted, salable mysteries that will appeal to today's editors and readers. *#10290/$13.99/224 pages/paperback*

The Writer's Complete Crime Reference Book—Now completely revised and updated! Incredible encyclopedia of hard-to-find facts about the ways of criminals and cops, prosecutors and defenders, victims and juries—everything the crime and mystery writer needs is at your fingertips. *#10371/$19.99/304pages*

Police Procedural: A Writer's Guide to the Police and How They Work—Learn how police officers work, when they work, what they wear, who they report to, and how they go about controlling and investigating crime. *#10374/$16.99/272pages/paperback*

Private Eyes: A Writer's Guide to Private Investigators—How do people become investigators? What procedures do they use? What tricks/tactics do they use? This guide gives you the "inside scoop" on the world of private eyes! *#10373/$15.99/208 pages/paperback*

Deadly Doses: A Writer's Guide to Poisons—This comprehensive reference book addresses the crucial issues you'll encounter when "poisoning off" a character. *#10177/$16.99/298 pages/paperback*

Scene of the Crime: A Writer's Guide to Crime-Scene Investigation—Save time with this quick reference book! You'll find loads of facts and details on how police scour crime scenes for tell-tale clues. *#10319/$15.99/240 pages/paperback*

Armed & Dangerous: A Writer's Guide to Weapons—You'll learn how to arm your characters with weapons to perfectly suit their crime. Hundreds of examples and easily understood language make complicated details completely accessible. *#10176/$15.99/186 pages/paperback*

Modus Operandi A Writer's Guide to How Criminals Work—From murder to arson to prostitution, two seasoned detectives show you how to create masterful crimes while still dropping enough clues to let the good guys catch the bad guys. *#10414/$16.99/224 pages/paperback*

Malicious Intent A writer's Guide to How Criminals Think—Find all the details you need to create chillingly believable villains. You'll get a compelling look into the criminal mind; who they are, why they commit crimes, how they choose their victims—even how police catch them. *#10413/$16.99/240pages/paperback*

Cause of Death: A Writer's Guide to Death, Murder & Forensic Medicine—Discover how to accurately "kill-off" characters as you're led step-by-step through the process of trauma, death and burial. *#10318/$15.99/240pages/paperback*